CRIMINAL POLICY IN TRANSITION

Oñati International Series in Law and Society

A SERIES PUBLISHED FOR THE OÑATI INSTITUTE FOR THE SOCIOLOGY OF LAW

General Editors

Professor William L.F. Felstiner
Professor Eve Darian-Smith

Titles in this Series

Emerging Legal Certainty: Empirical Studies on the Globalization of Law
Edited by Volkmar Gessner and Ali Cem Budak

Totalitarian and Post-Totalitarian Law
Edited by Adam Podgorecki and Vittorio Olgiati

Family Law and Family Policy in the New Europe
Edited by Jacek Kurczewski and Mavis Maclean

Foreign Courts: Civil Litigation in Foreign Legal Cultures
Edited by Volkmar Gessner

Procedural Justice
Edited by Klaus F. Röhl and Stefan Machura

(ALL THE ABOVE TITLES PUBLISHED BY ASHGATE)

Criminal Policy in Transition
Edited by Penny Green and Andrew Rutherford

Social Dynamics of Crime and Control
New Theories for a World in Transition
Edited by Susanne Karstedt and Kai-D Bussmann

Law and Poverty
Edited by ASbjorn Eide and Peter Robson

(PUBLISHED BY HART PUBLISHING)

Criminal Policy in Transition

Edited by
PENNY GREEN
ANDREW RUTHERFORD

OÑATI INTERNATIONAL SERIES IN LAW AND SOCIETY

A SERIES PUBLISHED FOR THE OÑATI INSTITUTE FOR THE SOCIOLOGY OF LAW

• HART •
PUBLISHING
OXFORD – PORTLAND
2000

Hart Publishing
Oxford and Portland, Oregon

Published in North America (US and Canada) by
Hart Publishing c/o
International Specialized Book Services
5804 NE Hassalo Street
Portland, Oregon
97213-3644
USA

Distributed in the Netherlands, Belgium and Luxembourg by
Intersentia, Churchillaan 108
B2900 Schoten
Antwerpen
Belgium

Hart Publishing is a specialist legal publisher based in Oxford, England.
To order further copies of this book or to request a list of other
publications please write to:

Hart Publishing, Salter's Boatyard, Folly Bridge,
Abingdon Road, Oxford OX1 4LB
Telephone: +44 (0)1865 245533 or Fax: +44 (0)1865 794882
e-mail: mail@hartpub.co.uk
WEBSITE: http//www.hartpub.co.uk

British Library Cataloguing in Publication Data
Data Available
ISBN 1 84113 188 1 (hbk)
ISBN 1 84113 189 X (pbk)

Typeset by Hope Services (Abingdon) Ltd.
Printed and bound in Great Britain on acid-free paper by
Biddles Ltd, www.biddles.co.uk

Foreword

Criminal Policy in Transition comes along at a time when the literature in criminology is desperately short of "global" perspectives. It helps fill that gap while it presents important new insights into changing penal policy and practice. That it raises as many questions as it seems to answer is one of its great strengths. The authors write knowledgeably about their home societies without being prematurely bounded by comparative criteria. As a result, they develop a complex and uneven image of similarities and differences, of divergence and convergence through time. In this sense the collection offers a model of how international collaborative work should proceed.

The book is the product of a workshop held several years ago at the International Institute for the Sociology of Law (IISL) in Onati, Spain. The IISL is a partnership between the Research Committee on the Sociology of Law and the Basque Government. For more than a decade it has conducted an international master's programme in the sociology of law and hosted hundreds of workshops devoted to sociolegal studies. It maintains an extensive sociolegal library open to scholars from any country and any relevant discipline. Detailed information about the IISL can be found at *www.iisj.es*. This book is the most recent publication in the Onati International Series in Law and Society, a series that publishes the best manuscripts produced from Onati workshops conducted in English. A similar series, Coleccion Onati: Derecho Y Sociedad, is published in Spanish.

William L. F. Felstiner
Eve Darian-Smith

Preface

This book took shape within two important institutional locations: the Faculty of Law at the University of Southampton, where the project was first conceived and later at the International Institute for the Sociology of Law in Oñati, Spain, the setting for a workshop which was convened to develop the themes which had emerged. Here, in the beauty and turbulence of the Basque country, a group of international scholars gathered to explore and make sense of the tremendous transitions facing criminal policy at the millennium, transitions which certainly in the short-term invite a bleak pessimism but which in the longer term may actually confront us with exciting possibilities. The debates and discussions which took place and the essays which emerged go to the core of criminal policy at the start of the twenty-first century. These underline its limited possibilities as well as its very real limits. The social justice issues around which much of the history of criminal policy has been framed—fairness, equality, inclusion, social responsibility, poverty, alienation, power, legitimacy, legality and ideology—have been pushed to the margins as extraneous impediments to mandates for managerial efficiency and the delivery of crime control. An overriding theme of this Volume is for the restoration of these values to centre stage.

These essays are intended to be accessible not only to criminologists but also to scholars of political science, sociology and social policy. They bring together political analysis, empirical research and theoretical developments to reveal the limits of criminal policy within democratic and democratising states. It is envisaged that the Volume will, therefore, attract a wide academic audience as well as reaching those responsible for issues which reach the heart of public policy.

We are pleased to acknowledge the support and encouragement we have received from the University of Southampton and the International Institute for the Sociology of Law at Oñati. We also much appreciated the advice of Bill Felstiner, editor of the Oñati series. Finally, our very special thanks are due to Emma Laurie and Debbie Malson of the Law Faculty at Southampton University for the diligent efficiency which they brought to the final stages of this project.

Penny Green and Andrew Rutherford
February 2000

Contents

List of Contributors

Hans-Jörg Albrecht is director of the Max Planck Institute for International Law at Freiburg. He is co-editor of *Drug Policies in Western Europe* (1989) and *Crime and criminal Policy in Europe* (1990).

Katherine Beckett, Ph.D., is Assistant Professor, Department of Criminal Justice, and Adjunct Assistant Professor, Department of Sociology, University of Washington, Seattle. Her research interests are in the areas of drugs and society; crime, law, and deviance; culture and media; political sociology; punishment and social control; and gender and society. Two recent publications are "How Unregulated is the US Labour Market? The Dynamics of Jobs and Jails, 1980–1995," with Bruce Western (*American Journal of Sociology*, 1999), and *Making Crime Pay: Law and Order in Contemporary American Politics* (1997).

Pat Carlen is currently Professor of Sociology at Bath University and before that was Professor of Criminology at Keele University. She has published 14 books on the relationship between criminal and social justice, including *Magistrates' Justice* (1976), *Women's Imprisonment* (1983), *Women, Crime and Poverty* (1988), *Jigsaw: A Political Criminology of Youth Homelessness* (1996), *Sledgehammer: Women's Imprisonment at the Millennium* (1998). In 1997 she was awarded the Sellin-Glueck Prize by the American Society of Criminology for international contributions to criminology.

David Faulkner is a fellow of St. John's College Oxford and a Senior Research Associate at the University of Oxford Centre for Criminological Research. He writes and lectures on various aspects of government, criminal justice and public service and works with a number of charities concerned with law reform and opportunities for young people. He served in the Home Office from 1959–92, becoming Director of Operational Policy in the Prison Department in 1980, Deputy Secretary in charge of the Criminal, Research and Statistics Departments in 1982 and Principal Establishments Officer in 1990.

Julia Fionda is a lecturer in law at Southampton University (formerly at King's College London). Her teaching and research interests lie in the fields of criminology, criminal law, youth justice and homelessness and the law. She has published widely in these fields and is author of *Public Prosecutors and Discretion: A Comparative Study* (1995).

Penny Green is Professor of Law and Crimnology in the School of Law at the University of Westminster (formerly at the University of Southampton). She is the author of *The Enemy Without: Policy and Class Consciousness in the*

Miners' Strike (1990) and *Drugs, Trafficking and Criminal Policy: The Scapegoat Strategy* (1998).

Thomas Mathiesen has been Professor of Sociology of Law at the University of Oslo, Norway since 1972. He has conducted research and published a number of books in a wide variety of areas such as sociology of law, criminology, political sociology and sociology of the media. He was one of the founders of the Scandinavian prison movement, in which he is still active. In addition to the Scandinavian languages, many of his books and articles have been published in English, German, Italian, French, Portuguese and Japanese.

Dario Melossi, having taught for a long time in the US, at the University of California, has now returned to teaching criminology at the Faculty of Law at the University of Bologna. He is the author of *The Prison and the Factory* (with Massimo Pavarini), *The State of Social Control*, and the editor of *The Sociology of Punishment*. His current research deals with the study of "crime and migration" in Italy, as well as the historical-comparative study of imprisonment's relation with a host of other social variables in Italy/Europe and the US.

Andrew Rutherford is Professor of Law and Criminal policy at the University of Southampton, UK. His publications include, *Prisons and the Process of Justice, The Reductionist Challenge* (1984), *Growing Out of Crime* (1986), *Criminal Justice and the Pursuit of Decency* (1993), *Transforming Criminal Policy* (1996) and (editor) *Criminal Policy Making* (1997). Between 1984–99 he was chair of the Howard League for Penal Reform.

Sebastian Scheerer, Professor of Criminology at the Faculty of Law, University of Hamburg, Germany, has a special interest in the analysis of drug legislation and in the construction of yet another general theory of crime.

René van Swaaningen is a Reader in Criminology at the Erasmus University Rotterdam, and Secretary of The Netherlands' Society of Criminology. He has published eight books and many articles on theoretical criminology, penal reform and community safety.

Bruce Western is an Associate Professor in the Department of Sociology and a Faculty Associate of the Office of Population Research at Princeton University. His interests include comparative sociology and statistics. His recent book, *Between Class and Market: Postwar Unionization in the Capitalist Democracies* (1997).

Gema Varona is a Research Fellow and Reader in Criminology at the University of the Basque Country, Spain. Doctor of Law, graduate in Criminology and holder of a Masters Degree in Sociology of Law, she is the author of books about human rights, immigration and restorative justice. She has written articles on prisons, victims and the police. In 1998, she received a Junior Scholar Competition Award from the International Society of Criminology for an essay on mediation within the gypsy community. She is at present working on a monograph about legal cultures and juries.

Part I

Political Trends and Criminal Policy

1

Introduction

ANDREW RUTHERFORD and PENNY GREEN

> "*It may turn out, then, that going back can be a way to go forward: that remembering the modernisms of the nineteenth century can give us the vision and courage to create the modernism of the twenty-first*" (Marshall Berman, 1982: 36).

So it may be with criminal policy.

The concept of criminal policy is no more than a century old and the contributions to this Volume suggest that the transitions faced as it moves into its second century are more substantial than anything previously encountered. These include punitive trends in the realm of punishment, expansive transitions from criminality to "sub-criminality", the extension from national to global control, the diminution of criminological knowledge in the formulation of policy by the rise of actuarialism,[1] technological transitions which bring more and more of the world's citizens under surveillance and a global populism which has eclipsed the truths and knowledge of the academy.

If criminal policy has its own *internal* logic, with formal plans and strategies, as well as being shaped and defined by a myriad of *external* structures, processes and pressures (Rutherford, 1997b: xiii), then the sources of contemporary change are evidently to be found in both arenas. This Volume explores the range of internal and external criminal policy dynamics both within and beyond the parameters of the nation state. Its interweaving themes of citizenship, globalisation, state power, managerialism, individualism and punitive populism provide the framework for understanding the volume as a whole. Indeed this is a book about democracy and the limits of criminal policy.

The central paradox of criminal policy is that it necessarily exists at the margins of much of what might be done to reduce crime. This Volume is replete with examples of tensions arising from the host of pressures to criminalise social policy. Criminal policy is not equipped, nor can it be given its essentially limited parameters, to address the wider structural and socio-economic roots of

[1] Perhaps the best definition of actuarialism is that offered by Malcolm Feeley and Jonathon Simon when they write, "It is concerned with the techniques for identifying, classifying and managing groups assorted by levels of dangerousness. It takes crime for granted. It takes deviancy as normal. It is sceptical that liberal interventionist crime control strategies do or can make a difference. Thus its aim is not to intervene in individuals' lives for the purpose of ascertaining responsibility, making the guilty "pay" for their crime or changing them. Rather it seeks to regulate groups as part of a strategy of managing danger" (Feeley and Simon, 1994: 173).

law-breaking behaviour. Furthermore, an appreciation of this fundamental reality demands the foregrounding of progressive economic and social policies if governments are to seriously impact upon crime. But, as Nils Jareborg has reminded us, dealing with crime represents only one dimension of criminal policy, and at least within a liberal democracy, one cannot lose sight of the "defensive" (principles and safeguards) function of the criminal law with respect to suspects, offenders and ultimately all citizens. This imperative is underlined in several contributions to this Volume and which draw attention to forces which are pulling policy both in terms of methods and consequences, in an "offensive" direction (Jareborg, 1995: 21–8).

WIDER CONTEXT

Transitions within criminal policy-making do not occur independently of wider socio-economic and political developments and, while intelligible within existing criminal justice paradigms, may only fully be understood in the context of those wider developments.[2] As reflected throughout this Volume, we are experiencing massive social, economic and political transitions at this point in our history. Globalisation, the unification of Europe and the concomitant increasing exclusion of the developing world, all have some bearing on the dynamic of domestic criminal policy—witness the ideological fusion of immigration, illegal drugs and criminality in shaping European and American criminal justice practices in the latter half of the twentieth century. These practices are not confined to the Western powers, however; rather, in their design and implementation they manifest a global reach. Criminal policy has now become an important forum in which the United States and, to a lesser extent, Europe exercise hegemonic claims on a global scale.

The direction and execution of foreign policy has now begun to parallel and reinforce punitive and pedagogical developments in criminal policy; criminal policy in turn has responded by accommodating to the economic and political power of the world's remaining superpower. In effect, patterns of criminal policy at the millennium are merging with aspects of foreign policy—the primary interests of American and European capital and their protection dictating the control of economic, political and social threat. Since the ending of the Cold War, Western foreign policy has become increasingly concerned with issues of criminal policy (Green, 1998: 31). According to an American political scientist, "Never before have US foreign policy and US criminal justice been so deeply entangled" (Nadleman, 1993: xiii). Perhaps the most illuminating evidence comes from the war against drugs. During the 1980s, for example, foreign aid and debt re-financing in the developing world became increasingly tied to com-

[2] See especially Garland (1990) for a socio-historical exploration of penal policy in modern Western societies.

pliance with United States drug control policy. The 1984 *National Strategy for Prevention of Drug Abuse and Drug Trafficking* called, "for US decisions on foreign aid and other matters, such as re-financing of debt, to be tied to the willingness of the recipient country to execute vigorous enforcement programs against narcotic traffickers".[3]

Accordingly, "if the President fails to certify a country, or if the Congress disapproves a certification, the United States must withhold most economic and military assistance, along with support for World Bank and other loans".[4] Mutual Legal Assistance Treaties (agreements between countries which attempt to overcome national legal impediments in the process of international evidence gathering) have become another means by which America has encouraged its own hegemonic claim over legislation, criminal law enforcement and specifically drug law enforcement. The resultant process (often encompassing "coercive inducements") has been one, ". . . in which the US has made modest accommodations to foreign legal systems and foreign authorities have made much greater accommodations to US demands . . ." (Nadleman, 1993: 315).

It should be noted here, and this is not a matter directly addressed elsewhere in the Volume, that the criminal policy orientation of the United Nations has not been immune to these broader political influences. Within the various agencies of the United Nations there has, over recent years, been a substantial shift towards "offensive" law enforcement at the expense of "defensive" human rights issues. This development carries significant messages to member states across a range of policy issues, from minimum prison standards to the status of juveniles confronted by the criminal law. Not least, in this regard, is the reinforcement of national inclinations to generously enhance resources for the hardware of criminal justice.

In Europe, we see the emergence of similar patterns of control—the difference only residing in the degree of coercion. The European Commission, for example, has declared that clauses on the "fight against drugs" and on "the fight against money laundering" must now be routinely included in any external agreement the European Community enters with third countries, "not only to provide a basis for the cooperation but also to develop the political dialogue" (European Commission, 1994a: 21). Further, and perhaps more tellingly, "[T]he political dialogue, the international commitments entered into by third countries on drugs questions, and the amounts of aid available, must be exploited so as to make third countries accept the fight against drugs as a priority aspect of the Union's cooperation activity" (ibid., 23). If third countries *"maintain a resolutely negative attitude"* then any envisaged cooperation between Europe and the third country may be reviewed or suspended. It is clear from the European

[3] Drug Abuse Policy, The White House, *National Strategy for Prevention of Drug Abuse and Drug Trafficking* (US Government Printing Office, Washington DC 1984), 11.

[4] The White House, *National Drugs Control Strategy* (US Government Printing Office, Washington DC 1989), 68–9.

Plan that available aid is indeed conditional on a third country's compliance with Western drug wars.

The desire for membership of the European Union by less developed but geographically proximate countries, will, in part, ensure the expansion of Western drug enforcement strategies and wider criminal policy. Any country seeking European Union membership must develop policing agencies, legal systems and political structures which are compatible with the models employed in democratic Europe. For those countries eligible for membership (for example, Poland, Hungary, Romania, Bulgaria, the Czech and Slovak Republics and most recently Turkey) the EU has instituted programmes (for example, PHARE) designed to facilitate "democratisation". For those countries eligibility will currently rest heavily on such compliance (Green, 1998: 28). As Dario Melossi suggests in Chapter 9, immigration discourse is also playing a central role in defining what it is to be European. Similarly, increasing national conformity on criminal policy issues may also be seen as a crucial part of the transition toward a European identity.

The development of globalisation has been accompanied by political trends which raise fundamental questions about the nature of state power. We are increasingly witness to right-of-centre social democratic governments strengthening the remit of criminal policy in order to secure individual and public order. In The Netherlands, order and managerialism have replaced liberal pluralism. In England and Wales, New Labour's approach to criminal policy is all-embracing, tightly co-ordinated and highly centralised. The integrity of individual government departments, once regarded as necessarily constitutionally separate, has been transcended by the insistence on "joined up" government. An example is the joint statement by the Home Secretary, Lord Chancellor and Attorney General on *Criminal Justice Planning Structures* in August 1998 which envisages a three-year strategic plan "for the criminal justice system as a whole", whose overarching aims are to reduce crime and the fear of crime, to dispense justice fairly and efficiently and to promote confidence in the rule of law. By comparison, the sheer modesty of an earlier Labour Government's view of this policy arena, two decades earlier, is especially striking (see Home Office, 1977). In this latter instance, the Government reflected a minimalist approach embodying a real hesitancy about what might be achieved by government. No such hesitancy exists with New Labour.

By contrast, in those societies with a strong state tradition and a lack of formal policy-making, the existence of "invisible criminal policy" (as highlighted in Chapters 10 and 11) creates particular paradoxes. Just as prisons in Turkey allow for relaxed and humane spaces, so criminal policy itself appears largely as a lacuna. Thus, states emerging from the shadows of authoritarianism may be relatively open to initiatives from within civil society.

MILLENNIUM ISSUES IN CRIMINAL POLICY

What frames liberal democratic criminal policy discourse at the end of the twentieth century? Certainly the re-emergence of a dichotomy between the deserving and the undeserving citizen; a preoccupation with administrative and managerial forms, underpinned by ideologies of individual responsibility, the unquestioned value of punishment in securing community safety and a political reliance on "punitive populism". Chief among the rhetorically undeserving are the visible and "noisy" poor, disenfranchised working-class youth, asylum seekers, those involved in organised crime and specifically, drug traffickers. It is these groups who are targeted as threatening community safety, often by their mere presence. It is the members of these groups who through individual irresponsibility are deemed to be undeserving of welfare solutions. Punitive solutions, however, are readily at hand. Thus we have a "criminology of the other", which coexists with an increasingly de-personalised and de-humanised administration of criminal justice, informed not by theories of punishment, social responsibility, human development or community, but by an overriding commitment to the internal and self-sustaining goals of an actuarial process.

The decline of the welfare state in the United States and throughout much of Europe has been accompanied by two parallel trends—an increasing resort to punishment as a solution to social and economic problems, and the rise of managerialism as a paradigm for running a "system" concerned with identifying, arresting, processing, convicting and punishing those pre-ordained as offenders. As Beckett and Western comment in Chapter 2, "the contraction of the welfare state and the expansion of the penal apparatus in the United States represents a new and unprecedented mode of state intervention in social and economic affairs". Liberal notions of social responsibility, rehabilitation, welfare and treatment, evidenced in criminal policy-making between the 1930s and 1960s have, since the late 1970s, given way to notions of individual responsibility and punishment based on "just deserts". Central to the decline of the rehabilitative ideal has been a return to a vision of the poor as "dangerous"—a "dangerous" rather than "deserving" class, or in late twentieth-century parlance, an "underclass".

Since the early 1980s criminal policy-makers in liberal democracies have increasingly resorted to policy justifications grounded in the lowest common denominator of "public opinion". Fears of crime, of strangers, of asylum seekers, of the young and so on are cultivated through populist mechanisms (mass media and government), to create a limited sense of community and rigid community boundaries which governments are in the business of preserving. Given the problematic nature of public knowledge about crime and punishment, based primarily, as it is, on mass-media paradigms, policy justifications are inevitably distorted and unscientific. Common sense is elevated to a status far above that of scientific knowledge and virtue is made of ignorance. Populist slogans such as

"Prison Works", "No More Excuses" and "Tough on the Causes of Crime" act as signifiers of ultimate and unchallengeable truths. As Sebastian Scheerer so powerfully warns of populism in Chapter 13, "While it pretends to please the public, it might be rather serving basic instincts. In the realm of criminal justice these instincts spell anger, revenge and retaliation, exemplary punishments and death penalty for abominable crimes." Populism is thus ultimately reactionary, retributive and increasing resort to it by new right and social democratic governments reaffirms the desire to place political expediency above empirically informed and rationally derived policy.

Although the majority of Chapters in the Volume examine themes pertinent to modern Western liberal democracies, we are acutely aware that criminal policy across much of the globe has to be understood within an authoritarian and undemocratic political context (see, for example, Radzinowicz, 1991). As Francis Allen has written, "We may trust such regimes to identify what is essential to their own existence, and the lesson they teach us is that massive assaults on the values of greatest importance to liberal societies will be preceded by extinction of the legality ideal" (Allen, 1996: 97). For the purposes of this Volume we have largely concentrated our analysis on Western liberal democracies, specifically avoiding authoritarian states such as China or Iraq. Where we have sought to analyse underdevelopment and its impact on criminal policy-making, we have chosen states in democratic transition out of authoritarianism (although clearly at different stages of transition), namely, Spain and Turkey. These states are also, for political, strategic and economic reasons, particularly vulnerable to the kinds of international policy pressures outlined above.

This Volume attests to the crisis inherent within modern criminal policy-making—a crisis, at least, for those concerned with the "targets" in the exercise of state power—and demonstrates the dangers of imagining that criminal policy offers solutions to the problems of "crime" and "criminals". While forces of punitive reaction and managerial efficiency dominate this field we are not without optimism. Criminal policy futures must be rethought and resistances harnessed. These futures and resistances are, however, unlikely to derive from criminal policy, which has shown itself incapable of dealing with the "problem" of crime.

In many senses, the key themes running through this Volume—globalisation, modern managerialism, punitive populism, the developing discourse on the nature of communities and terms of citizenship, the rule of law and democratisation—can all be understood as points of resistance. In order to do this, we must detach ourselves from the imperatives and sureties of "post-modern" criminal policy and return to the fundamental precepts of a just and egalitarian society. For as Marshall Berman argues, "the modernisms of the past can give us back a sense of our own modern roots", equipping us with the vision and courage "to confront the adventures and dangers that lie ahead" (Berman, 1982: 35–6).

THEMATIC STRUCTURE OF THE VOLUME

The Volume is organised into four thematic parts. Part One *Political Trends and Criminal Policy* explores the explicitly political nature of democratic criminal policy solutions in the late twentieth century. Katherine Beckett and Bruce Western begin by arguing cogently that populism or the politics of public opinion is a misrepresentation of the public's demand for punitiveness. The "democracy at work" thesis, so favoured by successive US presidents, is built upon a framework of politically distorted representation of public opinion. It is their central thesis that the decline in welfare, witnessed in the US, corresponds and is related to an increase in penal control. Penal developments cannot therefore be understood outside an analysis of political economy. In the US the sustained policy effect of low unemployment has been dependent on a policy intervention of ever-increasing magnitude—i.e. the incarceration of ever-increasing numbers of young men. What they describe is an incarcerative solution to problems of poverty, welfare and education—a criminology of "the other". As with David Faulkner and René van Swaaningen (in Part Two), these American authors document the transition from welfare to law and order through the administrative medium of managerialism.

Andrew Rutherford follows with a sharply critical analysis of New Labour's approach to criminal policy in Britain, with a particular focus on the Crime and Disorder Act 1998. He discusses three developments of major concern: an enhanced role for citizens in assuming responsibility for crime prevention and control; the reconceptualisation of crime prevention away from primary crime prevention to measures directed at "potential" offenders and tertiary prevention (aimed at convicted offenders); and the "quasi-criminal" and other disturbing pre-emptive remedies (i.e., the use of hybrid civil–criminal remedies) to criminalise sections of the community. Thus, to borrow Francis Allen's terminology, the "habits of legality" have become significantly weaker in the administration of criminal justice (Allen, 1996). From this perspective, tackling underlying social and economic issues is seen very much as a secondary strategy incapable of dealing with the "problem" of crime which is unambiguously presented as a matter of individual responsibility. These concerns are explored through a case-study of the "anti-social behaviour" order and the part it plays in creating a class of "sub-criminal" members of society, with "sub-criminality" forming the link between civil nuisance and criminality.

Pat Carlen examines the politics of late twentieth century British criminal justice with particular respect to young people and the issue of "citizenship". Her chapter examines the decline of the inclusive ideals associated with the welfare state, the shedding of major elements of the state's "welfare burden" and its displacement, in terms of responsibility, with the market, the public, the community and the individual. Concerns with youth, citizenship and exclusion have, she argues, become framed by a "culture of recrimination" in which individuals and communities must bear responsibility for crime and crime prevention. She writes of a cultivated fear of the young assisting this tendency with the unemployed, single parents and ethnic minority youth being targeted as the greatest criminal threat and not as the victims that they very often are. She argues for a "holism" in criminal justice which embodies youth citizenship and transparency of sentencing for all ages.

In Part Two, *The Managerial Agenda*, the contributors examine the phenomenon of "managerialism"—a rising paradigmatic universe which has, as the following three authors document, undermined not simply the way in which criminal justice policy and practice is organised but the very premises upon which criminal policy has traditionally been based. In his Chapter theorising the condition of criminal justice in England and Wales in the last decade of the century, David Faulkner writes of two parallel developments; the emergence of a deserving/undeserving citizen dichotomy, for whom inclusive and exclusive policies apply, and the rise of New Public Management strategies for organising public and criminal justice service where outputs of convictions and punishment are maximised as goals in themselves. He draws sharp parallels between the "exclusive" politics of the 1980s and 1990s, the elevation of individual responsibility over state responsibility and the popularity of New Public Management strategies. Criminal justice has become a victim in the devaluation of social sciences and academic research. Accountancy, economics, financial management, downsizing and cost-cutting have become reified—they, rather than ideologies, welfare or rehabilitation, have begun to define the content of criminal policy. His chapter is a call for the revitalisation of the liberal concepts of citizenship, inclusion, personal and social responsibilities, accountability, fairness, equality, respect, opportunity and proportionality.

Case-studying the Dutch probation service, René van Swaaningen explores the transition from ideologies of concern, welfare and rehabilitation around the offender to the de-humanised practice delimited by parameters of actuarialism and economic management. He documents the move from policies motivated by offender-focused content to managerially crafted economic form. Form becomes the *raison d'être*—content is regarded as largely superfluous. It is suggested by van Swaaningen that one result of the "McDonaldisation" of criminal justice (with its emphasis on performance targets, efficiency, goal orientation, value for money etc) is that ideas inevitably stagnate and the possibility of creative developments, in terms of an offender focus, are outside the actuarial schema. Lost is the notion of the value to society in attempting to keep offenders out of prison. His chapter concludes with an argument for the elevation of "some good old-fashioned commitment to social justice"; an elevation not possible within the current restrictive framework of managerialism.

In keeping with this theme Julia Fionda, in the essay which follows, argues that the rationale behind the criminal justice process as a whole has shifted fundamentally towards what she identifies as "managerialist principles" and that the process of punishment has changed concomitantly. Most disturbing, she argues, is the lack of "natural limits" inherent in managerialism. Thus expansion offers limitless possibilities for developing means of greater efficiency, independent of any sense of pain or suffering embodied in the actual process of punishment. She also suggests that the manipulation and management of public opinion is a central plank of new managerialism in its need to secure legitimation for an approach to punishment which is both sanitised and dehumanised.

In Part Three, *Exclusion in the New Europe,* Hans-Jörg Albrecht, Dario Melossi and Thomas Mathiesen explore some of the central criminal justice issues facing the New Europe. Hans-Jörg Albrecht examines the role of the immigrant in European criminal and social policy-making from a position of conceptual polarities: endangered and dangerous; victim and offender; included and excluded; discriminated against and affirmed; protected and controlled. He argues that the fusion of European immigration (and the related issues of race and ethnicity) with crime and criminal policy can only be understood in terms of five sub-categories; citizenship, victimisation, hate violence, discrimination within criminal justice and immigration laws and control—all of which gained political prominence in the 1980s and 1990s. The chapter reviews the methodological difficulties in undertaking accurate comparative research on immigrant involvement in crime and offers ways forward for the development of a comprehensive knowledge base.

Dario Melossi's empirical analysis of crime and migration in the construction of the European Union draws important parallels between the politically manufactured "fear of crime" and a similarly cultivated fear of the immigrant. In examining the economic and social underpinnings of these linked fears, he finds that those in positions of "social weakness" and vulnerability are far more likely to be seduced by moral panics and claims of threats of danger from outsiders. While acknowledging that a small proportion of immigrants may be drawn by the host country's illegal opportunities, he insists that this must also be understood in terms of wider political economy and the contribution this may make to the political discourse on immigration, crime and "otherness". The chapter concludes with a call for a struggle to ensure that an ethnic underclass does not become a reality in northern Italy.

The transition to a unified Europe, and the "free" movement of labour it espouses, have been accompanied by the development of a global European surveillance system which Thomas Mathiesen argues, in his chapter, threatens democratic processes. A variety of independent but interlinking police-based registration and surveillance systems is rapidly developing in the new Europe and Mathiesen's argument is that there is a powerful tendency toward convergence and integration—tendencies which will result in a gigantic and monolithic surveillance structure of panopticon proportions. This development has serious expansionist implications for criminal justice because only a minority of those registered will have or may have committed crimes—the majority will be those who, "in a diffuse sense are viewed as threats to public order and state security and unwanted aliens". To avert the further erosion of democratic processes,

Mathiesen argues for a resistance strategy which includes the development of a critical and alternative public sphere and for a continual monitoring and demystification of the expanding surveillant state.

Part Four of the Volume takes up global themes—state power, democratisation, globalisation and ultimately "futures". We are reminded of the limits of ethnocentrically liberal democratic approaches to criminal policy in Penny Green's cautionary chapter on Turkish criminal justice. She describes an authoritarian, racist, brutal but strangely *laissez-faire* dynamic in the construction and operation of Turkish criminal policy. She also describes what she terms the "New Policy-Makers"—a group of Turkish academics, politicians and judges who are keen (albeit in a pedestrian manner) to transform Turkish arrangements and processes in line with Western models of legal principle, managerial efficiency and consistency. Her major thesis is that the imposition upon (or willing importation by) democratising countries of Western models of criminal justice policy, without contextual appreciation, may have unforeseen repressive outcomes. In the case of Turkey, the formalisation of criminal policy may result in an expansion of criminal justice parameters resulting in the imprisonment or punishment of people who are currently defined out of the criminal justice process. In addition, current informalities and the reactive nature of Turkish criminal justice practice—usually resulting from a *lack* of policy (for example, in the prison system)—can result in certain "humane", or at least benign, outcomes for offenders (regular amnesties, considerable autonomy for prisoners, etc). "Ordinary" crime is not perceived as representing a significant social problem and fear of crime neither exists to any significant degree nor is it in any way influential in decisions of policy. Rather, it is the political and military conflict in Turkey's south-east; the perceived rise of Islamic fundamentalism and the state's general insecurity about its own national integrity which are central to shaping the reactive practice of Turkish criminal justice. Criminal policy, Green argues, is unable to offer any solutions.

Spain offers interesting parallels as a state considerably further along the democratic path than Turkey but still clearly in transition from the authoritarian legacy of Francoism. Gema Varona identifies a bifurcation within Spanish criminal policy between what she describes as "visible" and "invisible routine" criminal policy. On the one hand, the "visible" hand, formal rights and principles are enshrined in the 1978 Constitution, in statutes and articles; on the other "invisible" hand we have uncontrolled, managerially-driven, criminal justice practice which, it is argued, devalues the formal rights and principles of criminal policy. Her chapter also identifies the powerful role of political conflict (in this case Basque nationalism) in driving criminal justice policy and practice.

Sebastian Scheerer concludes the Volume by addressing the global malaise which has gripped criminal policy at the millennium. He begins by asking why, almost invariably, criminologists are so pessimistic about the future—why, given that the terror of early modernity has disappeared and approaches to punishment and crime control have been increasingly humanised, are we unable to look optimistically into the criminal justice future? His answer is "the disillusioning performance of the state"—its demonstrable exercise of violence has revealed it as aggressor rather than protector. Despite increasing democracy, the modern state has become stronger and less easy to control but that is not to say that the future implies an ever-strengthening state. Rather this essay, perhaps in contradiction to Marshall Berman, argues that such a vision, informed by "past futures", is no longer appropriate. Criminal justice futures must now be calculated on the basis of managerialism, populist nationalism, globalism and the possibility of a disorganised state.

Whatever "futures" we harness, we must be clear that criminal policy cannot be the vehicle for remedying that which is criminogenic in our society. To move forward we must, therefore, free our imaginations from the limiting constraints of modern criminal policy and work creatively to resist the repressive state and global developments which confront us at the beginning of the new millennium.

2

Crime Control, American Style: From Social Welfare to Social Control

KATHERINE BECKETT and BRUCE WESTERN

OVER THE PAST several decades, the United States has emerged as the leading example and advocate of the "get-tough" approach to crime. Since 1965, US crime control expenditures have grown from $4.6 billion to over $100 billion and the rate of incarceration in the United States is now one of the highest in the world (Danziger, 1996, 1). Increasingly, politicians agree that policies such as mandatory minimum sentencing laws and capital punishment, as well as aggressive tactics such as "quality-of-life" policing, are the best response to the crime and drug problems. US social policy has also become more punitive in recent years, especially programmes that provide cash and services to the poor. The simultaneity of these developments is not accidental, but reflects the ascendance of the notion that government's primary responsibility is social control rather than social welfare. This shift has, in turn, been facilitated by the construction of the poor as dangerous and undeserving.

Together, the state's expanded penal system and weakened welfare apparatus comprise a novel form of governance, one that has been called a "new government of misery" based on the criminalisation of poverty (Wacquant, forthcoming). US officials encourage governments around the globe—particularly those undergoing democratisation—to adopt the social and penal policies associated with this new form of governance. In recent years, this approach has been legitimated by apparently low levels of unemployment in the United States which allow the government to argue that the "American model" is far more efficient—and ultimately, more helpful to the poor—than the welfare states of Continental Europe.

This chapter analyses the process by which this mode of governance was adopted in the United States and examines the consequences of its adoption for international policy debates. In Part I, we argue that the ascendance of the "get-tough" approach in the United States is a consequence of the reorientation of government policy around social control rather than social welfare. To support this argument, we show that the discourse of "law and order" has been bound up with the attack on the US welfare state, and that the inscription of this discourse in penal policy and institutions cannot be understood apart from this larger debate over the proper role of government in society.

In Part II, we analyse the impact of growing rates of incarceration in the United States on assessments of the US economy and the welfare states of Western Europe. We argue that the incarceration of large numbers of working-age men in the United States conceals a high level of persistent unemployment, particularly among African-American men. The fact that conventional estimates of unemployment systematically ignore this population—located overwhelmingly at the fringes of the labour market—gives the false impression that the ostensibly unregulated US labour market is more efficient and productive than the welfare states of Continental Europe. This impression has been critical to international debates over social policy and has legitimated US attempts to export the "American model" of governance. We also argue that while, in the short term, the tremendous size of US prisons and jails obscures unemployment, incarceration will increase unemployment in the long run by reducing the job prospects of ex-convicts and disrupting their families and communities. The expansion of the penal apparatus in the United States thus represents a new and unprecedented mode of state intervention in social and economic affairs, one which will have long-lasting adverse consequences.

THE CHANGING FACE OF GOVERNANCE IN THE UNITED STATES

The spread and popularity of "get-tough" policies such as capital punishment and mandatory minimum sentencing statutes is, for many academics and legal professionals, something of a mystery. The most popular explanation of their adoption suggests that such policies reflect the public's preference for "cracking down on criminals". According to this "democracy-at-work" thesis, tough anti-crime measures are politicians' response to widespread popular punitiveness.[1] Although it is certainly the case that segments of the American public have become more punitive, the situation is more complicated than the democracy-at-work thesis implies. In the first place, "Public opinion is not an essentialist thing that exists outside of politics" (Fox Piven, 1998: 459). Attempts to identify the "true nature" of public opinion often reify it, implying that it is based on an experience of the world that is unmediated by culture and politics.

In addition, popular opinion regarding crime, punishment, and social justice remains heterogeneous, fluid and contradictory despite decades of political initiative on these subjects. Enthusiasm for the death penalty, for example, weakens considerably in the presence of alternatives and coexists uneasily with support for rehabilitative ideals (McGarrell and Sandys, 1996; Sandys and McGarrell, 1995). Widespread and growing support for mandatory minimum and three-strikes sen-

[1] We are indebted to Cullen, Clark and Wozniak (1985) for this term and their critique of the view that current criminal justice policies are a direct reflection of popular sentiment.

tencing laws coexists with ongoing support for policies aimed at crime prevention (Cullen, Clark and Wozniak, 1985; Cullen et al., 1990; Roberts, 1992). In fact, when asked to choose between spending money on punishment or prevention programmes, approximately two-thirds of those polled in the late 1980s chose the latter (Cullen et al., 1990). Similarly, a 1997 poll found that 82 per cent of those surveyed favoured investing in crime prevention rather than punishment, and 57 per cent would be willing to transfer money from the prison budget to community youth violence prevention projects. The fact that much of the public supports prevention and rehabilitation efforts challenges the argument that penal severity is rooted in a new, meaner political culture.

Furthermore, most versions of the "democracy-at-work" thesis cannot explain why public support for punitive anti-crime and drug policies (ambivalent as it is) has become more pronounced in recent years. More simplistic versions of this argument attribute this trend directly to a worsening crime problem, although this argument has become difficult to sustain in the face of consistent and steep declines in rates of crime. Since 1990, for example, the state prison population has grown seven per cent annually, despite significant drops in violent and property crime rates (as reported by both police and victimisation survey data) for seven consecutive years (Butterfield, 1998).

In a more sophisticated version of this argument, Garland (2000b) suggests that relatively high and growing rates of crime in the immediate post-war period mean that more people have directly or indirectly experienced criminal victimisation. Garland also argues that the professional middle classes are now less able to insulate themselves from the threat of crime. When combined with other social developments (including media accounts of crime) that heighten concern about social instability, this popular experience intensified public anxiety and triggered a long-term cultural adaptation to "crime as a normal social fact" that includes heightened efforts to enhance personal security. The punitive policies of the war on crime in the UK and US, Garland argues, are "conditioned by" this cultural context.

Garland's claim that penal policy developments have cultural underpinnings which include the experience of everyday life is undoubtedly correct, and his emphasis on the culturally mediated nature of this experience enables him to avoid reifying popular "experience" and "public opinion". In addition, the notion that popular measures aimed at enhancing personal security may, in the long run, undermine the sense that the world is a safe and secure place is an interesting one. At a more empirical level, however, Garland's argument exaggerates the fearfulness of the American public, ignores ongoing public support for rehabilitation and prevention efforts, and downplays continued racial, class and geographic differences that shape reactions to crime and punishment (see Beckett and Sasson, 2000). Furthermore, in the absence of any reference to political discourse, Garland's argument does not explain why heightened fear and anxiety (if they in fact exist) would necessarily give rise to greater support for punitive policies (see also Savelsberg 1999).

Indeed, survey research in the United States suggests that neither concern about crime as a social problem nor fear of personal victimisation necessarily give rise to punitiveness. For example, demographic groups that are relatively unafraid of being victimised typically express the highest levels of support for the "get-tough" approach, while those who are more fearful are often less punitive. Rural white men, for example, feel relatively safe but are quite staunch supporters of law and order policies. By contrast, African-Americans and white women are typically more fearful of being victimised but have historically been less punitive than white men (Stinchcombe et al., 1980). Although recent research suggests that increased risk of victimisation may be the primary cause of growing punitiveness among African-Americans, fear of victimisation remains unrelated to punitiveness among whites (Cohn and Halteman, 1991). And although there is evidence that concern about social and familial instability is widespread and related to support for punitive policies (Sasson, 1995; Tyler and Boeckmann, 1997), this connection is not immutable, but rather subject to cultural and political influence (Sasson, 1995).

Another explanation of US punitiveness stresses the fact that the United States is a more crime-ridden and violent place than other industrialised countries. However, according to international crime survey data, the US crime rate in 1995 was average when compared to ten other industrialised nations (Mayhew and van Dijk, 1997).[2] A comprehensive review of both survey and police data concluded that the incidence of non-lethal violence in the United States is similar to that in other English-speaking nations, while US rates of property crime are significantly lower than in comparable countries (Lynch, 1995). Although the rate of lethal assault continues to be exceptionally high in the United States—and it is possible that this contributes to public support for the war on crime (Zimring and Hawkins, 1997)—US punitiveness is not limited to those convicted of violent crimes. In fact, the United States incarcerates a much larger proportion of its property and drug offenders and does so for longer periods of time than other industrialised countries (Lynch, 1995).

To summarise, most accounts of the adoption of punitive anti-crime policies in the United States suggest that such policies are a reflection of popular attitudes, which are based at least to some extent on the experience or incidence of crime. More sophisticated versions of this argument recognise that crime rates do not correspond in any neat way to either cultural practices or policy developments, and that the experience of criminal victimisation is a culturally mediated one (Garland, 2000b). Still, without explicit reference to political struggle and debate, these accounts cannot explain why heightened anxiety about crime and other manifestations of social change and instability—whatever their source—would necessarily lead to punitive penal policies. In what follows, we argue that political discourse on crime and punishment has given expression to these preferences and anxieties in ways that generate support for punitive penal and social policies.

[2] Although earlier surveys did find that US rates of criminal victimisation were somewhat high, they were not exceptionally so (Tonry, 1995).

CRIME, PUNISHMENT AND THE RECONSTRUCTION OF THE STATE

In the late 1950s, Southern governors and law enforcement officials began to use the rhetoric of law and order in an attempt to heighten popular opposition to the civil rights movement. As the debate over civil rights became a national one and welfare rights activists pressured the state to assume greater responsibility for social welfare, the crime issue assumed a central place on the national political agenda. The debates over civil rights and welfare involved the question of whether government is obligated to assume responsibility for creating a more egalitarian society. Without being explicitly identified as such, competing images of the poor as "deserving" or "undeserving" became central components of this debate.

It was in this context that crime-related problems became staples of national political discourse. By drawing attention to the problems of street crime, drug addiction and delinquency, and by depicting these problems as examples of the immorality of the impoverished, conservatives encouraged the public to imagine the poor as dangerous and undeserving. Indeed, over time, race, crime, violence, delinquency and drug addiction became defining features of those now referred to as "the underclass" (Katz, 1993). Of course, the vision of the poor as dangerous and undeserving provides the "vocabulary of punitive motives" (Melossi, 1985) that justifies a more Hobbesian conception of government, according to which the state assumes responsibility for the maintenance of order but not for the reduction of the social inequalities that, ironically, threaten that order.

The politicisation of crime was thus a component of the effort to replace social welfare with social control as the principle of state policy. Toward this end, conservative politicians used discussions of the crime issue to ridicule the notion that criminal (or any other "deviant") behaviour has socio-economic causes, and promoted the alternative view that such behaviour is the consequence of "insufficient curbs on the appetites or impulses that naturally impel individuals towards criminal activities" (Richard Nixon, quoted in Marion, 1994: 70). This neo-classical view that the causes of crime lie in the human "propensity to evil" clearly calls for the expansion of the social control apparatus rather than policies aimed at ameliorating social inequalities. As then-President Nixon concluded, the "solution to the crime problem is not the quadrupling of funds for any governmental war on poverty but more convictions" (quoted in Matusow, 1984: 401).

In the decades that followed, conservatives continued to emphasise "street crime" and to promote individualistic understandings of its causes. President Ronald Reagan's first major address on crime, for example, consisted of a sweeping philosophical attack on "the social thinkers of the fifties and sixties who discussed crime only in the context of disadvantaged childhoods and poverty stricken neighborhoods" (quoted in Gross, 1982: 123). The need to hold individuals—not society—accountable for crime was emphasised again and again in Reagan's speeches on crime:

> "Here in the richest nation in the world, where more crime is committed than in any other nation, we are told that the answer to this problem is to reduce our poverty. This isn't the answer . . . Government's function is to protect society from the criminal, not the other way around" (Reagan 1984a: 252, our emphasis).

Somewhat contradictorily, conservatives also identified the "culture of welfare" as an important cause of "social pathologies"—especially crime, delinquency and drug addiction. For example, Presidential candidate Barry Goldwater argued in the 1964 election campaign that welfare programmes are an important cause of increased lawlessness and crime:

> "If it is entirely proper for the government to take away from some to give to others, then won't some be led to believe that they can rightfully take from anyone who has more than they? No wonder law and order has broken down, mob violence has engulfed great American cities, and our wives feel unsafe in the streets" (quoted in Matusow, 1984: 143).

Lest they be perceived as mean-spirited, these critics of the welfare state depicted public assistance programmes as detrimental to the poor themselves and conservatives as the true allies of the impoverished:

> "By nearly every measure, the position of poor Americans worsened under the leadership of our opponents. Teenage drug use, out-of-wedlock births, and crime increased dramatically. Urban neighborhoods and schools deteriorated. Those whom the government intended to help created a cycle of dependency that could not be broken. Government became a drug, providing temporary relief, but addiction as well" (Reagan, 1985: 1176).

Over the years, conservatives continued to argue that welfare programmes such as Aid Families Dependent Children (AFDC) not only reproduce poverty, but accounted, along with lenient crime policies, for the rising crime rate and problems such as drug abuse. Like individualistic interpretations of crime, this argument was used in an effort to legitimate reductions in welfare spending and the adoption of punitive crime and drug policies. President Reagan made this goal quite explicit:

> "This is precisely what we're trying to do to the bloated Federal Government today: remove it from interfering in areas where it doesn't belong, but at the same time strengthen its ability to perform its constitutional and legitimate functions . . . In the area of public order and law enforcement, for example, we're reversing a dangerous trend of the last decade. While crime was steadily increasing, the Federal commitment in terms of law personnel was steadily shrinking. . . ." (Reagan, 1984b, 672).

Despite their differences, then, the neo-classical and "culture of welfare" theories of crime initially promoted by conservatives, similarly imply the need to adopt policies that enhance social control and diminish government responsibility for the reduction of social inequality. Initially, the (Democratic) Johnson administration countered the conservative anti-crime campaign by stressing the social causes of crime and by questioning the accuracy of the reported increases in the official crime rate. But by 1965, liberals began to change course, and over time Democratic politicians have become even less likely to challenge the conservative approach to the crime problem. Particularly in response to the Reagan/Bush war on drugs, Democratic Party officials made the conservative rhetoric on crime and drugs their own.

The liberal about-face on crime-related problems reflects, among other things, conservatives' ability to disseminate law-and-order rhetoric through the mass media. The presence of political elites—especially politicians and law enforcement personnel—in news stories that focused on crime and drugs had a significant impact on the way in which the crime and drug problems were framed. For example, in the 1960s, news stories in which officials served as primary sources were far more likely to identify "liberal permissiveness" and the loss of respect for authority as the main cause of crime than were stories which relied on non-official sources. Similarly, drug-related news stories that relied primarily on politicians or law enforcement personnel in the 1980s were much more likely to emphasise the need for greater law enforcement efforts and/or punishment and were less likely to challenge the assumptions of the war on drugs (Beckett, 1995, 1997). While their capacity to shape media representations is not infinite, officials have been quite effective in using the mass media to disseminate images of the crime and drug problems which implied the need for greater punishment and control.

The capacity of elites to mobilise public opinion in favour of "get tough" solutions to the crime problem also reflects the fact that the symbols and rhetoric associated with the discourse of law and order resonate with deep-seated cultural "myths" and help to make sense of lived experience. The neo-classical depiction of crime as a personal and free choice, for example, is consonant with American individualism. Similarly, the argument that welfare programmes encourage family disintegration and crime taps into (and reinforces) widespread concern about social instability and the "breakdown" of the family (see Sasson, 1995). The fact that the discourse of law and order resonates with (and reinforces) these "myths" helps to explain its growing popularity.

The racial sub-text of the discourse of "law and order" helps to explain the particular appeal of this rhetoric among those who hold racially and socially conservative views. While many such voters are long-time supporters of the Republican party, others are economic liberals who have historically voted Democrat. In-depth interviews with these "swing" voters reveal that racially charged hostility toward those who "seek something for nothing"—criminals and welfare cheats in particular—is widespread, and that this hostility informs support for punitive anti-crime and welfare policies (Omi and Winant, 1987; see also Edsall and Edsall, 1991). The strength of these sentiments has had quite significant policy implications, as the Republican and Democratic parties have competed intensely for the loyalty of these "Reagan Democrats" in recent years.

Finally, while the incidence of violent crime probably did not increase in recent decades, the sense that it was increasingly pervasive and random in nature has generated anxiety and fear among some. When combined with anxiety about social change and instability, calls for "tough" anti-crime policies appear to identify a scapegoat for and resolution of these concerns (Garland, 2000b; Tyler and Boeckmann, 1997).

Although the policies associated with the war on crime are relatively popular, particularly among certain segments of the white population, it is important to recognise that the "success" of the campaign for law and order reflects the resonance of a particular discourse and set of images at a specific historic and political juncture. Those who attribute this success instead to a monolithic and immutable "American punitiveness" overlook the political origins of the campaign for law and order, as well as the complexity of popular beliefs about crime and punishment. This complexity is an important resource for progressives who seek to shift the terms of the debate in a more humanitarian and progressive direction. The fact that most members of the public continue to believe that crime has social causes and that rehabilitative programmes are an effective means of responding to crime suggests that the discourses of "root causes" may still be deployed with some success. Similarly, the fact that concern about the "breakdown" of the family (and social fabric more generally) informs assessments of the crime problem (Sasson, 1995) and support for punitive anti-crime policies (Tyler and Boeckmann, 1997) need not work exclusively to the advantage of conservatives; a progressive alternative to the rhetoric of the war on crime might stress the ways in which structural forces such as unemployment, low wages, inadequate medical care and limited access to child care can diminish the capacity of parents to care for their young (Sasson, 1995; see also Currie, 1998).

To sum up, the discourse of law and order has become more entrenched in American political culture and is especially popular among socially and racially conservative voters. Concerns about security, change and stability inform this shift, as do racial tensions and stereotypes. But it is also clear that political elites have played a leading role in calling attention to crime-related problems, in defining these problems as the consequence of insufficient punishment and control, and in channelling popular concerns in ways that generate popular support for punitive anti-crime and welfare policies. This ideological campaign has been a component of a much larger effort to establish social control rather than social welfare as the primary state responsibility.

FROM SOCIAL CONTROL TO SOCIAL WELFARE

The effort to reshape government policy around social control rather than social welfare has had important consequences for US social policy, and in particular, for welfare programmes aimed at the poor. Beginning as a pension programme for widows, Aid Families Dependent Children was gradually transformed into a cash support programme for single mothers after World War II and has remained the main cash assistance programme. In the 1960s, however, policymakers began to challenge means-tested welfare entitlement. In 1967, a Democratic Congress imposed the first work and training requirements on AFDC recipients, and additional work requirements were added in 1971 (Heclo, 1994). The redistributive effect of AFDC was further weakened by its variation across states: poor states offered small benefits with tight eligibility rules, while wealthier states could afford more generous support (Patterson, 1981: 162–3).

The already tenuous position of AFDC in the 1970s foreshadowed the welfare state retrenchment of the 1980s. Two pieces of legislation in the first year of the Reagan administration significantly eroded the redistributive role of American government. The 1981 Economic Recovery Tax Act effected a general 23 per cent cut in marginal tax rates. However, standard deductions and personal exemptions remained unchanged, providing minimal tax relief to low-income families. Because the tax cut was accompanied by a large increase in defence spending, unprecedented budget deficits resulted, placing strong downward pressure on social spending (Danziger and Gottschalk, 1995: 24). The declining economic position of the poor was further undermined by the Omnibus Budget Reconciliation Act (OBRA). Driven by a philosophy of self-reliance and justified by the notion that many welfare recipients were "cheats" or "greedy, not needy", OBRA reduced real spending on employment and training, unemployment compensation, and removed nearly half-a-million working families from AFDC rolls between 1981 and 1983 alone (Danziger and Gottschalk, 1995: 25).

The most recent revisions to the welfare system in the 1996 Personal Responsibility and Work Opportunity Act further tightened work and eligibility requirements. The average benefit payment to families entitled to AFDC has also declined considerably. In response to these cuts in state assistance to the poor, child poverty rates in the 1980s and 1990s have been about one-third higher than in the 1970s (Danziger and Gottschalk, 1995: 67). The severity of poverty has also increased: the average payment required to lift the poor above the poverty line was more than 20 per cent higher in the 1980s and early 1990s than in the 1970s (Danziger and Weinberg, 1994: 33).

The reorientation of government policy has had an equally dramatic effect on penal policy and institutions. Beginning in the mid-1970s, the US incarceration rate began to climb. Between 1980 and 1998, the number of people incarcerated in the United States increased by more than 300 per cent and now totals over 1.8 million (BJS, 1999). Approximately 1.2 million of these inmates are housed in federal and state prisons, up from 266,000 in 1980. The jail population also grew dramatically during this period, from about 183,000 to nearly 600,000 (BJS, 1999). The number of people on probation and parole has grown almost as rapidly as the inmate population, and by 1997 nearly 5.7 million adults (almost three per cent of the population) were under some form of correctional supervision (BJS, 1998, Tables 6.1 and 6.2). These developments have had particularly pronounced implications for young, male minorities. By 1995, one out of three (32 per cent) black males aged 20–29 were under some form of state supervision and nearly seven per cent of all black male adults were incarcerated (BJS, 1998).

Keeping this many people under governmental supervision is, of course, quite costly. Total criminal justice expenditures increased from approximately $36 billion in 1982 to nearly $94 billion ten years later (BJS, 1995a, Table 1.1). By contrast, only $41 billion was spent on all unemployment benefits and employment-related services in 1992 (Bureau of the Census, 1995, Table 585). While the budgets of all components of the criminal justice system have grown, spending on "correctional" institutions has increased most dramatically. By 1992, the public cost of correctional facilities alone totalled more than $31 billion (BJS, 1995a: 3).

The attack on programmes aimed at the poor has thus occurred alongside an unprecedented expansion of the social control apparatus. The simultaneity of these shifts is not accidental, but reflects a redefinition of the role and responsibilities of the US government that has been legitimated by the image of the poor as dangerous and undeserving. In what follows, we argue that by removing disproportionately working age and minority men from estimates of employment and unemployment levels, the expansion of the penal system has bolstered assessments of US economic performance. These falsely optimistic assessments have, in turn, been a crucial source of legitimation for those promoting the "American model" of governance.

INCARCERATION AND THE DEBATE OVER SOCIAL POLICY

The proper role of the government in social and economic affairs has not just been debated within the United States, but is the subject of intense controversy around the globe. In these debates, the "American model", ostensibly characterised by an unregulated labour market, is contrasted with the so-called "Continental model". Critics of the latter contrast high rates of European unemployment with the apparently strong performance of the US labour market and conclude that the decline of Keynesianism in the United States has produced a more efficient economic system. According to this argument, European welfare states, with their generous unemployment benefits, high levels of unionisation, and strong welfare programmes, are characterised by reduced market flexibility and work incentives and, therefore, high levels of unemployment.

But the estimates of unemployment upon which these arguments rest do not include the prison and jail populations, which in the US are now estimated at nearly 1.8 million. In what follows, we argue that apparently low rates of unemployment in the United States are in part due to the dramatic expansion of its penal system. When the incarcerated population is included in estimates of unemployment, it appears that European economies have had lower levels of male unemployment than has the US for most of the past two decades.

Social policy, penal institutions, and the labour market

It is often observed that the United States lags far behind Western Europe in industrial relations policy and welfare state development (see Table 1). The comparative weakness of US industrial relations is illustrated by unionisation and collective bargaining coverage statistics (Columns 1 and 2). Social policy is also less developed in the United States. For example, while approximately one-quarter of the gross domestic product (GDP) is devoted to social welfare in the large European countries, US social spending accounts for only 15 per cent of the GDP (Column 3). Similarly, both coverage of unemployment insurance and spending on employment-related services in the United States are quite low by comparative standards (Columns 4 and 5).

Although welfare and industrial relations statistics do illustrate the weakness of social protection mechanisms in the United States, this does not justify the claim that market principles alone drive the superior US employment record.

Table 1. Selected industrial relations and social policy characteristics of 12 OECD countries.

Countries	*Private Sector Union Density*	*Collective Bargaining Coverage*	*Unemp – Total Social Spending*	*Active loyment Benefit Coverage*	*Labour Market Spending*
Australia	32	80	13	82	0.34
Canada	28	38	19	129	0.68
Denmark	72	—	28	113	1.56
France	8	92	27	98	0.88
Germany	30	90	23	89	1.64
Italy	32	—	25	—	—
Japan	23	23	12	36	0.13
Netherlands	20	71	29	105	1.12
Norway	41	75	29	61	1.14
Sweden	81	83	33	93	3.21
United Kingdom	38	47	24	71	0.59
United States	13	18	15	34	0.25
Average excluding the United States	38	72	24	94	1.03

Note: Union density and collective bargaining coverage are expressed as a percentage of all employees. Data are for 1988, except for Canada and the Netherlands (measured in 1985) and the United Kingdom (1989). Coverage is expressed as a percentage of all employees. Data are for 1990 except for France (1985), Germany (1992) and Japan (1989). Total social spending is measured as a percentage of GDP. All data are for 1990. Unemployment benefit coverage measures unemployment beneficiaries as a percentage of unemployed recorded in labour force surveys. Data are for 1990–1 except for Denmark (1992) and Sweden (1992). Active labour market spending includes public spending on training, employment services, youth measures and subsidised employment expressed as a percentage of GDP. Data are for 1990–2.

Source: Western and Beckett, 1999.

Labour markets are embedded in and affected by a wide array of social arrangements that extend beyond the regulative mechanisms of the welfare state. As we have seen, market deregulation and welfare state retrenchment have been accompanied by rapid expansion of the criminal justice system in the United States. Public expenditures on the penal system are a significant and costly state intervention comparable in size to the large social programmes of European welfare states. Indeed, due to low levels of unemployment insurance coverage and high rates of incarceration, more American men were incarcerated than received unemployment benefits in 1995.

US incarceration rates are even more striking when compared to those of other industrialised democracies (see Table 2). In 1993, the US incarceration rate was five to ten times greater than other OECD countries (Column 1). These high rates correspond to large absolute numbers (Column 2). In the United States, prison and jail inmates are counted in the millions. In European countries, prison populations number in the thousands.

Table 2. Numbers of inmates and incarceration rates per 100,000 adult population, selected OECD countries, 1992–1993.

Countries	*Number of Inmates*	*Incarceration Rate*
Australia	15,895	91
Canada	30,659	116
Denmark	3,406	66
France	51,457	84
Germany	64,029	80
Italy	46,152	80
Japan	45,183	36
Netherlands	7,935	49
Sweden	5,668	69
United Kingdom	60,676	93
United States	1,339,695	519
US Blacks	626,207	1,947
US Whites	658,233	306
Average excluding the United States	26,988	78

Source: Western and Beckett, 1999.

The short-term effect of incarceration on unemployment

By moving more than one million able-bodied men of working age into prisons and jails, US criminal justice policy has had profound effects on estimates of employment trends. Because they are institutionalised, prison inmates are not counted by population surveys as members of the civilian labour force, or even among the jobless—those "not in the labour force". In the short-term, then, incarceration lowers conventional measures of unemployment and joblessness by obscuring significant numbers of working age men from the purview of census takers. These labour market statistics therefore give a falsely optimistic picture of labour utilisation when incarceration rates are high.

To remedy this limitation, we analyse unemployment trends that take account of the size of the incarcerated population. If the number of unemployed is given as U, and the total number of civilian employees E, the usual unemployment rate is calculated by:

$$u = 100U/(U+E)$$

To take account of the incarcerated population, P, we also examine the adjusted unemployment rate:

$$u^* = 100(U+P)/(U+P+E)$$

The importance of incarceration as a source of hidden unemployment varies by sex and across countries. More than 90 per cent of prison and jail inmates are male in the United States, so we focus on trends in the labour market conditions of men. From a comparative perspective, the short-term effect of incarceration is tiny in Europe because incarceration rates are so low (see Table 3). In most European countries, unemployed males outnumber male prison inmates by

Table 3. Male incarceration and unemployment rates in the United States and Western Europe, 1990.

	Number Unemp-loyed (U)	*Number Incar-cerated (P)*	*U/P*	*Unemp-loyment Rate (u)*	*Adjusted Unemp-loyment Rate (u*)*	*Difference between conventional and adjusted estimates (in %)* $u^* - u$
Austria	63	6.0	10.5	3.0	3.3	0.3
Belgium	143	6.7	21.5	6.1	6.3	0.2
Denmark	121	3.4	35.8	7.8	8.0	0.2
Finland	54	3.4	15.8	4.1	4.3	0.2
France	935	44.7	20.9	7.0	7.3	0.3
Germany	968	49.7	19.5	5.5	5.8	0.3
Italy	1102	11.4	96.7	7.6	7.6	0.1
Netherlands	228	6.2	36.9	5.6	5.7	0.1
Sweden	36	4.8	7.5	1.5	1.7	0.2
UK	1155	51.4	22.5	7.2	7.5	0.3
United States	3799	1087.9	3.5	5.6	7.0	1.5

Note: Data from all countries are for 1990, except Italy (1986). The unemployed and incarcerated populations are measured in thousands.
Source: Western and Beckett, 1999.

between ten and 20 to one. In the United States in 1995 this ratio had fallen to just under 2.2 (Column 3). Differences between the United States and Europe are also reflected in the relative size of the conventional unemployment rate, u, and the adjusted figure that includes the incarcerated, u*. In most European countries, counting prison inmates in estimates of unemployment only changes the unemployment rate by a few tenths of a percentage point. By contrast, prison and jail inmates in the United States added 1.5 points to the usual unemployment rate in 1990 (Column 5) and over two points by 1994.

Conventional estimates of US and average European unemployment suggest that unemployment in the United States peaked in 1983 at about ten per cent, dropped in the later 1980s, and rose again in the early 1990s—but recovered fairly quickly after each of these recessions. Although European unemployment rates were low compared to the United States until 1984, estimates of unemployment suggest that recovery from the recessions of the mid-1980s and early 1990s in Europe was relatively weak.

But US employment performance looks less impressive once we take the size of the prison and jail population into account. Our adjusted estimate adds inmates to the male unemployment count and shows that male labour market inactivity in the United States never fell below about seven per cent in the 1980s. By 1994, the prison and jail population had become so large that it added about two percentage points to the male unemployment rate. These modified estimates suggest that unemployment in the economically buoyant period of the mid-1990s was about eight per cent—higher than any conventional US unemployment rate since the recession of the early 1980s. When the incarcerated population is included in estimates of unemployment and joblessness, European rates of unemployment are actually lower than those in the United States for 18 of the 20 years between 1975 and 1995.

A more detailed examination of the US data allows us to identify the impact of incarceration on estimates of unemployment and jobless rates among black and white men. Observed unemployment, u, and the adjusted measure, u*, are shown in Table 4. In 1983, when the prison population is added to the unemployment count, the resulting unemployment rate for all men is just one percentage point higher. Estimates of unemployment among black men in 1983 increased by four percentage points to 23 per cent. The effect of incarceration on white male unemployment is smaller, raising the unemployment rate by only about half a percentage point. As the prison population grew through the 1980s, however, the labour market effects of incarceration became much larger. For all men, average unemployment in the 1990s was lifted to nearly eight per cent. When the incarcerated population is included in estimates of black unemployment we find that nearly one in five African-American men were without a job throughout the 1990s. Incarceration has a similar effect on estimates of black joblessness, a category that includes those no longer looking for work.

To summarise, the growth of US incarceration through the 1980s and 1990s conceals a high rate of persistent unemployment and joblessness. Adjusted

Table 4. Conventional and Adjusted (Incarcerated Population Included) Unemployment and Jobless Rates for Men, 1983–1995.

	All Men		*Black Men*		*White Men*	
Year	*Conventional* *u*	*Adjusted* *u**	*Conventional* *u*	*Adjusted* *u**	*Conventional* *u*	*Adjusted* *u**
Unemployment Rates:						
1983	9.7	10.6	19.1	23.0	8.6	9.2
1985–9	5.5	6.7	11.6	16.9	4.7	5.5
1990–4	5.9	7.7	11.3	18.8	5.2	6.3
Jobless Rates:						
1983	29.4	29.9	39.5	41.7	28.3	28.6
1985–9	6.2	27.0	34.0	37.0	25.3	25.7
1990–5	27.0	28.1	34.3	38.5	26.2	26.8

Source: Western and Beckett, 1999.

unemployment figures that include the incarcerated population suggest the United States labour market has performed worse than European labour markets for much of the past two decades. Incarceration has particularly strong effects on estimates of black unemployment: when inmates are added to jobless statistics, rates of joblessness among black men have remained around 40 per cent. It should be noted that because only approximately five per cent of inmates in the US worked in 1996 producing goods or services for external consumption,[3] omitting inmates engaged in this type of work would not significantly alter these revised estimates of unemployment. However, because our estimates do not reflect reductions in joblessness due to expanded criminal justice system employment, they may significantly underestimate the short-term impact of penal expansion on estimates of unemployment.

The long-term effect of incarceration on unemployment

Thus it appears that by removing large numbers of men from the labour force count, incarceration artificially lowers conventional estimates of labour inactivity. However, it is likely that the expansion of prisons and jails will increase unemployment in the long run. Research suggests that the prospects of job applicants with no criminal record are far better than those of demographically similar persons who were convicted and incarcerated. While convicts who acquire educational and vocational skills in prison are able to improve their chances of employment (Irwin and Austin, 1994), resources for education and

[3] This estimate is based on data provided in (BJS, 1995b) and by Rod Miller of the BJA Jail Work and Industry Center, personal communication, 1997.

vocational training in prisons and jails have declined in both absolute and relative terms, and the recent decision to deny inmates Pell grants to pursue higher education suggests that this trend is likely to continue in the future.

Our analysis of data from the National Longitudinal Study of Youth (NLSY) (not presented here) supports the argument that incarceration increases the likelihood of future joblessness. The results of this analysis indicate that youth incarceration reduces annual employment by about five percentage points, or about three weeks per year, controlling for education, work experience and local labour market conditions. The effect is larger for blacks, whose employment is reduced by about eight percentage points (more than four weeks in the year) by juvenile incarceration. In fact, the effects of youth incarceration on adult employment are larger than failure to graduate from high school or living in a high unemployment area. Even after 15 years, respondents who were incarcerated as juveniles worked between five and ten percentage points less than their counterparts who did not experience incarceration. The effects of adult incarceration on employment status are even greater, reducing employment by about one-fifth or about ten weeks per year. A variety of analyses thus strongly supported the conclusion that incarceration has large and extremely long-lasting effects on the job prospects of ex-convicts.

CONCLUSION

Over the past several decades, the crime issue in the United States has played a central role in justifying the reorientation of government policy around social control rather than social welfare. As a result, the already feeble protections offered to the poor have shrunk considerably, while penal institutions have expanded dramatically. In international policy debates, apparently low levels of unemployment in the United States are attributed to this uniquely "American model" of government.

By contrast, our research suggests that the US state has made a significant intervention in the labour market by expanding the penal system in the 1980s and 1990s. Consisting mostly of young, unskilled, able-bodied men of working age, large and growing prison and jail populations conceal a high level of joblessness that, if included in labour market statistics, would contribute about two percentage points to the male unemployment rate by the mid-1990s. These effects are especially strong for African-Americans: labour inactivity is understated by about two-thirds, or seven percentage points, by the conventional measure of black male unemployment. Despite claims of "Eurosclerosis" and the successful deregulation of the US labour market, our revised estimates show that unemployment in the United States exceeded average European rates between 1975 and 1993.

While incarceration has the immediate effect of lowering conventional estimates of joblessness and unemployment, it significantly increases the chances of unemployment among ex-convicts. With well over one million men currently in prison or jail, current levels of incarceration annually generate the equivalent of a full year of unemployment for more than 200,000 American men. In the aggregate, then, it appears that the high US incarceration rate will greatly reduce the productivity and employment of the male workforce.

How can these findings be reconciled? If incarceration lowers conventional measures of joblessness in the short-term but increases unemployment in the long-term, why does the US labour market still perform well according to conventional indicators? The steady expansion of the prison and jail population, combined with high rates of recidivism and re-incarceration, helps to explain this paradox. About two-thirds of young state prisoners are re-arrested within three years, removing many of those at risk of unemployment from the labour force. With high rates of recidivism and intensified surveillance of ex-convicts, the short-term negative effect of incarceration on unemployment dominates the long-term positive effect. Under these conditions, the appearance of strong employment performance has been assisted by an ever-increasing correctional population. Thus, far from being unregulated, the distinctively American mode of labour market regulation may be understood as *hyper-regulatory*. By this we mean that a sustained policy effect (low unemployment) depends on a policy intervention of ever-increasing magnitude.

It has been argued that some European welfare states may also conceal unemployment. Although there may be some truth to this charge, the dangers of US prison expansion are significantly greater than those posed by European welfare policies. Unlike welfare institutions, the penal system has unambiguously negative effects on the job prospects of its clients. Where many job training programmes and employment-related services expand human capital and strengthen social networks, incarceration devastates the market power and productive capacity of potential workers. Moreover, penal expansion exacerbates rather than alleviates racial and class inequalities. In summary, the massive expansion of the penal system is a uniquely American mode of state intervention that improves conventional indicators of labour market performance in the short-term—but will exact a high social cost in the long run. While some policy analysts celebrate the free market principles of the US model, these same principles should be assessed in light of the significant and coercive reallocation of labour through the expansion of American prisons and jails.

3

An Elephant on the Doorstep: Criminal Policy without Crime in New Labour's Britain

ANDREW RUTHERFORD

ALMOST IMMEDIATELY AFTER its landslide victory of May 1997, the Labour Government acted to widen the state's reach over "anti-social behaviour". The appearance of the anti-social behaviour order (ASBO), together with other pre-emptive remedies, suggests that a cornerstone of New Labour's emerging criminal policy is reliance on civil procedures with a criminal sting. This Chapter explores the origins and implications of New Labour's endeavour through the Crime and Disorder Act 1998 to bring "sub-criminal" conduct within the ambit of the criminal justice process.

The twin themes of the Crime and Disorder Act are those of prevention and intervention. A duty is placed on police forces and local authorities to formulate and implement strategies to "reduce crime and disorder". The substance of these strategies will depend on analyses of crime and disorder, augmented by a local consultation process. The statute also provides a highly interventionist framework, mostly directed at young offenders, embracing all stages of the criminal justice process from a "final warning" by the police to "youth offending teams" and "training and detention orders" for 12 to 17 year olds, with the possibility of reducing the minimum age for a custodial sentence to ten.[1] Indeed, the legislation is characterised by a bewildering array of civil, criminal and quasi-criminal orders reflecting the hard-edged approach to criminal policy pursued by the Labour Party since 1992.[2] Pride of place, at the head of 120 sections, is given to the ASBO, the most radical expression to date of New Labour's

[1] The interventionist agenda for dealing with young offenders was set out in a stream of consultation papers issued before and after the 1997 election, culminating in Home Office (1997c). Under section 37 of the Crime and Disorder Act 1998, it is "the principal aim of the youth justice system to prevent offending by children and young persons".

[2] For an early review of quasi-criminal remedies with reference to sexual and drugs offenders, see Rubin (1971); more recent discussions include, French (1988), Richards (1989); see also *Kansas v. Hendricks* (1997) 138 L Ed 2d 501 in which the Supreme Court upheld the Sexually Violent Predator Act 1994 in the state of Kansas under which a sex offender, prior to his release from prison, may face civil commitment. By a majority of 5–4 the Court held: "The Act does not establish criminal proceedings and involuntary confinement under it is not punishment."

penchant "to mix the best of the civil and criminal law".[3] By fashioning the prohibitions to a particular individual, it has been suggested that the order creates "a form of personalised criminal law" (Leng, Taylor and Wasik, 1998: 13). This new power, along with other orders directed at sex offenders,[4] children under the age of criminal responsibility and the parents of young offenders, is part of New Labour's endeavour to target selected categories of troublesome persons as one aspect of its strategy for crime and disorder reduction.[5]

As with much else about New Labour, criminal policy was in an embryonic shape when the Crime and Disorder Bill received Royal Assent in the summer of 1998. A close observer of the British political scene remarked at the time:

> "We know what the new regime is not; we don't yet know what it is . . . New Labour speaks and acts as though it embodies a national consensus—a consensus of the well-intentioned, embracing rich and poor, young and old, suburbs and inner cities,

[3] Jack Straw, 16 December 1996, H.C. Deb, 6th ser., Vol. 287, col. 791. In reviewing the origins and possibilities of the ASBO, this chapter takes account of developments up to the Orders taking effect on 1 April 1999.

[4] The construction of the sex offender order is largely similar to that of the ASBO. The police may make an application and the magistrates' court may make the order when the defendant is a sex offender and has acted "in such a way as to give reasonable cause to believe that an order . . . is necessary to protect the public from serious harm"; the minimum period of the order is five years. Alun Michael, the Home Office Minister, told Parliament that paedophiles are the true targets. "A sex offender order is a civil order, and that is its great strength. It will allow the police to intervene before a further offence is committed by someone who has committed a sex offence in the past. The idea is to stop him in his tracks when such behaviour by another person may be considered innocent." Mr Michael acknowledged that "we are treading a thin line in respect of human rights". He later added: "The sex offender order is near the limit of what is possible. If we were to go any further we would jeopardise the proposal and run the risk of being struck down by the European Court." The Home Office Guidance, published in 1998 stated: "What is being prohibited may well be actions or behaviour that for another individual would be unexceptionable."

[5] Other civil orders created under the Act include:

- parenting orders, under which parents (of children convicted for an offence or made subject to an ASBO) may be required by the court to attend counselling sessions and/or to exercise a measure of control over the child. Failure to comply, without a reasonable excuse, makes the parent liable to a fine of up to £1,000;
- child safety orders, to be made by the magistrates family proceedings court, are aimed at children under ten (i.e., under the age of criminal responsibility) when the child has committed an act which would have been an offence if the child was ten or over; in order to prevent anti-social behaviour or offending; or because the child has contravened a local child curfew notice (see below). Failure to comply may make the child subject to a care order;
- local child curfews enable local authorities to deal with unsupervised children on the streets late at night. If the local scheme is approved by the Home Secretary the police will have powers to take a child home or (if no-one is at home) into police protection.

New criminal powers include:

- drug treatment and testing orders for persons aged 16 and over convicted of crime(s) which fund their drug habit and who agree to undergo treatment for their drug problem for a period of six months to three years; failure to comply means a return to court to be dealt with for the original offence.
- reparation orders require young offenders (with their consent) to make reparation to the victim(s) or to the community at large;
- action plan orders are tailored to address the cause of a child or young person's offending behaviour over a three-month period.

hunters and animal rights campaigners, successful and unsuccessful. In place of the Thatcherite cold shower, it offers a warm bath, administered by a hegemonic people's party appealing to every part of the nation" (Marquand, 1998).

On the first anniversary of becoming Prime Minister, with Labour's lead in the opinion polls higher than a year earlier, Tony Blair made it clear that his Party was determined not to lose "the new support"—those people who once kept away from Labour but who had cast away earlier doubts.

> "The new support does care about the disadvantaged and the poor. It has a social conscience—that's why it voted for us. It is simply that it recognises that we also need economic efficiency, trade unions given their place in democracy but not confused with Government. It doesn't want penal rates of taxation; and though generally tolerant and liberal-minded, it does want strong defence and law and order."[6]

RECONSTRUCTING CRIMINAL POLICY UNDER NEW LABOUR

Labour's efforts to reconstruct its criminal policy, which began after its fourth successive general election defeat in June 1992, have to be placed within the context of the Party's "modernisation" project. For leading modernisers, having been out of office for so many years, this meant presenting "an image of the party . . . that chimes in with what people want to think" (Gould, 1998: 47). Tony Blair, the new shadow Home Secretary, told his immediate colleagues that the starting point had "to be what is right, not what has been our traditional position" (quoted in Sopel, 1995: 152). For much of the 1980s, the Labour Party had taken a generally liberal reformist stance in opposing much of the criminal justice legislation brought forward by the Conservative Government.[7] It was, however, consistent with this stance for Labour to support the Government's proposals to reduce reliance on prison sentences, culminating in the Criminal Justice Act 1991.[8] But by the time the 1992 General Election was called, the

[6] Tony Blair, *The Guardian*, 1 May 1998. At the Labour Party Conference in October 1997, Blair referred to New Labour's "compassion with a hard-edge". One of New Labour's principal strategists, Philip Gould, quotes Stanley Greenberg (a key adviser to Bill Clinton during his first presidential campaign and first administration), reflecting on the 1988 defeat of Michael Dukakis by George Bush that the Democratic Party had been characterised by its opponents as being "short on patriotism, weak on defence, soft on criminals and minorities, indifferent to work, values and the family and, inexplicably, infatuated with taxes." Impressed by his visit in 1992 to the Clinton campaign, Gould called for "a new populism", urging that Labour should announce it had changed just as the New Democrats had done. The Clinton victory gave the modernisers a road map. "To win", Gould wrote in May 1993, "Labour has to gain new support from new groups." A year later Gould wrote that the way forward for Labour meant persuading "ordinary working people that they will be financially better off under Labour; connecting with the populist instinct of voters through policies that are tough on crime; opposing welfare fraud; supporting individual responsibility" Gould (1998, 172–81).

[7] For a succinct overview of Labour's criminal policy before and after the General Election of 1992, see Anderson and Mann (1997, 229–70).

[8] On this unexpected period of criminal policy-making see Windlesham (1993), and Rutherford (1996, especially 87–123).

political mood was hardening and the ethos of the 1991 legislation was regarded with growing scepticism within the new Conservative administration.

Tony Blair, who asked for his new portfolio, allowed himself a few months before revealing too much of the hand he was about to play. Once he did so, it was evident that generational sentiments and attitudes were significant. "Blair wasn't a politician of the 1960s", argued one of his biographers.

> "[H]e was never part of the 'liberal' consensus, so he shared the gut instincts of many of his constituents; not the received wisdom of what the next Home Secretary, Michael Howard, disparagingly referred to later as the "do-gooders" who ran the criminal justice system. Blair saw the 1960s as a morally lapsed time when the distinctions between right and wrong had become blurred" (Sopel, 1995: 153).

He acknowledged the influence of his constituency, a former mining community in the north-east of England, which had

> "brought home very clearly that people understand that there are causes of crime we should tackle, but they also believe very strongly in personal responsibility. They don't believe that you can ever allow the identification of those causes of crime to become an excuse for not having an effective criminal justice system" (quoted in Perryman, 1996: 73).

During a radio interview in January 1993, Blair first used the slogan, which was to lose none of its political potency, on the need for a national strategy that was "tough on crime and tough on the causes of crime".[9]

Five weeks later, in the wake of the national trauma of the murder of the toddler James Bulger by two ten-year-old boys,[10] Blair talked about a disintegrating society, the solution to which

> "must come from a rediscovery of a sense of direction as a country and most of all from being unafraid to start talking again about the values and principles we believe in and what they mean for us, not just as individuals but as a community. If the value of what is right and wrong is not learnt and then taught then the result is simply moral chaos which engulfs us all."[11]

A few days later, in an article for Rupert Murdoch's daily tabloid, *The Sun*, Blair wrote: "It's a bargain—we give opportunity, we demand responsibility. There is no excuse for crime. None."[12] It was into this politically charged atmosphere that Michael Howard was appointed Home Secretary, determined, above all, that his Party would regain ownership of the crime issue. Howard's infamous "27 points" speech at the Conservative Party Conference in October 1993

[9] Interview by Nick Clarke, *The World This Weekend*, 10 January 1993. According to Rentoul (1997, 279), the phrase was actually coined by Gordon Brown.

[10] As Julia Fionda (1998) has commented, in the aftermath of the Bulger case, the reality was largely ignored that fewer than one child per year under the age of 14 commits murder.

[11] Tony Blair, speech to Wellingborough Labour Party, 19 February 1993. This has been characterised as a "seminal speech" for Blair. "[H]e had found his voice, and more than any other speech this one defined the man and imprinted his character on the public's mind, resulting in a huge postbag of support and encouragement." Mandelson and Liddle (1996, 47–8).

[12] *The Sun*, 3 March 1993.

was a crude preview of the Criminal Justice and Public Order Bill which appeared two months later. Blair, determined to avoid being wrong-footed by the Conservatives, persuaded John Smith, the Leader of the Opposition, that Labour should abstain on the Bill as a whole. In political terms, Blair's tactics were vindicated with a Gallup poll of spring 1994 placing Labour ahead of the Conservatives as being best able to handle law and order issues.[13]

It has been to the United States, rather than to Europe, that New Labour has looked for inspiration, in due course sharing a somewhat self-conscious discourse on "the third way" with the Clinton administration.[14] On the eve of leaving for an Anglo-American seminar on social policy issues, which included youth crime, at Camp David in February 1998, the Home Secretary, Jack Straw, declared that "the two governments are learning more from one another all the time. There is now a deep ideological relationship, but it's not one-way traffic."[15] The American connection began five years earlier for Blair when he and Gordon Brown, the shadow Chancellor of the Exchequer, made a four-day visit in January 1993 to meet with members of the successful "New Democrat" Clinton campaign team. They heard from Paul Begala, one of Clinton's strategists and speechwriters, that Clinton had "put personal responsibility back at the centre of an activist communitarian philosophy", and that he was a Democrat who was "very tough on crime" (quoted in Rentoul, 1997: 280–1).[16]

For Tony Blair, a connection with members of the Clinton administration flowed from Amitae Etzioni's communitarian notion that an obsession with individual rights leads people to lose sight of their mutual obligations and

[13] The passage of the Criminal Justice and Public Order Act 1994 is ably described by Windlesham (1996, 39–168).

[14] Tony Blair regards criminal justice as being "critical to the third way. It was essential for Labour to break free from the view that social considerations weakened personal responsibility for crime and disorder. Hence my call for a government that was "tough on crime and tough on the causes of crime". New Labour is adopting this approach in government—electronic tagging of criminals and tough new laws against racial violence; a £250 million crime prevention programme while imposing new sanctions (sic) on disorderly conduct" Blair (1998, 13–14); see also Anthony Giddens, who regards the "third way" as "a framework of thinking and policy-making that seeks to adapt social democracy to a world that has changed fundamentally over the past two or three decades. It is a third way in the sense that it is an attempt to transcend both old-style social democracy and neoliberalism" Giddens (1998, 26). Asked about Clinton's "third way", John Kenneth Galbraith has remarked that "the third way is a purely political concept. The increase in numbers and power of the middle-income groups means that governments choose to meet their needs first. The third way is a justification for that necessity" *The Guardian*, 17 October 1998. On the emergence of the third way with reference to both Clinton and Blair, see Gould (1998, 235–8). Philip Gould has commented that the third way is far from being an abstract idea to ordinary working people. "On a basic level people are tough on crime but supportive of a strong state role in education and health."

[15] Quoted in *The Observer*, 1 February 1998. This was the second of three "third way" seminars held during 1997–8.

[16] As Rentoul notes, it was three days after returning from the United States when Blair first used the phrase "tough on crime and tough on the causes of crime". Compare to the Declaration at the New Orleans Convention of the Democratic Leadership Council: "We believe in preventing crime and punishing criminals, not explaining away their behaviour". Fourth Annual Conference, Democratic Leadership Council, New Orleans, March 1990; on the DLC and Bill Clinton's bid for the presidency, see Greenberg (1995, 203–13).

responsibilities to their communities.[17] With specific reference to criminal policy, Etzioni has suggested as a legitimate community-building device the temporary "marking out" of convicted persons, as well as not allowing legal niceties to enable the "walking" of "real" criminals (Etzioni, 1993: 137).[18] In Blair's mind there was no doubt that "the breakdown in law and order is intimately linked to the break-up of a strong sense of community" (quoted in Mandleson and Liddle, 1996: 48).[19] If crime is "the most emotionally compelling symbol of lost community" (Abel, 1995: 118) a civil liberties framework might have to give ground. As Nicola Lacey has observed, "[i]t can hardly be doubted that a political theory which acknowledged more firmly (than liberalism) the inevitably social nature of human life would take a less stringent attitude towards the visiting of disadvantages upon persons in the expectation of fostering important social goals . . ." (Lacey, 1986). While these propositions would almost certainly gain Blair's ready concurrence, it has also been suggested that a moral communitarianism of the Right can be identified in New Labour's guiding philosophy where "the causes of crime and social breakdown are laid at the family and liberal and relativist ethics" (Driver and Martell, 1997: 39). The importance of the notion of community, he stressed in a speech immediately after the murder of James Bulger, is "that it defines the relationship not only between us as individuals, but between people and the society in which they live, one that is based on responsibilities as well as rights, on obligations as well as entitlements".[20] But the multi-faceted language of communitarianism, with its notions of "deficient we-ness", as David Faulkner notes in Chapter 5, may point either in an inclusive or exclusive direction. Although New Labour's social policy statements firmly placed the accent on social inclusion, as far as criminal policy issues are concerned the ambiguity has remained.[21]

With Tony Blair elected as leader of the Labour Party, following the unexpected death of John Smith in May 1994, the post of Shadow Home Secretary was entrusted to one of his leadership campaign managers, Jack Straw.[22] Without departing from the communitarian discourse,[23] Straw's distinctive

[17] See e.g. Etzioni (1993). In referring to crime, Etzioni is inclined to draw upon the work of James Q. Wilson.

[18] For useful discussions of Etzioni's influence on New Labour, see Hughes (1996) and Freeden (1999).

[19] Blair was speaking in June 1993; as a student, he was influenced by the writings of a Scottish philosopher, John MacMurray who interpreted the social commitment of Christianity through the concept of community (see Mandleson and Liddle, 1996: 32–3).

[20] Tony Blair, speech to the Wellingborough Constituency Labour Party, 19 February 1993.

[21] For an attempt to move beyond this ambiguity, see Leadbeater (1996).

[22] Jack Straw first came to public prominence as President of the National Union of Students in the late 1960s when many universities were in turmoil over student demands. For some years he was a political adviser to Barbara Castle, Minister for Health in the Wilson Government, and he succeeded her as MP for Blackburn in 1979. Prior to taking the lead on Home Office matters, he was Labour spokesperson for education and later on environmental issues.

[23] See, for example, "Put the heart back into communities", *The Times*, 8 November 1995, where Jack Straw wrote of the "over-emphasis on rights to the near exclusion of duties and responsibilities" and the "me-first society" which he contended had been encouraged during the 1980s.

theme was that the threat posed by anti-social conduct to the community needed to be addressed as much as serious crime. Drawing on meetings with his constituents in Blackburn, as well from personal experience,[24] he spoke out against "noisy neighbours", "the aggressive begging of winos, addicts and squeegee merchants", declaring that, "crime and insecurity creates a vicious circle of community decline in which those who are able to move out do so, whilst those who cannot have to modify their behaviour and avoid the streets, squares and parks which they used to use . . .".[25] During the summer of 1995 he visited New York to observe the "zero-tolerance" tactics of the city's police department, inspired by Commissioner William J. Bratton's reading of the "broken windows" article by James Q. Wilson and George Kelling (Wilson and Kelling, 1982) and by a seminar, led by Kelling, which he had attended at Harvard's School of Government.[26] As Wilson insisted, the policy imperative was to focus attention on "activities that are not crime in any real sense" (Wilson, 1983: 283). Straw was especially impressed by a recently completed study which drew from policing practice in New York and elsewhere to propose a model of "community-based prevention" (Kelling and Coles, 1996). In his foreword, Wilson maintained that "[a] rights oriented legal tradition does not easily deal with this problem . . . The judge sees a snapshot of the street at one moment; the public, by contrast, sees a motion picture of the street, slowly, inexorably decaying" (Wilson, 1996: xv).[27] Extending this thesis, Kelling and Coles contended that the crime problem for city dwellers does not begin with serious crime. "Conceiving of it and addressing it as such, as has occurred for thirty years in national debates about crime, leads to bad public policy, poor legal thinking and practice, and distorted criminal justice practices and priorities" (Kelling and Coles, 1996: 5). The authors stressed that "[w]hile many of these behaviours are criminal, they are usually classified as misdemeanours or petty offences" (Kelling and Coles, 1996: 15). Straw found himself to be totally in tune with the policy imperative for a new and broader conception of crime prevention and control alongside the delineation of a crucial role for citizens (Kelling and Coles, 1996: 230).

[24] He spoke of the misery his mother had to deal with when confronted by an awkward next-door family on a council estate in Loughton, Essex. This dispute between neighbours, with mutual accusations of assault, led to Jack Straw, then in his early teens, giving evidence on behalf of his mother who was vindicated when the neighbour was fined and bound over to keep the peace (*The Times*, 23 September 1998). On Straw's childhood and his politically active parents, see Anderson and Mann (1997, 250).

[25] Jack Straw, speech to the Howard League for Penal Reform, September 1995. This may have been one of the first uses in Britain of the American term, "squeegee merchant" (someone who washes your windscreen, often without invitation, as you wait at the traffic lights).

[26] Bratton and Knobler (1998); see also Bratton (1997).

[27] Compare: The main test to determine whether the use of an anti-social behaviour order might be appropriate "is that it represents a *pattern* of behaviour which continues over a period of time but cannot be dealt with easily or adequately through the prosecution of those concerned for a single "snapshot" or criminal event." Home Office Guidance (paragraph 3.10, 1999, emphasis in the original).

Remarkably, Straw owes more to American "new realists" of the right such as Kelling and Wilson than to the considerable body of work emanating from British "left realists".[28] For one of the founding fathers of left realism, Jock Young, the requirement was to break away from "left idealism or minimalism" and

> "to do something about crime, the need to have some audit of police practice, and the necessity of independent data. It was at this point that socialist politicians realised that it was their constituents—the working class, women and ethnic minorities who suffered most from crime—that radical criminology came of age" (Young, 1988: 171–2; see also Matthews, 1987).

So while Thomas Mathiesen has correctly observed, with regard to left-realists, that where their "analysis of social aetiology should lead to social remedies, it leads to more policing, more formal social control" (Mathiesen, 1990: 152), their policy agenda has remained rather threadbare[29] compared to the robust proposals of Wilson and his former students.

Mr Straw has observed that New Labour has broken with its past elitist inclinations by listening to what ordinary people had to say about crime and anti-social behaviour. But, the relationship between politicians and the public at large is more subtle than a mantra of this kind implies. René van Swaaningen has identified the active role of political actors with respect to criminalising social problems in the formulation of crime prevention policy.

> "Crime is used as a label for quite general feelings of anxiety, dissatisfaction and irritation. These feelings are the most common in areas with a high level of social deprivation, and can mostly be traced back to relatively small annoyances and social rather than crime problems: garbage in the streets, broken street-lighting, run-down houses . . . Crime in the strict, legal sense of the word is undeniably part of the problem, but because tackling the crime problem has such a high place on the political agenda, all misery is translated into a crime discourse. That is the most certain way to receive political attention" (van Swaaningen, 1997a: 213).

The crucial step, and one that is all too apparent in the New Labour context, is that "politicians stimulate people to interpret crime as something completely different from any other social problem, instead of acknowledging that the crime problem is an integral part of socio-economic problems" (van

[28] As Home Secretary, Straw fully accepted the Wilson–Kelling assertion that unchecked incivilities led to serious crime. In March 1999 he told the House of Commons that "where there are high levels of incivility in an area the chance of people suffering, for example, a violent crime is four times greater than in similar areas. If we deal with disorder, we can cut a great deal of crime" Jack Straw, 16 March 1999, H.C. Deb., 6th ser., Vol. 327, col. 910. It seems there was more contact between "left realists" such as Jock Young and Roy Hattersley, Mr Blair's predecessor as Shadow Home Secretary than in the period since 1992. One list of criminological texts consulted by Mr Straw did not include the work of any "left realists". "Challenges of the Future—Taking the Criminal Justice System out of its Secret Garden", speech given at the University of Salford, 18 September 1996. A small group with whom Mr Straw, as Home Secretary, had regular lunch meetings to discuss crime issues included very few academics, and none of the "left realist" persuasion.

[29] See, for example, Lea and Young (1984), Matthews (1992) and Young (1997a).

Swaaningen, 1997a: 213). The resort to civil justice procedures, such as the ASBO, in this process represents a perverse contradiction of the case made for "civilising" the criminal law by abolitionist criminologists (Hulsman, 1986; Christie, 1977; Scheerer, 1986). The changing stance of the Labour Party, during its long sojourn in Opposition, emerges from tracing the course of public order legislation since 1980 and the pursuit of civil remedies to anti-social behaviour which gathered pace 15 years later. By the close of this period, Labour's new face on criminal policy reflected a sense that conventional ways of using the law, both civil and criminal, had reached a cul-de-sac.

EXHAUSTION OF PUBLIC ORDER OFFENCES

During Margaret Thatcher's early years as Prime Minister there was, perhaps surprisingly, little enthusiasm to proceed further down the path of extending the range of public order offences. The Home Office, with an eye to the offence, created by section 5 of the Public Order Act 1936, of engaging in "threatening, abusive or insulting words or behaviour, in a public place", contended that "it has sometimes been suggested that the ambit of the section should be extended, but it is difficult to see how this could be done without bringing in behaviour or words which should not properly be regarded as criminal".[30] This resolve to maintain the status quo was reinforced a year or so later by Lord Scarman's inquiry into the Brixton disturbances (Scarman, 1981). However, by the mid-1980s, in the aftermath of the bitter and drawn-out miners' dispute, intensive lobbying by the Association of Chief Police Officers and other police organisations persuaded the Government to change course and bring most common law offences within an extended statutory framework. The new scheme included violent disorder (with a maximum penalty of five years' imprisonment) together with two summary offences, the first of these, section 4, being that of causing fear of or provoking violence.

In advocating what was to become section 5 of the Public Order Act 1986, it had been asserted by the Home Office that new criminal powers were required to combat a range of disorderly behaviour, including hooliganism on housing estates, groups of youths shouting abuse and obscenities, and rowdy behaviour late at night. Alive to the drafting complexities in ensuring that the offence met the normally precise requirements of the criminal law, the proposals referred to "*substantial* alarm, harassment or distress", and also held that the behaviour must actually cause someone to feel alarmed, harassed or distressed (emphasis in the original).[31] However, when the Bill was published both qualifications had been dispensed with and, together with extending the reach of the criminal law

[30] *Review of the Public Order Act 1936 and Related Legislation,* (1980) Cm. 7891, 29.

[31] *Review of Public Order Law,* Home Office and Scottish Office, Cm. 9510 (1985) 19. The words "harassment, alarm and distress" were to re-appear 12 years later as the basis for the anti-social behaviour order.

into areas of annoyance, disturbance and inconvenience, attracted considerable controversy, especially on the Labour benches. Referring to the Bill as it stood at Committee Stage, Gerald Kaufman, the Labour shadow home secretary stated:

> "The clause is so imprecise, loose and accessible to misuse that it poses inherent dangers to the liberty of the subject . . . we are discussing here the rights of young men who are in danger of being criminalised, for which the word of a police officer will be the only verification."[32]

In the event, the Government amended the Bill to require an actual bystander although this person did not have to be a witness and could be a police officer. This new summary offence of offensive conduct, for which the maximum penalty is a fine, applies if a person: "uses threatening, abusive or insulting words or behaviour, or disorderly behaviour, or displays any writing, sign or other visible representation which is threatening, abusive or insulting, within the hearing or sight of a person likely to be caused harassment, alarm or distress thereby". As with many of the Act's provisions, and in line with a growing legislative tendency, the burden was placed on the defendant to prove one or more specified defences, such as that his conduct was reasonable. Furthermore, a police officer was given the power of arrest if there was a further offence after a warning had been made.[33]

By 1986 the outer boundaries of legislating on public order appeared to have been reached (Lacey, Wells and Meure, 1989: 118; Smith, 1987: 164),[34] notwithstanding that eight years later yet another new offence was created (more serious than section 5) of causing intentional harassment, alarm or distress (by using threatening, abusive or insulting words or disorderly behaviour, or displaying any writing, sign or other representation which is abusive or insulting) with a maximum penalty of six months' imprisonment. Although the scope of public order was stretched to cover cases of "aggravated trespass" on private property (thereby criminalising the activities of people such as squatters, New Age travellers, gypsies and hunt saboteurs) and criminal sanctions were created for non-compliance with directions by the police,[35] it is reasonable to conclude that the 1986 and 1994 legislation

[32] Gerald Kaufman, House of Commons, Official Report, Standing Committee G Session 1985–6, Vol. VI, 11 February 1986, col. 205.

[33] This provision was amended in 1996 so that the same police officer did have to warn and later arrest. This short Bill was introduced by a Labour Member in June 1996. In contrast to ten years before the need for a broad public order offence was given only cursory attention and there was certainly no controversy. See Reid (1998).

[34] There is considerable variation in the use of section 5 across police forces, with Afro-Caribbeans over-represented among defendants (Brown and Ellis, 1994). During 1996 there were 15,000 successful prosecutions under section 5, reflecting a substantial decline since the peak of almost 27,000 in 1989. The number of formal cautions, by contrast, between 1989 and 1996 increased from 4,000 to 10,600 (Reid, 1998: 868).

[35] See e.g. section 76 of the Criminal Justice and Public Order Act 1994 under which failure to comply with an interim possession order became a criminal offence carrying a maximum sentence of six months' imprisonment.

> "had more to do with the symbolic affirmation of a political commitment to enforcing public order, maintaining public authority and expressing support for the agencies of control than it had to do with instrumental changes in criminal law" (Lacey and Wells, 1998: 152).

Important as symbolism was for New Labour, its sights were increasingly set on a view of the law which was explicitly instrumental.

ALTERNATIVE CIVIL ROUTES AND BEYOND

By the mid-1990s civil remedies appeared to offer a more potent approach to anti-social behaviour than further refinements to the criminal law. In contrast to the development of public order legislation, where police organisations have long been the main players, the new civil and quasi-criminal remedies largely originated within local government. Of particular significance was the Association of District Councils (now the Local Government Association) and the Local Authority Working Group on Anti-Social Behaviour, established in September 1995 by housing officials employed in Labour-controlled cities such as Coventry and Manchester.[36] This impetus, emanating from local authorities and their national associations at about the time that Jack Straw became shadow Home Secretary, opened up broad vistas for intervention and control.[37] Close consultation between Straw and local government representatives was in tune with Party policy. After all, Labour supported, just as the Conservative Government opposed, the conclusion reached in 1991 by a Home Office Standing Committee that crime prevention programmes should relate to local democratic structures.[38]

In the early months of 1994 the Labour Party highlighted issues such as racial harassment and domestic violence (Labour, 1994), but detailed attention was soon directed to how a new government might most effectively combat a wider spectrum of anti-social behaviour. Local government representatives, accompanied by a legal adviser, Duncan Forbes, found in Jack Straw an eager partner to the proposition that the existing law and criminal justice process fell far short of what was required to do the job. With the drafting entrusted to one of Straw's key aides, a small group met from time to time to work on a Labour Party consultation paper. In addition to Duncan Forbes, this group included Coventry's chief housing officer and representatives from Manchester City Council and the Association of District Councils. In June 1995, the opening sentences of *A Quiet Life, Tough Action on Criminal Neighbours* established the tone and target.

[36] Renamed the Social Landlords and Nuisance Group, by 1998 its membership consisted of some 75 local authorities.

[37] In the 1994 local government elections Labour's substantial gains had resulted in 12,000 councillors in office.

[38] Report of the Home Office Standing Committee on Crime Prevention (1991) (chair, James Morgan), London: Home Office.

> "Every citizen, every family, has the right to a quiet life—a right to go about their lawful business without harassment, interference or criminal behaviour by their neighbours. But across Britain there are thousands of people whose lives are made miserable by the people next door, down the street or on the floor above or below. Their behaviour may not just be unneighbourly, but intolerable and outrageous . . . Criminal procedures have never been designed to curb chronic and persistent anti-social criminal behaviour and so, as they stand, are themselves defective" (Labour, 1995: 1).

Two case studies were set forth in the consultation paper, both of which were to feature regularly in the presentation of New Labour's emerging strategy against anti-social behaviour. The background to the first of these case studies was that tenants of a council estate in Coventry had, it was alleged, been threatened and intimidated by two brothers, aged 30 and 27, who lived with their mother on the estate. It was alleged that the brothers had been seen carrying out burglaries and disposing of stolen property but that witnesses were reluctant to contact the police or give evidence in court. These circumstances led the local Tenants and Residents' Association to set up a support group which received information implicating the brothers. Because the police were unable to use this information to bring prosecutions, Coventry City Council agreed to pursue civil remedies. In February 1995, acting on the advice of Duncan Forbes, the Council's Housing, Environment and Public Protection Policy Coordinating Committee passed a resolution that an injunction be sought under section 222 of the Local Government Act 1972.[39] Three days later the High Court, after listing numerous offences for which one or both brothers were allegedly responsible, issued a provisional injunction restraining both brothers from entering a defined area of the estate.[40]

The defendants' mother was reported by *The Guardian* as welcoming the ban:

> "My boys have caused havoc around here and I feel extremely sorry for the other families. I am glad that all this has been sorted out for all the people who have been upset by what my lads have done. I never heard them say what they wanted to do for a job. I guess crime is their life. But they never did any harm to anyone; they just stole daft things like cassette players and TVs. I don't agree with anyone being burgled and I guess you have to put a stop to it."

It was, however, noted that had she opposed the injunction she faced eviction from her home. Approving remarks were also forthcoming from the head of the Council's neighbourhood management team. "These people, in common with others, have repeatedly targeted vulnerable people in the area. By ordering them off the estate we hope to restore the confidence of the vast majority of families who have felt intimidated by their presence." The local police superintendent was especially perceptive: "This is pretty radical stuff. We are taking crime pre-

[39] Under section 222 of the Local Government Act 1972 a local authority may institute civil proceedings in its own name.

[40] *Coventry City Council v. Finney*, [1995] QBD, 432.

vention into new territory. We are leaving the traditional area of locks and bolts and beginning to target prolific offenders."[41]

Two months after the exclusion order was issued, the Council brought contempt proceedings against one brother for entering the restricted area. He was committed to prison for six months, but this penalty was suspended on condition that he did not breach the injunction over the next two years. In August 1995, two months after the appearance of *A Quiet Life*, similar action was taken against the other brother who had entered the prescribed area on three occasions. However, in March 1996 both orders were discharged after the City Council, acting on the advice of a leading Queen's Counsel, abandoned the proceedings. Considerable costs had been incurred by the Council, with preparation of the case requiring four officers employed full-time over a four-week period, in addition to the legal team, but as one officer put it: "Despite our best efforts we had been unable to collect direct evidence as required for a full civil trial."[42]

The consultation paper's second case study involved "Family X", and was based upon a letter which had been sent by the superintendent of police in Blackburn to the local Member of Parliament, Jack Straw, a few weeks before he became Shadow Home Secretary. After outlining examples of intimidation by Family X, together with details of numerous arrests accumulated by five of its members, the superintendent stated that there was

> "no doubt that this family is responsible for many problems and the quality of life of people living in the area has been adversely affected . . . I have to say that residents in the area are looking for those in authority to help them. Blackburn police have done all we can and both we and the people living there hope that this awful situation will be reflected in the way these people are subsequently dealt with by the local justices."

It was further asserted that the conventional process was ineffective "because each incident of criminal behaviour was dealt with in isolation", and frequent court appearances were mostly dealt with by non-custodial sentences. Furthermore, the challenge posed by "Family X" extended beyond the council's property. While action by the police and the public landlord led to eviction "the family then emerged elsewhere in town to cause more trouble. They now live in private rented accommodation so the local authority has no locus to evict them" (Labour, 1995: 5).

The Labour Party contended that the criminal justice system was unable to respond effectively to the Coventry brothers or Family X because it dealt with the commission of crime as an acute, rather than a chronic condition. The system is therefore at its least effective where the offending behaviour is chronic and persistent, where the separation of incidents may lack forensic worth, where it is the aggregate impact of criminal behaviour which makes it intolerable and where the whole is much worse than the sum of its parts. But the

41 *The Guardian*, 25 February 1995.

42 Amon Lynch, telephone interview, 28 January 1998.

courts rarely treat such behaviour "as a serious pattern which is wholly destructive of the quiet life of a community . . . There is no opportunity, by definition, for bringing evidence of overall anti-social behaviour other than that relating to the specific charge—which may be very minor, for evidential reasons." A new composite charge, it was suggested, should be made available as a single criminal offence where there had been "a series of linked incidents of anti-social behaviour or harassment". In the event, this proposal was not pursued, no doubt because it was considered that a quasi-criminal remedy would more readily achieve its purposes.

Existing deficiencies in the criminal justice system, it was asserted, meant that "other, in principle less satisfactory, sanctions are now having to be sought" including administrative action by public landlords or civil injunctions. "The procedure and criteria for obtaining injunctions, as in the Coventry case, is far from easy and the substantive law is far from certain." In proposing a "community safety order", as it was first termed, Labour declared that, "new remedies now have to be developed to deal with the patent wrong of chronic anti-social behaviour". The application could be brought by the police or by the local authority—in either case the opinion of the other would have to be appended. The order could include "curfews, exclusion from a particular area, restraints on approaching individuals, uttering threats, making noise of specified kinds and desisting from racist behaviour. The principal aim of the order is *punitive and preventative*". Applications for the order might include circumstances where there had been multiple convictions (say five or more) related to the area, or evidence of such offences, "even where there had not been a conviction" or other evidence of unlawful acts (criminal or civil) "likely to interfere with the peace and comfort of a residential occupier" (ibid. 8–9, emphasis added).

At this point in the text the innovative cross-over was introduced, triggered by a breach of the order, from civil to criminal proceedings. Unlike contempt procedures (which carry a maximum penalty of two years' imprisonment as a civil prisoner), any breach would attract the full range of penalties, including imprisonment for up to seven years. "There should be a normal expectation that a breach of a community safety order would be punished by a custodial order in the case of defendants [aged] eighteen and over, and [punished] severely in respect of those under eighteen." Any alleged offender should, if necessary, be held in custody pending sentence and be treated as a sentenced prisoner (ibid. 10). As to safeguards, "(t)he police, local authorities and courts have sufficient discretion not to use the proposed powers save where it is necessary, and only where other remedies have failed" (ibid.: 2).

THE QUASI-CRIMINAL REMEDY COMES OF AGE

Labour's first opportunity to actively pursue its novel quasi-criminal remedy within Parliament arose when the Housing Bill was introduced in 1995, in part to toughen measures dealing with "nuisance" by council tenants and persons living in social housing. The new measures included widening the grounds for taking possession of a property to cover the behaviour of visitors to the property, and it became no longer necessary to prove actual nuisance which is continuing, as past conduct which caused a nuisance or was likely to do so would suffice. This could be established on the basis of evidence from third parties who were not themselves victims and might include "professional" witnesses such as council officials or police officers. The grounds for illegal and immoral use of a property were widened, in response to Labour amendments, and local authorities' powers were strengthened with respect to drug dealers and other categories of offenders. Any breach of an injunction against anti-social behaviour meant that the person responsible could be arrested without warrant. These new remedies, which reflected efforts within many local authorities over the previous two years or so to combat anti-social behaviour, meant that official action would no longer be restricted in the way Coventry City Council had been. A defensive and politically weak Government was anxious to assure both the Labour Opposition and local authorities that concerns about anti-social behaviour were being met.

None of these efforts to strengthen civil remedies, however, went anything like far enough for the Labour Party. To the shadow housing minister, Nick Raynsford, it was unacceptable for "local communities to go on enduring the behaviour of someone who has been convicted of an anti-social activity, but who can live in the community for several months while the normal, slow possession proceedings trundle through the courts". He tabled a highly elaborate amendment (which had been largely drafted by the indefatigable Duncan Forbes), introducing a "community safety order", broadly in line with the quasi-criminal scheme set forth in *A Quiet Life*, but qualified by a complex array of elaborate pre-conditions (which tightly restricted any resort to the order) and with a maximum of five years' imprisonment for breach. Mr Raynsford quoted a letter from Coventry's chief housing officer outlining the difficulties encountered in his city's notorious case of the two brothers. But this "harebrained scheme" was firmly rejected by the Minister, who, referring to a critical review of the community safety order by the Penal Affairs Consortium, placed the onus for the proposal not on Mr Raynsford but on the Member for Blackburn, Mr Jack Straw "who is lurching so far to the right that he is causing terrible difficulties for his own party".[43] The Minister's anxieties about the amendment undermining civil liberties received the support of a Labour backbencher, Andrew Bennett, who, after describing his Party's amendment as "ill conceived", argued that the real requirement was for adequate resources to back up existing legislation.[44]

[43] David Curry, House of Commons, Official Report, Session 1995–6, Vol. V, Standing Committee G, 29 February 1996, col. 439.

[44] Andrew F. Bennett, House of Commons, Standing Committee G, 29 February 1996, col. 442. While the Housing Bill was under consideration, Lord Woolf was persuaded to include a special

By now, Labour's ideas on community safety orders had broadened beyond "criminal neighbours" to encompass "criminal anti-social behaviour in neighbourhoods" (Labour Party, 1996a). It was noted that the Government had initially dismissed Labour's proposals as "merely window dressing" but was later forced to respond, reinforced by pressures from local authorities, with the measures contained in the Housing Act 1996. But these steps

> "do not go nearly far enough to deal with a problem that can affect those who own their own homes as much as those in local authority accommodation . . . To get the cases to court they require hard information within the rules of criminal evidence. But witnesses—other neighbours—are often intimidated into silence. And even where cases get to court, the charges and punishments may rarely fit the crime" (ibid. 3).

While the powers contained in the Housing Act were welcomed, "they do not overcome problems inherent in the section 222 (Local Government Act 1972) procedure nor do they tackle the appalling delays in many county courts". Furthermore, "a breach of the injunction may often result in a sentence of a few weeks only, and then as a civil prisoner enjoying greatly enhanced rights within the prison system . . . *Our approach seeks to address some of the conceptual failures of the criminal justice system and brings the system more into one based on a problem-solving approach*" (ibid. 10, emphasis added). The efforts of Labour councils were "severely hampered by delays and restrictions in our civil courts" and penalties on breach did not reflect the seriousness of the harassment involved. Any breach of a community safety order would be dealt with by a prison sentence of up to four years, with an expectation of a custodial sentence for adults, intensive community supervision for those aged under eighteen, although in serious cases juveniles would be placed in secure accommodation (ibid. 15).

A cuckoo's egg neatly placed by Labour in the nest of the Conservative Government was the next step in the road towards the anti-social behaviour order. In May 1996, following a spate of high-profile cases of "stalking", the Government were put on the spot by a Labour Member, Janet Anderson, who introduced a Private Member's Bill on stalking, which contained a much slimmed down and simplified version of the quasi-criminal procedure rejected by the Government three months earlier. Few Private Member's Bills proceed far but, in this instance, the Government was prompted into rushing out a consultation paper proposing that a stalker's victim might apply for an injunction "for the purposes of restraining the defendant from pursuing any conduct which amounts to harassment". It was contended that "[a] general tort of molestation

study of housing litigation in his Access to Justice Inquiry. This included a visit to a council estate in Manchester arranged by the Association of District Councils. He concluded that some modifications to the standard possession procedure were appropriate and that the procedures could be usefully expedited. Noting the use of professional witnesses and resort to hearsay evidence, Woolf commented that "it must be doubtful how much weight could be given to such evidence. In particular, it would be essential to ensure that the defendant had a proper opportunity to be heard, and to challenge evidence against him or her" (Woolf, 1996: 211).

on these lines might also catch a wider range of activities in disputes between neighbours or at work". The provision of remedies to deter stalkers may give further protection to people in these wider areas, although it was acknowledged "that if the scope of any new legislation to deal with stalking is not carefully defined it will criminalise the everyday behaviour of innocent people" (Home Office, 1996b). It was asserted that stalkers were unlikely to be deterred by the maximum of two years' imprisonment for breaching an injunction and therefore any breach should be dealt with as a criminal offence, punishable by up to five years' imprisonment.

The resulting Protection from Harassment Act 1997 provides an extraordinarily complex scheme, embracing criminal, civil and quasi-criminal remedies. Building on the Public Order Act 1986, the legislation creates two further criminal offences (pursuit of a course of conduct which amounts to harassment became a summary offence with a maximum prison sentence of six months; and a new indictable offence of "putting a person in fear of violence", carrying a maximum penalty of five years' imprisonment). On conviction for either offence, in addition to any criminal penalty imposed, a civil restraining order may be made for a specified or indefinite period. The behaviour to be restrained through such an order is "anything" described in the order. Breach of the restraining order became an indictable offence with a maximum penalty of five years' imprisonment. Furthermore, and in line with the consultation paper, the Act adopts the quasi-criminal formula, thereby creating a statutory tort of harassment, breach of which is an indictable offence with the same maximum penalty.

During the Parliamentary proceedings, Jack Straw explicitly noted the parallels between stalking and anti-social behaviour generally, commenting that the criminal law was "far less developed in dealing adequately with behaviour such as stalking or serious neighbourhood disruption . . . When the criminal justice system has tried to deal with stalking or neighbourhood harassment, on the whole it has failed."[45] Once again, it was the Labour Member, Andrew Bennett, who urged that, in making an order, the standard of proof should not be weaker than that applied in a criminal court. This objection was dismissed by the Home Office Minister precisely on the grounds that

> "one of the main reasons for introducing the civil tort is to gain access to that lesser test so that more victims or potential victims might be protected. I am confident that the courts will always act in a way that protects the civil liberties of those involved in a case."[46]

Enacted in March 1997, the legislation represented the first statutory expression of the formula originally promoted by the Labour Party in *A Quiet Life*, and in

[45] Jack Straw, H.C. Deb., 6th ser., Vol. 287, 17 December 1996, col. 788.
[46] Gary Streeter, H.C. Deb., 6th ser., Vol. 287, 18 December 1996, col. 968.

so doing provided a convenient precedent to be drawn upon a year or so later during deliberations on the Crime and Disorder Bill.[47]

Within four months of coming into office, and reflecting its manifesto commitment, the Labour Government published a consultation paper with the aim of helping to "build safer communities by protecting those whose only wish is to be allowed to live their lives in peace". The civil nature of the order was emphasised, with the intention being to protect the community from future anti-social conduct. The order's duration should therefore not reflect the conduct as such, but the period of time required to protect the community. On the basis of the Coventry case, the Government claimed the new power was likely to cut offending by those named in the order and by others (Home Office, 1997a).[48] The most notable departure from earlier versions was that the appropriate court venue would be the magistrates' court rather than the County Court. This change was unsuccessfully resisted by the housing lobby which believed that the experience and expertise most in tune with the proposed powers resided with the County Court (Home Office, 1997a).

PARLIAMENT AND THE ANTI-SOCIAL BEHAVIOUR ORDER

The main features of the ASBO, as laid down in the Crime and Disorder Act 1998, for England and Wales,[49] are:

- an application for an Order is made in a magistrates' court by the police or the local authority (after one has consulted the other);
- the defendant does not have to be present at the proceedings and the court may decide the case on evidence given by professional witnesses rather than hearing directly from actual victims;[50]

[47] The offence-creating sections (in the event of a breach of an order) of the 1997 Act were brought into effect by the Labour Government on 1 September 1998. For a useful appraisal, see Wells (1997).

[48] The paper mistakenly stated that the Coventry injunction had been overturned on appeal; this error was repeated by Jack Straw in April 1998 during the Second Reading Debate on the Crime and Disorder Bill, who added that after the injunction had been "quashed by a higher court" the brothers were allowed to return and "caused mayhem yet again . . ." H.C. Deb., 6th ser., Vol. 310, 8 April 1998, col. 371. The matter was only finally corrected in Home Office Guidance (1999) where the Coventry brothers and Family X were featured anonymously within an appendix.

[49] Somewhat different arrangements apply in Scotland. Of these, the most important are: only the local authority (and not the police) is able to initiate proceedings; and the defendant must be at least 16 years of age. These differences rest upon the view taken in Scotland that for many years the police had no role within the courts (although it might be argued that this has also applied in England since the establishment of the Crown Prosecution Service in 1986), and because of the "children's hearings" established in Scotland since 1968 to deal with children under the age of 16. For an overview of the more muted and considered approach in Scotland see Burney (1999); see also Collins and O'Carroll (1997).

[50] However, as noted by Leng, Taylor and Wasik (1998, 10–12), there is some uncertainty on these points. Under the Magistrates' Court Act 1980, a defendant may be summonsed, and in the event of non-attendance, a warrant for arrest may be issued. Furthermore, under the Civil Evidence Act 1995, the maker of the original statement may be called to be cross-examined.

- under the civil law test of the balance of probabilities,[51] the court has to determine whether a person, aged ten or over, has acted in an anti-social manner. This is defined as acting "in a manner that caused or was likely to cause harassment, alarm or distress to one or more persons not of the same household as himself";
- it is a defence for the defendant to show that his or her behaviour was "reasonable in the circumstances";
- disclosure of information is permitted, in a similar manner as where the issue is one of preventing or detecting crime, even though the order is a civil remedy;[52]
- the Order must be necessary to protect persons in the local government area (or specified adjoining areas) in which the harassment, alarm or distress was caused or was likely to be caused from further anti-social acts by him;[53]
- an Order, for a minimum duration of two years but with no maximum period, prohibits the individual from doing anything described in the Order;
- termination of the Order within two years requires the consent of both parties;
- any breach of the Order (without a reasonable excuse) becomes an indictable offence, carrying the full range of criminal penalties (but excluding a conditional discharge) including a maximum of six months' imprisonment in the magistrates' court and five years' imprisonment in the Crown Court;
- resort to an ASBO enjoys the same exemptions as criminal proceedings from the requirements of data protection legislation;
- there is a right of appeal to the Crown Court against the making of an Order.

By and large, the Crime and Disorder Bill was warmly welcomed by supporters of both main political parties, with the ASBO attracting little attention or controversy within or beyond Parliament. The first note of dissent had come from the Penal Affairs Consortium, representing twenty six organisations within the criminal justice arena. In September 1995, three months after the Labour Party first published its ideas on a "community safety order", the Consortium expressed alarm that fundamental procedural safeguards available to defendants in criminal proceedings should be jettisoned in a process which could result in a serious criminal conviction and a lengthy prison sentence. The following month, referring to the Home Secretary of the day, a group of six

[51] The civil test of proof compares with the more demanding criminal test of being satisfied "beyond reasonable doubt". It should be noted that the Home Office Guidance (1999) states "those applying for orders may wish to be aware that in some civil proceedings (for example, complaint for a binding over in the High Court) where the movement of an individual is to be curtailed, the court will take particular care in assessing the risk to the public and balance it with the loss of the freedom to the individual". See, *Middlesex Crown Court, ex parte Khan (1997)* 161 JP 240.

[52] This issue had been strongly pressed on the Government by local government associations, as the data control legislation was regarded as inhibiting collaborative efforts between local government departments and the police in dealing with anti social behaviour.

[53] The relevant local authorities in England are district authorities and London boroughs, and for Wales are county or county borough councils.

leading academic lawyers described the proposal as "Howardism with a vengeance", contending it would be an Undesirable Persons Act with no place in a free society (Ashworth et al., 1998). Two and a half years later, with the Bill before Parliament, the same group argued that the ASBO threatened "to criminalise people's activities by stealth" through the wide discretion entrusted to local officials and the courts. Implementation of these powers would send such people into "a kind of internal exile". The group was astonished

> "that a Labour Government would wish to give local officials this vast power to create a new breed of outcasts and outlaws, particularly in view of the Government's professed wish to remedy the social exclusion bequeathed by eighteen years of Tory rule" (Ashworth et al., 1998).

In a further article, written as the Bill proceeded through the House of Lords, these academics, with an eye to the European Court, argued that the order was civil only in a formal sense but in substance was a criminal disposal (Gardner et al., 1998). Likewise, in his capacity as editor of the *The Criminal Law Review*, one of the group, Andrew Ashworth, suggested that deployment of a "Trojan horse" to use civil procedures to gain access to the institutions of criminal justice would cut little ice with the European Court which seemed likely, in his view, to regard these proceedings as criminal for the purpose of the Convention's guarantees for a fair trial (Ashworth, 1997: 769–70).[54]

As Parliament commenced its deliberations, organisations raising serious misgivings about ASBOs included the Howard League for Penal Reform, Liberty and the Law Society. However, the various counter-arguments, which had been totally ignored in the Government's consultation paper, received only passing recognition in Parliament. In December 1997 the Bill commenced its untroubled journey in the House of Lords, despite the preponderance of Conservative peers. The Conservative spokesperson on home affairs, after quoting from a letter to *The Times* written by the director of the Howard League for Penal Reform, warned that such an order cannot be used "simply to penalise the eccentric and should be limited to very real anti-social behaviour".[55] And a leading Liberal Democrat peer wondered what limits would be placed on the reach of the Order, reminding the House that

> "the behaviour of minorities, especially immigrants, is often claimed to be anti-social when it is in an hostile environment . . . I would not trust every policeman fairly to invoke the provisions of Clause 1 if a manner "likely to cause harassment" is initially his to judge."[56]

But this line of reasoning was rebutted by a Labour peer who, in what became a familiar refrain, retorted that "those who suffer anti-social behaviour do not

[54] Article 6 of ECHR (right to a fair trial) is also raised as a potential problem for the ASBO by Leng, Taylor and Wasik (1998, 14).

[55] Lord Henley, H.L. Deb., 5th ser., Vol. 584, 16 December 1997, col. 539.

[56] Lord Rodgers, H.L. Deb., 5th ser., Vol. 584, 16 December, col. 545.

need to have it defined; they know what it is and experience it daily".[57] Four months later, when the Bill reached the House of Commons, Alun Michael, the Home Office Minister, defending the scanty criteria for seeking and granting an Order, maintained that "[f]or those who experience anti-social behaviour and harassment, such problems are very much an elephant on the doorstep, and they know what they want to be protected from".[58]

There were no divisions on clauses relating to the Order at the Committee Stage, where the detailed work takes place. None of the amendments aimed at tightening the definition of "anti-social" behaviour were pressed to a vote. The Government's position was that the Bill's language was sufficiently precise, and that the behaviour itself "is a significant social vice for large numbers of people who live in this country. They do not live in the leafy green suburbs. They live on mean streets."[59] It was reiterated that victims of anti-social conduct may well be "old, disabled, vulnerable, poor, or from a particular ethnic group". Striking a communitarian note, it was asserted that, "acting in an anti-social manner is something which is not consistent with the responsibilities of a citizen who derives rights and benefits from living in our society". The Order's civil, rather than criminal, status was continually stressed, with one Minister insisting that, "[t]his anti-social behaviour order is merely a prohibition. It is analogous to an injunction . . . What on earth could be wrong with that as a concept ?"[60]

At no stage in the Parliamentary proceedings did anyone urge abandonment of the proposed ASBO. While Lord Goodhart, for the Liberal Democrats, was among those few peers pressing for its scope to be tightened, he distanced himself from outright opposition. As to mixing civil and criminal procedures, a Government spokesperson declared:

> "Anti-social behaviour is a menace on our streets; it is a threat to our communities. We aim to prevent it as far as we may. A civil order is part of the regime for doing that. But ultimately, we regard such behaviour as criminal. If it cannot be stopped at stage one . . . it must be recognised and dealt with for what it is. That is why we made the deliberate decision to invoke the criminal law at the breach of the order stage."[61]

At the Report Stage, the Liberal Democrats tabled the only two amendments which were pressed to a division. The first sought to restrict the scope of the ASBO by requiring "intent" on the part of the defendant and that any alarm or

[57] Lord Watson, H.L. Deb., 5th ser., Vol. 584, 16 December 1997, col. 550.

[58] Alun Michael, House of Commons, Standing Committee B, 28 April 1998, col. 37. The familiar elephant analogy was used, for example, by Lord Justice Lawton in *Bradbourn* ([1985] 7 Cr.App.R. 181 at 183) in declaring with regards to the custody threshold in sentencing cases, that "courts can recognise an elephant when they see one, but may not find it necessary to define it". Compare Kelling and Coles (1997, 26), who drawing on the empirical work of Wesley G. Skogan, remark that, "people recognise disorder when they see it, and uniformly want something done about it". However, Skogan sensibly warns that "because many norms of public behaviour are uncodified, the potential set of standards which may be violated is larger and more amorphously bounded than behaviour prescribed by the criminal law" (Skogan, 1990: 5).

[59] Lord Williams, H.L. Deb., 5th ser., Vol. 585, 3 February 1998, col. 512.

[60] *ibid.*, col. 513.

[61] *ibid.*, col. 603.

distress caused be "serious". Opposing this move, the Solicitor-General once again stressed the civil nature of the proceedings, remarking: "Surely there can be no need to prove intent merely to seek an order which simply demands that a person act reasonably."[62] With Labour and Conservative peers joining forces, the amendment was rejected by 131–43. Also defeated, by much the same margin, was the attempt to give the courts a sole discretion to discharge an Order. Indeed, the Government's one concession during the Bill's passage through Parliament was to accept a Conservative amendment which widened the Order's scope, by reducing the number of potential victims of anti-social conduct from a minimum of two persons to a single individual.

In early April 1998, with barely a scratch inflicted and the ASBO intact, the Bill arrived in the House of Commons where the Second Reading Debate indicated that it would continue its smooth progress towards Royal Assent. The tone of the proceedings underlined the extent to which the face of criminal policy had changed under New Labour. According to the Home Secretary, the Bill's purpose was "to build a safer and more responsible society. My wish is that everyone should enjoy that most basic of human rights: the right to live life free from fear and free from crime." In terms evocative of James Q. Wilson, Mr Straw declared that the Bill "represents a triumph of community politics over detached metropolitan elites". Jack Straw added that in the early 1980s "my party lost its way not least by failing to listen to those whom we claimed to represent, and by failing to learn from them". Tony Blair had broken with all that by ensuring that "our policy making would be inspired above all by our constituents".[63] The order was warmly welcomed by the chair of the Home Affairs Select Committee and a chorus of Labour and Conservative Members. Gerald Kaufman, who had opposed the loose framing of section 5 of the Public Order Act 12 years earlier, caught the mood of the House by exclaiming that "this is a Bill for which my constituents have been waiting".[64] The only discordant note came from the Liberal Democrats spokesperson who complained that the standard of evidence required in some clauses was too weak.

As the Bill proceeded, it was Conservative Members, who urged tightening the definition of anti-social conduct, with one remarking "any type of action leading to "harassment, alarm or distress' could give rise to an order". A col-

[62] Lord Falconer, H.L. Deb., 5th ser., Vol. 587, 17 March 1998, col. 584.

[63] Jack Straw, H.C. Deb., 6th ser., Vol. 310, 8 April 1998, col. 370; see also Straw, (1998b) on the need to listen less to pressure groups and more to ordinary people. "For many years, the concerns of those who lived in areas undermined by crime and disorder were ignored or overlooked by people whose comfortable notions of human behaviour were matched only by their comfortable distance from its worse excesses." According to James Q. Wilson, writing in 1977, "[s]ince our current crime wave began in about 1963, popular opinion has been receptive to policies that elite and intellectual opinion is only now coming to accept the signs of policy change that we can detect seem to be caused by what the few now think rather than what the many long believed" Wilson (1977, 122–3); and also compare, "in popular debate about crime there has been an enormous and unbridgeable gulf between left-of-centre intellectuals and the general public—including the mass of Labour supporters" Mandelson and Liddle (1996, 133).

[64] Gerald Kaufman, H.C. Deb., 6th ser., Vol. 310, 8 April 1998, col. 388.

league complained that the Bill's loose wording was "a charter to punish the eccentric, the oddball and the person who does not conform". Another Conservative lawyer observed there was a danger that

> "we fool ourselves into thinking that passing these remedies, which every year become ever more draconian, will deal with the problem. However, most of the problems arise from the fundamental social, moral and ethical structures of society, which Parliament, acting through legislation cannot address."

The danger also existed that "we will suddenly trip into a repressive society . . . the Bill is a potentially dangerous departure from the way in which Parliament has protected civil liberties over the centuries". He recalled the debates on the Public Order Act 1986 which "went as far as advisable in a free society. The restrictions in section 5 of the 1986 Act do not apply to anti-social behaviour orders . . . that is why they are dangerous."[65] Alun Michael retorted that it was useful to have lawyers on the Committee, and that the courts and Parliament have their place, "but only if they serve the real world, which is inhabited by people who suffer from the behaviour that these provisions are meant to address . . .". Referring to the suggestion that the provisions overlapped with public order offences, Mr Michael remarked that the Order was to be used in circumstances which were neither more or less serious. The Orders differed in conception, operation and effects from the criminal law. Essentially, the Orders were directed at "criminal or sub-criminal activity . . . the behaviour prohibited in an Order should be serious enough to justify the available sanction".

The Minister's use of the term "sub-criminal behaviour" prompted the following (paraphrased) exchange between him and Edward Leigh, a Conservative Member:

Edward Leigh: Despite the Minister's efforts . . . he has been entirely unable acceptably or reasonably to define what sub-criminal behaviour means. Behaviour is either criminal in that it infringes an Act of Parliament and a provision clearly laid down, or it is not. There is no such thing as sub-criminal behaviour; there is behaviour and criminal behaviour . . .

Alun Michael: Sub-criminal behaviour is behaviour of a level that may be criminal, but to actually describe it as such, it would have to be proved to be so before a court. The question of proof may be a problem, but it makes perfect sense as part of a general pattern of activity, when evidence is given to a court as part of the civil burden of proof about the need for an anti-social behaviour order to be made to prevent the repetition of certain behaviour.

Edward Leigh: That is not good enough. It is not the way in which sensible criminal law is made.

[65] Edward Leigh, House of Commons, Standing Committee B, 28 April 1998, col. 31.

Alun Michael: I repeat very slowly, that we are not talking about a prosecution of an individual leading to punishment.[66]

For good measure the Minister later observed that,

> "individuals who are subjected to the sort of anti-social behaviour that the Order will target, and who are not protected by the law as it stands, would be stunned by some of the comments of Opposition Members. There is no place for the complacency which continues to leave people without the protections that they need."[67]

On 31 July 1998 the Crime and Disorder Bill received Royal Assent, with ASBOs available from 1 April 1999.

Alongside two or three other measures contained in the Crime and Disorder Act 1998, the ASBO is the clearest expression of New Labour's project to fundamentally refashion criminal policy.[68] By the spring of 1999, three inter-related features of this "progressive" endeavour can be highlighted in terms of the contribution of the ASBO, namely: (i) an enhanced role for citizens; (ii) a reconceptualisation of crime prevention; and, (iii) side-stepping the constraints inherent in criminal law.

ENHANCING THE ROLE OF CITIZENS

The ASBO offers a direct role for members of the community in terms of instigating action by the local authority and the police. In this sense, New Labour's project is consistent with the "crime prevention model" sketched by George Kelling and Catherine Coles which defines crime prevention in new and broader terms, with the emphasis on citizen or neighbourhood-based groups as a key element in restoring order. Within this model, a key role resides with citizen- or neighbourhood groups which have the common purpose of restoring order and "prod[ding] criminal justice agencies into helping them solve neighbourhood problems". Kelling and Coles cast citizens within a proactive role of setting standards and maintaining order in the neighbourhood, with the police and other criminal justice agencies seeing their role as that of supporting and aiding citizens (Kelling and Coles, 1996: 241). New Labour's hybrid remedy, with its broad sweep of civil powers, also exemplifies and appears to extend what David Garland has characterised as a "responsibilisation" mode for governing crime where the recurring message is that "the state alone is not, and cannot effectively be, responsible for preventing and controlling crime" (Garland, 1996: 466).

[66] House of Commons, Official Report, Standing Committee B, 30 April 1998. The notion of "sub-criminality" has been carried forward into the official guidance. "The orders are intended to be used for criminal or sub-criminal activity" Home Office Guidance (1999).

[67] Alun Michael, House of Commons, Standing Committee B, 30 April 1998, col. 71.

[68] See Andrew Rutherford, *Tough and Smart: Criminal Policy and the New Progressives* (forthcoming).

However, it remains to be seen what sort of behaviour is defined as "anti-social",[69] how ASBOs will be regarded by the police and local authorities within the overall crime and disorder reduction strategies envisaged by the Crime and Disorder Act,[70] and whether applications for Orders are made as an early or last resort.[71] In part, much may turn on how local audits of crime and disorder, required under the Act, are read by the parties involved, as well as the influence brought to bear by community groups within the consultation process and through informal channels, in addition to any pressures from central government. The Home Office Guidance coyly indicated that, while the audit may highlight individual cases of anti-social behaviour, decisions as to how to actually handle such cases "will obviously not figure in the strategies".[72] It also remains uncertain how much enthusiasm there will be for ASBOs within the (mostly lay) magistrates' courts. A few days before the Orders came into force the Lord Chancellor (that most constitutionally hybrid of figures) drew attention to the importance attached to this "major new development" by the Government in its programme of "modernising the delivery of justice". He told

[69] The Home Office Guidance (1999) suggests that anti-social behaviour, for the purposes of an order, does "not include run of the mill disputes between neighbours, petty intolerances, or minor or one-off disorderly acts". Examples of behaviour where an order might be appropriate include: individuals who intimidate neighbours and others through threats or violence or a mixture of unpleasant actions; families whose anti-social behaviour, when challenged, leads to verbal abuse, vandalism, threats and graffiti, sometimes using children as the vehicle for action against neighbours and their children; persistent racial harassment or homophobic behaviour; persistent anti-social behaviour as a result of drugs or alcohol misuse.

Alun Michael, as Home Office Minister, stated that "... in respect of juveniles, I must make it clear that they are not the main target of these orders. Their use against juveniles, especially those at the younger end of the range, would be exceptional" Standing Committee B, 30 April 1998, col. 51. While the Home Office Guidance (1999) states that, "it is unlikely that there will be many instances where anti-social behaviour orders will be appropriate against the younger age group of juveniles, e.g. 10–11 year olds except where the child's behaviour is part of anti-social behaviour by a family or group which includes older people", it went on to observe that in "the case of the older age group of 12–17 year olds, however, it is envisaged that applications may be made more routinely particularly if other measures have failed to prevent the offending and anti-social behaviour".

[70] In its Guidance on anti-social behaviour orders, the Scottish Office state: "It is expected that ASBOs will be seen as a last resort and that there will be relatively few orders across Scotland per annum" (August 1998, 5; See also Burney (1999, 89–92), on differences in the approach taken in Scotland). In contrast, the Home Office estimated there would be about 5,000 applications made annually in England and Wales (Home Office Guidance, 1999). An official of the Local Government Association remarked that this figure was "plucked out of the air", adding that she viewed the order as having a "powerful deterrent effect". Its advantage over existing civil remedies is that it can be targeted on specific individuals and their behaviour and does not carry the collateral consequences for other family members, inherent to powers of possession and eviction (Interview, Local Government Association, April 1999).

[71] The Home Office Guidance (1999) suggests that an application, as a general rule, should be made when other methods have failed or are deemed to be inappropriate. Given the background to the new Order, it seems likely that most applications will be made by local authorities rather than by the police. It is also possible that local authorities may use an ASBO as the basis for an eviction order when the individual is a local authority tenant (letter from Local Government Association to the Social Exclusion Unit, 3 March 1999).

[72] The Home Office Guidance (1999) suggests that the partnership responsible for implementing the strategy will provide the ideal forum for discussion of local uses of the ASBO.

magistrates that he was "placing great reliance on your abilities to use the powers and processes to make the justice of the magistrates' courts speedier and even more effective".[73] Furthermore, with local authorities and citizen groups mobilised to promote ASBOs and similar initiatives, pressures were quickly apparent to extend quasi-criminal remedies well beyond the 1998 legislation.[74]

RECONCEPTUALISING CRIME PREVENTION

Placing the ASBO together with the other civil orders, in Part 1 of the Act headed "Prevention of Crime and Disorder", highlights the question as to the interpretation to be placed on the second part of Tony Blair's slogan, "being tough on the causes of crime". It was originally taken to mean that social crime prevention strategies would be pursued alongside "being tough on crime", but, as New Labour's project proceeded, it became clear that prevention also embraces targeting individuals whose behaviour lies outside the scope of the criminal law. In terms of the conceptual framework, adapted from the public health arena by Brantingham and Faust (1988), the movement has been away from primary crime prevention (measures not directed at individuals) and is characterised by merging secondary measures (directed at potential offenders) with tertiary prevention (measures directed at convicted offenders). This reconceptualisation of crime prevention, largely unanticipated in the academic literature,[75] not only encourages resort to quasi-criminal and other pre-emptive remedies but seems

[73] Lord Irvine, speech to the Council of the Magistrates' Association, 25 March 1999.

[74] During the Committee Stage of the Crime and Disorder Bill the Conservative spokesperson proposed an amendment to create a "drug supply protection order". This was rejected by the Minister on the grounds that experience with the two new orders should be tested before the approach was extended. The Opposition also tabled an amendment, but did not put it to a vote, to introduce a "football behaviour order". In November 1998 the Home Secretary welcomed the third report of the Home Office Working Group on Confiscation which recommended the radical extension of civil forfeiture of cash and property in cases where there were no criminal proceedings (see Rutherford (1998)); a few weeks later the Home Office published another consultation paper urging consideration to giving the courts the power to prevent persons without convictions for football-related offences from attending football matches. The Crime and Disorder Act 1998 was cited as creating a precedent, and it was suggested that the ASBO provisions might be amended to enable the courts to impose a civil "Restriction or Exclusion Order (international or domestic banning order)", without requiring the person to be convicted of a football-related offence. In February 1999 Jack Straw informed the House of Commons that the Government would bring forward proposals for the reviewable, indeterminate detention of persons with "severe personality disorders" who may not have committed an offence and who lay outside the mental health legislation because of their non-treatability. H.C. Deb., 6th ser., Vol. 325, 15 February 1999, col. 601. These ideas were set out in Home Office and Department of Health (1999, esp. 16–18).

[75] See for example, Bottoms (1990); Tonry and Farrington (1995); and Waller, Welsh and Sansfacon (1997); but see Pease (1997, 981), who comments that the loosening of crime prevention to become community safety "probably means a de-emphasis of primary prevention in favour of secondary and tertiary prevention". This tendency, he notes, may be further encouraged by strategies based upon zero tolerance.

likely to divert attention from underlying social and economic issues,[76] despite Labour's expressed commitment to addressing structural considerations.[77] Indeed, as noted earlier, the ASBO provides a particularly striking example of the criminalisation of social policy (Crawford, 1997: 228–32; van Swaaningen, 1997a: 210–17; 't Hart, 1988).

SIDE-STEPPING CONSTRAINTS IMPOSED BY THE CRIMINAL LAW

New Labour's circuitous quasi-criminal path has gone some way towards neutralising the restraints imposed upon the state and official powers more generally. Under the limiting principle of ***nulla poena sine*** lege, as Francis Allen has reminded us, "persons become criminals because of their acts, not simply because of who or what they are" (Allen, 1996: 14–15). The rule of law restrains the definition of conduct as criminal and the methods available to law enforcement officers. Standards of conduct must "meet stringent tests of specificity and clarity, may act only prospectively, and must be strictly construed in favour of the accused" (Kadish, 1962: 904). The arrival on the scene of the ASBO should also be considered in the light of Leon Radzinowicz's warning of the displacement of a "socio-liberal" model of criminal justice by an "authoritarian" model and, in turn, encouraging imprecise definitions for many crimes, an absence of strictly enforced rules of evidence inspired by the presumption of innocence, and with the enforcement of criminal justice likely to be exercised not only by the courts but through administrative and police agencies. Furthermore, and especially evident in authoritarian states, this "hidden jurisdiction relates to a large area of behaviour vaguely disguised as anti-social, deviant or parasitic" (Radzinowicz, 1991).

By infringing the principle that the criminal law be divided from civil sanctions (see, for example, Ashworth, 1995b: 55–7), the ASBO and its promise of fast action in tackling social problems also underscores concerns expressed by Nils Jareborg, a Swedish legal scholar, of a general weakening of the "defensive" model of criminal law policy. Under this model, criminal law aims to protect individuals against the abuse of state power by insisting that legal certainty and justice are not subordinated to perceived needs for crime prevention. Unlike other forms of law, the criminal law does not primarily have the aim of problem solving, and instead imposes normative limits on the power of the state

[76] Further steps down this route lead to James Q. Wilson's dismissal of any consideration of "root causes" on the ground that this "inevitably detracts attention from those things that government can do reasonably well and draws attention toward those many things it cannot do at all" Wilson (1975, xv).

[77] The Labour Government has acted on a number of fronts for which it has claimed the purpose, *inter alia*, of tackling underlying causes of crime. These include the New Deal for long-term unemployed persons, additional resources for nursery education and setting up a Social Exclusion Unit within the Cabinet Office. Some of these developments are discussed by David Faulkner in Chapter 5.

by insisting that criminal conduct be tightly defined and that courts demand a rigorous standard of proof along with other procedural protections. Over recent years, however, and perhaps especially in those states where politicians of the social democratic centre are dominant, these presumptions have lost ground to powerful ideological counter-currents, fuelled by frustrations that existing law falls short of meeting particular problems at hand (see, for example Tham, 1995). Consequently, the "offensive" model of criminal law policy dominates, characterised by "linguistically indeterminate" definitions of crime, and with the goal of preventing harm (Jareborg, 1995). That criminal justice is regarded as a "potential repertoire of methods for solutions of social or societal problems" is echoed in the warning of the "common social enterprise", involving law-makers and law-enforcers, where the criminal law is regarded as "only one of several, legal and non-legal, formal and informal, alternative forms of social control from among which one has to choose a rational way, without being hampered by moral considerations" (Peters, 1988: 32). Viewing criminal law and law enforcement as "mere instruments for the implementation of governmental politics, as a means of social engineering" ('t Hart, 1999) of course, reaches its zenith with resort to quasi-criminal remedies and where the protective functions of the criminal law have largely been stripped away.

It is also not without some irony that the Government introduced the Crime and Disorder Bill at precisely the moment it embarked on legislation to incorporate the European Convention on Human Rights into the law of the United Kingdom.[78] Indeed, there are no indications that New Labour's enthusiasm for pre-emptive intervention has been dented by its reading of the Convention and Mr Straw has signed a clear statement to Parliament saying that the Government believes that the provisions of the Crime and Disorder Act comply with the Human Rights Act 1998.[79] But is not the ASBO a criminal remedy in all but name? Applying the test used by the European Court in *Benham v. The United Kingdom*, although civil procedures are relied upon, the Order is sought not by individual plaintiffs but "by a public authority under statutory powers of enforcement". Furthermore any breach is subject to penalties of imprisonment, considerably more severe than available in *Benham*.[80] At a jurisprudential level, the "geometry" of a criminal prosecution differs, as Ronald Dworkin has suggested, in terms of its symmetry from that of a civil proceeding. While in standard civil cases one of the parties has a right to win, in criminal cases, although

[78] Curiously, there were few references to the European Convention on Human Rights, or to the Human Rights Bill, during the proceedings on the Crime and Disorder Bill. Some commentators have wondered whether the Government had even begun to grasp the significance of its own human rights legislation, pointing out the rights bestowed by the ECHR are absolutes. See, e.g., Gardner et al., (1998).

[79] Jack Straw, H.C. Deb., 6th ser., Vol. 327, 16 March 1999, col. 906.

[80] *Benham v. The United Kingdom*, Judgment of 10 June 1996, Reports and Decisions 1996–111. Although the Government had argued that the proceedings in this Poll Tax case were civil rather than criminal, the European Court found that Mr Benham had been "charged with a criminal offence".

the accused, if innocent, has a right to be acquitted, the state has no parallel right to a conviction if the accused is guilty (Dworkin, 1987: 100). It is within New Labour's efforts to force a symmetry onto what, in reality, is a criminal procedure that the fundamental objections to the ASBO reside.[81] To apply Foucault's graphic terminology, these hybrid remedies can be located within the "[c]arceral continuity and the fusion of the prison-form [which] make it possible to legalise, or in any case to legitimise disciplinary power" (Foucault, 1979: 302).

As the twentieth century opened, the new discipline of criminology placed the spotlight on the individual, rather than the offence, thereby promising more effective ways of dealing with problem categories, such as the habitual offender, as well as reaching towards social concerns located beyond the borders of the criminal law. That liberal values prevailed at that time, expressed in the vitality of the rule of law, despite powerful pressures for radical solutions opened up through the biological sciences, was in no small part due to the distinctive determination of those "New Liberals" who sought to re-establish a connection between ethics and politics (Freeden, 1978). At the start of the new millennium with the re-emergence of powerful instrumental forces, driven by a zealously enthusiastic government, it is by no means clear that this connection is firmly in place. The rule of law is once again under severe strain, with the criminal policy agenda reaching beyond serious offences to encompass conduct not adjudicated as criminal.

[81] At the Labour Party Annual Conference in September 1998 Tony Blair, the Prime Minister, declared: "From April, anti-social neighbours can be taken to court and *punished*" (emphasis added).

4

Youth Justice? Arguments for Holism and Democracy in Responses to Crime

PAT CARLEN

THE CLOSING YEARS of the twentieth century in Britain witnessed major reconstructions in ideologies and strategies of governance and citizenship. Monetarist policies, primarily and explicitly designed to manage fiscal crises by severely pruning welfare expenditure, have concomitantly subverted classical discourses on citizenship: first, by effecting the exclusion of increasing numbers of young people from traditional opportunities for minimum need satisfaction via work, consumption or adequate welfare payments; and, secondly, by displacing responsibility for some of the staples of public governance (e.g. welfare, public order and citizen protection) onto the "market", the "public" (i.e. the media), the "community" and the "individual". Nowhere has this abdication of government, together with its accompanying subversion (through delegitimation) of the state, been more apparent than in law and order discourses.

As the increased use of imprisonment failed to halt rising crime rates at the end of the 1980s, official discourses on crime control facilitated reconstruction of the subjectivities of "good citizens" by heightening their awareness of both criminal risk and their own responsibility for diminishing it. Increased attention to personal risk-management, via private insurance, prudent investment, household crime prevention, responsible family management and "neighbourhood watch" membership, was officially touted as the most appropriate protection for the privatised consumer-citizen. Relieved of some of its welfare "burden" and some of its "softer" policing activities, the (supposedly) beleaguered state would then be free to protect "good" consumer-citizens by engaging in the actuarial targeting of whole groups of potentially "bad" (though not necessarily *criminal*) "outsider citizens". "Good citizens" would demonstrate responsibility by developing the siege mentality, which would produce a boom in private insurance, personal therapies and obligatory counselling for every occasion. The many young people already excluded from opportunities to demonstrate "good citizenship", via the trappings of employment, housing tenure or high consumption, would increasingly be *pre*cluded from the traditional protections of being allowed to pursue their lawful activities without official molestation, and of being judged on the basis of their behaviour rather than *pre*judged on the basis of their generational or ethnic affiliations.

So, on the threshold of the twenty-first century, British law and order discourses are still dominated by a culture of recrimination in which governments effectively displace some major responsibilities for crime control onto individuals, communities and the media. These latter, reconstituting such displacement as a tacit admission that the criminal justice system cannot deliver protection against criminals, have also exploited the ensuing legitimation deficit by promoting an unforgiving populist penality, dominated by an ethos of revenge and the practices of exclusion.

Against this backdrop of punitive despair and the almost pre-modern displacement of penality from state to populace, the focus of the penal gaze in Britain has fastened, with growing (and sometimes hysterical) fear, upon the young—the young unemployed, the young homeless, young single parents and the young of any ethnic minority group perceived to be economically or culturally threatening (see Albrecht, Chapter 8). And all this, too, in a situation of asymmetrical citizenship where much adult crime is not even seen as such, especially by its victims who are often the very same young people currently being processed by a variety of agencies as either actual or potential offenders themselves (see Boswell, 1995; Brown, 1995; Maung, 1995; Carlen, 1996; Loader, 1996)!

Thus it has come about that, at the time of writing in mid-1998, a majority of pseudo-community penal initiatives target young people; and the concept of "youth crime" has been widened until it has become a conceptual site wherein a whole range of youth behaviours are conflated as being crimogenic. It is therefore not surprising that three of the most fashionable pseudo-community penal concepts—"the three Rs" of "restorative justice", (individual) "responsibility" and "reintegration"—have been interpreted as referring almost entirely to the obligations of known young offenders to known victims—rather than to any possible obligations that the state has to all young citizens because of their varying degrees of dependency.

In some recent and influential statements on youth justice in Britain, the obligations of the state to its young citizens have indeed been recognised. However, redress of the civil and criminal wrongs perpetrated on children and youth whose young lives have been seriously blighted by poverty or adult abuse (physical, sexual or psychological) has not been officially argued for as a fundamental state obligation. Instead, its utility as a penal strategy has been emphasised (see Straw, 1998a: 2); and the blame for young people's disenchantment with the political and ethical values of their seniors has been attributed to parents, teachers and probation officers. Pragmatic populism of this ilk will not work. Redressing the wrongs of socially-blighted youth within discourses of penal strategy could counterproductively provoke the old anti-welfare control complaint that offenders should be less (rather than more) eligible for assistance than law-abiding citizens. Governmental attacks on parents and teachers for youth alienation obscure the need, and obstruct opportunities, for a more fundamental structural analysis of "youth exclusion" questions; and, moreover, could also rebound by provoking counter-attacks on the legitimacy of the attackers.

Fragmentation of social policies, short-termism in economic policies and the continuation of the erosion of the ethical state by governments who have abdicated their moral responsibilities to "market forces", have produced today's "high anxiety" societies, wherein young people are too often being placed under surveillance as "threats", rather than being cherished as "assets"; and where "uncertainty", rather than being seen as an inevitable part of human existence, is wielded as a sinister political weapon to keep citizen-consumers in awe of the market (cf. Elliott and Atkinson, 1998).

In this chapter, therefore, I shall argue the following:

(1) that criminal justice for young people raises issues of responsibilities and obligations (especially of adults to young people) which are distinct from those pertaining to adult crime; but
(2) that insofar as the present emphasis on "youth crime" separates out questions about "youth crime and justice" from other criminal justice and social issues (thereby ignoring some fundamental, but equally relevant, considerations such as "legitimacy"; "obligation"; and "sentence feasibility") the emphasis on "youth" rather than "justice" is misplaced;
(3) that governments should aim for a more holistic (less bifurcated and less fragmented) conception of criminal justice, through the development of fundamental sentencing principles that can be seen to be equally applicable to all offenders, young or old;
(4) that all sentences should, accordingly, require democratic justification under one or more of the following criteria: recompense, incapacitation, civil regulation;
(5) that, prior to sentence, an assessment of the "legitimacy", "feasibility" and "sustainability" of the sentence should be made;
(6) that sentencing practices should be monitored and reviewed; that sentencers should be made to clarify their sentencing objectives to the agents who have to operationalise them; and that sentencers should also be expected to weigh the costs of their sentences against the estimated value of attainment of the stated objectives.

The arguments for holism in criminal justice developed here are not put forward in praise of either a totalising state or a new welfarism. They are premised on two main assumptions: first, that there are two sides to the youth citizenship equation and that the corollary to young people's obligation to be responsible and law-abiding citizens is that they themselves should be endowed with full citizen rights, including minimum need satisfaction (Doyal and Gough, 1991); and secondly, that, if the criminal justice system is to be accorded any kind of legitimacy (in terms of being credited with developing consistent and transparent sentencing strategies), there should be a greater transparency in sentencing *whatever the age of the offender.* (See Bottoms, 1995 on the differing conceptions of personhood realised by the concepts of "just deserts/human rights", "managerialism" and "community".)

PRINCIPLES AND PRAGMATISM IN POSTMODERN YOUTH JUSTICE

The history of the twentieth century response to young people's crime in England has been one of oscillation between two opposing models: the punishment of offenders on the one hand and the "rehabilitation" of children in trouble (and their parents) via increased "welfare" support, on the other. Although proponents of each strategy in its pure form constantly accuse their opposite numbers of ignoring some essential components of any just (in terms of "justice as fairness") response to lawbreaking, there is no doubt that they both hold fast to some classical, though asymmetrical (to each other), notions of "justice". While the advocates of individual responsibility and punishment invoke a classic criminal justice model (the main concern of which is to inflict a just measure of pain on the guilty), the advocates of welfare intervention draw on a classical social justice model, with its recurrent concern about the possibility of criminal justice in a society where people's material life chances are so unequal from birth.

Neither model of youth justice has ever been implemented in its "pure" form. Strategies have often been pragmatically combined, though sentencing objectives in specific cases have seldom been made explicit. Undoubtedly, the emphasis on "children at risk" (social justice model) has repeatedly resulted in some "netwidening" programmes which have injudiciously lumped together the "depraved and deprived". Undoubtedly, too, both models, when operationalised by either the courts or social services, have too frequently punished children and young persons for the omissions, sins, crimes and misfortunes (especially of class, ethnicity and gender) of their parents or institutional guardians, rather than for their own misdemeanours. None the less, until the early-1990s, the official criminal policy emphasis was still primarily on the just (however defined) punishment of known offenders and the just response to young people at risk of offending. During this last decade, however, the regulation of young people in general has become much more surveillatory, punitive and pragmatic, with whole groups of young people seen as posing a risk solely because they are *young*, unemployed, homeless, and visibly hedonistic; and with speed of response, combined with value for money, being repeatedly put forward as prime criteria for evaluating all aspects of youth justice (Audit Commission, 1996, van Swaaningen, Chapter 6). What has caused this *fin de siècle* punitive pragmatism, and what are its distinguishing features?

Young people have been seen as posing greater risks in the 1990s than at any other time this century, primarily because of the new phenomenon of long-term youth unemployment, with its accompanying youth homelessness, very visible youth hedonism in public places, and the relentless search for meaning, status and income in a world without work; a search that may well be instanced by the focus on drugs and life-style, the increase in the founding of single-parent families, and the rise in acquisitive crime rates (Bourgois, 1995; Collison, 1995; Hale, 1998).

Although young people are nowadays dependent upon either their parents or the state for a much longer period than they have been in previous eras, the ethos of the postmodern consciousness is one that celebrates the very individualism and self-sufficiency that are not easily accessible (in either their psychic or material forms) to the young unemployed. Moreover, in the epoch of deregulated financial markets, heightened risk awareness and individualised anxieties, four further features of 1990s England increase the vulnerability of the young both to crime (as lawbreakers and victims) and to penal regulation.

First, over the past couple of decades there has been an erosion of many of the formal regulations and informal social controls which have traditionally been taken for granted as props to public probity and civility. Thousands of jobs have been lost in public transport, parks, council estate maintenance, environmental services, education and health. Rod Morgan and I have described the deleterious effects that extensive job losses have had in terms of the multiple insecurities now experienced in many public and semi-public places previously thought to be "safe"; and in the increased physical vulnerability of both property and persons in these newly dehumanised (though maybe electronically-eyed) spaces:

> "Previously, these posts, whatever their explicit job descriptions may have entailed, also effectively (and silently) fulfilled the functions of informally policing public and semi-public space outwith the confrontational apparatus often accompanying (or at least necessarily implicit in) formal policing activities. We think in particular of the regional railway and London tube stations that at certain times of the day and night are nowadays utterly empty of any kind of officialdom—porters, ticket collectors, or information providers . . . We think of the buses that do not seem safe to many people since they have become singly-operated by a driver and without the traditional bus conductor. We think of the vast tracts of public park areas which are now without park keepers on foot and often also without motorised patrols. We think, too, of the massive and modern public institutions with their downsized staffs; of hospital and educational institutions denuded of porters, receptionists, lift staff and cleaners; and of the long, empty corridors inside buildings and the vast derelict spaces surrounding them—too frequently occupied only by that thieves' delight—an unmonitored carpark, full of expensive vehicles. All of these landscapes of public sector neglect and urban de-socialisation not only heighten the unease of the remaining skeleton staffs and the stranger-citizens going about their legitimate business, they are also a godsend to those whose business is less legitimate or even downright criminal." (Morgan and Carlen, 1998: 206–7)

Secondly, the systematic implementation of closed circuit television (CCTV) in the town centres and out-of-town shopping malls which attract large concentrations of young consumers (Norris and Armstrong, 1998), together with the police and welfare bureaucracies' targeting of whole groups of young people for closer surveillance (school students roaming the streets during school hours, children out late at night, travellers, young people at pop concerts or dossing in city centres, single parents, and social security claimants) ensure that more young people than ever before unknowingly come under either official police or private security surveillance—even at times when they are innocently engaged in legitimate pursuits, and even though they may have no previous criminal records. (See Feeley and Simon, 1992 on the actuarial targeting of suspect populations; see Mathiesen, Chapter 10 for a bleak vision of an emergent and internationalised electronic panopticonism.)

Thirdly, racial discrimination, at all levels in the criminal justice system, results in disproportionate numbers of young Afro-Caribbean being remanded in custody or sentenced to a term of imprisonment (Audit Commission, 1996: 44–5), while unfounded scares about an increase in the numbers of violent young women, together with a pillorying of single mothers, were, not surprisingly, accompanied by an increase in the female prison population of 57 per cent between December 1992 and December 1995 (Penal Affairs Consortium, 1996: 2). "During 1996, 214 sentenced 15, 16, and 17-year-old girls were held in prisons in England and Wales. Of those, 68% were for non-violent offences . . ." (Howard League, 1997: 13).

Finally, young people as a group have been negatively portrayed by the media as being unendingly problematic and threatening, with certain newspapers playing unremittingly on a populist punitiveness which, with the honourable exception of the late 1980s Conservative Home Secretary, Douglas Hurd, few ministers have dared to gainsay.

"Would it pass *The Sun*[1] test?" continues to be the routine query of pusillanimous politicians and officials, reluctant to implement less punitive and more effective crime reduction policies (see Carlen, 1998). In fact, during 1998, a number of incidents involving media and ministerial pronouncements which provoked protesters to take to the streets over their fear of certain offenders already released from prison, makes it possible to argue that, at the time of writing, as the millennium approaches, the 1980s emphasis on the managerialists' three Es of economy, efficiency and effectiveness (see Fionda, Chapter 7 and van Swaaningen, Chapter 6), has been replaced in 1990s Britain by the three Ms of an unholy alliance of media, ministers and mob. As they bay for blood in their tabloids, in Westminster, on the streets, and outside the courts, the three Ms unequivocally and cynically (in the case of the media and the ministers) abandon rational models of criminal justice in the forging of a punitive, populist and premodern criminology.

In such an unfavourable and punitive climate, it is all the more admirable that some organisations have worked hard either to implement, or to persuade the

[1] *The Sun* is a daily tabloid newspaper, published by Rupert Murdoch.

new Labour government (which took office in May 1997) to initiate, some less punitive responses to crime, especially initiatives or blueprints involving notions of "restorative" or "relational" justice.

RESTORATIVE JUSTICE

In its theoretical lineage, "restorative justice" is an offspring of the old complaint that the classical fiction of a social contract between citizen and state which places upon the state an obligation to punish offenders, also results in the "theft of the conflict" from both offender and victim (Christie, 1977). In the subsequent court proceedings, where the social concern about the injury to the victim is translated into the legal concern about the violation of the criminal law, the victim is squeezed out of the reparative equation altogether (Pashukanis, 1978—first published 1929). By contrast, and in its contemporary policy applications in New Zealand (McElrea, 1994), Australia (Blagg, 1997) and Canada (Davies, 1997), "restorative justice" attempts victim empowerment at "restorative conferences" where the offence, and the appropriate penalty in response to it, are discussed with victim, offender and representatives of the appropriate criminal justice agencies. Exponents of restorative justice, however, though vocal about its speed and cheapness, are usually silent about the more difficult questions of legitimacy, obligation, feasibility and sustainability—all the awkward issues which, though an insistence on them here may seem to be wilfully subversive of both the pragmatism and the optimism which pervade the "restorative" approach, actually have to be confronted as soon as the more persistent, serious, or seriously damaged young offenders come into the frame.

LEGITIMACY AND OBLIGATION IN CRIMINAL JUSTICE

> "Putting it bluntly, if someone's got a stolen telly in their front room, no one round here gives a shit. But why should they? How can you expect people with no future, on the poverty line, to worry about a stolen telly when the chairman of British Gas has got his whopping pay rise and his millions in share options, while his own employees are getting the sack?" (Police Constable with 20 years' experience, quoted in Rose, 1996: 94–5; cited in Cook, 1997).

One of the main problems of separating out youth criminal justice from criminal justice in general and then attempting to address youth crime independently of questions of social justice, is that, increasingly, young people themselves refuse to make that distinction. Recent research indicates that high proportions of young people who end up homeless, in state care or penal custody have had serious crimes committed against them by adults who will never be brought to trial (Carlen, 1996). The same research suggests that these adult depredations often occasion their young victims' first steps (e.g. running away, playing truant, going into care, staying out all hours) into criminal trouble (Carlen, 1996). These youngsters, together with those living in poverty, have also had sufficient education in social adversity to see through the political hypocrisy of governments focusing on young people's relatively minor crimes, while youth unemployment, youth homelessness and youth poverty are represented as being, in part, the fault of the young persons themselves (see Cook, 1997). However, to insist that there is a positive relationship between the law-breaking of the most socially-deprived young people and their prior exclusion from the emotional and material goods that tie a majority of citizens into either law-abiding behaviour or the structures of respectability that will keep them out of the arms of the law even when they do commit crime, is not also to imply that young people are thereby licensed to burgle and batter with impunity. Nor is it implied that they should be allowed to deny all responsibility for either their present crimes or (especially) their future behaviour. But it does call into question the state's *right* to punish them as if they were *solely* to blame for their actions. And it also calls into question the *feasibility* of expecting young people to take control of their lives without any of the most effective regulatory controls—i.e. stakes in society such as decent jobs and homes—being provided by the state itself.

Insofar as young people themselves are conscious of the legitimisation and feasibility deficits described above (and the present widespread estrangement of young people from traditional party politics suggests that they may be—see McRae, 1987) the likelihoods of their feeling ashamed about their own criminal behaviours and the possibility of their integration—(the term *re*integration will obviously be inappropriate in many cases)—into law-abiding society is diminished. (See Blagg, 1997 for a similar analysis of why "restorative conferences" are unlikely to be legitimated by Aboriginal young people in Australia.) For, in any holistic and ethical-*state* programme of restorative justice (as opposed to the consumerist-ethical *community* model espoused by exponents such as Haln, 1998: 134), the question of "who restores what to whom and why" becomes central both to the quality of justice and to the quality of the reparation made. In cases where further inquiry reveals that the young offenders have themselves been either criminally victimised or grossly deprived of material or emotional nurture in childhood, it will certainly not be enough for a "restorative justice" programme merely to restore the "status quo". In such cases, a greater recognition and explicit reiteration of the state's obligation to all its young citizens will be required (see Cullen and Gilbert, 1982: 246; Faulkner, Chapter 5). For, as well as inducing a sense of responsibility and remorse in offenders, a truly restorative programme would also take steps to ensure that offenders' own exclusion from minimum need satisfaction be redressed (c.f. Pashukanis, 1978: 177; Carlen, 1983, 1989; de Haan, 1990). There is, moreover, no reason why this model of "state obligated rehabilitation" (Carlen, 1989), which emphasises the reciprocity of state-citizen obligations (and especially the special obligations of protection and nurture that the state has to its young citizens), should ignore the informal relations between individual victims and offenders. Indeed, young offenders are much more likely to take their own obligations to society seriously if they feel that, in the future, they themselves are to have a greater stake in that society, and that therefore the demands made upon them are *legitimate* (see Bottoms, 1994 for a similar point). At the same time, for any state-obligated programme to work, it would not be sufficient for it to be seen as being legitimate; the reparative and rehabilitative demands would also have to be feasible and sustainable. For why should any offender want to "restore" a situation riven with inequality?

SENTENCE FEASIBILITY

I have previously given detailed examples of some of the ways in which issues of sentence feasibility occur:

> "The problem of sentence feasibility and social circumstances comes about primarily in two ways. First many people . . . currently enduring domestic situations fractured by the pains of unemployment, low wages and poor housing are in no fit state to undergo further punishment in the community. Secondly, many areas of the country lack the communal facilities which provide for a decent standard of public life. Thus, while certain offenders might be willing to attempt compliance with [restorative justice] orders, probation officers might rightly calculate that, given the tensions and frustrations already existing in their homes, their clients would be unlikely to complete any order involving constant home calls, curfews or house arrest. Similarly, in other cases, officers might know that while a lack of child-minding facilities would prevent some parents from doing community service, a dearth of public transport would equally prevent some clients from getting to and from suitable schemes. Additionally, it might also be unrealistic to expect emotionally and mentally damaged recidivists to complete any punitive, as opposed to supportive, scheme" (Carlen, 1989; 120; 1990: 22).

Within such landscapes of deprivation, very substantial questions of "feasibility" need to be confronted in relation to restorative justice schemes involving either long-term "excluded" young people or seriously damaged victims of adult crimes, such as parental neglect, sexual abuse and physical abuse. They include, at a minimum, those which ask: Who is the relevant community? What are the objectives of the exercise? What changes in the offender's situation need to be made in order for these objectives to be achieved? What type of official help needs to be forthcoming in order for these objectives to be met? What is a realistic timescale in which to expect the offender to meet these objectives? Is any element of "shaming" appropriate to this particular offender? What could the offender possibly restore to the victim?

Answers to these questions would involve a variety of agencies, and they would not be cheap to come by in terms of either money or time. But they might help translate the presently partial rhetoric of "restorative justice" into more possible realities. (For further discussion of "sentence feasibility" see Carlen, 1983, 1989, 1990 and 1998.)

(i) The feasibility of "community" integration

Central to the "reintegrative shaming" theory which was first put forward by Braithwaite (1989) and which is either explicit or implicit in most theories of restorative justice, is an assumption of a "community" that the offender respects (see also Pavlich, 1998). If, because of the offender's exclusionary social circumstances, no such moral community exists, then it will have to be constructed. (The "foyer" movement is one imaginative scheme for creating new communities for the excluded young see, for instance, Shelter, 1992.) It is certainly not feasible to expect young people who have already been abused by adults, or excluded from education and the labour market, to be "defined back in" (Dahrendorf,1985) to the families, schools and exploitative jobs that they have already rejected.

(ii) The feasibility of the "time-scale"

If, because of emotional or physical damage inflicted on the offender as a child, he or she needs a great deal of time to be "persuaded" and/or empowered to enter into the designated moral and material community, maybe a long-term, tolerant and non-repressive and non-custodial regime of "respite care" (NACRO, 1997) will have to be risked—if only *because it is likely that all other known forms of intervention would be even riskier in terms of the likelihood of future recidivism.* The failure of traditional criminal justice mechanisms (see Faulkner and van Swaaningen, Chapters 5 and 6), together with the destruction of many of the informal controls previously inherent in "real work" and face-to-face controls on public space (see above), has created a social control vacuum in which there is an urgent need to create civil mechanisms for a newly legitimated but non-repressive social control. Unless it is appreciated that long-term objectives can be attained in a variety of ways, that the conditions for change are constantly changing, and that all methods for attaining long-term goals need to be adapted to the multiple historical realities of people differently placed according to class, gender and ethnic inequities, it is likely that the more imaginative responses to young people's unemployment and related problems which are currently being advocated, will once again be inappropriately monitored on far too short a timescale. Then, and as in previous eras, they will be found lacking and abandoned before they have been given a chance to have an impact on youth crime.

(iii) The feasibility of shaming

If, because of young people's poverty-stricken circumstances, the only thing that they have left is their pride, then as Blagg (1997, 489) has insisted in a different context, any attempt to "shame" them by a community which has never included them in its share-out of emotional and material goods in the first place, will merely be experienced as yet another imposition by an alien culture, and will be bitterly resisted. In this last example, above all, it is very apparent that in predicting sentencing efficacy in terms of the achievement of stated objectives, the questions of legitimacy and feasibility will often be closely intertwined.

(iv) The feasibility of "restoration"

The fundamental problem of feasibility behind the notion of restorative justice is the implicit assumption that, prior to the offence, the needs and assets of victim and offender are usually in a relation of symmetry to each other and that, therefore, the restorative process can once more bring them into balance. Not so. Many young offenders are not in a position to restore *anything* to their victims, and, in these cases, attractive as it may be to yearn for a system of justice which satisfies the "just deserts" of victim and offender in one single process, reparation for victims will have to remain a state obligation. (See Carlen, 1983; Bottoms, 1994 for further discussion of asymmetries in criminal justice.)

HOLISM AND DEMOCRACY IN CRIME REGULATION

> "They see you as a danger, a threat. Fuck knows why. Because you've got nothing and they've got something? That's probably it." (Homeless young man, quoted in Carlen, 1996: 121)

The concept of "restorative justice" is enticing. It appeals to several sentencing philosophies, and aspires to deliver in one coherent, cheap and efficient process, a range of sentencing objectives (e.g. rehabilitation, reparation, expiation, deterrence) that are often seen as being opposed to (and are certainly not reducible to) each other. Given the range of its appeal, it might even be argued that restorative justice is indeed "holistic" in its approach. But, conflation of objectives should not be mistaken for an holistic programme. In this chapter, it has been argued that, at present, "restorative justice" in relation to "youth justice" is an impossibly asymmetrical concept and that, in 1990s Britain, youth justice itself has been variously and contradictorily marked by: bifurcatory processes which distinguish between the structural causes of social exclusion and a personal responsibility for lawbreaking; fragmented welfare and rehabilitative policies which subvert each other's objectives; and a conflation of distinct processes such as reparation for victims and the state's obligations to youth citizenry (see also Faulkner, 1998). Moreover, although the poorest young offenders are sometimes in a position to make some kind of recompense to the victim, they seldom have their own citizenship deficits (in terms of unemployment, homelessness and the criminal injuries inflicted on them as children) redressed.

In view of the foregoing, therefore, it would seem that the "liberal" conceptions of "restorative justice" (as described by Davies, 1997) will only be appropriate when young offenders already have at least some community ties; in those cases, in fact, where they could normally have been expected to "grow out of crime" as a concomitant of "growing into" the responsibilities of adult work, home and family (Rutherford, 1986a). In cases involving young people with fewer pre-existing ties, however, a more holistically democratic approach is called for if the desired behavioural changes by the offender are to be sustained beyond the period of the formal restorative process. Such an approach should be expected to: recompense the victim; identify and help create material conditions for the offender in which he/she should be less likely to commit crime in the future; and work to reduce the gross social inequalities and unredressed crimes against minors by adults (especially those involving sexual and physical abuse). It would also have to make explicit the moral and economic bases of all sentences in order that they could be assessed for both legitimacy and feasibility.

To help make explicit the moral basis of "restorative holism" in sentencing, all sentences should be justified in terms of one or more of the following objectives: recompense; incapacitation (of the offender); and civil regulation (of the offender's circumstances). Sentencers should be made accountable to a Sentencing Council (Ashworth, 1983), and, through a Sentencing Council to the Prison Service, and any other agencies involved in carrying out the sentence of the court; and, finally, some measure of financial accountability should be introduced into the moral universes of magistrates and judges. (The new Youth Justice Board for England and Wales, as its title denotes, only deals with 18 year olds and under. However, the damage done to certain young people by early neglect, abuse or blocked opportunities will require a much longer period of reparative intervention.)

(i) Recompense

The most attractive aspect of fully restorative responses to crime is that they should aim, as far as possible, to repair the relationships between offender and victim (sometimes an individual, sometimes a whole neighbourhood) which have been breached by the crime. This, already the best known objective of "restorative justice", the so-called healing of the breach between victims and offenders, is also the most difficult to realise: primarily, because it is seldom that the interests of victims and offenders are symmetrical; and secondly and consequentially, because those often opposed interests, cannot usually be realistically dealt with by one and the same process. Yes, it is surely right that crime victims should have their losses and injuries taken seriously and that they should receive compensation and support in relation to them. Yes, it may help some victims to have a say in what happens to offenders. And, yes, it may be morally instructive for offenders to have the injuries of the victims brought home to them. But, when there are great class, gender and ethnic inequities between victims and offenders, it may not be at all cynical to assume that young people's citizenship deficits might possibly be matched by similar empathy deficits; nor to doubt whether, in such (or even *any*) cases, victims are the most appropriate persons to judge offenders, or the ones most likely to induce guilt in them. Therefore, it seems to me that sentencers should only include victim reparation in restorative orders on occasions when it is beyond doubt that victims and offenders belong to the same moral communities; or when the state-obligated support to be given to offenders is such that they will see that it is both legitimate for the state to demand, and feasible for them to make, reparation to victims.

(ii) Incapacitation

In fully restorative responses to crime, an incapacitative sentence would be justifiable in only two types of cases: in those where the crime was so serious that it would be deemed essential to public protection to stop the offender from committing further offences; and in those where social redress of the offenders' circumstances was either deemed unnecessary (corporate crime?) or had already been made, and where it could not be argued that any (further) support in terms of material redress or "time to change" would encourage the offender to desist from the specific law-breaking activities in question. However, in this latter instance it would have to be demonstrated that the previous demands made of defendants had been both: *legitimate*—in that a "community" either already existed, or had been constructed, for them; and *feasible*—in that they had not been prevented from meeting their restorative obligations by adverse social, mental or emotional conditions; e.g. it would not necessarily be feasible to expect drug users to give-up an addiction just as soon as there was a change for the better in their economic circumstances.

I have deliberately named "incapacitation" as one of the categories to be included in a sentencing tariff aimed at transparency, because it is a sentencing objective to which sentencers are loath to admit, and which is surrounded by humbug. The rhetoric that offenders will be "helped" by prison sentences, imposed purely for incapacitative purposes, should be prohibited, unless additional and specialised facilities are available to achieve some kind of "civil recompense" objective during the period of incapacitation. For, in a holistic system, prison and other agency staff should not only know exactly what the sentencing objectives are but should also be entitled to claim the wherewithal to realise them.

(iii) Civic regulation

Finally, civic regulation. In any fully holistic sentencing programme, notions of censure and regulatory social intervention should be separated from those of incapacitative punishment and reparation, and the ideal in cases involving young people would be to redress the wrong done to the crime victim, and to *address* any adverse social circumstances, such as unemployment or homelessness, which might make the offender more crime or arrest-prone in the future (see Beckett and Western, Chapter 2). Maybe it is in this context that the operationalisation of the idea of a citizen wage would be most pertinent: the suggestion being that *participation* would be the sole qualification for receipt of a citizen wage from the state and that in this context, too, participation could include child (and other types) of care, together with all types of educational courses and voluntary and non-waged creative work (see Atkinson, 1998).

(iv) Sentence accountability

Although the courts should still maintain control over individual cases, in any future system aimed at a holistic response to crime, sentencers should be required: (a) to justify to a Sentencing Council (for sentencing policy review purposes) all custodial sentences and remands of prisoners, in terms of their appropriateness to the offender, the offence and any pre-existing sentencing criteria for the award under scrutiny (see Ashworth, 1995: 342–52 for a very full discussion of all the complexities inherent in the inauguration and viability of any such sentencing policy-making body); (b) to make very explicit what they hope to achieve by the custodial sentence awarded; and (c) to make a calculation of what the *total* costs of the sentence are likely to be. (After all, the requirement of financial accountability is nowadays imposed on all other public servants. Why not make the same demands of sentencers?) The thinking behind this latter requirement is that if the courts are going to continue sending women and men to prison for trivial offences, they should publicise the financial and social costs of what they are doing, say what they hope to get for their money—and let the public also have a chance to count the costs of (too carelessly) assuaging its punitive urge. Adoption of this strategy would most likely achieve reduction of the numbers of young people given purely punitive orders, and might, via the reintegrative shaming of both the communities that have excluded so many poor youngsters and the sentencers who too easily send them to prison, restore the "justice" to "youth justice". For, if sentencers had both to name sentencing objectives, *and* calculate and pronounce publicly on the costs of their sentencing practices, (e.g. £2,000 per week in 1998 to lock up a juvenile in a secure unit), they might also be shocked and shamed into demanding more appropriate civil mechanisms for both the prevention and reparation of crime and the prevention and reparation of criminal and social injustices.

Part II

The Managerial Agenda

5

Policy and Practice in Modern Britain: Influences, Outcomes and Civil Society

DAVID FAULKNER

RECENT DEBATE ON crime and justice in England and Wales has been influenced by several complex factors. These include the following:

- The rise in crime, the perception that crime is becoming nastier, and an increase in the fear of crime, which together have had a corrosive effect on public confidence and the way in which many people believe they have to live their lives.
- Changes in social and economic conditions which have caused, or contributed to, a loss of security in employment, a loss of stability in families and personal relationships, and increasing isolation and exclusion of those who have come to be seen as "failures", or who refuse or are unable to conform.
- Changes in the management of public services—sometimes described as the New Public Management—which have emphasised markets, competition, short-term contracts, measurement of results and individual responsibility rather than the more traditional values of equity, objectivity, partnership and security of tenure.
- Changing attitudes towards the functions of state, the role of government, the rights and responsibilities of citizenship, and the relationships between them.
- A self-centred, though entirely understandable, obsession with risk and personal protection, combined with impatience with the real or supposed failings of the criminal justice process and hostility towards those perceived as dangerous or threatening.

Governments and political parties have occasionally resisted, but have more often promoted, exploited, or manipulated these influences, especially during the period when the Conservative Government had to overcome the divisions in its Party and regain the confidence of the country after the United Kingdom's withdrawal from the European Exchange Rate Mechanism and the signing of the Maastricht Treaty in the autumn of 1992 (Windlesham, 1996; Downes, 1997). The other political parties, the courts, the police and other criminal justice services have in their own ways shared and responded to the same feelings and attitudes.

EXCLUSION AND INCLUSION

One consequence of this combination of influences has been the emergence, and for a time the prevalence, of an "exclusive" view of society and human relationships. This view emphasises personal freedom and individual responsibility, but is inclined to disregard the influence of situations and circumstances. It distinguishes between a deserving majority who are self-reliant, law-abiding and entitled to benefit themselves and those around them without interference from others; and an undeserving, feckless welfare-dependent and often dangerous minority or under-class from whom they need to be protected. Human behaviour is thought to be motivated mainly by a desire for material gain or by fear of punishment or disgrace and not much by a sense of personal loyalty or social obligation.

A society which adopts this view will favour such measures as the elimination of undeserving claims for social benefits; the surveillance and reporting of suspicious persons or events; the carrying of identity cards; access to personal records, including criminal convictions, by those in authority; and the large-scale use of imprisonment. Such a society is likely to be unsure of itself, suspicious of strangers, hostile towards foreigners and fearful of those who do not conform to its assumption and stereotypes (see Melossi, Chapter 9). It will be much concerned with personal protection and the assessment and avoidance of risk. Its decision-making processes will be cautious, closed and secretive. An example of "exclusive" thinking can be found in the focus on the "underclass" by the American writer Charles Murray (Murray, 1990, 1994). Andrew Rutherford gives an account of its potential consequences in his paper on "Criminal Policy and the Eliminative Ideal" (Rutherford, 1997a).

The contrasting "inclusive" view has received less prominence. It recognises the capacity and will of individuals to change—to improve if they are given guidance, help and encouragement; to be damaged if they are abused or humiliated. It emphasises respect for human dignity and personal identity, and a sense of public duty and social responsibility. It looks more towards putting things right for the future than to allocating blame and awarding punishment, although the latter might sometimes be part of the former. The duty to conform to society's or the community's standards is seen as matched by the community's own obligation to support its vulnerable and disadvantaged members. Solutions to social problems or to crime are sought more by inclusion within the community itself—among parents, in schools, by providing opportunities and hope for young people—than by punishment or exclusion from it. Authority has to be accountable and legitimate, and respect for it has to be earned and justified. The "inclusive" view is likely to be characteristic of a society which is open and compassionate, which accommodates and respects diversity and which has some confidence in the future. It resembles, to some extent, the notion of a "stakeholding" society put forward by Will Hutton and John Kay (Hutton,

1995; Kay, 1996). The language of "communities" with which it is often associated is not without ambiguity: it can be used to imply either an inclusive or an exclusive approach—inclusive if it seeks to reform and integrate those who are troublesome or disruptive, exclusive if it seeks to remove them for the protection or benefit of others. The term needs to be used with care (Lacey and Zedner, 1995).

NEW PUBLIC MANAGEMENT

While the "exclusive" view of society and human relationships was becoming prevalent in political debate, the "New Public Management" was becoming established in public services, including the criminal justice system (Hood, 1991; Harden, 1992; Freedland, 1994; James and Raine, 1998). New Public Management was a reaction to chronic economic weakness which sought to make public services more economical and efficient by applying commercial methods and standards. Later versions involved the creation of "markets", or the use of the attitudes and language, and were associated with the "down-sizing" or "hollowing-out" of the state. Examples in Great Britain included the adoption, or imposition, of quantified targets and performance indicators, performance-related pay, and the contracting-out or privatisation of services or their transition to the status of executive agencies. Similar influences were at work in the United States, Australia, New Zealand and in other countries (Osborne and Gaebler, 1992; Pusey, 1991).

A change from the attitudes, outlook and culture which had been characteristic of public services in the 1960s and 1970s was undoubtedly needed. Public funds were too easy to obtain for some purposes, and too difficult for others. They were often spent with too little regard for the cost-effectiveness of the service that was being provided. Too little attention was paid to the feelings, expectations and reactions of those for whom services were provided or who came into contact with them, including the victims of crime. Most professionals were conscientious and (often supremely) hard working as individuals, but collectively they could be secretive, complacent and obstructive (Young, 1982). The change from a culture of performing a function to one of achieving a result was one which many public servants welcomed, at least so long as the results were ones to which they could feel personally committed and they had some part in deciding what those results should be. New Public Management, and especially the change to agency status, had in some instances an invigorating effect, transforming a troubled organisation with low status and poor morale into a more dynamic, confident, and forward-looking enterprise.

The New Public Management, and the reforms associated with it, have often been described as if they were common sense, practical, and even inevitable in a world of global markets and constraints on resources, as uncontroversial, and as politically and ethically neutral. In fact they involve fundamental changes in public and public service values, attitudes and expectations. They have profound implications for public law, the role of the state and the nature of its authority, and the rights and duties of citizenship (Foster and Plowden, 1996; Freedland, 1998a). Health, education, employment and housing are treated as commodities to be purchased and traded on the most competitive available terms, not as obligations to be undertaken, and still less rights to be protected by the state, provided by public services and enjoyed by the citizen. Citizens are defined as individual consumers of public services, rather than as people who share a sense of common interest or identity or who are joined by any sense of mutual obligation or trust (Freedland, 1998b).

Public service is defined by the achievement of internal targets and performance indicators, or as the accurate performance of an internal process; (perhaps accredited to a national or international standard such as ISO 9001) rather than by reference to any social or economic outcomes. The values of public service become those of managerial efficiency, to be achieved for its own sake and not in pursuit of any wider purpose or obligation. The state, or rather the political administration of the day, becomes increasingly powerful, centralised and remote, while divesting itself of many of its responsibilities towards its citizens and placing such responsibilities as remain in the hands of private or intermediate organisations with their own, often commercial or quasi-commercial, interests and objectives. The contracting-out of prisons, which commenced in Britain in the late 1980s, is an obvious example.

IMPLICATIONS FOR CRIME AND JUSTICE

A country in which the attitudes of social exclusion and New Public Management are dominant will not show much interest in the social causes of crime, in the conditions in which crime is likely to be committed, or in any responsibility which citizens or communities may have to prevent it. Responsibility for crime is placed firmly on criminals, either individually for the particular offences they have committed, or collectively as if they were a separate group who are outside normal or legitimate society. Unruly children, single parents, refugees, the mentally ill and social security claimants have all been described—or demonised—in this way. Dealing with crime and its consequences is seen as a matter for the police, the courts and other statutory services, not for society or communities, and the obvious and proper method is by detection and punishment.

Deterrence and incapacitation by imprisonment are regarded as the most effective means of prevention, and an indefinite rise in the prison population—by 50 per cent in five years, with further increases projected (Home Office, 1999)—with its associated costs, can be accepted without serious question. Justice becomes a process to be accelerated and made more efficient, and more effective in maximising its outputs, which are convictions and punishment.

Attempts to prevent crime, to the extent that they take place, are concentrated more on physical security ("target hardening") and surveillance (typically security cameras and other, sometimes more secret, devices) to increase rates of detection, than on measures which might affect the motivation to commit offences (for example opportunities for training, voluntary service, social activity or legitimate adventure and excitement). "Targeted" policing focuses on known previous offenders, sometimes with successful results in obtaining evidence or recovering stolen property, but with a risk of what may be seen as harassment and resulting alienation. It raises important issues of accountability and legitimacy (JUSTICE, 1997). Private space is created in shopping malls and certain housing developments—often deliberately advertised as "exclusive"—and is guarded to prevent the admission of those who do not have the right personal appearance or the required forms of identification (Jones and Newburn, 1998). For the probation service, "protecting the public", through the mechanical enforcement of orders and attempts to make them more "demanding", takes precedence over programmes to reform or integrate offenders themselves. Measures of this kind are generally welcomed as generating confidence and trust among those who are "included" but little attention is paid, or thought to be deserved, to those who are not.

In public services, the skills which seem to be most highly rewarded, and the values which seem to be most highly respected, are those of accountancy and financial management and of cutting costs. The disciplines of economics and accountancy are more highly regarded than those of social science, and management consultancy is more highly regarded than academic research.

Financial procedures and quantified, internal measures of performance take precedence over those concerned with quality or social outcomes. Public service is not so much seen as a career or a long-term commitment, but as an episode in an individual's personal advancement to be continued for as long as, but no longer than, it is the most financially rewarding option that is available.

Many of these beliefs and attitudes seemed to be in the ascendent in the period before the general election in May 1997.

NEW LABOUR—A NEW APPROACH

The new Government faced a precarious situation when it took office after the election. The previous Government had encouraged people to expect more from their public services, but its obsession with management and efficiency had led to an assumption that many of the issues facing the country could be dealt with simply by reorganising the relevant public services to make them more efficient and effective. The policy on health was the internal market, on education it was the local management of schools, on transport it was privatisation. In line with that assumption, it was supposed that improvements in the efficiency and organisation of the criminal justice process, especially if accompanied by greater severity of punishment, would provide an adequate answer to the problem of crime. That was a dangerous oversimplification, which overstated the capacity of the criminal justice process to prevent crime, encouraged the view that crime was "someone else's" problem, and distracted attention from the public's own responsibilities as citizens.

The new Government's approach to the problems of crime and justice had been expressed while Labour was in Opposition by the slogan "Tough on crime, tough on the causes of crime". Its Crime and Disorder Act, passed in July 1998, is based on prevention and support for people in difficulty, combined with the coercion of those who do not comply and reform of the youth justice system. The Government recognises that problems of crime cannot be dealt with in isolation from wider questions of social and economic policy in areas such as employment, education, health and housing. All these are receiving attention in their own right, but also with some recognition that the solutions may also help to reduce crime. Through the Unit set up for that purpose, it is making a special effort to tackle some of the problems of social exclusion. It is not obsessed with conviction and punishment for their own sake or as the country's principal response to crime.

In matters relating to the management of public services, the Government is continuing to insist on efficiency and effectiveness; but effectiveness is more often being defined in relation to final outcomes such as the prevention of re-offending than to internal processes (HM Treasury, 1998). There is a strong emphasis on "what works" in probation practice, and a proposal to re-form the probation service as a unified executive agency of government, with a new, as yet undecided, title (Home Office, 1998b). New Labour is not proposing substantial change in existing procedures and structures such as performance indicators, agency status for the prison service or the contracting-out of prisons, but it seems to be less concerned (for example in the health service) with markets, competition and short-term contracts. There seems to be less of a culture of insecurity and blame; the Government ostensibly respects and is accessible to professional as well as public opinion; and is committed to an evidence-based approach which takes account of academic research.

At the same time as the Government is paying attention to the preventive effects of its wider social policies, it is also developing more specific policies aimed at those at risk of offending, or thought to present a risk to others (Home Office, 1997c, 1998b). They include some of the groups who have been demonised in the past—unruly children, irresponsible parents, misusers of drugs and those previously convicted of sexual offences. Many of its proposals are "inclusive" in the sense described earlier in this chapter—the reparation and action plan orders, the approval for community (or family) conferencing and mentoring schemes, the emphasis on the principles of restoration, reintegration and responsibility, and the youth panels and "contracts" which are intended to give those principles practical effect. Measures of this kind, especially community or family conferences in which the victim is involved, are sometimes described as "restorative justice" (see Carlen, Chapter 4).

Other proposals introduce a range of preventive orders—anti-social behaviour orders, drug treatment and testing orders, parenting orders—whose purpose is to prevent irresponsible and socially disruptive behaviour, initially by imposing various conditions or requirements, but backed up by severe penal sanctions for failure to comply. Concern has been expressed that those sanctions may be used, not exceptionally and as a last resort, but routinely and oppressively (Ashworth et al., 1998 and Rutherford, Chapter 3), and in ways which criminalise larger numbers of vulnerable and especially young people for behaviour which is criminal only in the sense that it involves a breach of an order or condition. These and other proposals, such as the child safety order and local child curfews (for children under ten), and the new statutory provisions allowing children of 14, and perhaps eventually as young as ten, to be held in prison custody under a new detention and training order, can be seen as implying that there is a separate, recalcitrant and potentially dangerous class of people for whom integration is not practicable and from whom the rest of society has to be protected. They are therefore "exclusive" in the sense previously indicated.

Individual policies should not be approved or criticised simply because they appear to be "inclusive" or "exclusive" in the way that has been described. Instead, they must be judged on their operation and outcomes in the situation in which they are applied and in conjunction with other policies and practices to which they are related. In matters relating to crime and criminal justice, some punitive and sometimes exclusive sanctions, such as imprisonment, must be available as a last resort. But the scale on which they are used, and the spirit and culture in which the measures are applied, will have a critical effect on their success or failure in terms of their eventual outcomes. A culture of punishment and exclusion, for example in the police or the youth court, could cause even the "inclusive" measures to be operated as instruments of punishment and so undermine the principles of restoration, reintegration and responsibility which the Government itself has set out.

PUTTING POLICIES INTO EFFECT

The problems which the Government and the country have to tackle—like many other problems in the modern world—are intractable and complex. They need multiple, co-ordinated solutions which draw on different skills from diverse backgrounds, brought together in formations which share a sense of common purpose and accountability. Despite the efforts and experience of the last 15 years, it is still hard to achieve co-operation successfully on the ground. It is especially hard in circumstances of tight financial control and shortage of resources, or in a management—and political—culture which has previously insisted on uniformity, competition, short-term contracts, narrowly defined and quantified performance indicators, individual rather than collective responsibility and effective discouragement of risk-taking.

No-one should underestimate the practical difficulties involved in making the new arrangements work successfully. They include the formation of new, inter-disciplinary youth offending teams to assess and supervise young people who are in trouble or at risk. The teams' composition, relationships and accountability will all need careful attention, both in the pilot schemes which the Government has proposed and once they are fully in operation. The teams need leadership as well as management, and their members must be chosen as the best people for the job, not as those who can most easily be spared. They will need to relate to statutory and voluntary services; local government including elected members; courts; local businesses; local communities including minority ethnic groups; victims and their organisations; central government; and the new national Youth Justice Board which has been appointed to supervise the arrangements as a whole. There will also be sensitive relationships, both within the teams and with offenders and their families. Many of the relationships will involve some degree of accountability, and will need suitable mechanisms for that purpose. Purchasing and funding arrangements which can provide a reasonable degree of continuity and confidence will be absolutely crucial. Programmes to support the new preventive orders must be of suitable quality, and the sanction of imprisonment—which is by definition exclusionary in its effect—must only be used exceptionally and as a last resort. Teams and those who work with them must look beyond preventive orders and punitive sanctions to the more positive opportunities for personal development, self-fulfilment and service to others which are part of a healthy civil society. All the new arrangements will need, not only to be monitored in terms of internal performance measures and indicators, but also evaluated for their social outcomes and consequences. The latter requires external, high quality research, for which the Youth Justice Board must have an adequate budget. Managing complexity and diversity on this scale is a challenging and exciting prospect, but it demands skills which have not been much valued or developed in recent years.

CRIME, JUSTICE AND CIVIL SOCIETY

Programmes for crime and justice should be set in a wider context which includes the ideas and values of citizenship and civil society. The country is coming increasingly to realise that the world does not consist just of individuals on the one hand and the state and its institutions on the other. Questions of crime, and of social stability and social justice, are also the responsibility of civil society—that is to say, those associations, networks and relationships which are neither part of the mechanisms of the state nor run for commercial profit. Civil society includes the voluntary sector, but also the less formal meetings, groups and associations, and the individual acts of kindness, which provide opportunities for personal development, service to others, and support in times of difficulty. They are what hold communities together, and they can make all the difference to the quality of national life. Ideas of civil society and citizenship have attracted increasing attention during the last few years, for example in the debates on stake-holding and communities, and on relational and restorative justice, and in the present Government's programme of constitutional reform and its concern over social exclusion.

Citizenship has three elements—rights, responsibilities and a voice in the country's and the local community's decision-making processes. None of them should be pursued without regard for the other two. The notion of rights, including the rights of children, set out in the United Nations Convention on the Rights of the Child and those enacted in domestic legislation in the Children Act 1989, has been much criticised during the last few years. But the country should be thinking about how to clarify, interpret and apply the rights of citizenship in an inclusive spirit, and about how to balance them with responsibilities. It should not weaken or qualify them, still less remove them altogether, either generally or from "undeserving" individuals in the supposed interests of punishment or social control.

Responsibilities seem to be thought of mostly as "other people's" responsibilities to conform to "our" standards and comply with "our" requirements, including those requirements whose purpose is to protect our own safety and comfort. The notion of responsibilities is "exclusive" when it is used in this sense. There has been less emphasis on the equally important and more "inclusive" responsibilities of citizens to promote and protect the interests of the nation's children, or more generally to support or care for those who are vulnerable, disadvantaged or at risk of being excluded, whether they do so by their direct efforts as volunteers, by supporting charities, or through the payment of taxes. That emphasis should be revived, as Alun Michael, formerly Minister of State at the Home Office, has argued (Michael, 1998).

A voice in the decision-making process, and confidence that it will be heard, is what gives the institutions of state their legitimacy and authority. Legitimacy is closely linked with public accountability. It was once left to the democratic process, supplemented by the subtle workings of the English establishment and the less subtle influence of representative bodies such as trades unions. All these have lost authority and credibility, and there is now an array of new procedures which include the Citizen's Charter, focus groups, regulators and various forms of inspection, audit and ad hoc consultation. Most of those procedures are remote from the ordinary concerns of citizens, and inaccessible to all but a privileged few. Citizens need the resources of civil society if their voices are to be heard and made effective.

Public administration in a modern state involves the continuous resolution of conflicts—between the interests of the individual and those of the state, between personal freedom and the protection of the public, between diversity and uniformity, between devolution and centralisation, between risk and safety. Their resolution, whether as a matter of policy and legislation or in particular cases and circumstances, has come to be portrayed as a matter of practical, even technical, and value-free judgement. In fact it is often a matter of political, ethical or professional values, which should be acknowledged and made explicit.

A programme to put the ideas discussed in this chapter into practical effect might therefore start by establishing a number of principles. Some of them—accountability, legality, openness, procedural fairness, equality of respect, opportunity and impact—would be those which apply to public service generally. They would resemble some of the seven principles of public life which the Nolan Committee established to deal with problems of corruption and lack of integrity, set out in its first report (Nolan, 1995). Others would be more specific to crime and justice. For example:

- Measures to prevent crime and reduce re-offending are matters for civil society as well as for the state. They should emphasise personal and social responsibility, personal development, service to others, and legitimate opportunities for adventure as well as punishment and social control.
- They should be judged by an evaluation of their outcomes and of the fairness and integrity of their procedures, and not just by monitoring their quantified inputs, outputs and other indicators of technical performance.
- Punishment, when it is needed, should never be disproportionate to the seriousness of the offence—to the harm caused and the culpability of the offender. It should, wherever possible, be constructive and restorative rather than disabling or exclusionary, and it should involve the minimum possible interference with the rights and responsibilities of citizenship.
- Condemnation should be focused on the offences which have been committed and the harm they have caused. Offenders, or criminals, are still entitled to their dignity and respect as people and citizens, and should not be treated as a class apart.
- Offenders, victims and communities are all entitled to be heard, within a framework of civil society and civic responsibility.

An interesting subject for study, as the present Administration proceeds, will be the relationship between developments in criminal justice policy, legislation and practice, and those in public administration and public service, including constitutional law. In the former, this chapter has drawn attention to the bifurcation between relatively "liberal" or "inclusive" policies of support for those who are vulnerable or in difficulty, and punitive or "exclusive" policies for those who do not conform or comply. The (mostly) liberal intentions of restorative justice are matched by authoritarian measures designed to lower the standards of proof and the protection available to defendants in order to make it easier for courts to convict and to impose more severe penalities when they do. All these measures depend crucially on the ability and will of public services to put them into effect, the spirit in which they do so, and the willingness of civil society to give its support.

At the same time, the Government is, through the Human Rights Act 1998, introducing constitutional reforms which will give greater recognition to the rights of citizens, and a more purposeful debate is beginning to develop about the obligations and accountability of public services, their values and their position in public law. These matters have received relatively little attention in relation to the administration of justice or the operation of the criminal justice services, but their application in those areas may have an influence on the quality of justice, and on modern British society, which is at least as great as those of criminal justice measures themselves.

6

Back to the "Iron Cage": The Example of the Dutch Probation Service

RENÉ VAN SWAANINGEN

TODAY'S VOCABULARY AND practice of criminal justice and penal policy differs fundamentally from what we were used to. The traditional legal questions of legality or guilt, or the traditional criminological ones of stigma or rehabilitation, or indeed the visions behind a certain criminal justice policy, seem to have lost their meaning. Nowadays, officials mainly speak about criminal justice in terms of business management. The criminal justice system is treated as a company, which assesses and manages risks; it has become a kind of insurance company (van Swaaningen, 1996). This "company" has a managing director who determines the general profile, and unit managers who see to it that the same general politics are carried out at every level. "Justice Incorporated" mainly communicates with society through public-relations functionaries. The general public communicates with the "company" through the firm law and order statements of politicians, who in their actual legislative work occupy themselves mainly with technical questions. The internal management of the "company" is ruled by "communication plans" and "step by step plans". Through so-called "planning and control" cycles, notions of legality and legitimacy are implicitly replaced by notions of efficiency: just intervention is efficient intervention. Dealing with offenders becomes a measurable "product".

In The Netherlands, this development is notably visible in a series of reorganisations of criminal justice agencies such as the police, the prosecution service, the prison system and the probation service. A similar reorganisation of the judiciary, in which the human input, the discretionary power of the judge, is increasingly curtailed by sentencing guidelines, is on the way. This chapter briefly examines the social and political context, the administrative rationale and the key characteristics of a trend towards an actuarial interpretation of justice and a managerial approach of what used to be called policy.

As an empirical example of this tendency, I will analyse the development of the Dutch probation service. In its 1995 reorganisation, both the breach with penal-welfare ideals and the adoption of new trends in risk-management come very clearly to the surface. The example of the probation service also shows how an agency, which was for a long time referred to as the "human face" of the criminal justice system, could be changed into a primary partner in control and sanctioning without an explicit change of ideology.

THE EMERGENCE OF A RISK SOCIETY AND ACTUARIAL JUSTICE

If we are to understand how institutions can change fundamentally in character over a relatively short period of time, we must first look at the economic and socio-political context in which such changes occur. In the 1980s, the economic system of the European continent gradually changed from the traditional Rhineland, corporative model, in which the state has a clear regulatory function with respect to a fair distribution of welfare and social justice, to the Anglo-American, competitive model, which is characterised by a taken-for-granted belief in the regulatory capacities of the market. "Good" is what is good for the economy. Many public services are privatised, and both the business community and the individual citizen are invited to take up their own responsibility for the quality of society. With this "responsibilisation strategy", the state starts to govern mainly from a distance (Garland, 1996). It determines in which direction and under which conditions third parties are to take care of public welfare, whilst increasingly limiting its own activities to the management of various subsystems. Authorities no longer seek to legitimise ideological choices, but present these as inevitable measures, which find enough support in a hardly ever problematised "public opinion" or indeed in the "invisible hand" of the economy. Their discourse is focused on technical questions of implementation rather than on content. It is no longer informed by stilted visions or ideals, but by statistical scenarios about the costs, benefits and feasibility of certain measures. Thus, the role of the state shifts from *a priori* regulation from the era of the Welfare State to *a posterio* control in our present Security State.

The Security State is a reflection of a risk society (Beck, 1992). In a risk society the state, the business community and the individual citizens frenetically insist that all problems are manageable, whereas in reality our major problems have become less and less manageable. Exactly because old certainties (religion, family values, steady job, progress, etc.) have lost their influence or have indeed disappeared, the desire for control (over one's life and against all these new uncertainties) has increased. A risk society is no longer oriented to positive ideals, but to the negative rationale of controlling risk. Similarly, solidarity is no longer based on a positive feeling of connectedness, but on a negative communality of fear. The public image of society has changed along the same lines. Once "the social" was seen as the indispensable embodiment of collective values preventing social disintegration. Now it is largely portrayed as an annoying restraint on one's individual freedom. With the process of individualisation, traditional, sometimes very tight, systems of internalised norms and values have lost their central role in social control. The subsequently increasing importance of external, formal systems of social control, such as criminal justice, is quite logical. As criminal justice has always been an institution with limiting harm as its central goal, its internal development along the lines of the risk society is also very clear.

A first necessary step towards a managerial approach to social problems is to ensure a consensus about the nature of both the problem and the solution. The communality of fear already steers the consensus about law and order. Clifford Shearing and Philip Stenning (1985) have called the way in which social control agencies actively produce consensus a "Disney order". The rationale of the Disney order of social control is simple. The basic message it communicates is that everybody has the same interest in having a good time. In order to secure this, nobody should "disturb" other people (by organising one's own fun, getting drunk or just sitting in the grass). Disney offers a world of predictable orderliness, apparently without coercion. The success of this Disney order of social control becomes particularly clear if we look at the way young children are "seduced". They supposedly have more freedom than the previous generation did (as expressed in the populist platitude "there is no authority and discipline anymore"), yet the margins of what it requires to be a full member of the children's community have become rather small. McDonald's is not just a fast food store, the Spice Girls are not just a pop group and Nike are not just sports shoes; they are commercially very carefully designed products which have become important metaphors of the "young and fast" way of life which every kid "voluntarily" adapts to. If you do not adapt, you place yourself outside of the group—and being an outsider is the most terrible position a child can imagine.

A similar metaphor of social control in our era is the portrayal of public life as one big shopping mall. Zygmunt Bauman (1995) argued that there are fewer and fewer urban areas where one can just stroll freely without having any definite purpose. Everything is designed to address you as a consumer and as a consumer alone. The message is: "if you have not come to buy anything, what are you doing here?". Mostly this coercion to consume takes place in a rather implicit way, but also in more explicit ways: apparent "strangers in the consumer era", such as homeless people or "idle" youth, are explicitly treated as suspects by omnipresent private security staff. "Act normal: shop!" is the adage. These two metaphors point to a privatisation of social control, its seemingly non-coercive character, a standardisation of control methods and the creation of a standard of normality and deviance according to people's perceived spending pattern.

If these social control systems, which are amongst others oriented towards the creation of consensus, conformity and docility, fall short, there is the criminal justice system. This formal system of social control also carries the features of the risk society, but consensus about the goals of law enforcement is produced in a different way. The political leitmotiv is the following: crime is getting out of hand and society needs to be protected against this external threat. The "soft remedies" of the 1970s must be washed away and we need to be tough on "criminals". If we look at the huge expansion of the Dutch criminal justice system, with its five-fold increase of the prison population over the last 20 years as the strongest symbol, we have to conclude that this discourse has been particularly successful. This is not to say that crime would not be a serious problem, let that be clear, but rather that more law enforcement is not a serious answer. Everything which went wrong in society cannot be compensated for by expelling a, still relatively small, group of people from society for a, still relatively short, period of time. David Garland argued in this respect that "punitiveness may pose as a symbol of strength, but it should be interpreted as a symptom of weak authority and inadequate controls" (Garland, 1996: 445).

Current criminal justice politics echo, as David Garland (1996) has demonstrated so eloquently, a confused message. Whereas the development of social control in society reflects a "criminology of the self" (mainly repeating the age-old adage that "the opportunity makes the thief"), the punitive discourse of law and order witnesses a "criminology of the other", in which crime is portrayed as a problem very different from other social problems, and "criminals" as "foreign elements" who are very different from "normal" people. Garland (1996) called this ambiguous position in criminal justice policy "the contradictory dualism" between the "hysterical denial of the predicament" that the state is not the effective provider of security we like to think, and the "adaptation" to that "predicament". Severe law and order campaigns embody an "hysterical denial of the predicament". They serve to produce the consensus needed to actually carry through a mere managerial politics in which "the predicament" is long accepted—it can only not be said aloud.

This paradoxical relation resembles Ulrich Beck's (1992) analysis of the myth and reality of controlling risk. Whilst the belief in penality needs to be supported to uphold the system, it is actually in crisis. The media know more than ever that crime sells, and politicians use the crime problem for electoral purposes and raise high expectations about "manageable safety". But the system cannot live up to this media and political pressure; it takes too many inconsistent measures, makes too many mistakes for people to retain their trust in the system. So, the fear of crime and the concern for victims need to be mobilised again to save the system's credibility. Because there is no clear vision of how problems are to be handled, the response includes a bit of everything: with a shot of hail you will always hit something. We need more police and the police need more resources. But, alongside the expansion of police resources, many countries face a derailment of the Rule of Law by undercover operations and criminal informants. Court delays are followed by curtailing legal guarantees, which are sold to the public as more "flexible" and "efficient" criminal procedures. An increasing number of fines and community sanctions coincides with an increasing use of remand and prison sentences beyond the system's actual capacity. Massive prison building programmes, overcrowding, waiting lists for "less severe" cases, or actually sending remand prisoners home, mark a custodial crisis. Thus criminal justice politics has become a continuous process of crisis and crisis adjudication.

If we are faced with a system which is clearly in crisis, but which has no real choice except to try to live up to the increased expectations of politicians and the general public, we can take two ways. Either we accept that our expectations of criminal justice are too high and we try to "repair" the, implicitly crime preventive, social arrangements and networks which have been "economised away" after the decline of the Welfare State, or we accept the inevitability of the risk society, dominated by an economic rationale, and we try to "manage" the problem within the criminal justice system. The political choice has been the latter. When everybody implicitly agrees that crime control is merely an efficiency problem, the actual politics of risk management can begin. Stan Cohen has characterised the relationship between "criminologies of the self" as rational choice, self-control, routine activity, opportunity, etc., and penal politics as follows:

> "The new round of "the end of ideology" game has left its mark in social control systems and ideologies. In the crime control business, we see an ascendancy of managerial, administrative and technocratic styles. The old liberal ideologies (treatment, rehabilitation, social reform) are discredited. The goal is to keep the criminal justice system in reasonable shape. Prison directors are not the "moral architects" of the early nineteenth century, nor the professionals of the heyday of the treatment ideology; they are just likely to be accountants" (Cohen, 1994: 72).

Malcolm Feeley and Jonathan Simon (1994) have characterised these developments as the new penology of actuarial justice. The adjective "actuarial" comes from the insurance industry. Actuaries calculate potential risks and determine insurance premiums accordingly. "Old" penology is "rooted in a concern for individuals, and preoccupied with concepts such as guilt, responsibility and obligation, as well as diagnoses, intervention and treatment of the individual offender." In the "new" penology, crime is seen to be a normal phenomenon, and the key problem is how to manage it most efficiently. The answer to this question is a risk-calculation "concerned with techniques for identifying, classifying and managing groups assorted by levels of dangerousness". Administrators of justice have become the actuaries of a risk society.

Actuarial justice is nebulous, but it is significant. Actuarial justice involves how we conceive of and talk about crime policy, but it is not an ideology in the narrow sense of a set of beliefs and ideas which constrain action. It involves practices, but is not reducible to a specific technology or set of behaviours. Indeed it is powerful and significant because it "lacks a well-articulated ideology and identification with a specific technology" (Feeley and Simon, 1994: 174).

Actuarial justice consists of new models of rationality, new practices and new functions for old forms. "Their newness lies in their particular combinations and the particular micropractices that are embedded in the functions which they perform" (Feeley and Simon, 1994: 174).

The managerial method which supports actuarial justice follows the rules of "McDonaldisation" (Ritzer, 1996). McDonaldisation is the successor of the Weberian process of rationalisation, adapted to the reality of our era in which many state functions have been privatised or ideologically transformed into businesses. It is based on the assumption that public services can and should be run as a hamburger chain. Its main characteristic is that efficiency, calculability, predictability, control and rationalisation have become goals in themselves. This managerial preoccupation comes clearly to the surface in the new metaphor of criminal justice: a company consisting of a number of chains—police, prosecution service, judiciary, probation service, prison system. The re-design of the criminal justice system is accompanied by a whole new idiom of managerial metaphors (Rutherford, 1996: 59–83). In an era of free-market the-ology, terms and metaphors derived from the business community are to be expected. It is not argued here that trying to increase the efficiency of the police and the prosecution service would be worthless or fashionable ideas; they are not. But they start from a purely pragmatic, instrumentalist way of thinking about criminal justice which I do not share.

When the "production-unit" justice is fashioned on the corporation model we find no place for the power-critical dimension of due process.

The glossary of control talk of this criminal justice "company" seems directly derived from the "management consultancy manual". The fact that this dis-course is applicable to any company witnesses little understanding of the spe-cific sociological meaning of the public values embodied in criminal justice. It is highly questionable whether metaphors derived from production units are suit-able for criminal justice.

ACTUARIALISM AND MANAGERIALISM IN PROBATION

Now that the process of actuarialism and managerialism has been analysed in general terms, we can apply this thesis to the reorganisation of the Dutch pro-bation service. Before doing so, however, we need to take one more intermedi-ate step: something needs to be said about the specific nature and development of the Dutch probation service in order to clarify how strongly its character and working ethos have changed. The *reclassering* (as the Dutch probation service is called, and which literally means something like resettlement) is in many ways quite different from, for example, its British counterpart. Most importantly, the *reclassering* maintained a rather autonomous position outside the criminal jus-tice system from its foundation in 1823, until the 1995 reorganisation. A second feature of the Dutch probation service is that a large part of the money needed for probation work was, until the 1970s, raised by religious and humanitarian organisations, and indeed from individual citizens. A third important feature of the Dutch probation service is its focus on client-oriented social work, rather than on assisting the court.

One hundred and seventy-five years of probation work in a nutshell

We can distinguish six phases in the development of the Dutch probation service. In 1823, the Netherlands' Society for the Moral Improvement of Prisoners (the first probation service) was founded by businessmen from Friesland and Rotterdam, inspired by John Howard—and by the Gospel. In their footsteps, a network of various probation services emerged, structured along the denominational pillars of society—Protestant, Roman Catholic, humanist, etc. They consisted of volunteers and were generally monitored by progressive lawyers and clergymen. Initially, the different groups active in probation work provided mainly charity work to prisoners—and some material after-care. Soon, however, the probation service also became an important campaigning group for penal reform, and can be considered as a social counterpart of the Modern School in penal sciences—founded in 1889 (van Swaaningen, 1997a: Chapter 3).

By the beginning of the twentieth century, when the criminal justice system's focus gradually shifted from the offence to the offender, the state began to pay for social inquiry reports. In this second phase, the probation service received a formal legal status, and social inquiry reports became a normal element of the sentencing process. In the 1920s, socialist criminologist Willem Bonger argued that the probation service deserved more support from the workers' movement, because their social inquiry reports showed so clearly how common crime is a product of socio-economic misery (van Swaaningen, 1997a: 52). In the 1950s, the Utrecht School gave another strong impulse to the offender-oriented aid provided by the probation services, and a more professional social work approach was adopted. It is fair to say that from this third phase onwards, the probation service has become a central and well-established factor in the typical way criminal law is enforced in The Netherlands (Janse de Jonge, 1991: Chapters 2 and 3).

In 1975, in the aftermath of the depillarisation and secularisation of Dutch society, most of the private probation services were "professionalised" (both in an organisational and educational sense) and fused into a national framework called the ARV—General Association of Probation Services.[1] In this fourth phase, the probation service was still not a fully governmental agency, but an association of private services, which totalled some 1,100 members in the community and had, in addition to the Ministry of Justice, numerous other financial supporters –for example the churches and the national collection for the probation services amongst the population. The unique Dutch feature, that the social task to reintegrate offenders into society was carried out by the community, was still upheld—without any preceding "responsibilisation strategy" by the state (Garland, 1996). During the continued processes of secularisation and individualisation, and indeed when the Welfare State was in its heyday, community

[1] The probation service of the Salvation Army (*Leger des Heils*) and of the association Help to the Homeless (*Hulp Voor Onbehuisden—WS*) decided to stay outside of the ARV.

support for probation gradually waned. Private sources became insufficient and governmental funding became increasingly important. At the same time, probation officers felt that the twofold task, of providing social work and after-care to offenders on the one hand, and information to the judiciary on the other, disrupted the relation of trust they had with their clients. There was an obvious tension between complete financial dependency on the Ministry of Justice and the decreased willingness of probation officers to act as agents of law enforcement.

People within the various justice (-related) administrations pointed out to probation officers that society has become less committed to progressive penal politics, and that the probation service had lost its credibility amongst the population, because it was now seen as an institution which pampers criminals. They spoke of a breach of trust with society which has to be restored by enlarging the co-operation with the criminal justice system. The probation service was therefore thought to perform a third task: monitoring community service orders and other diversion-programmes. In a fifth phase, starting in 1986, the association structure of the ARV was abolished, and a federally organised, centralised probation service NFR (National Federation of Probation services) was established. The NFR was also more hierarchically structured than the ARV. Most probation officers kept their jobs, but critical voices about the new structure and goal setting were not appreciated within the new organisation.

Under pressure of major budget cuts in 1991, the fundamental reorganisation which will be analysed below, in which the probation service was transformed into a quango (ZBO in Dutch), steered from a distance by the Ministry of Justice, was enacted. In this sixth phase, the Ministry of Justice gained full power over the probation service, by linking its funding directly to the services it provides to the criminal justice system. The organisation of the service is now modelled as a production-unit of the "penal chain". The frequent use of terminology such as unit-manager, case-management, result-oriented offer, input-trajectory, process- and product-registration, result-measurement, etc. is significant.

The prelude to the managerial revolution in probation

It is not coincidental that the managerial revolution in probation took place in an era when ideas on crime control had become marked by risk management; but this does not mean that there were not also good internal reasons for a fundamental reorganisation of the probation service. An organisational chaos, marked by many personal conflicts and a super-bureaucratic routine characterised the organisation. I will try to do justice to both the ideological and the practical side; because I believe that the whole notion of actuarial justice can only be understood if serious attention is paid to the practical necessity of working more efficiently. The "ideology" of actuarial justice is only very implicit, the main drive is its claimed inevitability. The rationale is that the penal system cannot deal with the increased caseload and with the new forms of crime by relying on the traditional means, and that therefore new, more efficient means of crime control have to be developed.

The functioning of the 1970s probation service epitomised the opposite of any idea one may hold of efficiency. Han Janse de Jonge (1991) described the success of the probation service in the traditional Dutch model of criminal justice as a consequence of the growing offender-orientation of the legal doctrine. This orientation on the person of the offender experienced its heyday in the 1970s; an era in which a general rejection of "authorities" in society had also led to a "basic democratic" structure of the probation service. Probation officers argued they were independent, professional social workers, whose task was to help offenders, and not the criminal justice system. This was clearly also a reaction to the previous phase, in which assisting the courts with social inquiry reports was seen to have become too dominant a function. The argument Louk Hulsman put forward in 1971 (Hulsman, 1971), that the probation service's task was to undo the damage caused by the criminal justice system, was shared by many probation officers. It should, however, be stressed that the ARV-statutes of 1975 did not adopt Hulsman's conflict model, but a so-called "bridge-model", in which the probation service was seen as a bridge between the criminal justice system and society (Heinrich, 1995: 215–23).

Amongst probation officers there was, however, much resistance against what they felt to be undesirable control from the Ministry of Justice over their activities. This control would frustrate the relationship of trust with the client, needed for effective social work. The irritation from the Ministry also increased, because they felt they were pumping a lot of money into an institution which was just sand in the machine, spent too much time talking whilst doing too little, and which had, moreover, a very one-sided view on crime and a top-heavy organisational "chaos structure". After the "democratisation" of the early 1970s, virtually everybody with some higher education had become the boss of something and was paid accordingly: by 1985 the so-called executives in the probation service consumed 20 per cent of the whole budget (Heinrich, 1995: 273–87). This situation formed the overture for the reorganisation—with the federalisation of the different services in 1986 as an intermediate step. A drastic budget cut in 1991 turned out to be an effective means of breaking the resistance within the service. When the probation service accepted that monitoring non-custodial sanctions would be its new primary task, its budget was substantially increased again. This control task, which had been rejected for more than a decade, was now presented as something which logically followed from the probation service's task of supporting the rehabilitation of offenders: now we know that prisons do not rehabilitate, this goal is to be pursued with sanctions in the community.

As already acknowledged, there were good reasons for a fundamental reorganisation of the probation service. Yet, it should also be stressed that this development was strongly influenced by changing opinions on law and order, and that the reorganisation certainly implied a form of "ideological cleansing" as well. Many critics were sacked or "invited" to resign, whilst new, younger staff members were appointed who reflected the "no nonsense" spirit of the 1990s, and who were unaware of the ideological struggles of the 1970s and early 1980s. The service's critical, independent journal *KRI* was replaced (in 1986) by a staff-magazine, *Vrij spraak*, in which only "good news" was published. Business administrators, rather than social scientists, were newly appointed as unit managers or directors. For the preparation of this part of the chapter, I have used an earlier, Dutch language publication (van Swaaningen, 1997b). I have never before received such a reaction to an article. Assenting, letters and e-mails from older probation officers, who, and this is probably even more significant, often explicitly asked me not to publicly mention their names.[2] This implies two important things: first, there is apparently, to use Michel Foucault's words, a "disqualified knowledge" within the probation service of which the management does not want to know; and secondly, there is a working atmosphere in which people feel intimidated and are afraid to speak out.

The elaboration of the reorganisation

A blueprint for the probation service's reorganisation, entitled *Probation in Broader Perspective* appeared in 1993 (Blauwdruk, 1993). This paper precisely set the tone of what was going to happen. Though the title suggests differently, this report almost exclusively dealt with organisational perils: the necessary change of culture within the probation service would follow from a different management style. According to the blueprint, the probation service should become a flexible, result-oriented and entrepreneurial organisation, which can, by means of a wide delegation of powers, and by profiling and prioritising its activities, quickly capitalise the demands of the market. Since this 1990s-style "broad perspective", it has hardly been possible to count the number of feasibility studies, organisation plans, step-by-step plans, communication plans, planning and control cycles, etc. that have resulted. In the 1980s, social scientists were often accused of using woolly language, but the managers of the 1990s are unsurpassable in the realm of their meaningless platitudes. It remains completely unclear where the "demand of the market" with respect to probation work comes from, who the market's superintendent is, or indeed who the clients are. Markets are, moreover, characterised by competition, but with the reorganisation of the probation service, previous "competitors" have indeed been fused into one foundation, *Reclassering Nederland*, which operates under the

[2] Later, employees of the probation service were explicitly invited—in an internal staff publication—to react to my article. This resulted in some reactions from the management, which, of course, rejected my assessment, but did not deny the general line of the argument.

direct supervision of the Minister of Justice.[3] It is all very modern: the probation service is transformed into a quango, steered from a distance by the state.

According to a spokesperson of the Ministry of Justice, the goal of the reorganisation would be to create a "flexible, market-oriented probation service, which demonstrated a visible contribution to the offender's resettlement into society" (Verhoef, 1994: 31). With this demand for visibility, the Ministry has forced an extremely quantitative style of working upon the probation service. From now on, social inquiry reports, social work and non-custodial sanctions are quantifiable "products", with a planned "production", a "production process" ruled by standard procedures, and a standard number of hours per "product". Actual social work fits poorly in this measurability ethos; at least if one believes that providing aid starts with the creation of a relationship of trust and with personal attention and understanding of someone's problems, and not with filling out a form and signing a contract. How would it be possible to measure after-care, for example? Are we to conclude that those activities which cannot be measured and quantitatively justified can no longer be carried out? The fact that a rather coercive process of the resettlement of offenders into society is suddenly called a "contract" is a good example of woolly managerial "newspeak": free choice and open dialogue are suggested even in the most obvious cases of forced, one-way communication.

It seems quite banal to remark that figures suggest an exactness they do not possess. For example, the probation service's annual accounts dramatically show the Weberian iron cage in which the probation service is currently caught. In 1996, the probation service "produced" five per cent more social inquiry reports than planned, but they attended 26 per cent less than the planned number of court sessions, whilst the number of non-custodial sanctions lagged four to 39 per cent behind planned figures (Reclassering Nederland, 1997a: 5–6). But what does this mean? Are these "good" figures or not? Since when can the number of convictions be planned? Is this not determined by the judge? What should we understand by "assistance offered in vain"? What is a "finished product"? Not a single word is devoted to such obvious and simple questions. If we look in more detail at the "production figures" the whole story becomes ridiculous. It was planned that fifteen probationary releases would be supervised. The real number was three hundred and sixty seven. A deviation of 2,347 per cent from the norm was neatly calculated, but not a word was devoted to what this huge deviation meant (Reclassering Nederland, 1997a: 35). Looking more carefully at the non-custodial sanctions, we see that, in many cases, no planning was undertaken—simply because many new community sanctions were introduced—which make the signalised deviations from four to 39 per cent completely

[3] The independent (until 1995), CADs (Consultation bureaus for Alcohol and Drugs) and the HVO (Help to the Homeless) have become an integral part of the general probation service, in which the probation department of the Salvation Army and the NVIV (Netherlands' Association of Institutions for the Care and Treatment of Drug Addicts) only take a slightly more autonomous position.

fictitious figures. What follows is more than thirty pages of figures, which demonstrate the enormous variety of non-custodial sanctions in The Netherlands, but not much more than that. The next table in the annual accounts which gives an exact "cost price per product" is really laughable.

I do not claim that annual accounts are useless: it is interesting to know, for example, that in 1996, 15,687 social inquiry reports have been written, and 15,589 community service orders have been supervised. Of other non-custodial sanctions no reliable figures are available, because these are not imposed separately but in combination with another sanction—prison sentence, fine or community service order—or are diverted from the penal system in earlier phases of the process (van Swaaningen and uit Beijerse, 1993). It is also very interesting to see how much money is spent on temporary staff, redundancy payment schemes, travel costs or so-called "professionalisation courses": up to four million guilders per item. Yet, what these items consist of, in terms of their content, remains opaque. It is not surprising that the audit certificate to this account concludes: "Our control of the accounts has not given us the required certainty about the completeness and correctness of the production figures for 1996". The mock figures and incomprehensible phrases make the quantitative legitimation of probation work look like Hans Christian Andersen's Emperor's new clothes.

However, even more depressing is the probation service's planning and control manual (Reclassering Nederland, 1997b). Am I the only one who cannot make any sense of all these pages of input indicators, process indicators, output indicators, effect indicators and corresponding index numbers? If the relation between production and means is to be visualised; products rather than processes or formation are to be controlled; agreements with clients have to made in the form of management contracts; and costs are to be visualised and related to specific products, I fear the worst for the effectiveness. It costs more time to calculate your "product" than to do your actual work!

This is not to argue against controlling the costs of a public service, but to demonstrate that the nature of probation work changes fundamentally with such an organisational model. To phrase it in Andrew Rutherford's (1993, 18, 13) words, probation workers are forced to change their working principles from a "Credo Three" orientation, which embodies an "optimism that constructive work can be done with offenders" to a "prevailing concern of Credo Two (which) is to dispose of the tasks at hand as smoothly and efficiently as possible". The personal, human commitment and discretion of the probation officer is replaced by a formalistic rationality, and the multifaceted image of the offender is replaced by the flat character of the client. Such a managerial style makes it easier to carry out the politics of sheer risk control *within* the traditionally humanitarian working credo of probation officers: i.e. the ideology or rationale of probation work can remain the same, only the practice changes. In a managerial environment, people, whether they are public prosecutors, prison directors or indeed probation officers, need to act correctly as functionaries of the system. Their personal commitment and responsibility to do justice fall outside the relevant criteria for their behaviour, and will even be seen as an unprofessional attitude.

An important task of the probation service, providing after-care, has no proper place in the new quantitative "production" model. We have seen that it is very difficult to carry out tasks which are problematic to quantify. So, what to do if research continually reveals that both functionaries in the criminal justice system and offenders stress that the offender's return into society is unnecessarily complicated because the probation service provides too little after-care (Rood-Pijpers and Combrink-Kniters, 1991: 87, 135)? One applies a variation of the "responsibilisation strategy": citizens and volunteers' organisations should play a more active role in providing after-care. Internal research shows that most probation officers are also in favour of this solution. Many point to the fact that the probation service was originally a volunteers' organisation, and that one is, in a way, going back to one's roots. They are, however, also well aware of the fact that this step is mainly motivated by economic measures (Vogel, 1994). The probation service's "strategic long-range plan" does not, however, show such a renewed interest in volunteers—who had been put aside with the 1986 reorganisation (Reclassering Nederland, 1996: 11). This plan claims that the resettlement of offenders into society is something which can only be realised by professionals: only they can work according to a plan and only they are trained to solve problems. Volunteers can assist these professionals, and of course their experience and suggestions will be taken into account, but that is all (Reclassering Nederland, 1996: 12). The financial assistance to volunteers' organisations remains fixed at one per cent of the probation service's budget—the same level as when the probation service was still responsible for after-care. We should stress in this respect, that we are not speaking about upper-class ladies who want to do charity work in the penal sphere, but about people (amongst them many ex-offenders) who have for a long time been active in one of the approximately sixty NGOs in the penal sphere. For many years these volunteers have visited prisoners, offered shelter to ex-offenders or drug-addicts, assisted families of prisoners, run educational programmes about crime in schools and so on (van Swaaningen, 1997a: 155–63). The probation service's 1996 annual report offers more of an opening to these NGOs: by the end of 1999 each probation region should have a network of volunteers (Reclassering Nederland, 1997c: 51). It does not, however, discuss the necessary financial assistance, and that is exactly the problem David Garland (1996, 454) has highlighted: the responsibilisation of third parties is not a problem as such, the problem is that these organisations cannot do the job adequately because they have insufficient means and they are, moreover, forced to work according to methods which are not their own.

Actuarialism versus managerialism: policy or no policy?

Managerialism and actuarialism go hand in hand as means and goals—though it remains unclear what are the means and what is the goal. Sometimes, however, the desire to manage leads to an approach other than the actuarial desire to distinguish risk categories. In this instance, managerialism replaces a policy orientation (i.e. there is no explicit vision which informs policy), whereas an actuarial approach does require a policy in which special projects for risk groups are developed. This paradox becomes particularly apparent in the probation service's "policy" (or lack of policy) on ethnic minority groups.

Ethnic minority groups make up some 50 per cent of the Dutch prison population, and the level of anomie, especially amongst second generation Moroccan or Antillean youth, is currently widely considered to be very worrying. The probation service's annual report's chapter on "clients" distinguishes gender, age, employment status, level of education and drug dependency, but not ethnicity (Reclassering Nederland, 1997c: 28–9). Rood-Pijper and Combrink-Kniters's research shows that whilst most probation officers think they should know more about other cultures, a significant number of them also feel that taking account of cultural factors carries the danger that these factors are used as an excuse for bad behaviour: the underpinning idea being that offenders who live in The Netherlands are to be judged according to Dutch norms and values (1991, 110). Employing probation officers from ethnic minority groups is greeted with some scepticism: it could easily undermine the service's independence, because allochtonous social workers would be vulnerable to the pressure which may be put on them to support their own ethnic group rather than the service. The probation service's management (Reclassering Nederland, 1997c: 48–9) rejects completely the idea of a specific policy oriented at ethnic minorities, because its clients would mainly have been raised in The Netherlands, or have Dutch nationality. I fail to understand this explanation. First, it ignores the fact that those who probably need probation work the most have no access to it—for example, because of language problems. Secondly, if people are raised in The Netherlands, for example, second generation Moroccans, this does not imply they have had a (completely) Western education. And thirdly, if people have Dutch nationality, this does not mean that they speak (fluent) Dutch, have had a Western education, or are even raised here—for example, Antilleans and a number of Surinamese. But, according to the annual report, the problems of ethnic minorities are part of the wider problem of deprivation, which is already an integral part of the service's general policy (Reclassering Nederland, 1997c: 49).

Unfortunately, nearly all criminological studies on ethnicity and crime of the last decade show that the problem cannot be reduced to factors of deprivation, but that cultural factors also play a significant role in processes of social (and auto-) exclusion. In other words, the probation service's argument for not dealing with cultural differences is built on scientific quicksand. The annual report's paragraph on ethnic minorities is full of inconsistencies. It speaks, for example, about investing in means to increase the trust of ethnic minority groups in the probation service. Apparently it is acknowledged that there is something lacking with this trust, but the notion that this may be related to the fact that the probation service is an almost exclusively white organisation (certainly at management level) is not acknowledged. There is also mention of projects specifically oriented at Turkish and Moroccan boys. So, if there is apparently something special enough about them which would require a different approach, why not acknowledge this explicitly as well?

Characterised as a "bridge" between the criminal justice system and society, the probation service is likely to be touched by both the "new penology", as regards the organisational side of its work, and by the "Disney order of social control", as far as the actual content is concerned. This latter element is, however, not so easy to demonstrate, because, unlike organisational perils, visions of social control are not expressed in blueprints, annual reports and planning and control cycles. Looking, however, at the content of its various treatment, labour training, social skills or educational programmes (van Swaaningen and uit Beijerse, 1993); at the reformulation of rehabilitation as adapting people to a normal lifestyle; at the way coercion is obscured within contract terminology; at the way (potential) conflicts are ironed out with inconsistent and woolly language (as demonstrated by the case of volunteer work or of ethnic minorities); and indeed at the fact that the probation service wants to expand its market by developing projects to fight nuisance which is caused by so-called "potential customers" within the community (Reclassering Nederland, 1996: 9), we can deduce clear traces of the order-loving, seemingly non-coercive, consensus-creating, and even slightly infantilising vision of social control which characterises the Disney order. These elements are very clearly visible in the development of crime prevention politics (van Swaaningen, 1995), so the closer probation work moves to this side, the more "Mickey Mouse" the visions of social control will probably become.

It is, however, not coincidental that this chapter does not focus on the Disney order elements of probation work, but indeed on the other metaphor derived from US culture, namely the McDonaldisation of the way probation work is organised. Means have become purposes; one speaks exclusively about organisational perils because there is no clear vision, and thus no policy in the actual sense of the word. It is a "muddling on" approach, longing for credibility by dressing it up with suit-and-tie-discourse and reams of figures. Even the, in comparison with other reports, very concise, "strategic long-range plan" (Reclassering Nederland, 1996), in which one would expect a vision on the content of probation work, is again filled with sloganing about "the probation service as a partner in the penal chain". The few really surprising novelties, such as the above-mentioned expansion of probation work to prevention activities and the fact that the nuclear role of providing social work is rephrased as "supervision and control", are hardly made explicit: they are simply mentioned, but there are no reasons given for these policy changes. The obscurity of the actual content of probation work is all the more worrying, because the remarks made about the lack of policy on ethnic minorities can be repeated for "problem groups" such as drug addicts, multiple recidivists or people who have committed a crime of violence. For the large number of them, there are hardly any alternatives to long-term imprisonment available—and the alternatives which there are, are not carried out by the probation service. Maybe one cannot really blame the probation service. If it is to show a "good score" in mere quantitative terms, i.e. a high "success percentage", it is logical that it prefers to deal with the relatively easy cases, and not with the most notorious losers and drop-outs, who would probably have a negative effect on the success rate. Yet, in this way the probation service contributes to the emergence of a residue, a new dangerous class, who are just incapacitated.

Thus, the probation service has actually become an agent of the Disney order of social control: it addresses those people who can still be fitted into society. Those "bad asses" who do not want to adapt to a normal lifestyle, and whom we do not want to see in our streets, will get deeper and deeper into the criminal justice system. They will end up at the tough end of social control, which Nils Christie (1993) has captured in the metaphor of the "gulag Western style". He outlines a gloomy picture of what could happen if crypto-religious beliefs about criminal justice, managerial considerations and bureaucratic mechanisms of anonymisation coincide with profit-orientations of private enterprise. Notions like risk, fear and suffering have no intrinsic limits, and thus the symbolic display of power to compensate for these feelings may well be equally boundless. Sebastian Scheerer (1996, 333) has argued that with the current re-barbarisation of international relations, Shearing and Stenning's (1985) Disney order and Nils Christie's (1993) gulags Western style may well coincide. Only the "kind" of people that are controlled differs substantially in both models: the Disney order controls the insiders of society, the gulag the outsiders.

CONCLUSION

Looking at its recent reports, the probation service seems to have become a rather bloodless organisation without clear visions. This lack of content is obscured by a managerial sloganism, which every management consultant can deliver on request. It is unclear whether the service really believes that this is a particularly useful way to speak about probation work, or whether it is regarded as the only way to be taken seriously by its new boss, the Ministry of Justice.

Within the service there appears to be a gap between the new executives who think in managerial terms, and most field workers who think in social work terms. One cannot say that the old organisational problems have been solved, and that the probation service has really been as innovative as it promised. On the one hand, there are still some older probation officers who are not so convinced about the sense of the new politics and opt for passive resistance: i.e. they do their work as before, and do not take all those forms they have to fill out too seriously. It can, however, also be argued that they boycott any change, even when it is really necessary (such as in the case of ethnic minorities) for the rather mundane reason that keeping things as they are requires the least energy and keeps them safely in their "privileged" positions. On the other hand, there are now too many probation managers who will have administrative and management qualities, but will display little understanding of, let alone affinity with, the practice of probation work or of criminal justice. New probation officers who do want to innovate the content of probation work encounter problems on both sides.

This chapter does not question the need for the reorganisation of the Dutch probation service. It is only critical about the consequences of the reorganisation for the content of probation work. It concludes that the most pivotal issues remain hanging in the air, because there is no space for discussion or visions, and that the important values of "old style" probation work have been lost. Looking both at the spirit of the time in which the reorganisation was carried out, and at the specific experience of probation work in the 1970s, it is not surprising that a more hierarchical and more standardised working style has been adopted. According to Max Weber, such streamlining is even a key feature of any rational organisation and serves to keep arbitrariness and clientalism outside. Yet, already at the beginning of this century Weber warned that the formalistic rationality of bureaucracies will eventually result in an "iron cage" in which there is no place for the human size anymore. At present, authorities in the public sector are clearly caught in this iron cage, where rationalism has been pushed so far that it has stopped making sense (Garland, 1990: 178–92). That is the case—and cage—of the McDonaldised organisations we are now facing. George Ritzer (1996) has pointed out that the social consequences of McDonaldisation are a boundless uniformity, a blindness to moral dilemmas and a stamping out of everything which does not correspond with the standard norm. In order to safeguard the pluriformity of society and to take care that those who cannot keep up with the tempo of the social rat race do not perish, Ritzer argues that the process of an ongoing McDonaldisation of society should be broken by "carving out non-rationalised niches". He argues that

> "nonrationalized times and places tend to be conducive to creativity. It is difficult to be creative in the face of incessant, externally imposed, and repetitive demands. Thus working in a nonrationalized setting not only serves the individual, but many employers and society as well. They all need a steady influx of creative new ideas and products, which are far less likely to emanate from rigidly controlled bureaucratic settings than they are from skunk works" (Ritzer, 1996: 197).

In the recent past, the balance of Dutch probation work may have tipped too much in favour of independent, radical social work, but in those days there were at least creative ideas about possible ways to keep offenders out of prison and there was a clear vision of criminal justice. Now, the balance has tipped completely to the other side. The current probation service is a docile field organisation of the Ministry of Justice which no longer has any clear, autonomous vision of either its role in the criminal justice system or of its social tasks. The probation service has even become a supportive factor of actuarial justice. More than anything else, social inquiry reports now serve as means to draw up risk profiles. The difference between those people who are labelled as having some chance to be resettled "successfully" into the community, and those for whom this chance is thought to be rather limited, has become a watershed of the kind of social control they are subjected to. Of course, probation officers think about those cases which they can divert from the penal system, but the fact that there is no discussion at all about the other side of the coin, namely that by focusing so strongly on the provision of non-custodial sanctions for groups which are likely to have a high chance of success, an increasing residue of those people who never received, or failed to complete, a community sanction is created at the same time. It is quite likely that this residue, for whom there is hardly any normal social work and which is just bottling up in the penal system, will consist of an odd parade of "junkies, lunatics and foreigners". We will probably also have to add the so-called "administrative" detention and expulsion of foreigners as a new form social control, which will hopefully not set the ideological tone for developments in criminal justice. The cold, formalistic arguments with which so-called "illegals" or "economic refugees" are currently simply deported from The Netherlands, without having committed any offence, even if they have paid their taxes and contributed to the Dutch economy for many years, do not, however, make me too optimistic in this respect.

In the past, the probation service was an important force in keeping alive the social sensibility for what a decent criminal justice system needed to imply. Such moral pressure always formed an important impulse for penal reform (Garland, 1990: 247; van Swaaningen, 1997a: 135–69). Now such pressure from the side of the probation service has (virtually) disappeared, the professional ethics of the different criminal justice functionaries, to strive for as humane a system as possible, is also undermined. The "pursuit of decency" (Rutherford, 1993) is replaced by a "pursuit of efficiency" in which normative questions and commitments have become odd, irrational elements. This is why the current managerial, dehumanised professional culture and the seemingly rational standards by which risk-profiles are developed alarm me. It makes it too easy for the criminal justice system to derail into a more and more inhuman direction. Different as they are, both the tendency towards a Disney order and towards a gulag imply both an allegedly unequivocal and Manichaeist vision of social order and a completely instrumentalist and boundless vision of social control. If a new inhumanity is to be prevented, somebody has to do the "skunk work" of arguing forcefully against a further increase of managerial and actuarial tendencies, and advocating some good old-fashioned commitment to social justice, oriented at the problems of the early new millennium.

7

New Managerialism, Credibility and the Sanitisation of Criminal Justice

JULIA FIONDA

THROUGHOUT THE HISTORY of punishment it has been possible to trace a link between the methods used to punish and the principle behind the punishment being inflicted. As trends in the rationales of punishment change so too do the methods used and vice versa. For example, where general deterrence is thought to be the primary rationale for punishment, it would be natural for that punishment to be carried out in the public arena, using methods designed to instil fear. Similarly where restorative principles justify the infliction of penalties, those penalties and the process through which they are inflicted will reflect their reintegrative and reparative justification. This chapter will argue that, at the end of the twentieth century, the rationale behind the criminal justice system as a whole has shifted fundamentally towards managerialist "principles" (if such things exist) and that the punishment process has changed accordingly.

The urgent need for efficiency, constraints on the public purse and striving for optimum economy with resources are familiar notions to us all. New managerialism has permeated many areas of life, as the management of all resources (for example, time, money, energy, thoughts, compassion etc.) has become an essential reality. Indeed, in the field of public management there has been a distinct and much discussed shift towards managerialism. "Market-mimicking" (Harlow and Rawlings, 1997) in public management perhaps finds its clearest voice in the Citizen's Charter (Great Britain, 1991), which sets out minimum standards for the provision of publicly-funded services to the citizen as a consumer. Market forces are so endemic in public management that even one's inclusion in the definition of citizenship depends on one's ability to consume in a Thatcherite sense (Marshall, 1977).

The criminal justice system in many jurisdictions has not escaped, although the theme is much less well-developed here. Indeed, being one of the most expensive areas of public spending in terms of the resources listed above, it has been a natural target for managerialism for some time. The streamlining of the criminal justice system into a well oiled machine has become such a preoccupation that managerialist "principles" are now part of the criminal justice furniture. Indeed, it will be argued here that a new systems analysis has emerged where the criminal justice process in many jurisdictions is becoming a centrally controlled, multi-agency machine with a co-ordinated goal of achieving optimum efficiency in the process of punishment. "Good housekeeping" in the context of criminal justice in the 1990s, however, also requires the maintenance of credibility and the effective management of public relations by those in political control.

This quest for "good housekeeping" has, in turn, fundamentally changed the methods of punishment used and has prompted a major re-assessment of notions of "what works". Where efficiency and credibility are the central goals, punishment that "works" is clinical; a quick fix with determinate and visible results as opposed to a long-term therapeutic approach with uncertain outcomes. The end result is a loss of principle in the process of punishment and the concomitant loss of control over the nature and extent of punishment methods used. This chapter will provide a critique of this development in three parts; first the emergence of managerialism and credibility as central goals of the system and the return of a systems analysis of criminal justice will be traced. Secondly, recent procedural reforms in England and Wales and elsewhere will be examined as examples of the practice of "good housekeeping". Finally, the practical and political implications of the new managerialist approach to punishment will be discussed.

THE EMERGENCE OF MANAGERIALISM

Garland (1990) has traced the emergence of managerialism back at least 200 years. Indeed, the modern, centralised and state-run criminal justice process, which embodies this approach, has evolved over this period and many of its facets can be traced back this far. The development of the contemporary state-funded prison system (Morris and Rothman, 1995; Foucault, 1977), the establishment of professional bodies of public prosecutors, probation officers, prison officers, judges and the like, and the creation of centralised court systems have all occurred in most jurisdictions within this time scale.

Previously, Weber (1930) had argued that the emergence of managerialism within any social institution is an inherent product of its administration being carried out by bureaucratic organisations. The criminal justice system is no exception; it has undergone a transformation or "rationalisation" (Garland, 1990: 179), whereby punishment systems and methods based on emotional reactions and traditional practices or customs have been replaced by more mechanical, rational and bureaucratic practices: "In the course of this development, "science" (including social science) comes to replace belief, calculation replaces commitment, and technical knowledge replaces traditions and sentiments as the leading determinants of action" (Garland, 1990: 179).

Since the 1990s, however, managerialism has taken root in criminal justice systems in a much more literal way. It is now not so much a characteristic but rather a *raison d'être*, which governs perceptions of crime and offenders, the organisation of and choices for systems of punishment (James and Raine, 1998) and even criminological research (van Swaaningen, Blad and van Loon, 1992). More importantly, procedural reforms in England and Wales and elsewhere indicate that the pursuit of managerialist ideals has become a goal of the criminal justice system in itself and therefore a "principle" of punishment.

The activities of the criminal justice system require a powerful defence. The strength of such a defence may legitimise what would otherwise be systematic state violence and the unacceptable infliction of what Christie referred to as "pain" (Christie, 1982). Commentators have traditionally cited the prevention of crime through deterrence, incapacitation or rehabilitation (for example, Ashworth, 1995a; Honderich, 1969; Ashworth and von Hirsch, 1992; Walker, 1991) as a main function of and justification for the use of punishment (in its widest sense). Rehabilitation also served the function of expressing understanding and empathy towards the offender; an expression of what Rutherford called "decency" (Rutherford, 1993). Some have adopted the Durkheimian stance, arguing that the collective expression of rage, hatred, revenge or condemnation is both the purpose and justification of the punishment-using methods and systems which give voice to such emotions. More recently, the resolution of conflict created through criminal behaviour and the reparation of the victim's or society's material or emotional loss have been cited as purposes behind the criminal process (for example, Christie, 1977; Braithwaite, 1989; Cragg, 1992).

These purposes or aims have in common the expression or symbolisation of emotions and collective sentiments. It is argued here, however, that managerialism has become such a central focus of the criminal justice system that procedural reforms have been implemented without such emotive force on the part of policy makers but rather with a more self-fulfilling and self-satisfying sense of efficiency as their goal.

The Royal Commission on Criminal Justice, for example, conducted a major review of the criminal justice system in England and Wales, in the light of a number of serious miscarriages of justice in the early 1990s. The Report, published in 1993, made 352 recommendations for change, a large number of which were aimed at instilling notions of "good housekeeping" and which virtually lost sight of more fundamental concerns of defendants' due process rights and the need to prevent further injustice (Field and Thomas, 1994). Indeed the Commission made no apologies for their self-confessed adherence to principles of efficiency: "Although . . . every law-abiding citizen has an interest in a system in which the risk of mistaken verdicts is as low as it can be, there will always be argument about how much public money should be spent on arriving marginally closer to that ideal" (Royal Commission on Criminal Justice, 1993: 5).

In other words, this and other examples which will be expounded fully below, demonstrate that Garland's "limits of rationalisation" (Garland, 1990: 189) may indeed have been surpassed. Whereas van Swaaningen and de Jonge have claimed that the process of rationalisation has developed alongside the "moralistic discourse on law and order" (1995, 43), it will be argued here that the manipulation and management of public discussion and sentiment is in fact part of this new managerialism, which incorporates the need for credibility alongside that for efficiency and optimum control.

CREDIBILITY AND MANAGERIALISM

Towards the end of the twentieth century, criminal justice issues were high on the political agenda. Law and order are prioritised in manifestos and elections are fought as much on this issue as on the economy, social welfare, or foreign policy. It is therefore essential for political survival that criminal justice policy is palatable to public opinion. Policy must aim to secure public satisfaction with the punishment process and ensure that the public have confidence that it will protect their rights and freedoms. Therefore, as well as providing legal and physical protection to the public, the criminal justice system must also conduct its own public relations exercise and portray a satisfying image, most notably through the channels of the media. In addition, all this must be good value for money. This is a tall order for any government, since these various requirements may often conflict.

The direction of criminal policy in 1990s' Britain, however, has shown that it is possible for public opinion to be manipulated, via the media, towards support for those penalties and systems which are also efficacious in managerial terms. The creation of fear has been a powerful force in driving criminal justice policy towards the crime control methods which are usually the most efficient. Successive policy statements have made a point of directing their audiences towards thoughts of their own personal safety. In 1990, the Home Office began this trend by publishing proposals for legislation in a White Paper entitled *Crime, Justice and Protecting the Public.* The first paragraph of the White Paper illustrated its commitment to combining protection with efficiency:

> "Too many people in England and Wales are hit by crime. Being a victim of crime and being frightened by crime stunts many lives. Crime can drive out business from an area and destroy jobs. Dealing with crime is expensive; the annual expenditure on the criminal justice services in England and Wales is £7 billion. It has increased by 77% in real terms in the last 10 years. These facts reflect the government's strong and enduring commitment to sustaining the rule of law. This White Paper sets out the Government's proposals for changes in the way the courts deal with offenders" (Home Office, 1 990: 1).

In October 1993 this message was reiterated by the Home Secretary of the time, the Rt. Hon. Michael Howard, MP, in a speech to the Conservative Party Annual Conference, outlining twenty-seven major changes to the law which would protect the public even further. This would be achieved through "back to basics"—that is, by resurrecting traditional Conservative law and order values. There followed another White Paper in 1996, *Protecting the Public* (Home

Office, 1996a), whose title again appealed to those seeking protection from the dangerous criminal fraternity. This resulted in the Crime (Sentences) Act 1997 which is largely devoted to the significantly greater use of custody in many cases of violent or sexual crimes. Further, the Sex Offenders Act 1997 offers the community protection from dangerous paedophiles and others by creating a national register of all persons convicted of, or cautioned for, a sexual offence, thereby enabling the police to monitor their whereabouts and activities, if necessary.

The trend continued after the election of a Labour government in May 1997, which has introduced a number of new measures, again designed to maximise public safety. The Crime and Disorder Act 1998 contains, *inter alia*, provision for an anti-social behaviour order, a sex offender order, a child safety order and a local child curfew order which purport to satisfy these aims. These quasi-criminal orders, it is maintained, will protect the citizen from a new breed of social dangers, such as the undefined concept of "anti-social behaviour" (see Rutherford, Chapter 3). In this legislation the Government has even targeted the perceived threat posed by very young children, especially those under ten: "Unsupervised young children gathered in public places at night can cause real alarm and misery to local communities and can encourage one another into anti-social and criminal habits" (Home Office, 1997c: para. 113).

The 1997 British Crime Survey suggested that the message is getting through. This victimisation survey indicates that the British public mistakenly believe that recorded crime has rapidly increased and substantially overestimate the proportion of recorded crime involving violence (Home Office, 1998d). However, although this view is mistaken in the light of criminal statistics gathered during the same period, the fear that it reveals is a useful factor which the Home Office can utilise to justify the use of imprisonment and other criminal justice procedures which, it will be argued later, satisfy managerial ideals. "Rationalised" punishment requires that policy-makers carefully steer and manipulate the emotive fears of the public: ". . . correctional managers and administrators often seek to minimize the impact of political intervention and resist the 'irrational' forces of public sentiment, since these can lead to uncontrolled inputs into the system which may disturb managerial goals" (Garland, 1990: 187). Hence the growing role of the spin doctor, the advertising executive and the image consultant in the political arena.

The 1990s in England and Wales have also been the era of "soundbite justice". Media hysteria on a number of issues has prompted rapid changes in the law as successive governments struggle to maintain their popularity. So far this decade in England and Wales, dangerous dogs, beggars and the homeless, young people (whether offenders or not), those living a transient lifestyle, rave parties, firearms, and even eating some forms of beef, have been vilified in the press, resulting in rapidly drafted, knee-jerk, but often major, changes in the relevant law. The power of the media to pre-empt a moral panic and thereby bring about such changes, especially in the field of criminal justice, is well-documented

(Mathiesen, 1992; Goode and Ben-Yehuda, 1994; Cohen, 1972; Schlesinger and Tumber, 1994). Nowhere has this been more clearly demonstrated than in the media furore following the murder of James Bulger, by two ten-year-old boys, in England in 1993. The media gave vent to strong and powerful expressions of hatred, anger and rejection on the part of the public (Franklin and Petley, 1996). This coincided neatly with the new political rhetoric of "back to basics", thus enabling the government to focus public sentiment towards policies which could induce confidence and economise with resources at the same time. Again, the practical result has been a number of procedural and legal reforms which culminate in the greater use of custodial sanctions in relation to young offenders (particularly those aged under 15).

It can therefore be seen that the manipulation of these collective emotions is a necessary part of developing a criminal justice system based on managerialist principles. In order to implement a punishment system which is bereft of emotional symbolism, manipulation allows for these emotions to be vented through the media, at the same time as justifying the use of punishment methods which may otherwise be unpopular. The result is a criminal justice system whose central goal is to economise resources, run smoothly and generally demonstrate the principles of "good housekeeping".

"GOOD HOUSEKEEPING" IN PRACTICE

The end of the twentieth century witnessed a return of the systems analysis of criminal justice and a concomitant centrality of managerialist goals. The streamlining of the system is now openly discussed in policy documents and politicians are not shy to stress the financial and time-saving advantages of their proposed policies. This is a marked change since the late 1980s when Ashworth noted that the principal managerial developments at that time had taken place at a hidden and subversive level, so that "the law itself resembles at best a Gruyère cheese, with channels aplenty through which the *cognoscenti* can pass unhampered by rules" (Ashworth, 1988: 115). Indeed, at the same time Blumstein was advocating a greater concentration on the "macro concerns of system policy" as opposed to "the micro concerns over the handling of the individual defendant" (Blumstein, 1988: 247). By the beginning of the 1990s, the perception of the criminal justice system as a well-oiled machine or efficiently administered company was becoming much more the norm as it became increasingly run along corporate lines. Indeed, Dato Steenhuis, whose management philosophy has been extremely influential in the osmosis of managerialist principles into Dutch criminal policy, has drawn a powerful analogy between effective criminal justice systems and commercial enterprises:

> "The criminal justice company can, in my opinion, be defined as the totality of organs whose function, in mutual relationship to one another, is aimed at (or responsible for) the maintenance of the penal legal order. The different production phases of the com-

> pany are coupled to each other serially, like a car manufacturing factory or in a company where for example chocolate bars are produced" (Steenhuis quoted in Rutherford, 1996: 62).

Official policy documents are also unashamed in expressing their commitment to the managerialist goal. For example, the 1990 Policy Plan published by the Dutch Ministry of Justice did so very frankly, with large parts of it devoted to emphasising co-operation and co-ordination between its departments, and addressing organisational and managerial concerns, such as personnel levels and computerisation, as well as "intervention ratios", a sort of performance target for public prosecutors to observe in dealing with cases of petty crime (Netherlands Ministry of Justice, 1990; Fionda, 1995: 112). Equally, in England and Wales the Royal Commission on Criminal Justice has already been identified with a preoccupation with operational efficiency rather than due process rights. Indeed the Royal Warrant establishing the Commission requested that it should have "regard to the efficient use of resources" during their investigation of "the effectiveness of the criminal justice system . . . in securing the conviction of those guilty of criminal offences and the acquittal of those who are innocent" (Royal Commission on Criminal Justice, 1993: i).

This section will examine in more detail some selected examples of recent changes or developments in the criminal justice systems of England and Wales and other European jurisdictions. The centrality of principles of "good housekeeping" is evident from these developments and from the rationales behind them.

(a) Pre-trial procedures

One of the clearest examples of policy developments, aimed at conserving resources and streamlining the criminal justice process, has been the expansion of diversion at the pre-trial stages. Indeed, one of the primary rationales for diversion is to enable the criminal justice process to conserve its resources for the few, selected serious or complex cases which require the full panoply of the criminal trial. There are, of course, therapeutic and welfare reasons for diverting offenders away from the full criminal process which also justify the procedure. However, it is argued here that it is the managerial benefits of diversion that have provided the greatest momentum for almost unprecedented expansion in the late 1980s and 1990s.

In most European jurisdictions the implementation of the diversion process falls to the public prosecutor. In many northern European jurisdictions the prosecutor has taken on a managerial role over the last two to three decades, as the pressures on the resources of the criminal justice system have increased (Fionda, 1995). In The Netherlands, a rising crime rate led to concerns about overloading the criminal justice system. This prompted a reversal in the interpretation of the expediency principle during the 1970s. Prosecutors thereafter worked with a presumption in favour of diversion in a majority of cases, as a matter of practical necessity. When, in 1990, it emerged that such a policy had become politically unpopular, the Ministry of Justice continued to focus on the public prosecutor in the search for a solution. In order to reduce the number of unconditional waivers of criminal cases, which had apparently brought the law into disrepute by appearing to virtually ignore a large proportion of criminality, the Ministry sought to encourage the public prosecution agency ("Openbaar Ministerie" (OM)) to increase the number of conditional waivers. In this way public prosecutors became the " 'implementors' or executors of state policies instead of magistrates" (John Blad, quoted in Fionda, 1995: 123). This policy was severely criticised by some for harnessing the discretion of the public prosecutor and because of the civil liberties implications of increasing diversion at such an early stage. This did not prevent the Ministry of Justice from justifying it as a bureaucratic necessity (Netherlands Ministry of Justice, 1990).

In Germany a similar development has been emerging throughout the 1990s. The German criminal justice system also had to deal with a burgeoning crime problem and pressures on resources. This was a particular problem in the early 1990s when the boundaries between West Germany and the former German Democratic Republic were opened, and the personnel resources in the West had to staff the criminal justice system of the entire new, unified Germany. Again it was the public prosecutor who bore a large part of the responsibility for managing this change, using his/her powers to unconditionally and conditionally divert cases from the formal adjudication process (Fionda, 1995; Beckett and Western, Chapter 2). This development led some commentators to argue that, in the name of bureaucratic management, the fundamental constitutional principle of legality has been substantially eroded (for example, Bohlander, 1994; Weigend, 1983).

In Scotland, the introduction of procurator fiscal fines (a fine levied by the public prosecutor in lieu of prosecution) in 1987, and the expansion of the procurator fiscal's discretion to offer such a fine under the Criminal Justice (Scotland) Act 1995, is a further example of a similar process. This initiative was explicitly attributed to the valuable savings that could be made through diversion (Stewart Committee, 1983). Duff has also indicated that the fiscal fine was a deliberate attempt on the part of policy-makers in Scotland to widen the net of social control, without overburdening the criminal justice system (Duff, 1993).

In England and Wales the public prosecutor has not been such an important character in the implementation of the managerialist goal. The Crown Prosecution Service has nevertheless been subject to criticisms that it is embroiled with the managerialist culture: "[the CPS] is a bureaucracy whose sole purpose in life is to process files and churn them out like a machine in Willie Wonka and the Chocolate Factory" (Bennett, 1993). The CPS's diversionary discretion is virtually non-existent, aside from a power to waive cases where it would not be in the public interest to prosecute (Code for Crown Prosecutors,

1994). In 1993, the Royal Commission on Criminal Justice recommended that Crown Prosecutors be given powers to offer fines to suspects as a conditional diversionary option, similar to that of their European counterparts. Their reasoning was set out in a single paragraph of their report and mainly voiced their approval of the Scottish system (Royal Commission on Criminal Justice, 1993: 83). There were reservations with the creation of this system of pre-trial punishment, but these only served to re-emphasise the influence of managerialist principles on the Commission: "There would be a small cost to the magsitrates' courts' fine collection machinery but this should be considerably outweighed by the savings in magistrates' court trials" (Royal Commission on Criminal Justice, 1993: 83). Sanders was evidently correct when he forecast that ". . . there is little possibility of reducing punitiveness through diversion. The window of opportunity is only present at all because of financial pressures to reduce government spending" (Sanders, 1988: 529).

The development of diversion in England and Wales is rather more complex. The police, through the use of the caution, currently carry out diversion, conditional or otherwise. This has been widely used by the police, particularly in cases involving young offenders where a formal prosecution might be considered unduly stigmatising and damaging. Its development, however, has been at the relatively informal, practice level, not least because the caution remains, for adults at least, without any statutory authority. The expansion in the use of diversion for young offenders during the 1980s has been extensively documented by Rutherford (1992), and is claimed to be a central part of the "systems management" approach to youth justice (Cavadino and Dignan, 1997). However, systems management in this context is somewhat different to the managerialist processes thus far described. In the 1980s this was part of a sustained and general diversion of young offenders from custody and from the youth court, largely initiated by ground-level practitioners (Rutherford, 1992). The government openly supported the practice of cautioning in the 1980s for both therapeutic and managerial reasons (Home Office Circulars 14/1985 and 59/1990). By 1994, however, their patience with the therapeutic benefits of cautioning had worn thin and Home Office Circular 18/1994 set out less-encouraging guidance on its use. Since then the Crime and Disorder Act 1998 (sections 65 and 66) has placed the diversion process for young offenders on a legislative footing. The new system of reprimands and warnings, however, is designed around the guidance of the 1994 Circular, and the documents preceding the 1998 Act placed a great deal of stress on the need to combine a severe and deterrent punishment with a quick and simple procedure (Home Office 1997b: Part 2; Home Office 1997c; Beckett and Western, Chapter 2; Fionda 1999). The need to balance these police powers with adequate meaningful protection of the young offenders' civil liberties is not mentioned in either paper.

Plea-bargaining in England and Wales provides further evidence of the frankness with which managerial policies are now expounded. Until 1993, the process of negotiations between the prosecution and the defendant, resulting in the trade of a guilty plea in return for a lesser charge, inevitably took place. Nevertheless, the practice was taboo in a system where such practices were thought to compromise the process of justice for the inappropriate purpose of saving the time and expense of a trial. Indeed, this was one of the holes in the Gruyère cheese about which Andrew Ashworth wrote in 1988 (Ashworth, 1988: 115). The distaste for plea-bargaining was exacerbated by the findings of extensive research into the practice in the 1970s by Baldwin and McConville (1977). While the result of a plea bargain had a significant effect in determining the outcome of a case, they interviewed a large number of defendants who claimed to have pleaded guilty under pressure from lawyers, despite the defendants' innocence.

More recently, however, the Royal Commission on Criminal Justice not only openly revealed the practice but also recommended a detailed statutory framework for plea negotiations, sentence canvassing before a judge and a ladder of sentence discounts to be awarded to defendants who plead guilty. This was one of the few recommendations of the Royal Commission which Parliament implemented—in this case in the Criminal Justice and Public Order Act 1994. Sentence canvassing was still considered off-limits, but the sentence discount system has now attained legitimacy.

The Royal Commission was explicit in attributing their support for the plea-bargaining process to its capacity to substantially reduce the number of Crown Court trials. The triumph of such managerialism over due process principles has been strongly criticised:

> "To make acquittal of the innocent, *at any point*, [original emphasis] less than the primary consideration in a system that still deploys the due process rhetoric of preferring ten guilty going free to the single convicted innocent, is an important departure. The starting point of principle should have been to reject such a move" (Field and Thomas, 1994: 9).

The Royal Commission evidently also chose to ignore evidence presented to them that Afro-Caribbean defendants are substantially less likely to plead guilty than other ethnic groups and are therefore less likely to be in a position to take advantage of the discounts (Fitzgerald, 1993). Managerialism here is prioritised over the avoidance of indirect discrimination.

(b) The use of imprisonment

The use of imprisonment and policies on the expansionist track are not traditionally associated with managerialism. Indeed, custody in any form is expensive and not commonly utilised in a drive towards economy of resources. Yet, despite my argument that managerialism is becoming a dominant, possibly the dominant, theme in criminal justice policy towards the end of the millennium, many countries in Europe and worldwide have undoubtedly and deliberately increased their use of imprisonment. There appears to be a paradox. This section will first explore the pursuit of the expansionist track in both England and The Netherlands and will then examine this paradox in greater detail.

The movement towards severity and repression in Dutch penal policy has been a gradual process, beginning in 1985 with the publication of *Samenleving en Criminaliteit* (Netherlands Ministry of Justice, 1985), the first of several recent policy plans emanating from the Ministry of Justice. However, few observers in 1985 would have predicted the unprecedented expansion of the prison system and the use of imprisonment in the 1990s. The latest policy plan, *Werkzame Detentie* (Netherlands Ministry of Justice, 1993) prescribed an increase in the overall rate of imprisonment to 78 per 100,000 by 1998 (it was just 44 per 100,000 in 1990); a restriction in the use of early release procedures; and a fundamental change in the regimes of prison establishments, shifting the focus from rehabilitation to security, incapacitation and regimes involving hard labour and basic conditions. René van Swaaningen and Gerard de Jonge reported in 1995 that these plans were indeed being implemented (van Swaaningen and de Jonge, 1995: 25–36).

In England and Wales developments have been similar, although of course the starting point was very different. In 1990 the last Conservative government under the leadership of Margaret Thatcher, published a White Paper stating that prison is "an expensive way of making bad people worse" (Home Office, 1990: 6). The resultant legislation, the Criminal Justice Act 1991, which set out a framework for sentencing based on retribution and just deserts, aimed at reducing the use made of prison for many less serious offences, and confining its use to the deepest end of criminality. Most of the Act was implemented in October 1992, but only nine months later parts of it were repealed (Criminal Justice Act 1993) with the new government, embarking on its "back to basics" excursion, beginning to find the liberal emphasis of the 1991 Act a political embarrassment. The Home Secretary, Michael Howad, announced at the Conservative Party Annual Conference in October 1993 that "prison works" and proposed a series of measures designed to ensure that the courts made greater use of imprisonment for incapacitation and deterrent purposes.

These measures included: the "two strikes and you're out" procedure where mandatory life penalties are to be issued in respect of second or subsequent convictions for serious offences (Crime (Sentences) Act (C(S)A) 1997, section 2); mandatory minimum sentences for drug dealers and burglars (C(S)A 1997, sections 3 and 4) and the virtual abolition of parole (C(S)A 1997, section 11). When section 4 of the C(S)A 1997 (dealing with recidivist burglars) is fully implemented, it is estimated that this provision alone will add four thousand to the prison population. Young offenders were also targeted and in 1994 a new custodial order, the Secure Training Order, was created (Criminal Justice and Public Order Act 1994, Part I) which will detain 12–15-year-old "persistent" offenders in specially built institutions. The maximum period of detention to which offenders aged 15–18 could be sentenced was also doubled to two years (CJPOA 1994, section 17). More recently the Crime and Disorder Act 1998 introduced the Detention and Training Order (section 73) which potentially extends the use of custody to young offenders aged between ten and 12.

Mr Howard would not be disappointed with the results of these legislative changes. The prison population has risen steadily and consistently since 1993. In October 1993 it stood at 46,211; a year later it had risen to 50,000 and by November 1998 it stood at just over 66,000. Home Office projections anticipated that, by the end of the century, the prison population would reach an unprecedented 71,000. The use of community penalties has fallen correspondingly over the same period. These figures indicate unambiguously that the "just deserts" policy of the early 1990s failed to achieve the aims set out in the 1990 White Paper. Instead, they have taken England and Wales much further down the expansionist road.

It would appear that these expansionist policies represent the antithesis of managerialism, given that they are so costly in material terms. However, it is argued here that there is no contradiction or bifurcation in policy ideals and that the greater use of imprisonment is compatible with the pursuit of managerialist aims. There are two main grounds for stating this: first, in material terms imprisonment is much less costly than the hidden costs of some community-based alternatives; and secondly, imprisonment is undoubtedly less costly in terms of other resources such as human resources, political expediency and the energies associated with taking responsibility for society's maladies.

René van Swaaningen and Gerard de Jonge have indicated that a large proportion of the expanded prison population in The Netherlands are foreigners who have not committed offences, other than entering The Netherlands without valid authorisation to do so (1995, 28). Furthermore, statistics presented in the 1993 Policy Plan show that almost half of the prison population in Holland were unemployed at the time of their imprisonment and were claiming social security benefits. The proportions are similar in England and Wales. Not only are these people largely physically prevented from committing further offences whilst incarcerated, they are also not spending proportions of the government's welfare budgets. In England and Wales, assuming that offenders stay in prison long enough (usually in excess of one year), they will lose their right to claim housing benefit, unemployment benefit, income support and the like, as well as their capacity to take advantage of other welfare provision such as housing, social services and health care. Although it is estimated (by NACRO amongst others) that the cost of keeping a prisoner in a medium-security institution is around £500 per week, it is not inconceivable that to support the same person as a citizen in the community would be even more costly.

That this tortuous logic might appeal to governments whose political ideology is bound up with the pursuit of managerialism is clear when the following example is considered. In England and Wales, public opinion has recently been raging vehemently against a number of paedophiles released from prison at the end of their sentences and trying to settle back into the community. Local authorities are unwilling to house them (Fionda and Cowan, 1998) and local people are unwilling to accept them into their neighbourhoods. There are well-reported examples of paedophiles being hounded from one district to another, often violently (for example, "Jeering mothers drive paedophile off council estate" *The Times*, 11 January 1997). The government, responding to the lobby of public opinion, which claims that their children are in danger, have created a Sex Offenders Register in which the police will record details of all convicted and cautioned sex offenders, and pledge to monitor their whereabouts and activities. One paroled offender received 24-hour police protection from a Scotland Yard team of 30 officers in order to maintain his safety in the community (Fionda and Cowan, 1998). This has prompted the Home Secretary to consider expanding the mental health provisions in such a way that dangerous people with "untreatable" mental disorders (for example, a paedophile) can be detained mandatorily and indefinitely in a psychiatric hospital or elsewhere after their release from prison, or even without the need to convict them at all. Another alternative on the discussion table is to create a mandatory life penalty for offences relating to child abuse, so that paedophiles can be imprisoned indefinitely. This smacks of a desperate search for a custodial alternative to prison which, whilst costly, has been proved to be less expensive in financial terms than release.

Money, however, is not the only resource in respect of which incarceration is efficient. There is little doubt that the above-mentioned proposals for the treatment of paedophiles are politically efficient in the current social environment. So too is the use of prison. Imprisonment is popular with the electorate. Indeed, the return to expansionism in 1993 was part of the "back to basics" policy of the government of the day, which itself was a ploy on the part of John Major to recover valuable opinion poll ratings. The popularity of imprisonment may be explained in Durkheimian terms through the opportunity to collectively express powerful emotions towards those most vehemently condemned by society (there are elements of this in the treatment of paedophiles). However, there is another explanation which suggests that such emotive responses to crime are tinged with a managerialist ethos, and that collective sentiments have become a more anomalous "collective selfishness". In post-1980s Britain, the popular press was littered with protests at a variety of welfare-based practices to which the public, who foot the bill, object. John Kenneth Galbraith (1992) argued that in both post-Thatcher Britain and post-Reagan America the "culture of contentment" had instilled itself in society and that the materially contented middle class were no longer prepared to subsidise the "emerging underclass" (Murray, 1990). Indeed, to do so would be not only unjust to those whose wealth and contentment is acquired as a result of diligence and self-reliance, but would be manifestly unfair to those being subsidised who risk becoming dependent. Clarke et al. argued that this shift in the view of the benevolent state is part of a shift towards managerialism in society:

> "The Beveridge reforms and the post-war welfare state talked about the individual as a 'citizen', drawing on the ideas of New Liberalism about the reciprocal relationship between the state and the citizen. The citizen in this conception had both rights and

> obligations . . . The New Right, however, focused mainly on the citizen's obligations—talking about taxpayers and ratepayers, and the need to protect their interests against exploitation (either by 'public waste' or 'scroungers')" (Clarke, Cochrane and Smart, 1987: 141).

This view is not surprising given that these developments took place in a world where Margaret Thatcher famously claimed that "There is no such thing as society . . . There are families and there are individuals." In this environment managerialist principles would not allow for expenditure on activities and policies designed to alleviate the damaging circumstances of the undeserving or dispossessed in society. Such expenditure is not only morally wrong, but may be unproductive in the short-term: "The long run may not arrive; that is the frequent belief . . . the cost of today's action falls or could fall on the favoured community; taxes could be increased. The benefits in the longer run may well be for others to enjoy" (Galbraith, 1992: 20).

Hence the popularity of imprisonment. It is costly in terms of initial outlay, but economical in terms of its moral parsimony and its short-term results. It is a "quick fix" and does not present a response to crime where offenders (the morally undeserving) are seen to be getting something for nothing; a criticism often levied at more therapeutic responses. So, in credibility terms, expansionism is compatible with managerialism.

Imprisonment is also efficient in the sense that it is "clinical". It is easy in policy terms and requires little imagination on the part of policy-makers. It requires little emotional output and policy-makers need not trouble themselves a great deal about the ideology behind their actions. This is the very nature of managerialism; it turns politicians, policy-makers and criminal justice professionals into machine operators:

> "Advocates of the new penology profess no ideological affiliation, but see themselves as planners and systems engineers seeking to implement crime control policies aimed at the efficient management (rather than elimination or reduction) of criminal behaviour" (Beckett, 1997: 103).

The more technologically advanced the machinery, the more efficient those engineers will be, since human contact and time are expensive. Hence the development in America of the "Supermax" prison, and its recently opened imitation at HMP Woodhill in England. The principle behind the use of imprisonment as a punishment is lost. It is assumed to be justified and rational ideologically, and policy-makers focus their attention instead on the "management" of the system and the pursuit of optimum performance parameters.

It is noticeable in the English juvenile justice system that practitioners and policy-makers have toyed for over a century with welfare-based and punitive ideologies. However, there has never been any real imagination used in implementing these ideologies because of the frequent resort to detention of young people (Rutherford, 1992). The institutions have changed from time to time, as ideologically-driven policy-makers purported to be trying something new, but they have rarely had the imagination to do anything other than incarcerate. Incarceration is the "quick fix" with immediately visible results, which is so attractive to politicians, especially in the 1990s. New Labour expressed this in 1996 when they pledged to end the "confusion over punishment and welfare at national and local levels" (Labour Party, 1996b: 1) by adopting the less confusing punitive stance: "The welfare needs of young offenders should not be allowed to outweigh the community's needs for protection from offending behaviour" (Labour Party, 1996b: 3).

Imprisonment (or incarceration in other institutions such as psychiatric hospitals) is also efficient and economical with the conscience. Excluding the troubled and disadvantaged from the mainstream of society (or causing their "social death" as Rutherford described it (1997a)) is a clinical policy in that it enables both the government and the public at large to close its mind to the complex difficulties and painful experiences that they are surrounded by, and expend little time or effort addressing them. As long as the government justifies a clinical punitive approach to punishment, it can ignore the social and other factors which its policies may have caused and which in turn may contribute to offending behaviour.

(c) The transformation of community penalties

The pursuit of managerialism, and its associated lack of imagination mooted above, is also apparent in the transformation of community penalties in England and Wales in the 1990s. Far from attempting to carry out any sort of rehabilitative ideal, community sentences currently available to English courts increasingly mirror forms of imprisonment. Thus, all the arguments above relating to the use of imprisonment as an expression of managerialist principles, also apply here. However, policy in relation to community penalties also illustrates its own style of managerialism.

In 1988 a Consultation Paper was published by the Home Office which proposed that, due to the financial cost and ineffectiveness of custody in preventing re-offending, non-custodial penalties should be more widely used by sentencers. Community penalties have traditionally been viewed as the most efficient port of call in an expenditure storm: "Punishment in the community should be more economical in public resources. On average, holding someone in prison for a month costs twice as much as the average community service order" (Home Office, 1988: 2). However, in order to ensure that resort to community sentences would not cost dearly in credibility terms, the Consultation Paper also advocated strengthening them and making them "rigorous and demanding, otherwise the sentencers and the general public will not accept [them] as punishment" (Home Office, 1988: 4).

The resultant legislation, the Criminal Justice Act 1991, gave community sentences a more important role in the sentencing framework. They were no longer alternatives to custody but sentences in their own right, applicable in cases where the offence was of medium seriousness (that is, too serious for a fine and not serious enough for custody). Further, the Act introduced a new penalty, the curfew (section 12), which could be reinforced with electronic tagging (section 13), as well as a new strengthened community service order (section 10) and probation orders with a statutory list of requirements (section 8). All these community penalties were to be subject to the quality control mechanism of National Standards.

Curfews were criticised by many as inhumane, ineffective and, with electronic tagging associated with them, "incompatible with the essential fabric of a free society" (Howard League, 1988). They symbolised most clearly how community penalties had been transformed from therapeutic methods of rehabilitation to draconian instruments in the "punitive city" (Cohen, 1987). This comes as no surprise given the managerial benefits of imprisonment stated above. It is, therefore, also unsurprising that there has been a move towards expansion here. The most draconian of the community penalties, the curfew with electronic tagging, has been added to the Youth Court's powers and can be given to a young offender under the age of 16 (Crime (Sentences) Act 1997, section 43). New Labour's contribution to community penalties has simply been more of the same. For example, electronic tagging is now used as an alternative to continued custody at the end of a custodial sentence in an attempt to manage the numbers in a prison system which is rapidly becoming full to bursting point. Further, the introduction, in the Crime and Disorder Act 1998, of the reparation order for young offenders is one of a number of new penalties which are justified by the government by reference to their therapeutic or, in this case, restorative benefits. In reality however, this merely masks their managerialist aims. As Lode Walgrave has observed:

> "Governments do not let themselves be guided by scientific options or data. Governments use criminology, like a menu from which they choose à la carte what fits best into their political and electoral options . . . They pay lip-service to criminological options, like restorative justice, without really implementing the concepts behind the words" (Walgrave, 1998/99).

Further managerialist trends can be discerned, however, in the changing role of the probation officer. Probation, prior to 1991, was a supplementary order of the court, available where sentencers felt that the offender would benefit from some further assistance or advice. The probation officer used his discretion in deciding which facilities or treatment courses would be most appropriate for each offender and would design the structure of the order in terms of supervision and requirements. Since probation orders became sentences of the court in 1991, it is the magistrates who design the structure and framework of the order and the probation officer who implements it. This has prompted John Pitts to comment that the probation officer had ceased to be a professional, with autonomy and discretion and had become a technician who "applies techniques devised by somebody else to problems defined by somebody else" (Pitts, 1992: 143). Since they now have to write pre-sentence reports in a majority of cases appearing before the magistrates, their role as a social worker has also had to give way to their more time-consuming, but mechanical, role as administrator. The bureaucratisation of the probation officer is symptomatic of the managerialist ideal permeating the last bastion of the rehabilitative ideal. Rehabilitation is too costly and, in John Kenneth Galbraith's "culture of contentment", too uncertain, slow and open-ended for managerialist tastes.

THE SANITISATION OF CRIMINAL JUSTICE

The consequences of the adherence to managerialist principles in the formation of criminal justice policy are extensive. The abandonment of fundamental, constitutional principles and the wanton derogation of civil liberties under the cloak of managerialism have been widely discussed. Jones (1993) has voiced concern over the "trade-off" which often takes place between the interests of efficiency and those of natural justice:

> "As far as managers of the system are concerned, the exercise of due process rights thwarts the efficiency and effectiveness of the system. Improvement involves curtailing due process 'trappings', providing structural opportunities for 'opting out' of trial and applying penalties to those who 'opt in' " (Jones, 1993: 196).

The Report of the Royal Commission on Criminal Justice in England and Wales is an embodiment of this trade-off, as it trod clumsily over the right to silence (recommendation 83), the right to a jury trial (recommendation 114), the presumption of innocence (recommendation 156) and concrete evidence that some of its recommendations would result in racial discrimination (recommendation 156; see also Fitzgerald, 1993). It has also been accused of overlooking the opportunity to afford the defendant further protection from injustice in the police station and in the courts (Field and Thomas, 1994).

Other important principles have been trampled over; in Germany it has been shown how increased administrative sentencing by the public prosecutor has substantially compromised the legality principle. Indeed, prosecutorial diversion is generally fraught with civil liberties dangers which are often overshadowed by the more material benefits that it offers (Fionda, 1995). The expansion of the Dutch prison population in recent years has also prompted the breach of the principle of one prisoner to a cell, for the first time in over fifty years. The Ministry of Justice, anxious to avoid a large number of prisoners being released from prison due to space constraints, issued a Royal Warrant in July 1994 allowing cell sharing to take place, initially as a temporary, emergency measure.

There is also a problem with accountability. The more complex bureaucracies become, especially in the light of privatisation, the more difficult it is to trace a clear line of democratic accountability for the operational policy of the criminal justice system. This problem will grow as control of criminal justice agencies increases from the centre, but the application of policies diversifies at the local level. The newly appointed national Youth Justice Board in England and Wales, (Crime and Disorder Act 1998, section 41) provides a pertinent example. At the national level, a single board will monitor and co-ordinate policy in the youth justice system whilst maintaining a close relationship with the Home Office (Fionda, 1999: 40). At the local level, the operation of these policies will fall to local youth justice boards and multi-agency youth offender teams. To whom an aggrieved young offender complains is extremely unclear. Jones has suggested that criminal justice accountability in a managerialist system will become the responsibility of those who manage the public purse: "Auditors would become society's 'watchdogs of the night' " (1993, 188). The Audit Commission in England has already embarked on taking a close interest in the running of the youth justice system and its first report on the subject carried a heavy managerialist tone (Audit Commission, 1996).

However, this chapter has sought to demonstrate that the consequences of adopting a managerialist ideology are more widespread. As the process of punishment becomes more bureaucratic and criminal justice policy-makers become more akin to corporate managers, the punishments themselves become increasingly unemotional, clinical and "sanitised". We are in danger of losing sight of the fact that imposing punishment on others is more than a technical process; that is, we are losing sight of Christie's vision of punishment as the infliction of pain (Christie, 1982). The penalties being inflicted reflect the lack of emotion in the "ideology" behind them. Community penalties become less compassionate and empathetic and custodial penalties more basic and security-oriented. Whereas the demise of the rehabilitation model has, in the past, been hostage to the rise and fall of the "nothing works" philosophy, it would now appear that it has fallen prey to the "nobody cares" outlook.

The root of this movement towards sanitisation is political. Managerialism in criminal justice fits squarely with the social and economic philosophy of the New Right and the New Centre Left. In 1980s England, for example, Thatcherite Conservative principles consisted largely of:

> ". . . a determined campaign to replace socialism with a market economy . . . to reduce State involvement in the field of welfare provision and to break the power of the trade unions . . ." (Brake and Hale, 1992: 2).

Brake and Hale go on to argue that, in order to demonstrate the authority of the government planning to implement these social and economic dreams, the government first had to pursue a tough law and order policy. Garland (1996) has similarly argued that a government's stance on law and order voices underlying levels of insecurity about the power of the "sovereign state". The argument here is that crime control policy has simply become a part of the market economy. Like the running of any other industry, it has become embroiled with the need to ride the tide of market forces and to become financially self-governing. Moral discourse has no relevance in relation to such a criminal justice system. The expression of a moral standpoint and the emotions which accompany it therefore have no relevance in the practice of punishment. Just as political correctness has neutralised language, so managerialism has sanitised criminal justice.

CONCLUSION

Michael Howard's statement, "prison works", has an Orwellian logic to it—"Imprisonment is Freedom". For the penal policy-makers, prison works in the sense that it has an economic self-justification to it, in the same way that Orwell suggested that "war is peace" because the nation was economically dependent on it (Orwell, 1948). Nils Christie's haunting message about privatisation in criminal justice was similar. The "war on crime" will never end as long as there is an economic justification to keep it going: "The fascinating question, seen from an outsider's perspective, is why the inner cities of the USA are seen as targets for war rather than targets for drastic social reform" (Christie, 1993: 198).

One of the greatest dangers of managerialism and its concomitant sanitised punishment system is that it has no natural limits. The expression of retribution in punishment is, in most Western societies, tempered at least by some adherence to a concept of just deserts and commensurability. However, in contrast, managerialism has every incentive to evade limitations. Expansion offers greater opportunities for the pursuit of greater efficiency, although this line of reasoning may ultimately defeat itself. Christie (1993) has argued that the limits to expansion in the industry of criminal justice must be man-made. Willem de Haan called them the "politics of bad conscience" (de Haan, 1990). The argument here is that managerialism may have instilled the "politics of no conscience" into the process of policy-making in this field. The question at the end of this millennium must also be, where are the limits to sanitisation? Numbed to the infliction of pain through the process of punishment, it is argued here that the logical end to the managerialist argument lies well beyond the limits of humanitarianism.

Part III

Exclusion in the New Europe

8

Foreigners, Migration, Immigration and the Development of Criminal Justice in Europe

HANS-JÖRG ALBRECHT

ETHNICITY, IMMIGRATION AND foreign nationals have become major issues of concern in Europe since the second half of the 1980s (Tonry, 1997; Palidda, 1996). However, debates in Europe so far display elements that make the topic rather distinct from the "race and crime" and immigration debates in North America. Ethnic minorities in Europe are cornered between the crime issue and immigration, while in North America the immigration issue is dealt with quite independently from ethnicity or "race" which appear as distinct problems. The immigration issue has, it seems, been settled in North America, for quite some time leaving ethnicity (or race), and its assumed links to crime and criminal justice, as the prominent topic in the debate. In European countries, on the other hand, emigration originated primarily during the last 200 years (although examples of intra-European migration can be drawn from the beginning of the twentieth century and even from the nineteenth century). But, it is only since the 1960s that immigration to European countries has become a visible and long-term phenomenon, with "guest-workers" being attracted to the major European industrialised countries through recruitment policies designed to satisfy the demands of various industrial sectors for additional labour. For quite some time, therefore, immigration to the north and west of Europe was encouraged. Recruitment policies came to a sudden end with the first economic crisis which hit Europe at the beginning of the 1970s and set off an ongoing process of rationalisation, sending most European countries into a spiral of unemployment.

Today, crime, fear of crime, safety and justice have become central topics in the European debate on immigration and migration as well as on immigrant (ethnic and foreign) minorities in most European countries and look set to continue as such in the decades to come (Tonry, 1998: 60). Within the European context ethnicity and crime are strongly linked to immigration. In both Western and Eastern Europe, we can observe basic changes since the 1950s and 1960s in the very conception of immigration as well as changes in the political and social responses to immigrant and ethnic minorities. There, changes climaxed in the 1990s after the opening of borders between the east and west of Europe into a wave of hate violence.

While during the 1950s and 1960s a rather positive attitude towards labour immigrants found its expression in active recruitment policies, since the mid-1970s control of immigration has been significantly tightened in most Western European countries. This process has accelerated with the socio-political and economic changes in the east of Europe.

Immigration and immigrant resident groups have become a major concern for European and national policies, policy makers and political parties. The dominant perspective on immigration and ethnic minorities today is characterised through crime, deviance and conflict. Assumptions which suggest causal links between immigration (or the minority status) on the one hand, and crime and deviance, on the other hand, indicate powerful belief patterns concerning the potential of conflict and instability associated with immigration and the "alien".

The topic "immigration, ethnicity and crime" is therefore highly sensitive as it facilitates polarisation and is susceptible to political exploitation. Indeed, the issue of ethnic minorities (particularly asylum seekers) and their perceived potential for threatening public safety has become a rallying point for authoritarian sentiments in European societies, as well as for New Right political parties and extremist groups.

CONCEPTS, RESEARCH QUESTIONS AND MEASUREMENT

The ethnicity, immigration and crime topic as it emerged in Europe during the 1980s and 1990s may be broken down into five rough sub-issues. First, the topic of immigrant involvement in crime, an issue which has preoccupied criminology, crime policy and the media. The issue of crime necessarily raises the second issue of "immigrants, ethnic minorities and victimisation" (although for decades an almost completely disregarded issue). A third category refers to hate violence and inter-ethnic conflicts, as well as criminal law instruments devised to protect minorities from being preyed upon. Fourth is the problem of discrimination against ethnic minorities and immigrants in the justice system and in society at large, which has always had a prominent place in debates on "strangers" and minorities. The final issue concerns the physical control of illegal immigrants and "legal" immigrants selected for expulsion. Imprisonment and administrative detention have emerged as major problems and the links between immigration laws and criminal law, as well as between administrative and criminal authorities in controlling immigrant populations, have become an important field of research.

Through an examination of these topics it becomes clear that the debate on immigration, foreign nationals, ethnicity and crime/criminal justice is caught between several polarised positions; between immigrants as victims and immigrants as criminal offenders, between immigrants as endangered and immigrants as dangerous, between discrimination and affirmative action, as well as between protection and tough control or even exclusion.

The debates and discourses on whether racial, ethnic or national identifiers should be used in official data collection at all, whether for criminal justice or administrative purposes, demonstrate very clearly how sensitive the issue is. There is wide concern that the type of information produced by police information systems will be used to discriminate against ethnic or immigrant minorities (Killias, 1997: 381). Despite the purported salience of immigration, ethnic minorities and crime, most European justice systems do not provide accurate and specific data on ethnic or immigrant sub-groups particularly within the prison system. As a consequence, it is difficult to conduct cross-national research on ethnicity and crime, at least at the level of official crime statistics where most of the research on crime and criminal justice in Europe can be located (Tonry, 1998: 62).

Essentially, it is the lack of valid and reliable ethnic identifiers that make the comparative analysis of the involvement of immigrant and ethnic minorities in crime problematic in most European countries. Ethnic identifiers currently in use in European countries concern race and nationality. While the "race" identifier is confined to England and Wales (with some European countries even threatening criminal penalties for using race as a distinct category in any administrative environment), nationality or citizenship are used in continental European countries for the purpose of criminal justice, prison or other administrative statistical information systems. However, there are huge variations in the differentiation of nationality, as well as the depth into which sub-categories such as criminal suspects, prisoners, as well as immigrants, are broken down according to the national identifier. But, for both of the ethnic identifiers to be observed in criminal justice information systems (race and nationality), as well as research based on such information, it is clear that these represent over-aggregated categories which are possibly masking important differences. For both race and nationality not only can over-aggregation occur but also under-aggregation. So, for example with nationality, it is well-known that a proportion of second- and third-generation immigrants adopt the citizenship of the immigration countries. This holds true, for example, for Maghrebian immigrants to France, as well as for most ethnic minorities emigrating to England and Wales. It is also true—although at a somewhat lower level—for labour immigrants who came to other European countries, for example Germany, Switzerland, Austria and the Scandinavian countries, in the 1960s and 1970s. Furthermore, the reliability of the very denominator of ethnic minorities" involvement in crime is threatened by the phenomena of the illegal immigrant and the asylum seeker which emerged during the 1980s. While migrating groups are a well-known phenomenon throughout Europe, with gypsies representing the core of such migrating or non-resident groups, recent decades have seen a hitherto unknown increase in migrating populations. It is essentially illegal immigrants and asylum seekers, but also migrant workers, who expand populations but are not accounted for in official registers on residency, and thus are not counted in population surveys and statistics.

But it is not only over-aggregation that arises with categories like race and nationality; under-theorising can also be observed (Holdaway, 1997). It is clear that the umbrella categories of "race" or "citizenship" involve variables which condition those wide processes and which should be addressed when studying minority and immigration issues.

ETHNICITY, FOREIGN CITIZENSHIP AND CRIME INVOLVEMENT

In summarising the state of knowledge on links between immigration, foreign citizenship, race or ethnicity, on the one hand, and crime and deviance on the other (Tonry, 1998), we may conclude that:

- some immigrant groups exhibit much higher proportions of crime participation or involvement than do majority groups;
- however, some immigrant groups display the same degree of crime involvement (or even less participation) than is observed in the majority group;
- first-generation immigrants of the 1950s and 1960s have been involved in crime much less than second- or third-generation immigrants and those arriving in the 1980s and 1990s;
- research on immigration and crime during the twentieth century has shown that more attention should be paid to the motives underlying immigration, as well as the push- and pull-factors which trigger immigration and migration;
- what most immigrant groups have in common is a socially and economically disadvantageous and precarious position;
- however, cultural differences between groups which are similarly situated structurally can result in quite different crime patterns; different in terms of both the structure and the magnitude of criminal involvement;
- cultural differences between immigrant groups concern the phenomenon of community building and the preservation of the homogeneity of the immigrant group;
- such cultural differences are clearly important in explaining varying degrees of social and economic opportunities, legal or illegal, in different ethnic or immigrant communities and social groups.

When addressing the topic of disproportionate involvement in crime of immigrant or foreign/ethnic minorities, data drawn from police information systems of the Federal Republic of Germany may serve as an example of the type of differences masked by using categories such as nationality or citizenship. In the Federal Republic of Germany, the proportion of foreign suspects rose continuously until the mid-1980s, reflecting fairly accurately the increasing number of immigrants in the 1960s, 1970s and 1980s. In 1953, when police statistics were published for the first time after World War II, the rate of foreign suspects was as low as two per cent (Albrecht, 1997). By the mid-1990s, the share of foreign suspects stood at some 30 per cent. Information from other European countries confirms the significant share of foreign nationals in the group of criminal suspects but also points to significant differences between countries, as shown in Table 1.

Table 1: Proportions of foreign suspects for selected criminal offences, 1990

Offence	*France*	*Germany*	*Sweden*	*Switzerland*
Murder	15	28	26	52
Assault	17	22	19	42
Rape	17	33	26	58
Robbery	19	36	26	40
Theft	14	27	23	39
Burglary	10	22	13	33
Drug offences	22	23	20	36
Drug trafficking	38	33	25	43

Source: International Police Organisation: International Crime Statistics, 1983–95.

It is possible that differences in national citizenship policies might produce such variations. For example, Switzerland has a rather restrictive policy, while in France a substantial number of immigrants from Maghreb countries have adopted French nationality. These differences become even more marked when looking at the percentages of foreign suspects in murder cases and their development over time. While proportions of foreign murder suspects remained at a fairly stable and low level in Spain and France between 1983 and 1995, Germany, Austria and Switzerland exhibit significant increases, the onset of which coincides with the opening of borders between Eastern and Western Europe. It is also evident that there is not a stable involvement of foreigners in violent crime.

German police information systems which break down aggregate crime data along specific nationalities demonstrate that offender rates among certain groups of minorities are two to four times those of offenders observed in society at large. However, as previously outlined, some minorities (for example Spanish, Portuguese and Chinese) do display below-average offender rates. What can also be observed is that crime rates among labour immigrants throughout Europe were fairly stable during the 1980s and 1990s, and did not demonstrate any upward trend (Albrecht, 1997). As regards crime participation rates, data from England and Wales point to vast differences between black and Asian minorities, as do data from North America and other European countries.

An examination of the trends in foreign offender and population rates points to clear patterns which can be interpreted as the combined results of changes in the behaviour patterns of second and third generations, as well as of changes in migration patterns. While in the 1960s, rates of suspects and rates of immigrants followed each other quite closely, the gap became wider during the 1970s and the trends then took completely different courses. Disproportionate involvement of foreign minority members in police recorded crimes can be observed, in particular, in the age groups of 14–17 and 18–20-year-old suspects. A tentative explanation is that first-generation immigrants (in particular labour immigrants) did, and still do, experience improvements in living conditions in terms of better housing, better medical care, etc., which outweigh still existing differences in socio-economic placement between minority and majority groups. Furthermore, one can argue that selection took place through workforce recruitment schemes, interaction patterns of first-generation immigrants remained largely bound to the ethnic group itself, while contacts with the majority group were confined to the work environment. Second and third generations, then, are more likely to become conscious of deprivation and socio-economic inequality as well as experiencing conflicting expectations between themselves and those of the minority groups who are still bound to traditional values. Moreover, the density of interactions with the immigration society increases and with it the risk of conflict. Research on social and economic integration of ethnic and immigrant minorities throughout Europe reveals that major parts have slipped into marginal positions as regards socio-economic status, income, housing conditions, education and employment. Basic conditions for social and economic integration have worsened steadily during the 1980s and 1990s. Two groups in particular have been affected by this development of "the disappearance of work" (see Wilson, 1997). The first group comprises the subsequent generations of the first labour immigrants, who on average have a lower class background, poorer education and professional training and who are therefore particularly exposed to the risk of unemployment, moreover to the risk of never being able to enter the labour market.

New immigrants arriving in the second half of the 1980s and in the 1990s constitute the second group. These groups immediately adopt marginal positions in terms of either falling into social security dependency, being dependent on solidarity networks provided by resident ethnic minority groups, or entering the shadow economy and respective black markets. It is probably essentially ethnic solidarity networks, and the capability as well as potential within ethnic groups to build up ethnically homogenous communities, which work in favour of low crime participation (and also perhaps serve as major obstacles for attempts to penetrate ethnic groups through traditional policing and control strategies). In turn, such ethnically homogenous communities may be affected by larger proportions of hidden victimisation as a consequence of less accessibility to formal control agencies. What can also be observed among certain ethnic groups (in particular in Asian communities) are high rates of self-employment and the emergence of rather closed communities. This is true of England and Wales where Asians are reluctant to engage with the host society, while black people are much more "outgoing" and therefore also more likely to experience discrimination and hostile treatment (Smith, 1997: 174).

In establishing the framework within which the topic of immigration and crime may be analysed, we also have to take account of two levels of defining motives which underlie immigration: the official level, which produces categories reflecting the legal opportunities to enter European territories (labour immigration, tourism, asylum), and the factual level (or push- and pull-factors) associated with ongoing immigration. Some of the crime information systems cover (in addition to the category of nationality) the motives linked to a foreign offender's stay. Aside from education, it is essentially employment, tourism, asylum and finally illegal immigration which operate as factual-level motives. Here, too, we have to acknowledge that these categories are certainly under- or over-aggregated, as it can be expected that immigrants restrict their officially documented responses to such motives that, in their view, have the best chances of success in applying for legal residence.

The development and trends in police crime statistics, as regards the legal status of foreign offenders, clearly demonstrate marked changes in the official version of immigration motives. While in the 1960s, 1970s and early in the 1980s labour immigrants dominated the picture of foreign suspects in the Federal Republic of Germany, at the end of the 1980s and in the 1990s, it is foreign suspects either classified as asylum seekers, refugees or illegal immigrants who make up the bulk of foreign offender suspects. This change is certainly not indicative of changes in the motives to migrate or emigrate (with the exception of perhaps the wars in Bosnia and Kosovo) but rather reflects changes in immigration laws and policies. It is evident that the search for employment opportunities and the associated goal of improvement in life conditions are still the main forces driving people to emigrate to European countries. The distribution of various ethnic groups across Europe certainly follows the distribution of existing immigrant populations which developed in the 1960s and 1970s. The latter is partially explained by historical conditions (immigration from former colonies) as well as the feasibility of immigration (language, self-employment within ethnic groups).

Returning to the example of the Federal Republic of Germany and the crime data collected there, we may differentiate at least four groups of immigrant offenders exhibiting distinct offence patterns and indicating the need for different theoretical approaches to account for involvement in crime by various ethnic groups.

A first group of nationalities is characterised through offence patterns that are dominated by immigration offences and fraud/forgery. These offences are typically associated with attempts to enter the country without proper permission (forgery refers mainly to the use of false documents or passports). In Germany, it is essentially immigrants from India and Pakistan, as well as Afghanistan and Sri Lanka, who display this offence pattern. Leaving nationality aside and focusing on the actual push- or pull-factors, a rather homogeneous group emerges despite differences in nationality. In this group, labour and employment are certainly among the dominant push- and pull-forces.

A second group within the foreign offender population at large is characterised by an extremely high proportion of both property offences and immigration offences. Such offence patterns are prevalent among nationals from the former European socialist countries (Poland, Romania, Bulgaria, Russia). With this group, foreign suspects are isolated who have obviously one characteristic in common. This characteristic refers to small-scale theft, a pattern which falls in line with the development observed during the socio-political change behind the formerly sealed borders of Eastern Europe. Here, it is especially shoplifting occurring during—one can assume—short-term visits to Western European countries. Opening the borders after the breakdown of the communist regimes in the east of Europe has stimulated a sharp rise in property offences, mainly of a petty nature, committed by short-term visitors, the overlapping categories of tourists or asylum seekers. The wealth on display in department stores in border cities continues to serve as an important pull-factor for those coming from the East. This is underlined by the huge increase in shoplifting figures experienced by some German cities located near the border to eastern European countries. Furthermore, huge black markets in the east of Europe have emerged with a growing demand for all types of goods which are not produced, or not produced to a sufficient degree, and which are available in eastern European countries.

A third group of foreign offenders is comprised of nationalities which belong to traditional "guest-worker" countries. This group is characterised by a large and fairly stable resident population in Germany (as well as in other European countries). In this group, represented in Germany mainly by the Turkish offender population, more or less "ordinary" offence patterns can be observed (including a large share of property offences and a somewhat elevated level of violent offences), while immigration offences are marginal. It is in this group that socio-economic marginalisation is most prominent, with most of the labour immigrants as well as their offspring relegated to the lowest segment of European society. A certain trend towards ghettoisation—observable in most European metropolitan areas—reinforces obvious marginalisation and social exclusion. However, it is also in this group that crime involvement may vary considerably along either nationality or ethnic lines. It is clearly the degree to which social solidarity, community building and self-employment develop within these minorities that is decisive for the structure and size of visible crime involvement. However, it might also be the case that as stronger social solidarity develops, the less crime is reported, and the more difficult crime investigation becomes.

A fourth distinct group concerns nationalities with a significant share of drug offenders. Here, several sub-groups can be differentiated. The extreme example of some African nationalities emerged at the beginning of the 1980s in several German metropolitan areas, with arrests based almost exclusively on drug offences. These groups were involved in drug distribution, largely at the level of street dealing. In the second half of the 1980s Senegalese and Gambians disappeared from police statistics as a result of two factors: increased pressure on the drug distribution schemes and the lack of a significant resident Senegalese or Gambian population in Germany. Colombian nationals also seem to belong to this extreme group, being mainly arrested for cocaine trafficking (as well as immigration offences). A second sub-group concerns nationalities for whom the share of drug offences is rather high, although not particularly dominant in the general distribution of offences. Here, Moroccans can be identified as being heavily involved in cannabis trafficking and distribution. But, besides drug trafficking groups, there exists in this case a rather small community of Moroccans (contributing toward the adjustment of the structure of offences towards normal distribution). A third sub-group comprises Spanish, Italians and Turks for whom drug offences are somewhat above average, indicating that some groups within these populations are currently considerably involved in all types of drug offences. Drug markets in Germany as well as in other European countries continue to generate supply which is serviced by various ethnic and foreign national groups (for example South Americans in the case of cocaine, North Africans and black Africans, Kurdish and Arab groups in the case of heroin and cannabis). Black markets today involve international networks, thus necessitating the participation of nationals from other countries either on the supply or demand side of the illicit markets. As trafficking routes change because of continuing police pressure at borders and in terms of controlled delivery, the structure of nationals involved in drug trafficking and arrested in various European countries also changes.

With the particular importance of drugs attention is drawn to the black market in general, as well as to the informal or shadow economies. The market approach explains why particular ethnic minority offenders or foreign national suspects show up in various European countries. It may also serve as an approach to explain the crime participation of resident foreign nationals. However, the shadow economy provides employment and income for certain marginalised groups and in certain fields opportunities for upward mobility (Tarrius, 1997). For example, it is estimated that as many as ten thousand Vietnamese out of a total of thirty thousand living in the east of Germany survive on the trafficking and distributing of untaxed cigarettes (Lehmann, 1998).

In this respect, particular attention should be paid to the concept of organised crime which since the 1980s has become a major concern for crime policy makers throughout Europe (Fijnaut, et al. 1995). On the one hand, the organised crime debate adds a new dimension to the discussion on ethnicity, immigration and crime in Europe (focusing in particular on the import theory of organised crime). On the other hand, organised crime in terms of black-market organisation as well as the organisation of sub-cultures (or self-organisation of ethnic minorities) may serve as a promising way to achieve a deeper understanding of how crime develops in some minority groups. The discourse on organised crime is evidently relevant to the debate on immigration and crime. Organised crime is still conceived as a threat posed by alien groups, for example the Sicilian,

Russian or Chinese mafia, groups which—according to official statements—are assumed to extend their scope of criminal activities to Western European countries (Krevert and Kohl, 1996). It seems clear that the American debates have had considerable influence on the conception of organised crime in Europe (Fijnaut, 1990). It is essentially based on the belief that organised crime will ultimately be transformed into crime syndicates and the belief that crime syndicates are the result of an "alien conspiracy" (Potter, 1994). Ethnic and foreign communities in Western European countries are believed to provide logistical support for foreign crime syndicates, serving as "bridgeheads" and a safe environment for organised criminals.

VICTIMISATION

While discussions on organised crime are underpinned by assumptions of ethnic minority involvement, they also acknowledge ethnic minority victimisation. Ethnic minorities are assumed to be particularly vulnerable to organised crime, in particular racketeering and systematic extortion. While research in this area is problematic (Kelly, Chin and Fagan, 1993), surveys carried out in The Netherlands and Germany suggest that extortion patterns may be observed especially in the restaurant business (Ohlemacher and Pfeiffer, 1997; Mertens, 1994).

The topic of victimisation has not until recently received much attention in European criminology and crime policy. Few studies have dealt with the problem of victimisation, although there is evidence that members of ethnic minorities are disproportionately affected by victimising events, both in terms of criminal victimisation as well as other, non-criminal victimisation (Pitsela, 1986; Albrecht, 1987). Although differences in victimisation rates between ethnic minorities and majority groups may be reduced when other variables are controlled (in particular socio-economic status and marginalised positions in society), effects of criminal victimisation will be more severe at least for certain sub-groups among ethnic minorities than they are for members of the majority group. When considering, for example, intra-family violence, the vulnerability of minority women and children is likely to be reinforced by their weak legal position which may be adversely affected by permanent separation or divorce. Furthermore, knowledge about the availability of victim support services is not widespread among these groups. The traditionally weak position of females in certain ethnic minorities, as well as language problems, may add to the extent of victimisation and its impact on the individual. The bias against research on victimisation and foreign and ethnic minorities surely also reflects biased treatment of foreigners in criminal justice information systems. Police statistics published in most European countries do account for the citizenship of criminal suspects but not for the corresponding status of the victims of crime.

Recent studies on victimisation within ethnic minorities in Germany demonstrate that—as might be expected—illegal immigrants and asylum seekers are virtually non-existent among complainants (Steffen, 1996). For these particularly vulnerable groups of individuals the criminal justice system is—as a consequence of their precarious legal situation—not accessible. Non-criminal victimisation should also be taken into account. Workplace accident rates, abortion rates and rates of psychiatric and psychological problems are all higher in most ethnic and immigrant populations (Albrecht, 1991). Moreover, migrant workers are more at risk from exploitative employment conditions.

Since the beginning of the 1980s, trafficking in women and children as well as labour immigrants has attracted attention in crime policy and research. Trafficking in children has become a topic in the field of international adoption, while trafficking in women[1] has become an issue in gender research. Research has shown considerable problems in implementing and enforcing anti-trafficking laws which, to some extent, can be traced to the precarious legal situation of women being trafficked as prostitutes from non-EU countries to Europe (Heine-Wiedenmann and Ackermann, 1992). However, trafficking in women, and the placement of foreign prostitutes in red-light districts throughout European metropolitan areas, would seem to demonstrate a remarkable process of the successful integration of sub-cultures which to some degree parallels globalisation processes in the conventional economy.

HATE VIOLENCE

Victimisation of immigrant minorities has still another facet which has to be explored. Increasing numbers of police-recorded incidents of violence against ethnic minorities have directed scientific attention to the question of inter-group tensions and conflicts. In particular, violence against minorities may be conceived as a consequence of rapid socio-political transition and its impact on social disintegration. Moreover, this phenomenon extends beyond mere individual acts of violence to the potential for inter-group conflicts which are associated with societies disintegrated into segregated ethnic groups. Modern sociological theory cannot account for such developments because of its emphasis on describing and explaining post-industrial societies. In explaining social integration in modern and post-modern societies, the focus is placed on rationality. However, the perspective of social solidarity grounded on common beliefs and values, as well as feelings of belonging to a certain group, must not be forgotten. In analysing hate crime trends since the 1980s we have to consider why national or ethnic ideologies are on the rise again in virtually all European countries (including eastern European countries). The concept of culture conflict provides a means to understand the nature and extent of risks and dangers posed to social stability and integration inherent in the phenomenon of hate

[1] Trafficking in women refers to the phenomenon of organised recruitment and transfer of large numbers of women from South America, Africa, South-east Asia and Eastern Europe to Western European countries for the purpose of prostitution.

crimes. These dangers and risks are the product of collective reactions, manifested in violent behaviour and justified on grounds of defending cultural or national identities. It may be argued that in modern industrialised countries the locus of stability and integration is no longer a culture based on shared values and collective morals. Instead, it has been replaced by a material culture which does not refer to shared values or cultural consensus but allows for and even demands individual choices in lifestyles, careers and behaviour. Under stable and growing economic conditions which provide access to education, employment and careers, social integration takes place as a consequence of rational choices made individually. But in the case of larger segments of society which are denied access to the labour market, and thus denied the material basis for the emergence of rationality, the potential for the formation of collective reactions increases. Thus, people denied access to the material culture become susceptible to all types of social, religious or political movements, which stress the importance of collective values and responses to social and individual problems. The consequences, then, could be the segregation of societies along various solidarity-producing mechanisms, among them ethnicity and nationality (Münch, 1995).

CRIMINAL JUSTICE AND DISCRIMINATION

Theoretical approaches to the issues of discrimination and biased law enforcement must first be differentiated into those approaches which refer to the emergence of ethnic minorities and crime involvement as an eminent social problem, and those which focus on decision-making in the administration of criminal justice. Approaches to the former category may be divided roughly along the following lines. Scapegoating seemed to be a favourite analysis throughout the 1970s and 1980s, with social and economic competition between disadvantaged resident groups and newly arriving immigrants. Furthermore, the search for new social problems by administrative agencies has been put forward as a partial hypothesis, as has the functional role of the social problem in stabilising political power and attracting support within majority groups. However, with respect to discrimination within the criminal justice system, two dimensions must be differentiated: a subjective dimension which refers to perceptions of discriminatory treatment, and an objective dimension which refers to the outcomes of decision-making in terms of arrest, rates of non-prosecution, adjudication rates, sentencing as well as decision-making in the correctional system (type of prison regimes and parole). Discrimination defined in objective terms can be broken down into two models. The first is the individual discrimination model, the second the group discrimination model (Tonry, 1998). Individual discrimination refers to illegitimate or even illegal consideration of ethnic or racial variables in individual decision-making, be it sentencing, or other decisions. Group discrimination refers to neutral criteria in decision-making which, due to the particular position of minority groups in social and economic structures of society, operate to the systematic disadvantage of those groups.

As far as attitudes and perceptions are concerned, there is some evidence that racist attitudes can be observed in police forces (essentially to the same degree as in the population at large). Basically, one may assume that criminal justice staff and police do not differ greatly from the public at large in terms of attitudes and perceptions. In the area of decision-making, the data available do not indicate bias in making arrests or stop and search activities, although complaints about police harassment of minority juveniles are quite often made. The gap between patterns of decision-making on the one hand, and perceptions and attitudes, on the other hand, can, it is argued, be traced to different motives which are assigned to police activities by various ethnic and majority groups, not necessarily to biased strategies adopted by police in controlling minority and other youths. It is essentially group discrimination that prevails in European criminal justice systems. This is true for pre-trial detention as well as plea bargaining procedures. Neutral case-processing practices and guidelines in deciding upon pre-trial detention may operate to the systematic disadvantage of immigrant minorities. Elevated rates of pre-trial detention among immigrants are common. As immigrant minorities belong to segments of society with the least settled lives, legal grounds for pre-trial detention are found comparatively more often in criminal cases with (especially newly arrived or even illegal) immigrants. Research on plea bargaining shows that minority members are less likely to plead guilty (Tonry, 1997, Smith, 1997). This might be explained by alienation from the justice system and a belief that the system is biased against minority defendants. However, this may work to the systematic disadvantage of minority defendants as trial outcomes are usually more severe than the results of bargains from a guilty plea.

It is evident that the increase in prison populations in most European countries during the 1990s has been due to a heavy increase in foreign nationals and ethnic minority members either remanded to detention facilities or serving prison sentences. For example, between 1990 and 1992 Italian prisoner rates doubled (Pavarini, 1994). This rapid increase was explained by tougher responses to both immigrants and drug offences, reflecting the preoccupation of criminal justice systems with drug markets and drug trafficking, which—as part of shadow economies—are attracting sections of the immigrant population. Incarceration rates for some immigrant groups are much higher than those for the population at large. "Race and prison", once a topic thought to be exclusively North American, now also emerges as a major issue in Europe. For England and Wales it is estimated that the rate of imprisonment for blacks amounts to some 600 per 100,000 of the population, while in Germany corresponding figures of imprisonment exist for Romanians, Turks and other ethnic minority groups (see Albrecht, 1997). Comparing US and European prisoner rates it is clear that a vast difference exists which is ordinarily explained by differences in sentencing styles and the preference for long-term imprisonment in

North America. However, it has also been argued that the difference might be explained by the variations in the size of those ethnic minorities which are attracting prison sentences. The basic difference between the US and Europe would then be reduced to the fact that Europe displays much smaller groups of socially excluded and economically marginalised minorities. If European countries had the same proportion of blacks and other ethnic minorities as the US, it could be concluded on the basis of current knowledge on crime and sentencing patterns that differences in prison rates would disappear.

Prison populations in Europe have undergone considerable changes, with increasing proportions of foreign nationals, in particular among younger age groups. The data in Table 2, drawn from German prison statistics, provides an overview of such changes. Other European prison systems have experienced the same type of developments.[2]

The data in Table 2 demonstrate that there are two processes taking place: first, a long-term trend with a steady increase in the proportion of foreign nationals in the prison population at large which reflects the corresponding trends in immigration. However, a second trend seems to have emerged around 1990 (with the abolition of border controls between the east and west of Europe), leading to immediate, drastic increases in the share of young foreign nationals in the prison population. This trend seems to level off during the mid-1990s.

IMMIGRATION LAWS AND IMMIGRATION CONTROL

Around 1990 a process began in the Federal Republic of Germany which centred on administratively detained immigrants. From several hundred detained persons at any given date in the 1980s, the figure rose dramatically with several thousand illegal immigrants detained (prior to deportation) in the 1990s. This rapid increase in the number of detained immigrants indicates important changes. The roots of these changes are found first in the transition in the east of Europe with the opening of the formerly tightly sealed borders and growing numbers of migrants, poor tourists as well as asylum seekers; and secondly in the Schengen treaties of 1985 and 1990 and their demand for uniformity and in European immigration policies. Thirdly, we must consider those developments in detention practices which are related to changes in the social and legal conception of immigration.

What we observe with respect to immigration and the responses to it are both the emergence and construction of a new social problem, as well as the emergence of social controls devised to respond to that problem.

Migration and immigration are part of the transitional processes which European societies are now undergoing. Eastern Europe, for example, is experi-

[2] The same pattern seems to emerge in Belgian and French prison data, see Brion, (1996, 166).

Table 2: Age Patterns of (Sentenced) Foreign Prison Populations in Germany (per cent of total prison population) 1971–1997.

	14–17	*18–20*	*21–24*	*25–30*	*31–40*	*41–50*	*51–60*	*>60*
1971	2.3	3.2	4.3	3.2	2.9	5.3	4.6	3.0
1972	3.8	3.3	5.5	4.3	3.4	4.9	5.5	3.4
1973	3.9	4.3	6.3	5.1	3.8	5.2	6.6	2.2
1974	3.3	4.6	6.1	6.4	4.6	5.7	7.8	3.4
1975	4.9	4.3	6.3	7.3	4.7	5.5	8.4	2.7
1976								
1977								
1978	6.3	4.1	4.9	7.0	6.5	5.6	8.8	4.6
1979								
1980								
1981	11.9	6.9	7.0	8.1	9.6	6.9	8.9	5.5
1982								
1983	19.2	8.9	7.7	10.4	11.0	8.3	8.3	7.3
1984								
1985	17.9	10.0	8.7	10.0	11.1	8.0	7.6	7.1
1986								
1987								
1988	28.6	16.6	11.9	10.5	10.9	8.5	8.1	6.8
1989	34.9	17.9	13.4	12.3	11.6	9.0	8.4	9.6
1990	35.5	22.5	14.4	13.5	13.0	9.9	8.4	10.2
1991								
1992	43.4	30.9	18.9	17.4	14.1	12.5	9.0	11.2
1993	34.7	34.6	25.7	19.5	15.8	13.5	10.3	11.5
1994	35.1	35.4	31.3	22.9	18.0	15.2	11.5	9.4
1995	31.9	33	33.6	25.3	20.2	15.2	10.5	10.2
1997	30.6	30.2	39.3	29.6	22.6	16.7	10.4	10.5
Ratio 1971/ 1997	1:13	1:9	1:9	1:9	1:8	1:3	1:2	1:3

Source: Statistiches Bundesamt (Ed.), Strafvullzugsstastik, Wiesbaden, 1970–1998

encing social change at a much faster pace than the West, but is catching up rapidly in the field of immigration in terms of concepts, strategies and laws. The construction of immigration problems seems to be heavily influenced by a mix of concerns including crime, unemployment, poverty, illicit drugs and informal economies. Immigrants have certainly added to the list of precarious groups. Illegal immigrants now seem to have slipped into the role of the "Lumpenproletariat" in the nineteenth century. They have become part of the new "dangerous classes" in post-modern societies, or in modern sociological terms: migrant and immigrant populations have become manageable risks. In the analyses of how manageable these risks actually are, however, we also have to consider that besides normative questions related to immigration and asylum, other related issues emerge which in turn shape the manageability of such risks. A black market for illegal immigration now operates and is permanently adjusting to changes in the legal framework of immigration within Europe. Related to it is the informal or shadow economy which operates very efficiently as a result of the ongoing, cheap supply of "black" labour. The more tightly immigration is controlled, the more expensive it becomes and the more it will be organised in order to reduce the external costs for those organising illegal immigration. With this process a basic dilemma emerges: immigrants may, as a group, contribute to the risks of modern societies but as individuals they are vulnerable and endangered persons. Moreover, immigration and responses to immigration are sensitive political issues which can serve as rallying points for political campaigning. Throughout Europe during the 1980s and 1990s new radical and extremist political parties and political movements emerged. These groups have a common and very simple political agenda: immigration, crime, social order, the nation state, and political solidarity concepts based on national (or ethnic) identities.

Reports for most of the western European (and some of the eastern European) countries have demonstrated common features in the creation and implementation of immigration laws and policies (Albrecht and van Kalmthout, 2000). Among these commonalties there is a strong push towards reducing legal opportunities to immigrate (including asylum laws); reducing access to the labour market, welfare and other services; widening criminal law and increasing penalties for illegal immigration, clandestine labour and the organisation of immigration activities; stepping up enforcement of immigration laws in terms of extending capacity for detention, expulsion and deportation; and increasing the capacity for physical control of sub-groups of illegal aliens in terms of secure detention facilities, thus linking administrative and criminal law in important ways.

New criminal law has been created in the field of immigration and asylum, representing a mix of criminal and administrative offences. These offences are directed at illegal immigration itself, as well as at trafficking in immigrants, sharp restrictions in the free movement of asylum seekers (who are placed under the threat of criminal punishment if they leave their assigned districts), and the tightening up of labour in response to clandestine labour. These developments are part of the move from a rather liberal concept of labour immigration in the 1960s towards the conception of migration and immigration as a social problem.

Basically, there are two approaches to controlling immigration and migration:

- Exclusion from entry (in terms of entering a detention centre or airport detention);
- Exclusion after having entered and lived in a country through the withdrawal of a residence permit or exclusion simply because of over-staying or being denied asylum status.

With the first approach a preventive model of control is established which has led, in Europe, to the phenomena of both airport detention and immediate deportation back to the country of origin on the basis of "safe third country" rules.

The second approach implements a mix of preventive and repressive measures. The grounds to withdraw a residence permit essentially refer to those risks which through immigration policies and enforcement of immigration laws should be prevented. These grounds concern basically: having committed criminal offences, having created other dangers and finally poverty or becoming dependent on social security. A combination of administrative and criminal control is thus established which provides for much more flexibility in responding to criminal offences committed by immigrants than does criminal law alone. Expulsion and deportation thus become repressive measures and a punishment which is added to, or exchanged with, ordinary criminal penalties. Administrative procedures may replace criminal procedures, providing greater administrative convenience and fewer safeguards derived from the rule of law. Statistical information available on the number of immigrants detained prior to deportation shows similar trends throughout Europe. It is obvious that administrative detention became more important at the end of the 1980s. This coincided with the political and economic change in eastern Europe, as well as the implementation of the Schengen treaties and the emergence of the European Union as defined by the Maastricht treaty. It is remarkable then, that administrative detention accounts for an increasing proportion of immigrants placed in custody.

As regards the length of confinement of illegal immigrants prior to detention, wide variation exists in Europe. The upper limits vary between three months and indeterminate detention, limited only by the principle of proportionality. In fact, the detention of illegal immigrants was not until recently provided for by Italian law. However, an amendment to the Italian immigration law has revised this position. Comparatively, however, Italian immigration law permits a rather modest period of administrative detention.

On average, detention duration seems to be rather low, with up to several weeks or approximately one month representing the mean. Thus, it is a typical short-term imprisonment, with all its associated problems. However, some cases exhibit detention periods of well above one year. Although long detention periods affect only a small sub-group of detained immigrants, for this group the detention regime which is applied becomes of paramount importance. Although, in principle, all systems accept that detained immigrants should be separated from sentenced and remand prisoners, the practice of detaining illegal immigrants together with sentenced and remand offenders is still widespread. As illegal immigrants are not serving prison time, they should be separated from prisoners in order to avoid the ideological identification of immigrants with crime. Illegal immigrants represent a category of persons who in principle should not be treated the same as criminal offenders. On the other hand, separate and specialised facilities for administrative detention also have disadvantages. Private security staff are frequently used for supervising and controlling illegal immigrants in detention as well as for delivering services. It is questionable whether the combination of specialised units of detention and private security staff actually leads to safety becoming the major goal in detention regimes.

An examination into the relationships between criminal justice procedures and administrative immigration procedures reveals a process of intertwining criminal and administrative approaches in the control of immigrant populations. First, in criminal procedural laws devices have been introduced that allow for the consideration of administrative decision-making when deciding upon the dismissal of cases. Secondly, sentencing decisions may consider administrative decisions on deportation and expulsion as mitigating criminal sentences. Thirdly, the enforcement of prison sentences in the case of immigrant offenders increasingly allows for the consideration of deportation decisions as a means of reducing time served prior to parole. Particular attention should be paid to the length between pre-trial custody, on the one hand, and administrative detention for illegal immigrants on the other. It seems clear that both may serve as functional alternatives, with administrative detention being used to back up criminal justice policies, and pre-trial custody serving to reinforce immigration policies. It is significant that the concept of deterrence becomes central to the arguments on immigration policy, while a review of decision-making in sentencing immigrants reveals that immigration policy goals are taken up—in particular as regards drug trafficking offences—in determining the criminal penalty.

SUMMARY AND CONCLUSIONS

In summarising research on immigration, crime and criminal justice in Europe, we may conclude that

- research on ethnic and immigrant minorities, crime and criminal justice is biased towards the issue of crime-proneness;
- research on ethnicity, race and crime is highly sensitive because of its potential to encourage political and ideological conflicts;
- the categories used to identify ethnic and immigrant minorities—essentially nationality—are over-aggregated, masking significant differences between immigrant and ethnic groups;
- in general, crime among ethnic and immigrant minorities reflects an economically and socially marginal position in society. With increasing and continuing immigration to European societies, ethnic segmentation becomes visible, adding to the 1980s' prevailing conception of societies as segmented along class lines;

- a sharp distinction must be made between resident immigrant populations, migrating groups, and black market participants. The latter two should not be analysed from an immigration or a minority perspective but rather from an economic perspective;
- research carried out on discrimination in the justice system reveals that there is less evidence for biased treatment at the front end of the criminal process, while differential treatment can be observed in prison regimes;
- group discrimination clearly takes place. In particular, pre-trial detention laws work systematically to the disadvantage of immigrants.

The finding that, on all levels of the criminal justice system in the 1990s, immigrants are involved in a substantial proportion of cases, indicates the need to study the general performance of justice and correctional agencies under such conditions.

A substantial proportion of immigrant encounters with the criminal justice system include the risk of expulsion and deportation and the associated risk of administrative detention. This concerns responses (in terms of criminal penalties) towards "old" and "new" crime phenomena. Criminal sanctions for "old" crime phenomena will develop along two dimensions. On the one hand they will differentiate between resident and immigrant offender populations, while on the other hand penal responses will differentiate between criminal offenders who belong to criminal networks or criminal organisations, and individual offenders.

Research into suspects, sentenced offender groups and prisoners have demonstrated in the last decade that immigrant and migrant populations have become the fastest growing groups in the respective populations. By comparison, little has changed for the resident and individual offender in the last decade. Most probably, these offender groups will be subject to the trends in sanctions which have been developed since the 1960s and 1970s. Intermediate or community-based sanctions will play a major role as diversionary practices and non-prosecution policies are implemented. In turn, the role of imprisonment for these groups will continue to decline. An example can be drawn from the Federal Republic of Germany where imprisonment rates for German nationals are still on the decline, while the overall increase in prison populations can be explained by the tremendous (and ongoing) increase in the number of foreign nationals. The migrant and immigrant offender will furthermore provoke the emergence of a new mix of administrative and criminal sanctions, a process which can be partially explained by economic reasons. This mix of administrative and criminal sanctions consists of administrative measures rooted in immigration laws, as well as criminal sanctions which take into account the administrative (immigration) response. For example, a new Spanish criminal law accepts that prison sentences of up to six years should not be enforced if the offender is deported to his or her home country. Similar mechanisms affect the enforcement of prison sentences in virtually all European countries. The administrative detention of illegal immigrants (and immigrant offenders to be deported) is of particular concern. As more and more new detention centres are established, and increasing numbers of illegal immigrants and asylum seekers serve substantial periods of time prior to deportation in these centres, serious questions must be raised about the very nature of such detention.

9

The Other in the New Europe: Migrations, Deviance, Social Control

DARIO MELOSSI

ONE OF THE main recent developments in Southern European societies has been the massive appearance of immigrants on the scene. This has quickly connected with the diffusion of the idea that immigration is linked to all kinds of social evil, including the import of crime. That such a link between immigration and crime is established in popular imagination is not, of course, new. Sociological contributions from famous theoretical essays on "the stranger" which span the development of social theory from Simmel (1971) to Schutz (1944) to Sayad (1996) and Bauman (1997), to a sociologically oriented criminology (Sutherland and Cressey, 1978: 148–55; Ferracuti, 1968), have traditionally countered such a popular idea.

More recent criminological investigations (Tonry, 1997), have accepted that received wisdom but have also pointed out that, in contemporary Europe, specific ethnic and/or immigrant groups are disproportionately involved in criminal activities. This chapter addresses the point of connection between this traditional sociological concern and the construction of a European Union, a process which is characterised by a number of aspects, not only political but also economic, social and cultural. It is contended that, within such an overall process, one finds the reasons why specific contemporary immigrant groups appear to be at the same time more involved in criminally defined activities and more easily identifiable as such. The available research evidence—accumulated within the *Citt à sicure* (Safe Cities) project of the Italian Region of Emilia-Romagna—allows me to discuss only the second aspect of this question, the social, political and cultural context of the "targeting" of such minorities.[1]

THE STRANGER

The stranger has always been a matter of deep interest for sociologists, probably because, as Alfred Schutz (1944) noted, the attitude of the stranger and the attitude of the sociologist have something in common. The stranger is obliged

[1] Further research will be devoted to the more strictly criminological aspects of the investigation.

to behave as a practical sociologist in trying to decipher the obscure messages coming to him or her from a social group with which he or she has no familiarity. Georg Simmel (1971) wrote of the stranger as the visitor who is with us to stay, somebody we can identify as foreign but who, at the same time, remains with us. He is different and carries with himself an air of dangerousness. We do not know what gifts he is bringing for us, *Timeo Danaos et dona ferentes*! Even if his gifts are gifts of trade and knowledge—and not of subversion or illness—they somehow challenge the established ways of our group, they oblige us to question the established way of doing things, they upset us. Of course, much depends on the relative position of each individual in the social structure of the receiving society, as well as on his or her awareness of occupying that position. Those who occupy positions of power will always have a vested interest in reproducing the status quo and will have reasons, therefore, to be more cautious about strangers. Those who have nothing to lose, might only expect good things coming from strangers, given that for them the assumption can be made that any change is better than no change.[2] However, as long as a traditional attitude prevails, an attitude which is often fostered by elites' manipulation of each country's resources of racist and xenophobic discourse (van Dijk, 1993), there will always be, as Sayad (1996) has written, a double suspicion towards the immigrant. The stranger, being already at fault for his strangeness (his accent, his lack of etiquette and manners, his unrefined coarseness in the eyes of the natives, not to mention, his different religion, colour of skin, or politics) will easily be the target for suspicion of all kinds of deviant and criminal acts. If only some stranger will engage in such acts, not least for the reasons that labelling theorists explained so well, the viciousness of the circle will be perfect and the stranger will be found doubly guilty, for his strangeness and for his deviance, already implicit and wholly predictable in his being a stranger (see also Bauman, 1997: 35–45).

CRIME AND MIGRATION

A sociologically oriented criminology emerged this century in the United States in a period when the process of immigration (largely European) was so prevalent that it became one of the main foci of investigation for American sociologists. Indeed, for the most prominent sociological "School" of the time, the Chicago School, the migration process became almost a leading paradigm of sociology. Not only was the migration process a general metaphor for "the social process" but was also seen by Park and his colleagues, as a very positive

[2] One might add the consideration that the current history of the construction of a European Union (Favell, 1997)—in itself a massive experiment at dealing with strangers—could be told from such a perspective, because the divisions within each country between those who have something to gain from openness to Europe and those who have something to lose from it, will increasingly replace the traditional divisions following national border-lines.

process indeed. Migrations (as well as, not by accident, deviance) were not seen as something negative, threatening the purity of the race, or resulting from such impurity, as had been quite common in late nineteenth-century European thought, but as something positive, if not for the individual, certainly for society. Implicitly developing the ideas of Georg Simmel (1908), much loved at Chicago, and explicitly taking a position against the racial theories of Arthur de Gobineau, Robert E. Park wrote:

> "In fact, races and cultures, so far from being in any sense identical—or even the product of similar conditions and forces—are perhaps to be set over against one another as contrast effects, the results of antagonistic tendencies, so that civilisation may be said to flourish at the expense of racial differences rather than to be conserved by them. At any rate, if it is true that races are the products of isolation and inbreeding, it is just as certain that civilisation, on the other hand, is a consequence of contact and communication. The forces which have become decisive in the history of mankind are those which have brought men together in fruitful competition, conflict, and co-operation. Among the most important of these influences have been—according to what I have called the catastrophic theory of progress—migration and the incidental collisions, conflicts, and fusions of people and cultures which they have occasioned" (Park, 1928: 194–95).

These historical conditions produce, on the one hand civilisation, on the other the ambiguous condition of the "marginal man", fraught with possibility but also with pain and anomie (Park, 1928: 205–6; Stonequist, 1937). According to the ecological (cultural) determinism of the Chicago School, the first generation of immigrants would reproduce the characters of the native ecology and therefore the type and quantity of crime of the place of origin. At the turn of the century, for instance, southern Italian immigrants would therefore present high levels of violent crime of a passionate nature, reproducing the reality of southern Italian culture at that time (Sutherland and Cressey, 1978: 148–55). The Chicago School's ecological determinism would not, therefore, predict higher or lower levels of crime for immigrants. The outcome of their move to the new country would depend on the levels and types of crime of the sending country. Indeed, against the sensationalism of the press, sociologists were quick to note that immigrants' involvement in crime was lower than that of the indigenous population. Already the US Immigration Commission of 1911 had pointed out that the "foreign born" were less criminal than the native, a finding repeated in the Report of the Wickersam Commission in 1931 (Yeager, 1997: 147–9). If anything, the problem was instead with the second generation, located between the world of the parents and the new world they had found and characterised by anomie, or "culture conflict" in the words of the sociologist Thorsten Sellin (1938), himself a child of immigrants.

The ending of immigration in the 1920s in the United States also redefined the issue of migration and crime for criminologists. They became more and more interested in the crime of the children of immigrants, on the one hand, and the crime of domestic ethnic immigrants, on the other. Black Americans started migrating from the southern sections of the US towards the great urban centres of the east, mid-west and later of the west. Chicago was once more at the very centre of this movement: on the "mean streets" of Chicago the children of the Italian, Jewish, Irish and Polish immigrants fought among themselves and with the African-Americans recently arrived from the south. For criminologists, the problem of immigration became, therefore, the problem of ethnicity and race, at the same time that American jails were filling more and more with Americans of African ancestry.

It is therefore unsurprising that the immigration and crime theme reappeared at another time and another place, in Europe towards the end of the 1960s, in response to the movement of southern European and Mediterranean people towards central and northern Europe. The criminality of southern Italians in northern Italy and of Italians *tout court*, Turks, Spaniards and Yugoslavians in Switzerland or Germany became the focus of criminological research (Ferracuti, 1968). Methodologically, it was pointed out that the demographic composition of the population was very different for immigrants and for natives and therefore it was necessary to compare the rate of crime of immigrants with the rate of crime of the same group of the native population, especially in terms of age and sex. It was evident that the rate of crime among immigrants was not higher, but was indeed lower than that of the natives.

More recently, there has been a re-emergence of interest in the topic extended to all of Europe. This is because not only the northern and central European countries, but also the southern European countries, have become goals of immigration movements from northern and central Africa, the Middle East, Asia and Latin America. The picture portrayed in a number of recent collections, such as Tonry (1997) and Marshall (1997), in which certain ethnic groups are tied to higher levels of involvement in crime than others, is very uneven. It is also true, however, that these contributions often mix the issue of migration with that of race and ethnicity, blurring boundaries that are quite problematic. From Tonry, for instance, we learn that aboriginal peoples have higher rates of criminal involvement in Australia and Canada; that people of colour have higher rates of criminal involvement in the United States, United Kingdom and sometimes in Continental Europe, and so on. Even where very careful methodological care was taken in scrutinising the composition of the criminal statistics regarding immigrants, as in the case of Tournier's work on France (Tonry, 1997: 523–51), some ethnic groups are found to be involved in crime at a much higher rate than others. However, some of these studies also show that even where intentional (meaning, racist or prejudiced) discrimination was not found, there are forms of "structural" discrimination in the criminal justice system, which are directed specifically at foreigners. This refers to those crimes that only foreigners can become involved in, such as breaking immigration laws. There are also lengthy periods in custody which foreigners have to endure in systems where the way to avoid custodial remand is to be able to show exactly what foreigners are often not able or willing to show, that is, stable and legal residence, work and income, sometimes even their identity. Criminological explanations, such as anomie theory or some variant of culture conflict theory, are then mobilised in order to explain the still apparent high rates of criminal involvement for specific groups of immigrants. Because in the early stages of our study of the Emilia-Romagna situation we were able to concentrate only on the first aspect, the interaction between the native and the immigrant population, this chapter touches only briefly on the more strictly criminological questions.

RACISM AND XENOPHOBIA IN THE NEW EUROPE

As often happens in sociological matters, an element of paradox seems to preside over migration issues in Europe today, largely because those mechanisms which have created the conditions for migration, both at an international and at a domestic level, have also created, at the same time, the conditions for immigrants' involvement in crime and for an "amplified" fear of it.

There is certainly a crisis in Europe today. It takes different forms in different European countries, but there is enough commonality to, and enough spread across, the whole social spectrum, for the designation "European". It is a crisis which is at the same time political, social and cultural. In a sense, the most obvious aspect is the political aspect: the creation of a European Union, and the speedy transfer of sovereignty from the individual European countries to the European Union—a transfer which is becoming even more apparent with a common currency.

The speed and nature of this process is setting the stage for deep troubles in terms of loss of national identity and difficulty in acquiring a problematic new "European" identity. It has already been noted by many commentators that the making of Europe is, by necessity, accompanied by the resurfacing of traditional "sub-national" or "stateless national" regional identities. At the same time, the lack of an actual European system of democracy, for reasons too long even to summarise here, in one way or another can be traced back to the lack of a genuine European "public sphere" (Trenz, 1997), which in turn hampers the efforts at building a type of European "common house" which groups larger than the European elites may recognise as their own. This political, and specifically European, political crisis is happening together with—and it is also, at least in part, a response to—that crux of issues usually referred to as "post-Fordism". In other words, the processes of globalisation and restructuring of the economy, under the leadership of the United States, have put in question the accustomed way of living that emerged from post-war reconstruction. The decisive move of the centre of production from the industrial to the service sector, and the loss of centrality of the old factory-based production in favour of lighter, decentralised and much more flexible electronic information-based production, have combined with the loss of centrality of a male- and union-dominated working class in favour of a sharply divided, largely poorer, disorganised and increasingly female working class. Socially speaking, the wealth of upwardly mobile sectors, eager to consume licit and illicit goods, has accompanied what could be described as a true deconstruction, not only in numbers and power but also morally, of the traditional working class. This has accompanied a political and economic emphasis which has encouraged ever-newer forms of individual entrepreneurship.

It is easy to hypothesise that the principal figures of deviance linked to immigration—drug trafficking, prostitution, black market entrepreneurship—find their roots in the increased demand and opportunity that the above-described situation has contributed to creating. At the same time, it is easy to hypothesise that the traditional sectors of the working class, which have seen themselves displaced by this overall socio-economic change, may identify the arrival of immigrants and their occupation of specific niches in the licit and illicit labour market as the cause of the transformation. Whereas it would be disingenuous, and offensive towards the skills and entrepreneurship of the new immigrant groups, to portray them as simply "victims" of circumstances out of their control, it is clear that their entrepreneurship has in large part been in response to the increased demand and opportunities originated within European societies.

This set of hypotheses is consistent with the results of much recent research on racism and xenophobia (Wimmer, 1997) which has shown that the intensity of xenophobic conflict depends much more on the perception of the threat posed by immigrants than on the reality of economic competition, and that such perceptions are amplified by the accompanying presence of a social and/or economic crisis, to the point of assuming the characteristics of a situation of true "moral panic"—a term that students of ethnic relations seem to have adopted unaware of its long history in deviance studies (Wimmer, 1997: 30). Last but not least, these hypotheses are tied to the fact that such perceptions are not equally spread socially but are the property especially, and unsurprisingly, of the weakest sectors of the working class, those who have been hardest hit by the restructuring process. The fear of the "stranger" would therefore follow patterns of development with which students of deviance and social control are familiar from studies on the fear of crime and deviance. Indeed, the otherness of the stranger and the otherness of the deviant are collapsed in the social portrayal of the criminal immigrant—in the same way in which the reference to immigration largely overlaps, especially in much local and tabloid press, with reference to crime.

Such European concerns with immigration, remind one of the thesis by the American sociologist Kai Erikson who many years ago wrote a remarkable book on the sociology of deviance, *Wayward Puritans* (1966), where he described the "waves" of deviance that had shaken New England Puritans in the seventeenth century. He connected such waves to historical situations of crisis in the colony. His theory was that a community publicly debates its norms and values through the notoriety of famous cases of deviance. I would like to follow Erickson in submitting that, through this central and vexed issue of immigration, we Europeans are conversing about ourselves; who we are, and where we want to go.

The talk about immigrants' criminal and cultural deviance, with which European mass-media are replete (van Dijk, 1993; Ter Wal, 1991), is only in part a vehicle for controlling immigrants' behaviour. It is especially a vehicle for intra-European debate about the existence, nature and essential characteristics of a European identity which appears to be very problematic (Schlesinger, 1992). It seems to oscillate, in fact, between images as different as those conjured up, on the one side, in Habermas's view of a democratic and federalist Europe held together by loyalty to a "constitutional patriotism" (Habermas, 1992), and, on the other, in Alain de Benoist's view of a renewed Holy European Empire (de Benoist, 1991).

At the closing Conference of the European Year Against Racism, held in Luxembourg on 18 and 19 December 1997, the results of a Eurobarometer poll taken about racism and xenophobia in Europe among the citizens of the member-states were presented. The authors of the poll expressed a certain preoccupation with the results, because nearly 33 per cent of those interviewed openly described themselves as "quite racist" or "very racist", Belgium leading the way, with 22 per cent stating they were "very racist", followed by France and Austria (the lowest scores pertaining to Spain, Ireland, Portugal, Luxembourg and Sweden). As may have been predicted, based on the analysis sketched above, feelings of dissatisfaction with one's life circumstances and anxiety about the future were highly associated with negative views of immigration. Other factors that proved to be associated with the expression of racist feelings were: a position to the right on the political spectrum, older age, less education and opposition to one's country's membership of the European Union. Because these findings are highly consistent with those of our Emilia-Romagna sample, we will return to a discussion of these results in conjunction with the discussion of our own research results.

EXPERIENCE WITH AND ATTITUDES TOWARDS IMMIGRATION IN THE ITALIAN REGION OF EMILIA-ROMAGNA

As already mentioned, starting in the mid-1980s, for the first time Italy went from being a source of migration to being a receiving country. In 1997, there were more than one million foreigners residing regularly in Italy and of these the great majority were from non-European Union and developing countries. In Italy most immigrants come from Morocco, Tunisia, Albania, the former Yugoslavia and the Philippines. Whereas many of these people enter the country from the south, most end up living in northern Italy and in the capital, Rome, basically where the jobs, or the chance of making a living, seem to be. In comparison with other European countries, the total number of foreigners is quite low, slightly above two per cent of the population. However in the north, in the centres with higher influx, we easily reach percentages of around ten per cent or higher for mixed marriages and for elementary school pupils who have at least one foreign parent. In the centres of the north, where unemployment hovers around five per cent and is much lower than the Italian average, the presence of immigration is quite visible and in certain sectors of the economy is probably, at this point, indispensable. This is particularly the case in Emilia-Romagna where, in spite of having around the Italian average percentage of immigrants, there is a much higher percentage of regular immigrant workers. Together with Veneto, Emilia-Romagna has been a central driving area of economic development in Italy in the last two decades—a development largely connected with export-oriented, high-quality production by small companies.

According to some, in the same way in which foreigners have replaced Italians at the lower end of the legal job scale, so they seem to have replaced Italians at the lower end of illicit trade, especially drugs and prostitution (Palidda, 1994). In addition, immigrants seem to have replaced much of the Italian "underclass", in terms of their enhanced visibility, with the police and with social reaction in general. Immigrants account for about two per cent of the total population and yet yielded, in 1996, nine per cent of those charged with a criminal offence, 13 per cent of those convicted of a crime and 28 per cent of those admitted to prison during the course of the year. Pre-trial detention is certainly an explanatory factor for this extremely high number, given that foreigners represented "only" about 15 per cent of the prison population at any given moment during the year. In the large prison institutions of northern urban centres, in any case, the presence of foreigners has now reached about half of the total prison population.

This situation, while not reaching the highest levels in northern Italy, is, however, a source of concern in Emilia-Romagna. The regional Government has sought to investigate the connections between immigration and the question of urban safety by commissioning research within the overall "safe cities" regional project. In the spring of 1997, at about the same time as the Eurobarometer Poll was taking place, we surveyed a sample of the population of Emilia-Romagna and, shortly after, a separate sample of the (regular) immigrant population in the region, about their experiences of contact with the "others", and their opinion and attitudes towards them—surveys that were to be preparatory of a second phase of the overall study on the connection between criminal deviance and immigration.[3]

Characteristics of the sample

The sample of the population of Emilia-Romagna (reflecting, as it should, the characteristics of the overall population of the Region), expressed a rather sta-

[3] A full account of the study is found in Melossi (1999).

ble, hard working, well-educated, prosperous, progressively-leaning population; a type of population which should predict low levels of racism and xenophobia. About half of the sample was born in the city of residence, and another quarter in the county, with only about one out of four born either in the rest of the Region, in another region or abroad (only one per cent abroad). More than half had at least a high school diploma and the rate of work activity was very high: full-time workers and the inactive population was about the same (46 per cent) with the rest working part-time (the non-workers were retirees (23 per cent), students (12 per cent) and housewives (ten per cent)). Only two per cent stated they were unemployed or looking for work (the official unemployment rate in Emilia-Romagna is about four-five per cent). Of those working, blue- or white-collar waged work largely prevailed (28 per cent). The average family unit was made up of three people with almost two (1.77) working. Three out of four owned their own home. All were Italians except for three foreigners.

They were quite an enlightened group, it would seem. Only (for Italy) 80 per cent defined themselves as "Catholic" with the remainder stating they were atheists or agnostics. They leaned decisively to the left: about one-third did not answer the question about political leaning, but those who answered defined themselves as left (26 per cent), centre-left (16 per cent), centre (ten per cent), centre-right (ten per cent) and right (five per cent). We also asked a question about their sense of belonging: 15 per cent identified with the city of residence, 13 per cent with the Emilia-Romagna Region, 39 per cent with Italy, nine per cent with Europe and the remaining 20 per cent stated they were "citizens of the world".

Experience of contact with immigrants

How did they know about immigration and immigrants? Most of them indirectly (58 per cent from television and 23 per cent from the press) and only 17 per cent from any direct relationship. However, about half the respondents stated they had known immigrants, particularly in the context of work (18 per cent), or as friends or relatives (16 per cent). The immigrants they knew came from Africa and Eastern Europe. Largely they were very satisfied with these relationships (in 70–90 per cent of the cases). Had they had negative experiences with foreign immigrants (been threatened, assaulted, or experienced in any way unpleasant situations caused by immigrants)? Fourteen per cent said they had. One third of these referred to various forms of harassment and incivility, for instance the insistence of ambulant vendors; 13 per cent had witnessed what they defined as unpleasant situations (public drunkenness, drug dealing), 27 per cent mentioned generic "threats" and finally almost 35 per cent mentioned events that may come closer to being defined as "crimes" (completed or attempted thefts, muggings, robberies and assaults). This amounted to about six per cent of the total sample, not a trivial percentage.

Perceptions of the immigrant

Who are the immigrants, in terms of the respondents' perceptions? Four types of answers were given; about one quarter gave a rather literal and "neutral" definition; there were also those who attached the image of the immigrant to specific geographic origins, usually African or Albanian (nine per cent), or to hard conditions of life (26 per cent). Finally 27 per cent connected the immigrants with feelings, two-thirds of which were quite negative and about one-third sympathetic. We asked whether there was something the respondents liked or disliked about the immigrants. Remarkably, 49 per cent of the respondents found something they did not like and only 28 per cent found something they did like. They liked the immigrants' skills and entrepreneurship, their contribution to cultural diversity; they did not like their insistence and overbearance, their refusal to adapt to local customs, their apparent connection with crime and various social problems. We also asked about the degree of agreement and disagreement of the respondents with a battery of statements, some hostile to immigrants, some favourable, some neutral, which we used to build a scale of prejudice. The general picture emerging from these first questions about perceptions was not reassuring; there seems to be a connection, in public opinion, between immigration and all kinds of prevailingly negative feelings, some openly related to very negative issues (the purportedly criminal or hostile behaviour of immigrants) and others marking immigration as negative *even where they might have been expected to be sympathetic*. Immigration is more easily perceived as something connected to misery and suffering than to social change and cultural enrichment.

The preoccupation with immigration clearly emerged from another question in which we asked respondents to estimate the proportion of immigrants in Italy; the average answer was 12 per cent, an over-representation of about six or seven times (however the sample from the immigrant population gave basically the same answer!). They also thought that there were "too many" immigrants (65 per cent agreed); however, as is usual in these cases, if asked whether immigrants were many or few in the area where they lived, the answer distributed evenly among the various possibilities.

Attitudes towards immigrants

We asked whether we should welcome immigrants openly, welcome them with restrictions, or not welcome them at all, and repeated the question for each main "type" of immigrants, based on their geographic origins. The most favoured were the ones coming from the European Union; followed by non-EU Westerners, Asians, Latin Americans, Central Africans, Northern Africans, Eastern Europeans (the survey was conducted at the time of the "Albanian invasion" scare in the spring of 1997) and finally gypsies. It should be noted, however, that even for the preferred category, the Europeans from the EU, four per cent stated that we should not welcome them at all and 41 per cent stated that they should be welcome only with restrictions, in spite of Maastricht. This shows that attitudes of welcome and cosmopolitanism are quite indivisible, even if within a scale of preference (where prejudice and racism have a role, to a greater or lesser degree, for all respondents). It does not seem to be true, however, as the "Fortress Europe" stereotype would have it, that Europeans unite against outsiders. Rather, it seems that the opposite is true: those more open towards, say, French and German people, are also more open towards, say, Moroccans and Australians, and vice versa. This, in part, has to do with the fact that we still consider the other European peoples, even if in the EU, as different peoples, even if we nominally share a European citizenship. Another characteristic of the respondents appears to be the rather "normal" distribution of their xenophobic attitudes: most have some, with two small radical sectors of quasi-racists and extreme cosmopolitans.

Very few took a segregationist position about schools (six per cent); most thought that immigrants' religions should be taught in public schools; about the same believed that it would be right to build a mosque in the area where they live; only 17 per cent were worried about the diffusion of Muslim faith. Finally, only 22 per cent of the respondents expressed feelings of preoccupation about the possibility of immigrants coming to live in their neighbourhood.

A structural model of prejudice and attitudes towards immigration in Emilia-Romagna

Figure 1 (under the title *campione generale* "general sample"), presents the graphic illustration of a structural model of the material discussed up to this point, connecting a number of "independent" variables such as religion (relig), political leaning (att pol), attitude towards Europe (att eur), education (educazi), occupation (occup), relationship with immigrants (rapp imm), age (eta), identity (identita), to a "dependent" variable which I have called the "prejudice" variable (pregiu), constructed out of the agreements and disagreements with twenty one statements about immigrants.

The variables which appear to contribute to a more prejudiced attitude towards immigration are: a localised identity, a leaning towards the right-wing of the political spectrum, a negative attitude towards the construction of Europe, the fact of not having had relationships with immigrants, and finally being older, employed, less educated, male and Catholic. The results of the Emilia-Romagna 10 sample, then, are very consistent with the results of the European sample, as far as age, education, right-wing leaning and attitude towards Europe are involved, even in a region which is more developed and much more to the left of the political spectrum than the average European region. Furthermore, the observation about the anti-European sentiment is

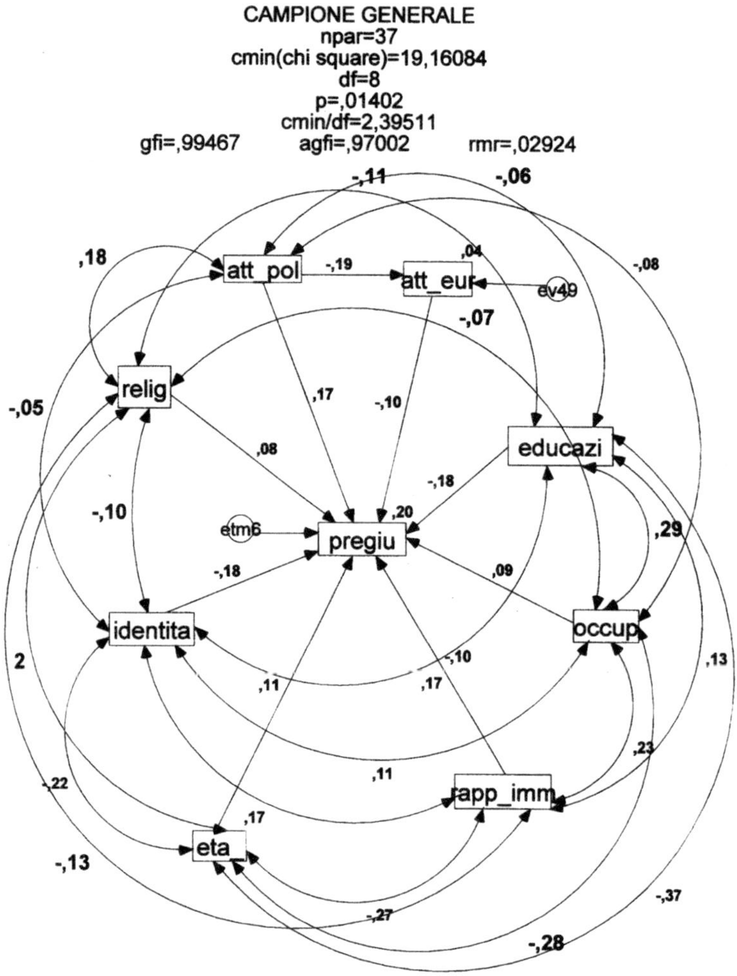

FIG. 1

reinforced by the effects of localised identity: clearly, a higher level of cosmopolitanism is associated with a more positive attitude towards immigration. Other traits, usually associated with conservatism, are also predictable, such as age, a lower level of education and religion (which in Italy essentially means Catholicism). Rather less obvious is the effect of being employed. This can probably be explained by the high percentage of students in our sample, more than offsetting the even higher percentage of retirees because the status of being retired is probably picked up by the effect of age. A quite interesting result is the positive effect of having had relationships with immigrants in terms of reducing the level of prejudice, all else being equal, a result that should be connected with the fact that respondents defined all types of relationships with immigrants as largely "satisfactory".

However, the statistical power of this general regional model is rather weak. Figure 2 (entitled "Bologna"), the same model is tested on a separate sampling centred on the capital of the Region, Bologna. As can be observed, the estimates of the paths are all in the same direction but the statistical power of the model is considerably higher: this is probably because in the main cities of the Region, and particularly in its capital, the question of immigration is much more alive to the public and the currents of opinion about it are stronger and more deeply rooted.

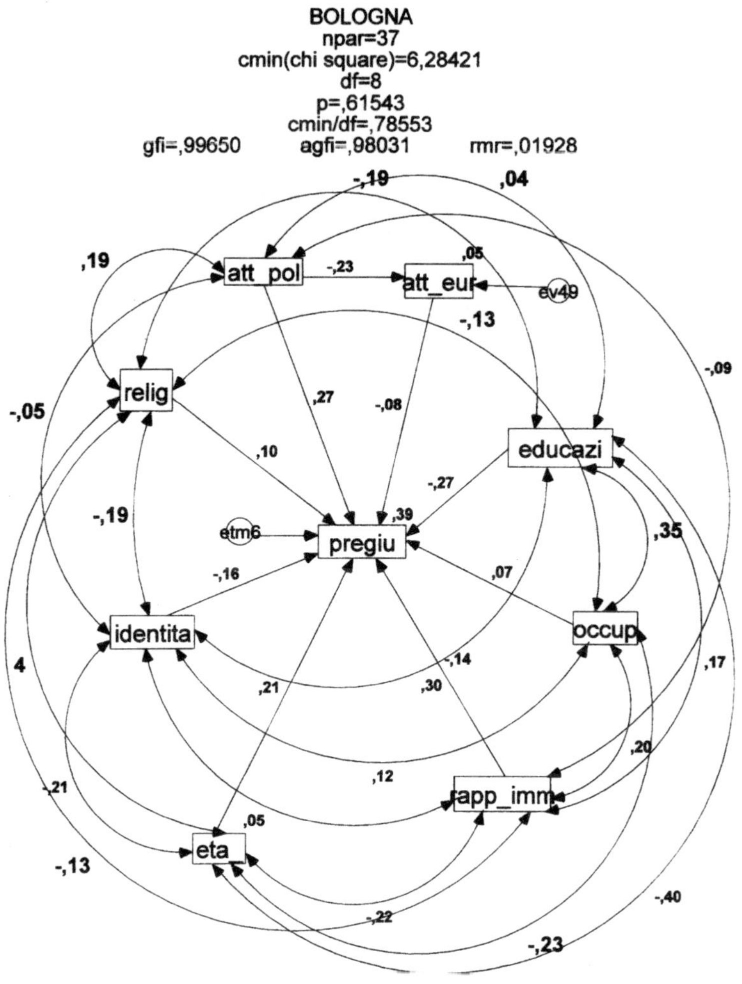

FIG. 2

To summarise, we can conclude from these initial results that:

(1) Factors of self-perceived weakness and vulnerability (such as older age, lesser education, isolation) seem to be connected to a higher level of anti-immigrant sentiment.
(2) Cultural attitudes mainly linked to conservatism (localism, right-wing politics, religion) are also connected with anti-immigrant sentiment. It is hard to tell how much points (1) and (2) overlap but because of the multivariate character of the analysis, I would tend to say that they are at least in part independent (that is, for example, older age and lesser education tend to "correct" the pro-immigrant attitude of those who are ideologically more progressive in the same way in which a conservative leaning tends to "correct" the pro-immigrant attitude of those who, by age and education, should be more inclined to an open attitude towards immigrants, such as students).
(3) Integration is effective in reducing the level of prejudice: relationships with immigrants, in and by themselves, have an impact on a more realistic and less anxious attitude towards immigration.
(4) Our starting assumption, that xenophobic sentiment is certainly racially weighted but indivisible seems to be true: all indicators of cosmopolitanism (a universalistic attitude, pro-European sentiment and an interest in international politics) are associated with openness to immigration. This also seems to be true at a European level and goes against the "European Fortress" stereotype. (This can be read in a positive but also a negative way: positive because obviously Europeans do not see immigration as conflicting with the construction of Europe; negative because probably this depends, in part, on the permanence of xenophobic attitudes within Europe itself, so that Europeans tend to see all those who do not share their (old-State-) nationality in at least some xenophobic way (and in fact we have seen that even if EU foreigners are preferred to everybody else, attitudes of restriction tend to remain towards them)).

DISCUSSION AND CONCLUSIONS

Research about crime and deviance has shown that some factors which increase the fear of crime are exactly the same as those which have an impact on fear of immigration, particularly those factors associated with a feeling of social weakness and vulnerability such as lower socio-economic status, older age, isolation (Hollway and Jefferson, 1997). Andreas Wimmer, in summarising results from current research on xenophobia and racism, has noted:

> "The 'others' become strangers, intruders in an ideal community of nation or race—even the causes of the break-up of this communal harmony and therefore responsible for the many insecurities that the future seems to bring. A kind of 'moral panic' spreads" (Wimmer, 1997: 30, also quoting Werbner, 1996).

"Moral panic" is, of course, a mainstay concept in the sociology of deviance. We have to go back to one of the most basic insights of the literature on the stranger, the idea that the stranger is deviant by definition, the one who is suspect for the very fact of not being of the place, for not belonging. In the popular imagery therefore, especially in the imagery of those who are more vulnerable and less connected with actual social relationships with immigrants, the two images of the criminal deviant and of the stranger tend to overlap and mix together. This is a process that is also fostered socially by specific institutions. Research on the mass-media has shown that most news dealing with immigration relates to criminal stories (such as drugs, prostitution, clandestine entry into the country (D'Elia, 1997)).

The operations of police forces, furthermore, follow the same logic. In a recent intervention at a meeting in Milan, a representative of the police officer union stated that:

> "police officers are not more racist than the average citizen, it is rather that, exactly as the average citizen, they cannot recognise an act as a racist act. From the newspapers, one learns that immigrants are all criminals. To this, one should add the fact that the police officer categorises the world between suspects and non-suspects; and that for him [sic] to find a foreign drug dealer in the street is the simplest thing of all. Then we can start to understand why the courts are replete with foreigners" (*Il Manifesto*, 22/2/1998).

A vicious circle seems to be triggered therefore between objective circumstances and the social reaction to such circumstances. In particular:

(1) A host of socio-economic developments, in both sending and receiving societies, has created the condition for the import of a (potential) workforce from the former to the latter, as well as a very divided welcome in the receiving countries. Whereas employers and the most cosmopolitan sectors of society welcome immigrants as a cheap labour force and as elements of social and cultural renewal, those sectors of society which have been the hardest hit by the social transformations, tend to overlap with those who express feelings of resentment (the older sector of the working class which has lost its centrality in the production process—older, less educated, male, conservative).

(2) A host of central social institutions, for their own reasons, tend to amplify the problems associated with immigration and to behave as tried and true "moral entrepreneurs" *à la* Becker (1964). On the one hand, the mass-media—especially those local mass-media which find their audience in the most backward, conservative and localised sectors of society, and on the other hand the police, for whom immigrants represent at the same time an emergent and unpleasant overburden and a perfect example of what Nils Christie defined as a "suitable enemy" (Christie, 1984). If we couple these pieces of the overall puzzle with the presence of political forces which find the immigration theme a useful card to play in the political arena—and

legitimise, therefore, a racist and xenophobic discourse which in all cultures is there to be tapped into, according to authors such as van Dijk (1993)—then a complex systemic machine is set in place. This is made up of socio-economic change, both in the sending and receiving countries, de-centred, autonomous institutional factors at the grass-roots level, and national politics.

(3) There is however a third element, which we have not yet considered. This is the behaviour of a small section of the immigrant population, attracted to Italy by openings in the illegal job market, exactly in the same way in which most of the other immigrants are attracted by the possibility of work in the regular job market. This is particularly the case for drugs and prostitution, where it is likely that some of the transformations we referred to, in the political and moral economies of the receiving countries, may have led to an increase in demand by Italian consumers. It may very well also be that, to a certain extent, it is the case of an offer-induced demand. It seems to be the case that specific groups of immigrants have specialised in offering certain products, such as specific drugs or prostitution (this will however be the focus of the second stage of the research).

It is necessary to close on a cautionary note, which is precisely relevant to these latter immigrant groups. Because some of these groups, particularly those of African origins, are commonly perceived as carrying somatic markers, towards which there is a tradition of racism in Italy, the danger that the vicious circle mentioned above may end up crystallising the constitution of a true racially defined underclass of the North-American or French variety (Wacquant, 1996), as a classic social reaction or labelling thesis would predict, is a very serious danger indeed. All kinds of social intervention should be mobilised to the end of combating, in the most decisive manner, the possibility of such a development becoming a reality in Italy and in the other "new" immigration countries of southern Europe.

10

On the Globalisation of Control: Towards an Integrated Surveillance System in Europe

THOMAS MATHIESEN

In 1985, Germany, France and the Benelux countries entered an agreement in the little town of Schengen in Luxembourg. The agreement, which was formulated in general terms, aimed at mutual recognition of visas between the countries and strengthened police cooperation. The major point of the agreement was to abolish national border controls between the countries, while at the same time strengethening controls along common external borders. Strengthened police cooperation was envisaged as a method of enhancing the external border controls as well as making up for the internal "deficit" created by the disappearance of national border controls.

In 1990 the same five countries entered a new agreement, again in Schengen. This agreement, which is usually referred to as the Schengen Convention, is a convention implementing the Schengen agreement of 1985. It regulates a long series of crucial questions concerning national and common external border controls, police cross-national "hot pursuits", police cross-national data cooperation, including registration of persons and objects, and so on. In effect, the Convention allows for wide-ranging registration and surveillance of large population groups in the countries concerned.

Full membership of the Schengen cooperative arrangement has always been restricted to EU countries. Until 1999 the Schengen Convention was an intergovernmental agreement outside the EU, and the individual member states had the right of veto. After the Convention was signed by the original five countries, Italy, Spain, Portugal, Greece and Austria joined the agreement. Great Britain and Ireland stood outside, wanting to maintain their national border controls intact.

An important change in Schengen matters took place in 1999. At the EU summit in Amsterdam in June 1997, which concluded a lengthy conference with complicated negotiations (de Zwaan, 1998) between the governments of the EU countries, the EU ministers decided to integrate the Schengen system, lock, stock and barrel, into the EU structure, partly in the first (supra-national) pillar and partly in the third (intergovernmental) pillar. The Schengen Executive Committee was to be supplanted by the Justice and Home Affairs Council (JHA) in the EU structure. The Amsterdam Treaty was signed by the foreign ministers on 2 October 1997 and entered into force on 1 May 1999.

The integration of Schengen in the EU structure will give the various Schengen arrangements, including the vast data-based registration and surveillance system, added momentum and influence. In addition, the "disappearance" of the whole Schengen arrangement into the hundreds of fragmented EU bodies and work groups, and among the tens of thousands of intricate EU documents, will make the Schengen activities, which have been difficult enough to monitor as separate Schengen activities, even more hidden and almost impossible to scrutinise and criticise—at least for outsiders.

The Nordic EU member states—Finland, Sweden and Denmark—have also ratified Schengen within the EU, and the Nordic non-EU members—Norway and Iceland—have entered a so-called "agreement to collaborate" in Schengen matters with the EU (the latter countries do not have access to the EU decision-making bodies, but are members of a so-called Joint Committee outside the EU structure, and may make suggestions and proposals, but do not have the right to vote). At the time of writing, Great Britain and Ireland still stand outside, but on 20 May 1999 the two states formally applied for participation in some of the Schengen activities, notably those related to law enforcement, including participation in the joint data-based registration and surveillance system. The application was made pursuant to Article 4 of the Schengen protocol of the Amsterdam Treaty, and was favourably received by the JHA.

Through Schengen, then, a widespread system and network of police cooperation, data registration and surveillance—from Iceland in the north to the Mediterranean in the south, and from the tip of Portugal in the west to the German/Polish border in the east—is in the making, and is a reality as the 2000s begin.

Space forbids discussion of all aspects of the Schengen system. In this chapter, I will concentrate on the cross-national, data-based registration and surveillance system, with its auxiliary system for supplementary information exchange, which has been operative since 1995. After having reviewed the major Schengen institutions and relevant issues, I will discuss some of the many other data-based registration and surveillance systems which are in the making within the EU. Towards the end, I will raise the question of whether we are moving towards an extensive, integrated registration and surveillance system—a vast, amalgamated police-based data system, with various specialised branches, which, if this is the developmental direction, may function both on the individual and the aggregate level. Individuals may be subjected to particular scrutiny, while large population groups may quickly be sorted out for surveillance and "special treatment".

The development which seems to lie ahead is another aspect of the so-called globalisation process which is currently taking place in economics, politics, and so on. At present, police control is also being globalised, based on advanced information technology.

Bureaucratic registers have been used before in European history for both of the above-mentioned purposes—individual and aggregate registration, surveillance and "treatment". On the individual as well as the aggregate level, the fate of the Jews and other population groups in the 1930s and 1940s is a case in point.

A tragic and concrete example is the way in which the German occupation forces in Norway during World War II used various existing registers, established for other purposes, in persecuting the Norwegian Jews. Over 50 per cent of the 1,400 Jews in Norway in 1942 were exterminated, while the figure for Denmark was under one per cent out of 5,600 (and under 0.5 per cent out of 2,300 for Finland). Why the much higher percentage for Norway? There are several reasons, one being that Norway had excellent registers pertaining specifically to Jews. The Norwegian Constitution of 1814 barred the entry of Jews to Norway, a prohibition which was abolished in 1851, but as a kind of substitute, separate registration was undertaken. From 1866 on, the Norwegian Census Bureau specifically registered Jews as a separate group of dissenters. The census was useful for German occupation forces and for the Norwegian Nazis. The register of the Norwegian Radio Authorities also proved useful. In 1940, immediately after the the German invasion, the German authorities ordered radios belonging to Jews living in the capital to be confiscated. The radio authorities had a register which could be used for this purpose. Consequently, the Jews themselves could also be tracked down (Sørbye, 1998).

Bureaucratic registers may be used for such purposes by police forces out of control, but also by political authorities when the political time is ripe, as it was in Norway during World War II. The new, technically innovative, compatible, hidden and cross-national uncontrollable data-based registration systems which are presently rushing forward, constitute an increased and enormous threat which cannot be ignored by anyone preoccupied with police and political control after 2000.

IN SCHENGEN: SCHENGEN INFORMATION SYSTEM

There are two comprehensive registration and surveillance systems in operation and continual development in Schengen: a data-based registration and surveillance system, and an auxiliary system for supplementary information exchange. The first is called Schengen Information System or SIS. Article 93 of the Schengen Convention states the purpose of SIS:

> "The purpose of the Schengen Information System shall be in accordance with this Convention to maintain public order and security, including State security, and to apply the provisions of this Convention relating to the movement of persons, in the territories of the Contracting Parties, using information transmitted by the system."

As the provision shows, the stated purpose is very wide and comprehensive, comprising *both* "public order" *and* "State security". No further definitions of these terms are given, which means that just about everything may be included, from acts of qualified terrorism through various forms of social unrest to political demonstrations deemed to be a threat to public order and/or State security by the governments concerned.

Broadly speaking, the information which may be stored in the system may be viewed in terms of three major levels or tiers. First, Article 94.3 of the Convention specifies the items which may be included in respect of persons: name and forename, and any aliases possibly registered separately; any particular objective and permanent physical features (an example would be skin colour); first letter of second forename; date and place of birth; sex; nationality; whether the persons concerned are armed; whether the persons concerned are violent; reason for the report; and action to be taken. In other words, the basic information system combines objective (for example, sex) and evaluative (for example, estimated violence) items.

But this is just the beginning. The second tier concerns who or what may be registered, and begins with Article 94.1, which stipulates that the items of information may only be supplied when this is required for the purposes laid down in Articles 95 to 100. Articles 95 to 99 refer to persons, while Article 100 refers to objects. Article 95 refers to persons wanted for arrest for extradition purposes; Article 96 refers to aliens who are reported for the purposes of being refused entry ("unwanted aliens"); Article 97 refers to persons who have disappeared or persons who, "in the interests of their own protection or in order to prevent threats", need to be placed provisionally "in a place of safety"; Article 98 refers to witnesses, persons summoned to appear before the judicial authorities in order to account for acts for which they are being prosecuted, or persons who are notified of a criminal judgment or of a summons to serve a custodial sentence; Article 99 refers to persons who, in compliance with national law, are to be subjected to "discreet surveillance" or "specific checks".

The third tier provides the conditions under which a person may be subjected to "discreet surveillance" pursuant to Article 99, and the information which may be communicated about a person to the police of another country who have entered an alert for discreet surveillance in the SIS about that person. Article 99.2 provides some of the conditions under which discreet surveillance may be used. They are partly rather precise, but partly extremely vague, allowing for discreet surveillance of broad categories of people. Furthermore, and most importantly, Article 99.3 permits discreet surveillance of political behaviour. Article 99.3 states that "a report may be made in accordance with national law, at the request of the authorities responsible for State security". In Norway, "authorities responsible for State security" is equivalent to the Secret Police. Such reports may be made when "it is necessary for the prevention of a serious threat by the person concerned or other serious threats to internal or external State security". There is not one word in Article 99.3 about offences or qualified criminal acts. The procedure to be followed by "the authorities responsible for State security", when requesting discreet surveillance, is detailed in a secret so-called SIRENE manual, which I will return to later.

Article 99.4 stipulates the additional information which may be collected and transmitted to the police of another country who have entered an alert for discreet surveillance. The information includes persons accompanying the person concerned or occupants of the vehicle. The Norwegian translation of the Convention makes clear what the latter term means: passengers.

In short, the criteria for storing information in the SIS is wide and discretionary, many items of information are subjective, and "discreet surveillance" quite clearly allows political surveillance and surveillance of a wide circle of individuals around the main person.

The SIS has a central database in Strasbourg, and national SIS bases in all of the Schengen states. The national databases are supposed to contain identical information, and this information is in turn supposed to be identical to the information stored in Strasbourg. In 1997 the number of access points thoughout the nine states which were then on-line was approximately 48,700.[1] The number of records ("gespeicherten daten", "record entries") stored on 26 March 1996 was close to four million. Germany and France were the largest users.[2] Information was stored about hundreds of thousands of persons and the capacity of the system was, at that time, estimated to be nine million records. For each succeeding year the numbers went up, from 5.6 million in 1997 to over 8.8 million in 1998. The figures are based on the total number of record entries in the SIS on a single day (for 1998: 5 March), and do not reflect the numbers deleted or added during the course of a year.[3] In any event, the system is very large. And, primarily due to the increasing number of states joining Schengen, it will become larger. Further development and technical upgrading of the central SIS base in Strasbourg, final integration of the Nordic countries into the system, increased compatibility between SIS and numerous other European registration systems, among others.[4]

[1] Source: *Statewatch European Monitor* No. 1, (1998) Vol. 1, p. 30, with full text reference to Report dated 25 September 1997 from the SIS Steering Committee.

[2] Source: The Annual Report of 26 March 1996 from Schengen's Central Group.

[3] The figure for 1998 as reported in *Statewatch* (1999), May–August p. 22. The figure for 1998 includes 1.2 million personal data entries and 7.6 million entries relating to objects. As a result of the high number in the so-called alias groups, that is, people who have a false second identity, "only" 795,000 of the 1.2 million personal data entries match actual people. Almost 5.3 million—(70 per cent—of the 7.6 million) entries relating to objects concerned lost or stolen ID papers. Only about 13 per cent of the entries relating to objects concerned vehicles, and other objects—banknotes, firearms, etc.—showed even smaller percentages (only 2–3 per cent concerned firearms); source of statistical information: *Statewatch* (1999), May–August p. 23. In other words, a vast majority of the entries concerned unwanted aliens, deportation matters, lost identity papers and so on, and not qualified crime. I will return to this point below.

[4] Sources: *Work Programme of the Austrian chairmanship in Schengen* (1997) Fall, p. 8; see also minutes from the meeting of 7 October 1997 of Schengen's Executive Committee, as well as *Information News Letter: Information for People Working in the Ministry of the Interior,* No. 1, Sept. 1997, p. 3.

In Schengen: SIRENE

SIS, however, is only one of the systems for information exchange in Schengen. The other system, closely related to and intertwined with SIS, is called SIRENE, an abbreviation for *Supplément d"Information Requis a l"Entrée Nationale* (Supplementary Information Request at the National Entries). SIRENE is intended to facilitate bilateral and multilateral exchange, mainly of supplementary information about persons and objects registered in the SIS, between the national police authorities in different Schengen countries. The well-informed journal *Fortress Europe?* comments on the SIRENE system as follows (December 1996–January 1997, p. 5):

> "SIRENE could best be described as a complex, network-like structure for bilateral and multilateral police and security cooperation between the Schengen countries, including central national offices and a sophisticated computerised information system, enabling the exchange of 'supplementary' data on persons and items prior to the entry of a report in the SIS, or following a hit (positive search) in the SIS."

Through the SIRENE system, police authorities in one country who have arrested a person who is registered in the SIS by another country, may require supplementary information, not stored in the SIS, from the latter country. The SIRENE system has developed alongside SIS, and is far less well known and not even mentioned in the Schengen Convention.

The system *is*, however, mentioned in a draft convention intended for the European Information System, EIS, within the EU. With the integration of Schengen in the EU, the SIS will take over the functions of EIS and be called SIS. But the original EIS draft convention clearly shows that the SIRENE system is designed for exchanging information which is extremely broad and virtually without limits. After having explicitly stated that each of the member states shall establish a SIRENE office with central responsibility for the exchange of supplementary information, the draft stated:

> "When a report is included or action to be taken is performed, the SIRENE offices shall exchange, in compliance with this Convention and their national law, *such further information as is necessary* to identify the persons or objects reported *as well as other information and documentation relevant* to the follow-up action taken" (emphasis added).

SIS, after all, stores fairly limited and standardised items of information. The national SIRENE units, on the other hand, handle far-reaching, non-standardised information or "soft" data. "[S]uch further information as is necessary", and "other information and documentation relevant", are all-embracing concepts or terms, which may include almost anything. This is also explicitly pointed out by people working in the SIRENE offices. The director of the Portuguese SIRENE office boasted of the SIRENE system in the following terms on Norwegian television on 10 March 1997.[5]

[5] Translated from the Norwegian subtitles by the author.

> "The Convention stipulates who has access to the system. But generally speaking, the police have access. They are, of course, at the airports, in the seaports, and can intercept mobile phones. It follows that they have access to masses of information all the time. They don't need to look for faxes. This is a rapid system. It is updated. There is masses of information and naturally the efficiency of the system is much greater than that of the traditional Interpol system."

The police intercept mobile (and other) phones. The information is exchanged between the SIRENE offices. Communication is SIRENE's main task. Communication of information between the police in different states has been on the increase for several decades. The SIRENE system formalises and legitimises the activity, thus greatly strengthening it. There is a comprehensive manual for SIRENE. The manual is secret (confidential),[6] but major parts as well as summaries have leaked out and have already been published (see for example, *Fortess Europe?,* December 1996–January 1997). Clearly, the range of applications is very wide indeed. First, in a relevant article in the Convention which is applicable here reference is made to "helping prevent future crime"—an imprecise category indeed, which implies that no concrete suspicion is necessary. Secondly, reference is made to "preventing offences against *or* [my emphasis] threats to public order and security". The word "or" indicates that the range of applications *goes explicitly beyond any reference to offences or crimes whatsoever.*[7] The article therefore allows for bilateral/multilateral exchange of information concerning highly diffuse matters; matters which may certainly include political activities when defined as a threat. *Fortress Europe?* makes this telling comment (December 1996–January 1997, p. 5):

> "Compared with the amount and sensitivity of information that can be stored and exchanged by the SIRENE offices, the SIS is actually little more than an Index system."

Like SIS proper, the SIRENE system is undergoing continual expansion. The Work Programme of the German chairmanship in Schengen, Fall 1998 (p. 9 in the Danish translation) has this to say about plans for the SIRENE system: "[M]odernization and acceleration of information exchange on the basis of the final implementation of the SIRENE network, phase II [will be implemented]".

[6] The SIRENE manual is a part of the Schengen acquis—over one thousand pages of binding decisions and declarations made by the Schengen Executive Committee. The comprehensive manual is, along with some other parts of the acquis, secret, pursuant to a decision made by the Executive Comittee of 14 December 1993 (itself a part of the acquis, and thus binding on the participating states). The decision states that the manual (along with the other relevant parts of the aquis) "shall" or "should" (from the French "doivent", in the intermediate zone between "shall" and "should") remain confidential "[i]ndependently of the different national rules". This decision, which has largely remained unnoticed, is actually sensational: by internal decree it obliges the participating states to keep the relevant documents secret regardless of what national legislation has to say about the matter. Citations from the Schengen acquis are translated from Norwegian or Danish texts by the author.

[7] The crucial word "or" appears not only in the English translation of the Convention, but in the French original text as well as in all the Scandinavian translations.

IN SCHENGEN: CRIME PREVENTION?

But what about crime? Is not serious, organised crime a worthy goal for surveillance, Schengen, SIRENE and the lot? Statistical information from Germany, as well as statistical information and reports from Schengen itself, show that the Schengen system of cooperation, to a very large extent, is focused on *identity papers and unwanted aliens*, such as asylum seekers who have been refused entry and have gone underground. Despite what political authorities and the police say, crime is not a primary target. This is apparent when we look in more detail at a Report from the German Ministry of the Interior, Fall 1995. The report showed that close to 70 per cent of the 2.3 million records ("datenzätze") which up to that time were entered in the SIS by Germany alone, concerned unwanted aliens and identity papers. Of the 2.3 million records, about 700,000 concerned persons. Of these, 600,000, or about 86 per cent, were registered pursuant to Article 96 in the Schengen Convention, concerning aliens who are reported for the purposes of being refused entry. Some of these may have committed serious, traditional crimes, but surely not the majority. The same report reviews the SIRENE system, which is more detailed, and which indicates that the aliens, to a large extent, were asylum seekers who had been refused entry in to Germany, and who had gone underground (Mathiesen, 1997a: 51).

The same results appear from the German Ministry of the Interior *Report about the Schengen Cooperation in 1996*, delivered to the Federal States in June 1997, and again from the *Annual Report on the State of Affairs along the External Schengen Border during* 1996, published on 20 March 1997, only more clearly so. *The report says nothing about serious control of cross-border crime.* Rather, the returning of third-country citizens to third countries, the control of visas, forged documents and so on are reported. Crimes in a traditional sense may be hidden in this material, but they are hardly conspicuous. A total of 563,423 control actions are reported at the external borders, 41 per cent concerned refusal of entry from third countries, 28.5 per cent concerned third-country citizens apprehended without a residence permit near the border, 24.5 per cent concerned the returning of third-country citizens to third countries, three per cent concerned third country citizens in the possession of forged documents and 0.5 per cent concerned "apprehended people smugglers" ("festgenommenen Schleuser"). Four point eight per cent were unclassifiable due to unreadable reports. It appears abundantly clear that *the crux of the matter is a policy of shutting out aliens* (A policy which has systematically remained uncommunicated by the media and the authorities). It also appears that, in so far as the apprehension of organised people smugglers is a Schengen goal, Schengen border control is a complete failure.

That the crux of the matter is such a policy, is also abundantly clear from an important and honest report from the Belgian SIRENE office.[8] The Belgian

[8] Entitled *The Schengen Information System and its Implementation in Belgium* (1994).

report explicitly states that the SIS is not a "criminal police service", but a service responsible for the control of all aliens who have been or will be refused entry into the Schengen territory.

The Belgian SIRENE report also shows, most importantly, that *the policy of shutting out aliens is intimately related to the maintenance of public order and State security*, thus corroborating in a very concrete way our earlier reading of the Schengen Convention and other authoritative documents. The report states that the SIS is responsible for storing information about "persons reported by the State security" (that is, the secret police). Such persons may also be aliens, including aliens who reside in the Schengen countries, but they may of course also be other kinds of "troublemakers". The secret SIRENE manual mentioned earlier provides the procedure for this.

The emphasis on public order and security in a broad sense of the word is also documented in the "Draft Schengen Manual on Police Cooperation in Maintaining Public Order and Security", prepared by the Schengen Working Group I on Police and Security on 11 June 1997. The draft manual is based on Article 46 in the Schengen Convention—a very broadly drafted article (see above). On page two, the draft manual says (emphasis mine):

> "Cooperation pursuant to the manual shall apply, *inter alia*, to events where *large numbers of persons from more than one country congregate in one or more Schengen States* and where the main purpose of the police presence is to maintain public order and security and prevent criminal offences. Examples of these are sports events, rock concerts, demonstrations or road blockades."

But not only "large numbers of persons" may be involved, because the manual continues as follows (p. 2, my emphasis):

> "This cooperation shall not be confined to large-scale events but *can also apply to the movement and activities of concentrations of persons, regardless of size*, which may pose a threat to public order and security."

Small groups of people may, in other words, also be scrutinised, on very vague grounds.

The cooperation may involve more than two neighbouring Schengen States, and may be extended through the Schengen realm. Liaison officers can attend and work with the police of other Schengen States, and should the cirumstances give cause (p. 5), "police authorities of Schengen States concerned may, with a view to coordinating operations, set up joint command and coordination centres".

In short, while governments and other authorities emphasise the struggle against traditional, serious international crime as Schengen's main goal, all of the empirical and documentary material available clearly shows that the goal is to be found at the cross point between the shutting out of aliens and the protection of vaguely defined public order and State security. The latter concepts may mean almost anything, and may certainly include politically-oriented behaviour. Though non-aliens may be involved, now or in the future, aliens presumably constitute the main threat to public order and State security. The Muslim "threat", for example, represents "a new enemy" after the breakdown of the Soviet Union and disappearance of "the communist enemy".

This is the reason why Schengen has been called "Fortress Europe". We are reminded of our own historical past.

IN SCHENGEN: DATA PROTECTION?

The SIRENE offices in the various countries also administer the national SIS bases. As far as SIRENE goes, there are *no* common data protection regulations (SIRENE is not even mentioned in the Schengen Convention). The absence of a common set of legal rules regulating the SIRENE network has been emphasised as a serious defect by JSA—the Joint Supervisory Authority concerning data protection in Schengen.[9]

As far as the SIS goes, there are data protection rules specified in the Convention. It is presupposed that the contracting parties have taken measures at least on the level of the Council of Europe Convention on Data Protection of 1981. The specific rules are fairly detailed, and many of them may be loosely grouped under two headings: rules concerning *information quality* and those concerning *application security*. Rules concerning *information quality* are those intended to secure the correctness of the information. Rules concerning what I call here *application security* are those intended to secure the proper use of the information.

However, a whole series of decisive problems are attached to rules such as these. *First,* a number of the most important rules concerning information quality—the right of citizens to have inaccurate data corrected or deleted, the right to ask the national supervisory authority to check data, and so on—depend entirely on the practical possibility of having access to the data. If people do not have access, the rules are of little help. In the Schengen Convention, there are wide mandatory exceptions, and in many countries the work registers of the police are, as a general rule, exempt from access.

Second, the application of the rules is, to a large extent, dependent on police practices in various countries, and it is well known that police practices vary greatly. As the Danish Professor of Law, Peter Blume, has formulated it: "Such differences in legal culture [are] an Achilles heal of such regulations" (Blume, 1992: 70). Actual data protection is further reduced by the fact, mentioned above, that there is a total of about 49,000 access points to the SIS throughout Europe, and by the fact that the usage of the system is, in practice, far from limited to the border police.

[9] Source: *Fortress Europe?* December 1996–January 1997, p. 5.

Third, the common JSA, which has been established to control the SIS in terms of data protection, is a very weak agency, largely lacking practical powers and certainly lacking sanctions. The JSA has two representatives from each country. The director of the Norwegian National Supervisory Authority is one of the Norwegian representatives. He had *inter alia*, the following to say about the JSA at a hearing on Schengen in the Foreign Committee of the Norwegian Parliament on 5 May 1997:[10]

> "It is a small agency. There are two [representatives] from each country. They have no sanctions, no secretariat, and as of today they do not even have a phone. A substantial part of the documents which we were supposed to relate to, did not exist in an English translation and not in any of the Nordic languages, so if this is not improved, our possibilities of being an Authority—that is, an authority which is listened to and which is taken seriously by the executive institutions—are probably rather small."

The problems emphasised by the Norwegian director will hardly disappear if the JSA, at long last, is provided with a phone. The JSA issued its first activity report in the Spring of 1997. The report covers the period between March 1995 and March 1997, and confirms that the JSA does not have any sanctions at its disposal, that its work is often obstructed by various Schengen authorities (the agency had at that time considerable difficulties in getting access to the necessary documents), that its budget is very small, its personnel small[11] and its authority weak. The JSA is worried about the many systems of police cooperation which are emerging in Europe (more about this below), and characterise the various sets of data protection rules which exist as a "legal labyrinth".[12]

[10] Translated from the Norwegian by the author.

[11] The 1999 budget proposal for the JSA was 1,050,000 Danish crowns, an increase from 1998. Out of this, 535,000 Danish crowns were earmarked "personnel". Compare this with the budget proposal of 44,110,000 Danish crowns for the central SIS database in Strasbourg (in addition, the national SIS bases are paid for by the individual countries). Of the 44,110,000 crowns, 33,470,000 crowns were proposed for establishing *SIS I plus* and *SIS II* (source: Memorandum from the Danish Ministry of Justice to the Legal Committee of Parliament, 4 December 1998). Establishing the new SIS generations will take much more than one year, and continual modernisation is expected.

[12] See *Activity Report* March 1995–March 1997 of the Schengen Supervisory Authority. For a more detailed and excellent review of the Activity Report, see *Fortress Europe?*, June 1997. The criticism is followed up in later Annual Reports of the JSA. Within the context of the action plan on the so-called "common area of freedom, security and justice" (more about this below) ideas about data protection within the third (interstate) pillar of the EU have been debated for several years. A report of 4 February 1999 (5643/99 LIMITE JAI 3; reference documents an Italian initiative, JAI 15, and a resolution by the European Data Protection Commissioners, JAI 16; presented in full text in *Statewatch European Monitor* (1999), Vol. 1, No. 2 pp. 12–14), sets out—as *Statewatch* summarises—three distinct areas: (1) the exchange of data between EU member states, (2) "common data collection" (e.g. Europol, Eurodac, SIS), and (3) exchange of data by "other bodies". The report (the Italian initiative) "deplores, against the background of increasingly intense cooperation in the Third Pillar, the fragmentation of data protection provisions for various complex information systems (e.g. SIS, Europol, CIS) . . .", and "suggests devising uniform standards which would have to be developed and could then be incorporated into new systems (e.g. EIS) as established elements". This says a lot both about the increasing integration of the information systems, which is openly admitted, and about the problems of regulation. But, as *Statewatch* comments (p. 12), the report "does not address the powers and resources which are essential if supervisory authorities are to be meaningful".

A telling example of the JSA's lack of control of the SIS system was revealed in November/December 1997. Secret documents with sensitive personal information were found at a train station in Belgium. The documents were accessible to everyone who passed by. Sensitive material was also seized in the apartment of a Belgian who had been arrested. The Danish Minister of Justice, Frank Jensen, characterised what had happened as "a serious breach of security in the SIS".

Fourth, even the most precise rules are likely to be inadequate in this area in the light of the rapid and enormous development of IT and other relevant technology.

A PLETHORA OF FURTHER SYSTEMS

Schengen does not stand alone. As I have intimated already, during the 1990s a whole plethora of other proposals, drafts and actual establishments of registration and surveillance systems has developed in Europe. A *surveillant state* is rapidly becoming a reality. At present, Schengen appears to be a core system, to which the other systems relate and are drawn. I shall very briefly give three examples, or sets of examples, of other systems.

It should briefly be mentioned that there are also other systems in the making, such as the CIS or Customs Information System, which according to a German initiative is also to include "suspects" who are, or have been in the past, subjects of investigation, whether or not any evidence of unlawful evidence has been found.[13] The CIS in itself represents fundamental problems of civil liberties.

EURODAC

The so-called *Dublin Convention* (Convention Determining the State Responsible for Examining Applications for Asylum Lodged in one of the Member States of the European Communities) establishes the principle that a single state is to have the responsibility for handling an application for asylum. The Convention contains a series of rules about asylum.

Related to the Dublin Convention there are concrete plans (in the form of a Convention on EURODAC) to establish a so-called *EURODAC register*. EURODAC is designed as a register storing the fingerprints of asylum seekers, but also of other personal data. The register is supposed to be[14] "a European central register". Forced registration of all asylum seekers over 14 years of age in all EU member states is envisaged. Fingerprints are supposed to be "stored temporarily" in EURODAC's central register "for a period of 10 years". There

[13] *Statewatch European Monitor* (1999), Vol. 1, No. 2, pp. 14–15.

[14] Quotes translated from the Danish version by the author.

are only two exceptions to this. The files of persons who have been granted citizenship in a member state are to be deleted and the files of persons who have been granted status as refugees pursuant to the UN refugee convention are to be barred from general use, and may only be used for statistical purposes. At the earliest, five years after the establishment of the central database, the Council shall consider whether the latter files are to be stored or deleted.

Certain rights to have data corrected or deleted pursuant to national legislation are proposed, but since EURODAC will be a work register for the police, those registered will (like those registered in the SIS, see above) be barred from access to the data in many countries. In order to invoke his or her rights to have information corrected or deleted, the registered person may—again pursuant to national legistation—bring an action before the courts or pursue the issue as a complaint to the competent authorities. But to bring an action before the courts is very complicated in general, and certainly an enormously complicated road for asylum seekers in an uncertain life situation.

The JHA reached political agreement ("global agreement") on the contents of the draft convention on 3–4 December 1998.

Independently of Schengen's integration in the EU structure (through the Amsterdam Treaty), Schengen will be provided with EURODAC. The Dublin Convention, which constitutes the basis of EURODAC, has already replaced the Schengen rules about asylum.

Recently it was proposed that the scope of EURODAC is extended to the collection, storage, exchange and comparison of fingerprints of so-called illegal migrants, and not only asylum seekers (van der Klaauw, 1998: 7). In practice, this means the storage, etc. of persons who are crossing the EU border without valid documentation—undocumented migrants. Large numbers of undocumented migrants are in practice political refugees from third-world countries where visas are necessary in order to enter the EU. The extension of EURODAC is planned as a protocol attached to the EURODAC Convention. The draft protocol was up for discussion at the JHA Council meeting held on 3–4 December 1998, but postponed with a view to further political preparation. Agreement was reached at the JHA Council meeting in March 1999. In view of the entry into force of the Amsterdam Treaty on 1 May 1999, the Council presupposed that the EU Commission would prepare a common instrument to supplant the convention as well as the protocol, with a view towards final agreement by the end of 1999.

The history of the issue of fingerprinting "illegal migrants" illustrates how Schengen and EURODAC are intertwined. The issue was, notably, raised in a decision by the Schengen Executive Committee on 15 December 1997, which advocated the "taking of fingerprints of each illegal third country national immigrant whose identity cannot be established beyond doubt . . . and storing of the data for information exchange with other authorities of the member states".[15] The decision on fingerprinting was part of a larger Schengen action

[15] Source: *Statewatch* January–February 1998, p. 1.

plan effecting, "without delay", a whole string of specific measures against so-called illegal immigration.[16] The electronic exchange of fingerprints is possible via the SIRENE network,[17] and the proposed fingerprinting would, as *Statewatch* comments (January–February 1998, 1), "create a major source of information to be entered into the EU's EURODAC computerised fingerprint database when it comes on line . . ."

A Joint Control Authority (JCA) will monitor the processing of data in EURODAC, and check the lawfulness of transmissions.[18] But while it will have rights to "control" and "examine", as well as make "suggestions for improvement", it will, as *Fortress Europe?* points out (January–February 1998, 7), "have no powers to sanction practices in breach of the Convention or of international obligations with respect to the protection and security of personal data".

EURODAC as a "European central register" is so far without precedent in European history. It will imply long-term or permanent registration and surveillance of (and throw lasting suspicion on) large population groups throughout Europe.

Europol

The convention which lies at the basis of Europol, (The *Europol Computer Systems)*, is ratified by all EU states. The Convention came into force on 1 October 1998 and Europol became operational on 1 July 1999. Europol is a joint police unit within the EU, originally—before ratification—established as a Europol drugs unit (EDU), but with an enormous potential for development. In contrast to Schengen, Europol is aimed at serious international crime. At the same time, the data protection problems and other issues are formidable.

As a *Statewatch* publication has put it

> "Europol is one of a number of inter-linking EU-wide computer databases being set up which, once created, will potentially impinge on the rights of a whole range of people for the forseeable future" (Bunyan, 1995: 2).

The Europol Computer Systems will have three main subsystems.

First, there is a *central information system* (Article 8 Europol Convention). Information may be entered about persons who under national law are suspected of having committed or of having taken part in criminal offences under Europol's competence, or persons about whom there are serious grounds, under national law, to believe will commit such offences (Articles 8.1.1 and 8.1.2). In

[16] Source: *Fortress Europe?* January– February 1998, pp. 3–4. *Fortress Europe?* observes that less than a month after the meeting of the Schengen Executive Committee, on 8 January 1998, a secret police meeting took place in Rome, where "police chiefs from the six Schengen countries most concerned by illegal immigration met . . . with the Turkish police chief to discuss practical cooperation in the fight against 'illegal immigration' . . .".

[17] Source: *Fortress Europe?* January–February 1998, p. 3.

[18] Source: *Fortress Europe?* January–February 1998.

other words, the system is clearly geared not only towards persons suspected of having committed any of the offences in question, but towards persons suspected of participation in a wide sense of the word as well as towards a broad category of possible future criminals and possible future offences—certainly, a very extensive and diffuse category.

What kinds of information may be included in the central information system? The system may be used to store, modify and utilise (Article 8.2) certain standardised personal data (name, aliases, date and place of birth, nationality and sex), and, "where necessary, other characteristics likely to assist in identification, including any specific objective physical characteristics not subject to change". The most obvious other "objective physical characteristic" is a person's race. In addition (Article 8.3), certain "details concerning the persons referred to" may be included: "criminal offences [and] alleged crimes", "means which were or may be used to commit the crimes", "departments handling the case and their filing references", "suspected membership of a criminal organization" and relevant convictions. The latter data may also be included "when they do not yet contain any reference to persons". For example, "alleged crimes" may be included without reference to any person.

Furthermore, (Article 8.4), "[a]dditional information held by Europol or national units concerning the groups or persons referred to in paragraph 1 may be communicated to any national unit or Europol should either so request. National units shall do so in compliance with their national law". In short, from Articles 8.2 through to Article 8.4 the information which may be included/communicated is continuously widened, ending with the catch-all "[a]dditional information".

Second, there are the *work files for the purposes of analysis* (Article 10 Europol Convention). These are special, temporary work files set up for the analysis of specific areas of activity. The work files may contain extensive personal data, not only (Article 10.1 No. 1) about persons registered in the central information system pursuant to Article 8.1, but also (Article 10.1 Nos 2–5) about:

- possible witnesses ("persons who might be called on to testify");
- victims or persons whom there is reason to believe could be victims (". . . with regard to whom certain facts give reason for believing that they could be victims . . .");
- "contacts and associates"; and
- informants ("persons who can provide information on the criminal offences under consideration").

In short, a very wide circle of individuals loosely tied to persons who have been sentenced or are under suspicion.

Third, there is *an index system*, designed in such a way that it is possible to determine whether or not a given item of information is stored.

Let us look more closely at the second of these levels, *the work files*. The kinds of personal information which may be stored in the work files are not specified in the Convention, only in so-called "implementation rules", given pursuant to the Convention. The implementation rules are not to be approved by parliaments, only unanimously by the Council (Europol Convention, Article 10.1). There is already full agreement on the final proposal for implementation rules in the JHA Council (according to minutes from the JHA Council meeting on 24 September 1998). The rules were approved by the Europol Management Board in October 1998, pending formal adoption by the Council. The implementation rules stipulate that, under certain conditions, sexual inclination, membership of political organisations and the like may be registered. It should be noted that the EU data protection Directive 95/46EF (Article 3.2) explicitly exempts the Directive *inter alia*, from being applicable to "the activities of the State in areas of criminal law". Inclusion of the sensitive information mentioned here, in other words, falls outside the jurisdiction of the Directive.

The final proposal for implementation rules applicable to work files (doc. 6100/4/97) allows (in Article 6) the processing of 53 types of personal data about persons registered in the central information system. The 53 types of personal information are grouped in ten categories, for example "personal details" (14 types of data), "physical appearance" (two types of data), "identification means" (five types of data; including forensic information such as fingerprints and DNA evaluation results, though "without information characterizing personality"), occupation and related qualifications (five types of data), "economic and financial information" (eight types of data), "behavioural data" (eight types of data; including "life style (such as living above means) and routine"), "danger rating" and "criminal related traits and profiles") and so on.

One of the other categories is named "references to other databases in which information on the person is stored", including Europol, police/customs agencies, other enforcement agencies, international organisations, public bodies and private bodies.

To reiterate, the above-mentioned types of data may not only be included about persons registered in the central information system, but also about possible witnesses, victims or persons whom there is reason to believe could be victims, contacts and associates, and informants.

To be sure, a joint supervisory body will be established pursuant to Article 24 in the Europol Convention. The draft rules of procedure for the Joint Supervisory Body were considered by the JHA on 24 September 1998, and again on 3–4 December 1998. In the minutes from the latter meeting, taken from the Internet, vague terms like "reviewing" the activities of Europol to ensure that the rights of the individual are not violated and "monitor" the permissibility of the transmission of data originating from Europol are used.

A protocol attached to the Europol Convention, pursuant to Article 41.1 of the Convention, gives diplomatic immunity for Europol officers within the EU countries. Article 8 of the protocol grants all Europol staff "immunity from the legal process of any kind in respect of words spoken or written, and of acts performed by them, in the exercise of their official functions". The protocol on privileges and immunities is ratified by all EU states. With the Convention as well as the protocol ratified, and agreement on the rules of procedure for the Joint Supervisory Body, Europol is ready to become fully operational, and is expected to be so before the end of 1999.

The system is planned with a view to far-reaching integration, *inter alia*, with the SIS. For one thing, Article 10.4 Nos 1–3 in the Europol Convention establishes a whole range of authorities and bodies within the EU from which Europol may request information. In a secret proposal of 9 April 1997 the so-called High Level Group on Organised Crime explicitly recommended, in line with this, that Europol is given access to the information stored in the SIS.[19] This and other recommendations were on the agenda of the Justice and Home Affairs' council meeting held on 3–4 December 1998 in connection with the action plan on establishing an area of freedom, security and justice, and were also discussed in a report of 26 February 1999 (6245/99 Europol 7). The report *inter alia* discussed the issue of whether Europol's authority should be extended to actual searches in the SIS.[20] Pursuant to the Europol Convention Article 3 (1) point 2 Europol has the task to obtain, collate and analyse information and intelligence, but no authority to search. Furthermore, concrete work directed towards facilitiating and easing compatibility between the two systems has been going on for a long time (Frigaard, 1996). After the Interpol meeting in Oslo in the Spring of 1999, the head of the Criminal Investigation Department, which will become the SIRENE office and in charge of the SIS when it is established in Norway, made the following interesting statement:

> "The Department is already connected with Interpol, and the contact with Schengen is also with us. If Norway gets an agreement with Europol, we will use the same people in our contact with them. . . . It is important to get an agreement with Europol, especially when you see how closely Denmark, Sweden and Finland are tied to the activity there. Norway has to become a part of the big family" (*Aftenposten* (1991), 31 May).

Once more, such access and integrative cooperation will be greatly facilitated through the Amsterdam Treaty.

Surveillance of telecommunications

In November 1995 a *Memorandum of understanding on the lawful interception of telecommunications* was signed by the EU countries. The Memorandum emphasises that law enforcement ("combating serious crime and protecting national security") requires such interception. The Memorandum refers in general terms to "law enforcement agencies", without any clear delimitation. In the background was an FBI initiative and an important meeting at the FBI academy in Quantico, Virginia. The initiative comprises a group of 20 countries, either

[19] Source: Personal communication from Nicholas Busch, editor of *Fortress Europe?*

[20] See *Statewatch European Monitor* (1999), Vol. 1 No. 2, pp. 14–17

meeting in Quantico or joining later, the "Quantico group". The group established the so-called "International Law Enforcement Seminar", ILETS, which has operated as a pressure group in the area of interception. Currently, the Memorandum is being updated within the EU. A new EU Draft Convention on Mutual Legal Assistance in Criminal Matters will *inter alia,* legitimise such surveillance. Referring to Article 6.2, a–c in the draft Convention, *Fortress Europe?* (May 1998, 4) comments:

> "The rules are worded so as to enable the interception without interruption in the whole territory of the EU, even of persons, quickly moving between different Member States and using any type of fixed or mobile telecommunication devices and structures."

Currently, bodies within the EU structure are working to extend the telecommunications plans to the Internet (e-mail) and to the new generation of satellite mobile phones.

The plans may be found in what has been named the "ENFOPOL papers". The documents are very secret. The journal *Telepolis* has, however, revealed some of its activities.[21]

Plans are in the making for monitoring any and all kinds of telecommunication data, whether encrypted or in clear form, mobile telephony, the new Iridium system and other satellite mobile phone services. Armin Medosch commented in a summary of the reports on the ENFOPOL papers, they are

> "aiming at the central terrestrial master station of Iridium in Italy as an ideal spot to monitor telecommunications traffic. But also large clearing houses which handle international phone call billing for the big national operators are mentioned as potential sources for the kind of information European police forces are interested in" (Telepolis, 30 November 1998 (www as above)).

At the moment, the plans are not a reality, but a set of proposals. But discussions have commenced in the JHA. Are, then, plans of this kind technically feasible? The so-called *Echelon* system, which *is* a reality, shows that they are.

While the FBI–EU initiative and related activities mentioned above will serve the "law enforcement community", Echelon serves the "military intelligence community". Unlike many of the electronic military intelligence systems developed during the cold war, Echelon is designed just as much for non-military targets—governments, organisations and businesses throughout the world. The US, Britain, Canada, New Zealand and Australia are the main participants, with the US as senior partner. A report to the European Parliament by Steve Wright[22] describes the activities of Echelon in the following words which, in terms of the technology described, is also relevant to the plans relating to law enforcement:

[21] (http://www.telepolis.de/tp/deutsch/special/enfo6329/1.html).

[22] Steve Wright: *An Appraisal of Technologies of Political Control*, PE 166.499. Revised September 1998.

> "A wide range of bugging and tapping devices has been evolved to record conversations and to intercept telecommunications traffic. . . . However, planting illegal bugs . . . is yesterday's technology. . . . [T]hese bugs and taps pale into insignificance next to the national and international state run interception networks. . . . Modern technology is virtually transparent to the advanced interceptions equipment which can be used to listen in. . . . Within Europe, all email, telephone and fax communications are routinely intercepted by the United States National Security Agency, transferring all target information from the European mainland via the strategic hub of London then by Satellite to Fort Meade in Maryland via the crucial hub in Menwith Hill in the North York Moors of the UK. . . . The Echelon system works by indiscriminately intercepting very large quantities of communications and then siphoning out what is valuable using artificial intelligence aids like Memox to find key words. Five nations share the results. . . . Each of the five centres supply 'dictionaries' to the other four of key words. Phrases, people and places to 'tag' and the tagged intercept is forwarded straight to the requesting country . . ." (pp. 18–19).

Echelon's technology is geared towards the interception of telecommunications via satellite. A substantial part of telecommunications today is transported via submarine cables across the oceans. Submarine cables are more difficult to intercept (though easy to intercept as they enter into or come up from the ocean). But the future is with the satellites. On 1 November 1998 the world's first global, mobile telephone network was launched (and called the world's first "virtual nation" by its promoters). The network is named "Iridium". Others will follow. For example, the satellite network Teledesic (with Microsoft's Bill Gates as one of the owners) is planned to be launched in 2003, and will be used for high velocity Internet. *Echelon's technology is apparently well suited to the interception of all these networks.*

It is Steve Wright's point that the US National Security Agency is deeply involved in Echelon. The US National Security Agency, NSA, was established in 1952 by president Harry Truman. This powerful agency plans, coordinates and executes signal intelligence as well as tasks concerning information security. It is concerned with non-defence as well as defence issues. A main point is to break through and understand foreign communications while at the same time protecting the nation's own communication systems. In this double task lies NSA's main goal and competence. NSA is the world's leading cryptological organisation.

The NSA is indeed an active agency. In July 1999 *The New York Times* revealed that the NSA had developed a plan for massive electronic surveillance. The plan, entitled "The National Plan for Information Systems Protection", was presumably directed towards protecting US data systems against hackers, data terrorists and enemy states; in other words, information security. The plan, however, included strategies to establish a large-scale domestic and international Internet monitoring system, to be used by the FBI. One of the plan's proposals called for the creation of a Federal Intrusion Detection Network, FIDNET, to monitor all network activity involving civilian government departments and agencies. FIDNET was to be linked to a similar system in the Defense Department known as the Joint Task Force-Computer Network Defense (JTF-CND) that monitors all Defense Department networks. Both of them were in turn to be linked to private sector Information Sharing and Assessment Centers (ISAC), which would monitor network activity in telecommunications, banking and other sectors. The plan was an outgrowth of recommendations made in the October 1997 Report of the President's Commission on Critical Infrastructure Protection (PCCIP) and in Presidentlal Decision Directive 63 (PDD 63) on Critical Infrastructure Protection issues in May 1998. Civil rights organisations, such as Electronic Privacy Information Center (EPIC), launched a massive criticism of the plan, arguing that the authorities would be able to monitor all data traffic, including private e-mail, whereupon the White House stated that the plan had not yet been approved by the President and that it would be undergoing a legal review. The House committee sent the fiscal 2000 budget to the full House with language barring the Justice Department spending on FIDNET. Thus, the plan was temporarily aborted, but it will no doubt be rephrased and will turn up again. This is not the first time the NSA has tried to introduce massive monitoring systems. The "Clipper Chip" was its first attempt, also under the Clinton Administration. A chip was to be installed in all telephones, modems and faxes which would make the communication content understandable to law enforcement agencies. Again, massive protests followed.[23]

The relationship between the recent NSA initiatives and Echelon is unknown, but no doubt one does exist.

TOWARDS AN INTEGRATED SYSTEM

The basic point of this chapter is that there is a tendency towards convergence and integration between the various registration and surveillance systems—established or in the making—in Europe. Though there are obstacles and different or conflicting interests involved, the tendency has a momentum on the political as well as the policing levels. The Amsterdam Treaty, which integrates Schengen into the EU structure, will give added momentum to this tendency. A Schengen which has "disappeared" into the EU structure, will no longer have its own decision-making structure, so that amalgamation with Europol, EURODAC and so on will be much closer at hand.

On the horizon we may envisage the contours of a vast, increasingly integrated multinational registration and surveillance system, with information floating more or less freely between subsystems, at any time covering large population groups. A full technical integration, in the sense that virtually everyone

[23] Sources: the civil rights' organisation EPIC, and the Internet journals Digi.no and ZDNet; http://www.epic.org; http://w3.digi.no; http://www.zdnet.com; http://www.wired.com.

in the police would have access to almost all information, would undermine secrecy, and secrecy is a dominant police value and functional necessity. In fact, this is already considered to be a problem in the Schengen context by the Secret Police in several countries (for example Norway). However, as previously alluded to, the point would be to have special branches catering to special issues, but with extensive cooperation between key people and numerous links between the various branches. Thus, the various systems which I have described could well continue to exist, and there could well be barriers between them, but the barriers would not exist for key personnel or groups of personnel, who could avail themselves of the continually expanding number of links. Judging from SIS figures today (available sources indicate that about 700,000 persons are at present registered in the SIS), we must reckon with millions of people in a more or less integrated future system. A minority of persons will be registered because they have demonstrably committed crimes, and another minority because they are concretely suspected of crimes. A large majority will consist of people in an extremely wide circle around such persons, as well persons who in a diffuse sense are viewed as threats to public order and state security and unwanted aliens. The system will be future-oriented, geared towards presumed or possible future acts.

A vast, amalgamated police-based data system of the kind envisaged above, with various specialised branches, may function both on the individual and the aggregate level. Individuals may be subjected to registration and surveillance, while whole population groups may quickly be sorted out for "special treatment". The system may be used for political purposes by police forces as well as through political institutions.

I have suggested that, at present, Schengen is a centre of gravity among the plethora of other systems. Schengen is already on wheels. But this may change as the systems proceed towards integration. Now that Europol is operational, and when the Europol Computer Systems become fully operational (probably towards the end of 2001), those systems may well take the lead and become the central locus of the integrated system. The enormous potential of the Europol Computer Systems, with the various work files in addition to the central information system, as well as the development of operative functions and the immunities and privileges of Europol's personnel, suggest that Europol in the (near?) future will become a centre of power, with communication channels and power lines to the other systems.

THE PANOPTICAL MACHINE—AND SYNOPTICISM

Michel Foucault's description of modern society as a "panoptical machine" (Foucault, Eng. edn, 1979: 217, original French edn, 1975) was even more apt than he thought back in 1975, when he wrote his famous book on surveillance and punishment.

The concept of "panopticism", which Foucault borrowed from Jeremy Bentham, derives from the Greek word *pan*, meaning "all", and *opticon*, which represents the visual. In a panoptical situation, a small group of observers—in principle one observer—is able to watch a whole multitude of people, and, in a panoptical society, a large segment or the whole population is similarly watched. Foucault, like Bentham before him, described the development of the modern prison as a development towards panopticism. But Foucault goes further. "In appearance", Foucault says, panopticism "is merely the solution of a technical problem, but, through it, a whole new type of society emerges" (1979, 216), transported "from the penal institution to the entire social body" (1979, 298). Though he did not discuss modern computerised registration and surveillance systems, his analysis may well be utilised as a theoretical framework for an understanding of the development of such systems. The likely development towards a more or less integrated, totalised registration and surveillance system in Europe implies a development towards a vast "panoptical machine" which may be used for registration and surveillance of individuals as well as whole categories of people, and which may well become one of the most repressive political instruments of modernity.

To be sure, panoptical registration and surveillance systems have existed before in history. The Church had them, the Inquisition had them, the Military had them; in a sense, they are archaic (see Mathiesen, 1997b). But never before in history have they been so inclusive, and so technically advanced and innovative, and never before in history have they developed so suddenly and rapidly. Within the span of 30 years the computerisation of registration and surveillance has suddenly become a reality and has developed in leaps and bounds, thus reaching a new and entirely different level of sophistication, and, as I have said, a developmental tendency towards integration.

This is all the more threatening because few institutions exist which might monitor critically what is going on. The various national supervisory committees, Schengen's Joint Supervisory Authority and similar institutions, are, as we have seen, close to worthless from the point of view of control. Parliaments are not equipped with enough knowledge and insight, and not with enough power, and the mass media—the only set of institutions which in principle has significant power to monitor and even control developments—is not doing their job.

As a parallel to the developing panopticism, there is, through the mass media, a developing *synopticism*. The concept is composed of the Greek word *syn* which means "together" or "at the same time", and *opticon*, which, again, has to do with the visual. Not only are we increasingly moving towards a panoptical situation where the few may see and monitor the many, we are also—especially through television—increasingly moving towards an opposite synoptical situation where many may see and monitor the few. I have outlined the details of this double development elsewhere (Mathiesen, 1997b); suffice to say here that synopticism, where the many see the few, is also archaic: Rome's Colosseum, the emperor admired by the crowd when returning victoriously from battle and the Catholic priest giving his sermon from the pulpit in the cathedral are only a few of the many examples. But like the development towards panopticism, the synoptical development, through television, has accelerated tremendously in modern times. Millions, at times hundreds of millions, watch the few that television focuses on. Historically, we have seen many examples of panopticism and synopticism combined. But the recent acceleration of the two developmental trends shows particularly striking concurrences in time, as if they were synchronised, and striking similarities in technology as well as overlap in personnel (Mathiesen, 1997b).

The synoptical mass media, especially television, contain great possibilities for aggressive and critical control of panoptical institutions. But the opportunities are not utilised. As the synoptical mass media developed, they became increasingly and almost unavoidably commercial targets. The commercialisation of television, and the emphasis on profit following from that, has transformed the latent possibilities of television into an enormous entertainment industry (Postman, 1985)—the ancient Colosseum one thousand times enlarged. The few who are watched by and produce messages to the many are the VIPs, the entertainers, the celebrated stars, almost a new class in the public sphere and, on the political level, key political figures in highly staged settings. All of them become entertainers in the service of the entertainment industry, as do the participants in the many television "debates", tranformed and degenerated as they are into regular talk shows. Though there are exceptions, in so-called critical journalism a president's sex life is much more important than his policies. In such a situation, the development of panopticism, though politically threatening and potentially extremely dangerous, is left almost entirely untouched. Monitoring such complex phenomena is left to the narrow journals, conferences and books, in the remote and uninfluential outskirts of public space.

With the start of the twenty-first century, this is what lies ahead in the West; a population born and raised in the age of synoptical entertainment, consequently entirely unprepared for the great potential of growing panoptical power.

Reminiscent of the 1930s, extremist right-wing movements are largely left unresisted and thriving by the unprepared population. Indeed, they are pushed forward by being invited to participate—and wave the flag—in the synoptical entertainment business, not because of any democratic right to participate, but because they fit excellently into the many polarised entertaining "debates" on the television stage. This is not the only reason why the right-wing is on the march, but it is one of them. In the hands of an extremist right wing regime, the potential of panoptical power will be even greater. Watchful panoptical surveillance of and action against dissident individuals and groups, will be coupled with the political peace, quiet and absence of criticism created and maintained by the synoptical entertainment industry.

CONCLUSION: AN ALTERNATIVE PUBLIC SPACE?

The situation requires resistance. A full analysis of resistance strategies goes beyond the limits of this chapter (for a discussion, see Mathiesen, 1982); here I will consider only *one* line of thinking.

The key phrase is "alternativ offentlighet" in Norwegian, "Alternative Öffentlichkeit" in German, and in English the much more cumbersome "alternative public space". The point is to contribute to the creation of an alternative public space where argument, well-founded criticism and principled thinking represent the dominant values. I envisage that the development of an alternative, critical public space, whether targeted against the globalisation of surveillance or other issues, would contain three ingredients.

First, liberation from what I would call the absorbent power of the mass media, which I have touched on elsewhere (Mathiesen, 1996). The definition of the situation implies that one's existence is dependent on media interest, media coverage and especially television coverage. Without media coverage, presumably I do not exist, my organisation does not exist, the meeting has not taken place. Relying on that definition of the situation, the actor is inescapably absorbed into the media entertainment business as the only alternative to non-existence, whereupon the content of the actor's message dwindles at the expense of his or her entertainment value. In Western society, it is probably impossible to refrain completely from media participation. At certain crossroads you are faced with a conflict: if you do not say something on television, others holding the opposite opinion will fill the empty space. But it is certainly possible to be very selective, and to say "no!" to the many talk shows and entertainment-like "debates" which flood our various television channels. Most importantly, it is certainly possible not to let the definition of one's success and very existence be dependent on the media.

The second ingredient is a restoration of the self-esteem and feeling of worth on the part of the grass-roots movements. It is not true that the grass-roots movements, emphasising network organisation and solidarity at the bottom, have died out. But with the development of the mass media, with television as their modern spearhead, these movements have lost faith in themselves. There is an important example from recent Norwegian history of the vitality of grass-roots movements. In 1993, thousands of ordinary Norwegians participated in a widespread movement to give refugees from Kosovo–Albania long-term refuge in Norwegian churches throughout the country. The movement ended in a partial victory, in that all of the cases concerning Kosovo–Albanian refugees were reviewed again by the Ministry of Justice. The example suggests that grass-roots solidarity even with "distant" groups like refugees did not die out with the Vietnam war.

The third ingredient is a restoration of the feeling of responsibility on the part of intellectuals, comprising a broad range of artists, writers, scientists—and certainly social scientists. That responsibility should partly be directed towards a refusal to become a part of the mass media show business, and partly towards re-vitalisation of artistic work, writing and research taking the interests of common people as the point of departure. This point is not new, but goes back many decades in Western intellectual history. The area is full of conflicts and problems, but they are not unsolvable.

In the area of penal policy, we have tried to achieve some of these objectives in Norway, in the organisation KROM, the Norwegian Association for Penal Reform. KROM is a strange hybrid, comprising intellectuals and prisoners, with a common cause. By organising large conferences on penal policy every year (holding them in the same place—a mountain resort outside Oslo—to create a tradition), with wide participation from the whole range of penal policy professions and agencies as well as many prisoners, and also by organising regular seminars and other activities, we try to create *a network of opinion and information* crossing the formal and informal borders between segments of the relevant administrative and political systems. The point is precisely that of trying to create an alternative public space where argument, well-founded criticism and principled thinking are dominant values, a public space which may at least, to some extent, compete with the superficial public space of the mass media.

The same may be achieved in the area of surveillance. Again, the public sphere of television and other mass media is not the only public sphere. The point would be for criminologists, sociologists of law and other social scientists, but also for a wide cross-section of professions such as teachers, authors, songwriters, actors, musicians and so on, to develop jointly a public space of critique and discussion of the deeply disturbing issues involved. This would necessarily imply some limited participation in the public sphere of television, but mostly it would imply independent public work and publicity through the various channels of communication and networks in which such a broad spectrum of professionals is involved. The *joint* character of the effort would probably be achieved gradually, as the movement developed. The excellent journals *Fortress Europe?* and *Statewatch* constitute important beginnings by continuously providing precise details of what is going on. Others would have to follow, in and across their respective networks. Plays and novels would have to be written, for example, a modern version of *1984*. Through the development of such an alternative public space of discussion and critique of the surveillant state, warnings and information could reach sizeable segments of the population. When people are informed beyond the intricate technicalities which are so difficult to comprehend, and get a gut feeling of what is going on, they become worried and engaged. Also, considerable pressure could be brought to bear on the political system. Concern about environment and pollution—an equally technical area—developed in this way: from almost nothing to a broad and powerful movement. Why not global surveillance? The mass media, including television, might even to some extent follow suit, cynically geared as they are towards being "where the action is". They did so in the area of environment and pollution. But because of its basic role in the entertainment industry, television is a distrustful ally, and great care should be taken to prevent the surveillant state from becoming an entertainment object where entertainment is figure rather than ground, to use a phrase from gestalt psychology. Entertainment may be a method to further information and engagement (remember Dario Fo), but when entertainment in itself becomes the goal, there is danger. The issue of environment and pollution has unfortunately partly become such a goal for television. The Norwegian soap opera "Off-shore", which portrays life and sex on an oil rig, is an example. We should learn from the errors of the past.

We should also note that an alternative public space of the kind I am suggesting has one important advantage over television as well as other mass media. It would be based on the actual and organised relationships between people. The public space of the mass media, especially television, is in that sense weak. It is a public space which is unorganised, segmented, splintered into millions of unconnected individuals—this is its truly mass character—and equally segmented into thousands of individual media stars on the media sky. This is the Achilles' heel of the public space of the media, where an alternative public space would have the upper hand. A model—probably unattainable in practice but at least challenging as an ideal—would be the political and critical kind of *bourgeois public space* which developed in the "salons" and coffee houses of France and England through the 1700s. This was a public space which finally competed successfully with—and neutralised—the once splendid public space of the Court and the old regime, thus preparing the ground for the great French Revolution of 1789 (Habermas, 1962).

To repeat, this is one line of thinking, and there are obviously others. None of the roads are broad and easy to walk. Let me conclude by saying that the expanding surveillant state, threatening the democratic fabric of our society as we know it, represents a permanent challenge to those of us concerned, politically and/or scientifically, with the sociology of social control in the widest sense of the word.

Part IV

Democracy, State Power and Globalisation

11

Criminal Justice and Democratisation in Turkey: the Paradox of Transition

PENNY GREEN

THIS CHAPTER IS concerned with the relationship between crime control, criminal justice policy and democratisation in the context of the Turkish state.[1] What happens to criminal justice in an authoritarian regime struggling with democracy, and what specific impact does the process of democratisation have on the development of state strategies of containment and control? The tentative answers emerging from this research suggest that crime control and criminal justice operate in Turkey independently of any coherent and formalised policy-making, and that the absence of such may have a benign impact on certain aspects of criminal justice in a society well acquainted with state repression.[2] This has cautionary implications for those European and American criminal justice entrepreneurs concerned with the export of Western policy models.

Turkey lies on the periphery of Europe, neither included nor totally excluded. The possibility of inclusion will be dependent upon the Turkish state meeting a set of economic, political, social and human rights criteria determined by the European Commission. As a consequence, issues of criminal justice policy and

[1] Preliminary research was carried out on drug offenders in Turkish prisons in the summer of 1993 and interviews were conducted with Turkish lawyers, academics, human rights activists and officials from the Turkish Ministry of Justice between 1997 and 1998.

[2] This chapter is exploratory, in the sense that there appear to be no critical expositions of Turkish criminal justice written in English in which to locate my study, and I have found no evidence of work, Turkish or English, which centrally seeks to understand the process of criminal policy-making. Part of the problem in writing this Chapter, then, has been the lack of a critical criminological tradition within the Turkish social sciences in which to ground my research. Criminology is a particularly undeveloped social science in Turkey. It has been dominated by biological determinism and other variants of positivism and by administratively-oriented criminal law. Neither criminology nor criminal justice are taught in law faculties and the subject has not been adopted by critical sociology as it was in the West. The experience of acute social injustice and severe violations of human rights (throughout the past four decades) has not, unlike the Latin American example, led to the development of a highly critical discipline of criminology (see Bergalli, 1997: 36–7). Rather than criminologists there are criminal lawyers with an interest in criminal procedure or psychologists locked into biological determinist analyses of the criminal mind. This condition was exacerbated by the expulsion of left-wing academics following the 1981 coup, thereby denying the social sciences of any real critical input until their reinstatement towards the end of the decade.

practice seem set to play a crucial transitional role in the "Europeanisation" of Turkey. Yet while the Turkish state is well known for its torture and degrading treatment of political and social dissidents (see Parliamentary Human Rights Group, 1993; Amnesty International, 1998; European Commission, 1998; Medical Foundation, 1999; Human Rights Watch, 1999), less is known of the criminal justice or penal processes under which these abuses take place, nor of the countervailing forces, both formal and informal which mediate their practice.

Democratisation is generally suggestive of more liberal, humane and consensual criminal justice practices, especially when contrasted with the arbitrary terror and human rights abuses characteristic of authoritarian regimes.[3] Yet the drive for democracy in repressive states may result in criminal justice practices which are, paradoxically, less humane than those they seek to replace. This may also take place alongside an amelioration in general human rights abuses.

The study of transitional states (i.e. states moving from authoritarianism towards full democracy), seems particularly useful in illuminating the relationship between democracy and criminal justice policy and practice.

DEMOCRACY IN TURKEY

> "A form of control based on consent—'social control' proper—is connected to the emergence of democracy. It is a powerful form of control because it produces behaviour. A form of control based on coercion, instead, is weak—in spite of its arrogance—because it is merely a form of censorship, and has no productive character" (Melossi, 1990: 175).

In light of the work by Dario Melossi (1990; 1997) and Roberto Bergalli (1997) on state and social control, it would seem that the most useful means of understanding and theorising the processes of criminal justice in Turkey is in the context of democratisation. The emergence of a concept of social control, Melossi argued, is directly linked to the coming to maturity of a democratic form of polity. The paradox (the ultimate paradox according to Melossi) of democracy is that social control becomes stronger as the state grows weaker. Democratisation, therefore, leads to more effective, more pervasive methods of social control. Is social control, or more specifically criminal policy, therefore, less "controlling" in the political arrangement which characterises modern Turkey?

Turkish democracy is precarious. Since 1996 three governments have fallen—the first was dissolved as a result of internal disputes, the second over charges of corruption and the third because of the perceived threat to Turkish secularism

[3] This despite the example of a return to "barbarism" most notably in the USA (see for example the re-emergence of the death penalty in the majority of states; the re-emergence of the chain gang and mandatory life sentences for repeat offenders).

that it posed.[4] Turkey's post-war history has been punctuated by periodic waves of mass political protest, public disorder, mass strikes, political violence and military coups. The Kurdish struggle for self-determination, the rise of Islamic fundamentalism as a political force and the continuing conflict over Cyprus, coupled with periodic economic crises, provide a context in which criminal justice has developed as a reactive force. Criminal justice thus operates without a framework of elucidated objectives. The military are centrally involved in Turkish political life and remain independent of civil control. Since the foundation of the Republic, the military elite has assumed the role of custodian of the Kemalist secular state and has intervened whenever it perceives the "integrity" of the Republic to be under threat. Thus, it was with the military coups of 1960, 1971, 1980 and again in 1997 when the military "quietly" intervened to remove the democratically elected Islamic government by outlawing the Refah (Welfare) Party. On each of these occasions, the army has succeeded in suppressing dissident forces and shoring up the "indivisibility" of the secular Turkish state.

Links between social groups and the political elite in Turkey have been characterised as weak (Powell, 1981: 866). The notion of institutionalised consultation between interest groups and political parties has, therefore, been effectively absent in Turkish politics. Interest groups thus have only a very limited role in the development of policy (see below) and because of the weak relationships thus cited, "regulation from above" continues to dominate the process of policy-making (Heper, 1992: 186).

According to American political scientist, Robert Putnam, whether a state is corrupt, inefficient, authoritarian, etc. is very much dependent on the extent and integration of civic associations in the society. In Turkey, with a population of some 62 million, only one million people are involved in civic organisations.[5] Political institutions have thus been distorted by the generalised lack of civic organisation. And according to Robert Putnam "By far the most important factor in explaining good government is the degree to which social and political life in a region approximates the ideal of the civic community" (Putnnam, 1993: 120).[6]

Turkey, as a young republic, emerged in 1923 out of the ruins of the decaying Ottoman empire. "Everything had to be rebuilt, above all a new identity" (Pope and Pope, 1997: 58–9).

[4] The minority coalition led by Prime Minister Mesut Yilmaz (ANAP) came to power in June 1997 following weeks of crisis brought about by the dissolution of the government led by the Islamic Necmettin Erbakan (Refah) and Tansu Ciller (DYP). In January 1998 the Turkish Constitutional Court dissolved the Islamic Refah Party, confiscated all its property and banned its leaders from joining any political grouping for the following five years. Most of its Deputies (MPs) and general membership joined the newly formed Islamic Fazilet (Virtue) Party.

[5] Douglas Johnson speaking at *Human Rights in Turkey: The Way Forward* Conference—organised by Amnesty International and the Istanbul Bar Association, 20 November 1998.

[6] Putnam defines *civic community* as "patterns of civic involvement and social solidarity" (1993, 83).

And through the dictatorial imposition of Western "democracy" by the Republic's charismatic founder and president, Mustafa Kemal Ataturk, the Turks were catapulted through a series of radical reforms. Between 1923 and 1926 the ancient institutions of the caliphate and sultanate were abolished and replaced by a secular state; clothing symbolic of the Islamic religion—the fez and the head-scarf (*türban*)—was forbidden in 1925; Shari'a or Islamic courts were abolished in 1924 and, with the transfer of the entire court system to the new Ministry of Justice, the judiciary was, for the first time in Turkish history, legally independent of Islamic control.[7] What remained of Shari'a law was replaced by an array of imported European legal codes—Mussolini's Italian penal code and the Swiss civil code in 1926 and in 1929 the German code of criminal procedure.[8] In 1928 the Latin alphabet replaced the Arabic alphabet, amidst a nationwide literacy campaign.

Ataturk's vision, of a relaxation of strong state control, once a new Turkish identity with accompanying values had been developed, has not eventuated. Rather, Ataturk's legacy has been one of what Turan (1984) has described as "cyclical democracy" (cited in Heper, 1985: 19).

> "Ataturk spoke for a Western system but his autocratic tendencies and his vanity required that he be sole leader of a hierarchical state. Furthermore, founded by army officers, the new state naturally had militaristic tendencies. As a result the Turkish republic, although a parliamentary democracy, never really developed the concept of teamwork central to party politics. . . . Rather than improving upon the incomplete, however, Ataturk's successors froze the picture when he died: the Turkey he had delivered was taken to be a finished product. Any change from then on was portrayed as straying from the path laid down by the ebedi sef, or Immortal Leader (Pope and Pope, 1997: 64–5).

The death of Ataturk in 1938 paved the way for elites to introduce elements of democratic practice previously forbidden. Multi-party political competition occurred between 1945 and 1966, with the first two-party elections in 1950. Multi-party competition led to an increased significance in interest groups, most significantly Islamic interest groups (Starr, 1992: 17).

Turkey, in the early twenty-first century, has satisfied at least some of the criteria normally required for conferment of the status of democracy—civilian rule, multi-party, freely contested elections, an administrative framework capable of framing and applying legislation compatible with the European Commission's *aquis communautaire* and a free press.[9] The 1982 Turkish con-

[7] While the structural reforms to the legal system were radical indeed, they were nonetheless structures which were well entrenched in Ottoman society. Seventy-five years earlier, secular courts had been established to resolve conflicts between non-Islamic merchants in Constantinople and only 15 years later to decide on criminal cases. Secular European ideas about law and education were part of the earliest challenge by the Ottoman bureaucratic elites to the Ottoman Islamic elites (Starr, 1992: 176).

[8] Ceza Muhakemleri Usulu Kanunu (the Turkish Code of Criminal Procedure) is a translation of the 1877 German Code of Criminal Procedure.

[9] Membership of the EU requires states to be both liberal and democratic. The Treaty of Rome did not, however, specify precise conditions of membership but given the nature of the criticisms levelled at Turkey by the EU its record on human and political rights is its major stumbling block.

stitution provides for the full range of political and human rights; since 1987 Turkey has recognised the competence of the European Court of Human Rights to accept complaints against the Turkish state; and in 1988 Turkey ratified the European Convention on the Prevention of Torture and Inhuman or Degrading Treatment or Punishment. But in practice, Turkey continues to restrict the political rights of its minorities (most significantly the Kurds) and human rights abuses continue both within and outside the criminal justice process. Cases of torture, disappearances, murders by unknown assailants and extra-judicial executions occur regularly, particularly in the south-east region. The trial process, particularly those political trials held in the State Security Courts, has been internationally condemned as unfair and incapable of providing justice.[10] Many of these human rights and criminal justice abuses are justified in Kemalist political terms and enshrined in the Constitution—Article 14 of the 1982 Constitution thus declares:

> "None of the rights and freedoms embodied in the constitution shall be exercised with the aim of violating the indivisible integrity of the state with its territory and nation, of endangering the existence of the Turkish State and Republic, of destroying fundamental rights and freedoms, of placing the government of the State under the control of an individual or a group of people, or establishing the hegemony of one social class over others, or creating discrimination on the basis of language, race, religion or sect, or of establishing by any other means a system of government based on these concepts and ideas" (cited in Dodd, 1990: 157).

The continued political power of the military, the size of and resources injected into the state apparatus and the underlying principle of the strong state in Turkey have ensured that, despite the country's significant steps toward democracy (see below), the transition has not been easy (Heper, 1992; Dagi, 1996). The implications for criminal justice practice and policy are many.

COUPS AND CONSTITUTIONS

For the purposes of this chapter, it is useful to review briefly the impact of Turkey's last military coup because its impact in recent history has important continuous resonances with the process of criminal justice and the strictures on policy-making today.

Of the 1980 military coup Feroz Ahmad has written,

> "The public, worn down by the breakdown of law and order, the galloping inflation and shortages of basic goods, the squabbles among parties and the paralysed parliament, welcomed martial law and the promise of stability it offered. Few bargained for what the commanders had in mind or the ruthless manner in which they implemented

[10] The very existence of the State Security Courts for political offences, with their reliance on confessions and elevation of the prosecution over defence counsel, act against the possibility of a fair trial. One in three of the State Security Court judges are military personnel.

their policies. The generals' agenda soon came to be seen as a counter-revolution whose aim was nothing short of revoking all the political and socio-economic gains made by the country since 1960" (Ahmad, 1993: 182).

The period of martial law which followed the 12 September coup saw widespread political arrests, thousands detained, thousands more beaten, intimidated and released, and the systematic and increased use of torture. All political parties and trade unions were abolished, their assets and their archives confiscated, strikes were outlawed and the Constitution suspended. Universities were de-politicised through the expulsion of all centre-left academics. According to Feroz Ahmad "Arrests and trials . . . were the principal features of daily political life in the 1980s" (1993, 185).

The National Security Council (NSC) appointed a cabinet led by retired admiral Bülent Ulusu, which significantly included Turgut Özal as Deputy Prime Minister. Head of State General Kenan Evren was appointed President for a period of seven years and the remaining four members of the NSC were to form the Presidential Council for the same term (Ahmad, 1993: 187). In November 1983, during the period of "transition to democracy", Turgut Özal, as leader of the Motherland Party, was elected Prime Minister. Under Özal's leadership, however, issues of democracy were secondary to those of economics. Thus it was that no reforms were forthcoming in relation to the undemocratic legacy of martial law. Law and order remained in the hands of the military. There were no changes to the penal code, to the laws relating to press freedom, nor to trade union and higher education laws.

The 1982 Constitution, drawn up under the auspices of the National Security Council, following the coup, was singularly preoccupied with preventing any reappearance of political disorder. It remains, as one important commentary observed, a document of "partial freedoms"[11] and one which has considerable significance, both for the nature of Turkish criminal justice and for the characteristic inertia associated with its policy-making process. At the heart of these "partial" freedoms lie the Turkish state's fears of separatism and territorial claims made, most significantly, by the Kurds but also by the Greeks and Armenians. Thus, while "everyone has the right to life" those who apparently threaten the integrity of the state security forces do not. As Hugh and Nicole Pope observed, "self defence" was to "become a morbid mantra as police reported that yet another group of 'terrorists' lying dead in an apartment in their pyjamas had 'returned fire when called to surrender' " (Pope and Pope, 1997: 148).

Martial law was finally lifted in July 1987, though a special government, with special powers, was appointed in eight of the eastern provinces and another eight provinces remained under a state of emergency.[12] Today, five provinces in

[11] Pope and Pope (1997, 148).

[12] A Report by an Independent Delegation, 22–27 August 1991, *An Investigation of Ten Killings by Turkish Security Forces on 12 July 1991.*

south-eastern Turkey remain under a state of emergency (Human Rights Watch, 1999).

The return to democracy took place during an increasingly unstable period—growing Kurdish insurgency in the south-east of Turkey, political assassinations, an increasing fear of Islamic Fundamentalism, sky-rocketing inflation and a public anxiety that again the military would intervene in the running of the state. Throughout the 1980s, the rich in Turkey grew considerably richer, such that the World Bank could, in 1993, cite Turkey as the seventh worst country in the world for income disparity cited in Ahmad (1993, 204). Feroz Ahmad has reported findings from the State Planning Organisation which show that the:

> "share of wages in the country's GNP declined sharply from a high of 36 per cent in 1977 to 21 per cent in 1983, and a low of 18 per cent in 1987. Real wages declined by about 45 per cent after 1980 while unemployment hovered at around 15 per cent (higher if unofficial figures are to be believed) throughout the decade" (1993: 204–5).

Dramatic rates of internal migration (Anatolian rural poor to the growth cities of Istanbul, Ankara and Izmir) have contributed to a real growth in urban poverty and to certain cultural and religious tensions between the new immigrants and the long-Westernised urban elite. In addition, some 40 per cent of Turkish workers have no social security, aside from family and mosque-based charity (Brewin, 1996: 46).

Despite this drastic worsening of economic conditions, Turkey has, it appears, seen no appreciable rise in property crime as might be expected in light of Western research linking recession with increases in particular forms of crime.[13] Gema Varona has noted a similar experience for Spain under Franco's authoritarian regime (see Chapter 12).

In addition, the Turkish population is demographically a very youthful one—62 million in 1998 estimated to rise to 70 million by the start of 2000. Again, the Western link between youth and criminal activity does not appear to have been borne out, with any significance, in the Turkish context.

ANOMALIES AND CONTRADICTIONS: THE STRANGE CASE OF TURKISH CRIMINAL JUSTICE

Criminal justice in Turkey is driven by the wider political problems confronting the Turkish state. It is reactive rather than proactive and operates in what we might describe as a policy vacuum. The following observation by Hugh and Nicole Pope characterises the crisis in criminal justice which has thus emerged:

> "Dangerous fault-lines have appeared inside the Turkish state. Its institutions, their roots deep in the Ottoman past, have responded to the inadequacy of politicians by

[13] Box, S. 1987, "Recession, Crime and Punishment", London: Macmillan.

> trying to take matters into their own hands. Above all the state is failing to hold the keystone of justice in place. Court cases drag on for years and witnesses are easily intimidated. Poorly paid judges, especially in commercial and political cases bend easily to the strongest wind. The police force operates as a state within a state with its own brutal methods; some policemen are hand in hand with the mafias whose gunmen learned their trade in the right-wing gangs that plagued the 1970s. Turks are learning to overcome their age-old belief that anything not specifically permitted by the state is illegal. But with no legal framework to take its place, people feel that the pendulum is once again from strong government towards a kind of anarchy in which only the rich, big business and Turkey's many mafias hold sway" (Pope and Pope, 1997: 339–40).

Turkish criminal justice is fraught with contradictions: authoritarian and repressive on the one hand, inert and inadvertently benign on the other. Those who threaten the integrity or "indivisibility" of the Turkish state may face the death penalty or be imprisoned for many years,[14] yet periodically, by executive decree, the prisons are emptied of all their inmates in an attempt to win electoral support. Similarly, if the prison population climbs too high to be adequately managed, then the widespread use of the conditional discharge is entertained. There is no concept of community-based punishment, nor of prisoner welfare, yet if a firm or company employs more than 50 workers, legislation provides that former prisoners must be recruited as employees.

Despite its appalling human rights record and internationally infamous penal reputation, Turkey has long been overtaken by European states as the great incarcerator of the region. Council of Europe data show Turkey's prison population at 1 September 1994 to be 43,432 (compared with 49,392 for England and Wales and 5,594 for Scotland). For the same year, Turkey's rate of detention stood at 72.4 per 100,000 of the population, compared with 96 per 100,000 in England and Wales. While Turkey's total prison capacity stood at 80,502, its occupancy rate was 54 per cent. England and Wales with a total prison capacity of 49,085 had an occupancy rate of 106 per cent.

Turkish prison statistics may be less than reliable but interviews with leading academics, lawyers and Ministry officials suggest that the Council of Europe figures (derived from Ministry of Justice data) are reasonably accurate. The periodic enactment of widespread amnesties, or the conditional discharge, explain the apparently puzzling dramatic decreases in Turkey's prison population every decade or so.

Oltan Sungurlu,[15] the right-wing ANAP Minister of Justice in 1997, experienced three periods of office in this role. Under Turgut Özal's presidency, he was involved in overseeing a substantial reduction in the prison population: "I was last Minister in 1991—I left with a prison population of 28,000—we enacted an amnesty on conditional release in 1991—a conditional release for *all*

[14] See the case of eight Kurdish MPs including the celebrated Leyla Zana (from the now non-existent DEP), imprisoned in March 1994 for periods of up to 15 years for declaring Kurdish nationalist sentiments in the Parliament, in conversations and interviews.

[15] Oltan Sungurlu was replaced in 1998 by the more liberal (DYP) Hasan Denizkurdu.

prisoners. It was an administrative procedure, the courts continued as usual".[16]

But while the short-term impact of executive release is to dramatically reduce the prison population, the reductionist results may be comparatively short-lived. According to the Ministry of Justice, the Turkish prison population at December 1997 stood at 60,000 (including 9,000 political prisoners), while the equivalent figure for England and Wales was in excess of 65,000.

Executive adjustments to prison populations have been used in a variety of other countries (notably Italy, France, Poland, Japan and Israel).[17] Fascist regimes have often resorted to amnesties for "minor" offenders who were distinguished from serious (political) offenders (Rutherford, 1986b: 58). In Turkey, amnesties have also included serious and political offenders. In a seminal analysis of criminal law in Nazi Germany, Otto Kirchheimer analysed the use of amnesties in terms of securing obedience: "Administrative penal procedure does not necessarily imply that the offender fares badly in the individual case, as its foremost task is not one of punishing but of enforcing the obedience of the individual to the administrative policy with its rapidly changing needs" (Kirchheimer, 1940: 456). In a review of the impact of amnesties and administrative early release schemes, Zimring and Hawkins have cautioned that the decarcerative results of such executive interventions may be "understated" by reasonably rapid rises in prison populations that may follow. They argued, however, that "If a sharp upward pressure on prison populations is the motive for administrative release, the return to pre-amnesty levels may still be significantly less than it would have been without the release programme" (Zimring and Hawkins, 1991: 197).

In Turkey, where the amnesty is more commonly used as a "corrupt" political device to secure electoral popularity, the decarcerative result is distanced from any reformist penal philosophy. While the desired ideological outcome is that of endowing the state with the character of mercy, the effect of executive releases on a population so familiar with political repression may rather be to suggest that prisoners are less harmful to society than the institution of prison itself.

MIDNIGHT EXPRESS RE-VISITED

In the Western consciousness Turkish jails conjure up lurid and frightening images of squalor, violence, torture and despair, and Alan Parker's famous portrayal of a foreigner's Turkish prison experience in the film *Midnight Express*, "fixed a prejudice that somehow all Turks were corrupt, sadistic and dangerous" (Pope and Pope, 1997: 60).

The situation in the prisons remained grim throughout the 1980s, characterised by often appalling conditions, torture and violence, prison riots and

[16] Personal communication December 1997, Ankara.

[17] Rutherford (1986, 186*n*).

routine hunger strikes. According to Human Rights Watch (1999), prisons are under-funded and poorly administered. A parliamentary human rights commission reported a catalogue of "atrocious" conditions, including torture and the beating of juveniles, following its investigations in April 1999.

Prisons I visited—Bayrampasa Cezavi and Özel Tip—were squalid and sometimes fearful places, where violence, bribery and corruption were evident, yet interviews with a range of Turkish and foreign prisoners (and former prisoners) revealed a much more complex experience of incarceration, involving a high degree of autonomy and free association enjoyed by those incarcerated. Prisoners, if they can afford to buy food, have facilities to cook their own meals. The experience described by one male prisoner is typical: "The prison food is very poor—beans and bread every time, so we buy food and cook it ourselves—we must also pay for the cooking gas. You pay for everything except the bed . . . In Bayrampasa [Prison] we pooled our money and bought two fridges and two TVs."[18] Prisoner testimonies suggest, paradoxically, that imprisonment in a Turkish jail may be less of a de-humanising experience than incarceration in many western European establishments. According to one North American woman, sentenced in Istanbul to eight years for the exportation of 15 kilos of heroin:

> "I can tell you stories about that prison that would stand your hair on end and sound like I survived hell, but to be living it at the time for me was not so bad . . . there were things, really nice things, that outside could not have happened. There was a sense of belonging together, of camaraderie that you cannot duplicate anywhere . . . So I cannot tell you it was hell, that it was terrible, it wasn't. It can be if you want it to be—if you want to walk into one of their fights, or talk about the bad food."[19]

Security in Turkish prisons, to a significant extent, ends at the prison walls. By UK standards it is lax. Turkish prisoners are housed not in cells but in dormitories. Dormitories may sleep up to 40 people:

> "Our cell-block was two large rooms, one upstairs one downstairs . . . both rooms were virtually wall to wall beds. There were between 70 and 80 women there and . . . about 10 babies and little children. And we lived in that area. We had a little courtyard. At the time there were two toilets upstairs but one didn't work so effectively you had one toilet for 80 people. We had two showerheads downstairs, one of which rarely worked and we had hot water most days, not every day, for about an hour in the morning. We were free to walk upstairs, downstairs and in our garden, from morning to evening. In the winter they closed the doors earlier because it was dark, 5.30 or so, in the summer they left them open until 8.30 or 9 o'clock. But we were not free to leave our "kush unless we had a visit."

The issue of how prisoners are to be housed has become an important question for the Ministry of Justice—very much driven by the existence and organisation

[18] "Anderson" a West Indian inmate convicted of exporting ½ kilo of heroin; serving 12 years but was to be released after serving less than two and a half years as a result of Temporary Article 1 1991 which offered a four-fifths dispensation of sentence for offences committed before 8.4.91.

[19] "Rose" foreign prisoner, Bayrampasa Cezavi, personal communication, September 1992.

of political prisoners. According to a report in the *Turkish Daily News* (27 January 2000), and a fact acknowledged by the Ministry, Kurdish and Islamic prisoners exert considerable control over their prison dormitories which may house hundreds of prisoners at any one time. One response to this perceived lack of control has been the replacement of dormitory style accommodation with cells in the planned expansion of the prison establishment. Two new, general prisons are to be built in Diyabakir and Aydin in eastern Turkey; both will be based on cells accommodating two to four prisoners—the official calculation being that this will break the influence of political and organised prisoners. These proposals have been met with widespread and militant protests across Turkish prisons. In 1996 12 political prisoners died on hunger strike in protest over (among other issues) the planned introduction of cell-based accommodation. In September 1999 11 political prisoners were killed and another 30 injured when state security forces were sent to Ulucanlar Central Prison in Ankara to suppress protests over prison accommodation.[20] These protests have caused widespread disruption in prisons throughout Turkey. Given this level of resistance, the cost of refurbishing existing prisons and the fact that the target population is limited, it is unlikely that the transformation to cell-based accommodation will be widespread in the foreseeable future.

Prisoners organise the details of their daily lives to a considerable extent, independently of the authorities. The prison authorities are thus absolved of many of the responsibilities they might otherwise be expected to assume in the daily management of inmates.

The introduction of formal mechanisms and principles of criminal and penal policy may not necessarily, therefore, improve the conditions or quality of prison life.

PEDAGOGY, POLICY AND THE REACTIVE STATE

Where in the UK ministries have become increasingly formalised, bureaucratised, driven by ideology and assuming previously unheld powers (see Rutherford, Chapter 3 and Faulkner, Chapter 5), the Turkish Ministry of Justice appears to be surprisingly inactive, driven less by concerns of crime control than by knee-jerk responses to political crises. It can certainly be argued that the Turkish state has "public enemies", other than criminals, and political and economic problems which eclipse the issue of crime. It might, therefore, be argued that, to date, the development of Turkish criminal justice has remained embryonic—essentially non-ideological in its "design" and reactive in its practice.

[20] These killings have been described by the Human Rights Foundation of Turkey as a "massacre". They write, "That this massacre has been put into practice after discussions about prisons in the National Security Board and the declaration of the Prime Minister Bülent Ecevit that "the authority of the state would be proven in the prisons" is a sufficient implication that it has been planned at the highest level" (Human Rights Foundation of Turkey, Press Release 5 October 1999).

The history of democratisation, and the demands set by the European Commission for Turkey's admissibility into the European Union,[21] suggest that criminal justice reforms will, in all likelihood, feature more prominently in Turkey's future. There is tentative evidence to suggest that criminal justice reform is now on the Turkish agenda—not as a major political priority, but as part of the general drive toward democratisation. After 70 years a new penal code is soon to pass through parliament; revision of the Criminal Procedure Code is almost underway; a punishment code is planned and the development of formal mechanisms of policy-making is being advocated by academics advising the government.

The administration of criminal justice in Turkey is viewed by those centrally involved as a pragmatic, rather than an ideological, responsibility, although, as noted below, it is imbued with political pedagogy. It is shared essentially by three Ministries: the Ministries of Justice, the Interior and to a lesser extent, Foreign Affairs as well as, in a quite specific context, the Military. The Ministry of Justice has four main roles: a duty to maintain the building structures of the courts; to prepare legislation for the "proper function of criminal justice"; prison administration and to oversee the drafting of the new penal code. The Ministry of the Interior has ultimate responsibility for the police and for the Jandarma (a force made up of unpaid army conscripts responsible for "public security" in rural and urban areas outside the main cities). But while the Jandarma is officially under the control of the Ministry of the Interior, "its real patrons are the Military".[22] Despite this acknowledgement, the Minister of Justice asserted that, "the Military have no role on the subject of criminal justice".[23]

Turkish law derives from the Continental, civil law tradition and the nature of its trial process is inquisitorial. Judges are appointed by the Supreme Council of Judges (*Yüksek Hâkimler Kurulu*), the institutional framework which provides for the close supervision of all judges and judicial apprentices. The role of *Yüksek Hâkimler Kurulu* is significant to understanding the lack of criminal policy development, given it is charged to, ". . . protect the system from infusions of influence and also act to constrain radical legal change in process and in deciding cases" (Starr, 1992: 181). From the inception of secularisation, judicial decisions were imbued with a strong "public interest" component—that of educating the citizens of the new Turkey around the structural values of Turkish nationalism, populism, secularism, individualism and gender equality. The values of the ruling elite were now to imbue the "periphery" (Starr, 1992: 17). In order to achieve these reforms through law, the new ruling elite,

[21] Among the Union's primary conditions are a stable democracy, an end to human rights abuses and the reunification of Cyprus (Brewin, 1996: 40). In 1993 the European Union established the "Copenhagen Criteria" i.e. that candidate countries establish stable institutions that guarantee democracy, the rule of law, human rights and respect for and the protection of minorities—as a basic requirement of membership.

[22] Oltan Sungurlu, Minister for Justice, personal communication, December 1997.

[23] Oltan Sungurlu, personal communication, December 1997.

> ". . . aimed at transferring to Turkey the constitutional blueprints from the Anglo-American democracies, that is, weak states. They placed emphasis on individual rights and liberties, but, at the same time, they tried to develop, through education, a political culture that placed emphasis on the collectivity. They also assumed that by mere exhortation, the people's attitudes and deep cultural values could be changed" (Heper, 1992: 186).

While the legislative process, courts and the justice system are driven by the pedagogic process of inculcating national cultural values (particularly to those from rural areas)—overseen by *Yüksek Hâkimler Kurulu*—the constraining influence of Kemalist authoritarianism on criminal policy development is evident.[24]

INTRODUCING WESTERN MODELS OF CRIMINAL POLICY: TURKEY'S "NEW POLICY-MAKERS"

> "Policy—no there is no policy, the government does not have a word for criminal justice policy-making; 'policies' are dictated by daily needs, they just want to cover their daily needs" (Feridun Yenisey).[25]

It is clear from interviews with both the authors of criminal policy and their critics that there is no real sense in which criminal justice is conceived of as a process by those in power. The relationships between the agencies—police, courts, prosecution and prisons—are not regarded as integral to the totality of the administration of justice. Rather they are viewed theoretically as autonomous institutions whose interactions are simply operational and mechanical:

> "When we prepare a new draft to change 'policy' we are obliged to take views from other institutions (e.g. the High Court, the universities, the Bar Associations and so on). If we prepare a draft with a view to change policy we have to take the views of the other ministries involved, so if we are regulating on the implications of investigations we would have close contact with the Minister of the Interior; on questions relating to custody, how long to hold without charge, how to conduct investigations—these are settled with the Jandarma and the Ministry of the Interior" (Oltan Sungurlu, Minister of Justice).[26]

[24] The criminal court structure is divided into two types: general and special. General courts include Justice of the Peace Courts (minor offences and arrest orders issued); Courts of General Criminal Jurisdiction (all cases which fall outside the jurisdiction of the other criminal courts) and Aggravated Felony Courts (for serious offences requiring a minimum of ten years' imprisonment). Both the Justice of the Peace Courts and the Courts of General Criminal Jurisdiction have one judge presiding and are located in county capitals. Aggravated Felony Courts are composed of three judges, and are located in the provincial capitals.

The High Court of Cassation is the court of last instance for reviewing decisions and judgments of the other criminal courts.

Courts of special jurisdiction include Military Courts (for military personnel), the Constitutional Court (examines the constitutionality of statutory law and government decrees) and the State Security Courts, long attacked by human rights defenders, which deal with political offences against the indivisible integrity of the state.

[25] Feridun Yenisey, personal communication, 31 March 1998.

[26] Personal communication, Ankara December 1997.

Criminal policy is, in the broadest sense then, fixed by the Constitution and from a limited array of relevant imported European codes and regulations. Within the Parliament there is a Justice Commission which is composed of 15–20 members from across the range of political parties. The commission is also attended by officials from the Ministry of Justice. All drafts relating to criminal justice are discussed by this commission. There are currently two codes relating to criminal policy—the Penal Code (adopted in its entirety from the Italian penal code in 1926), and the 1929 Criminal Procedure Code which is a translation of the 1877 German Code of Criminal Procedure. Occasionally, special laws are introduced to reinforce existing provisions of the Penal Code. The Law on Associations, for example, prohibits any form of political statement or activity by any organisation other than a legal political party while Law Number 413, a law aimed specifically at south-eastern Kurdish regions of Turkey provides the Minister of the Interior and regional governors with wide, unreviewable powers to control trade union activities, to prohibit publications and to relocate individuals or groups considered to be acting against the state.[27]

Criminal justice reform suffers from an extreme form of inertia, exacerbated by Turkey's wider political and economic crises which, as I have argued, effectively sideline the issues of crime and crime-control. There is, in any event, little domestic pressure to address the issues of crime and its control, featuring, as they do, rather less prominently than political corruption, state violence, the activities of the mafia, the Kurdish crisis and economic instability. Nonetheless there have been amendments to these codes over the years—most notable the 1992 liberalising amendment which went some way towards improving the position of the defendant and which introduced regulations relating to the inadmissibility of improperly obtained evidence.[28]

For the past 15 years the Ministry of the Interior has been involved in overseeing the drafting of a new penal code.

> "Everyone has complaints against justice in Turkey now but the Commission to revise the penal code was not formed reactively to these sentiments. It was formed by the Ministry of Justice many years ago and it has seen at least four different ministers of justice from four different governments."[29]

A commission composed of criminal law professors, a Court of Cassation judge, a representative from the Turkish Bar, experts from the Ministry of Justice and lower court judges was established to draft the new code. Now in its third draft, the code has gone for review to a special commission constituted by the Minster of Justice and is expected to go before parliament during 2000. If accepted, the new code will replace the 1889 Italian Penal Code. Criminal justice may not be "on the march" but it is beginning to walk. Whether or not criminal justice

[27] A Report by an Independent Delegation, 22–27 August 1991, *An Investigation of Ten Killings by Turkish Security Forces on 12 July 1991.*

[28] Biçak (1996, 13).

[29] Feridun Yenisey, personal communication, 31 March 1998.

reforms are occurring within a new "culture of democracy", as Bergalli has described for Spain (1997, 151), is less clear. Those who make up the reform commission speak of "modernising" principles, consistency and efficiency as the fundamental tenets of the new code. Once the Penal Code has been adopted, then work will commence on a new criminal procedure code. A new punishment code is planned but given the bureaucratic inertia which is still endemic to the "policy-making process" it may be many years before either come to any form of fruition.

The "new policy-makers"[30] seek to reduce levels of punishment and imprisonment, to abolish the death penalty,[31] to introduce community-based strategies for rehabilitation, to introduce a more effective system of fines, to incorporate the perspective of the victim and to remove the anomalies and irregularities which characterise Turkish criminal justice practice. Above all there is an expressed concern that criminal policy, criminal procedure and punishment be seen as an efficient, integrated whole rather than as the discrete and disparate practices they currently are. The approach, however, is a considerable distance from the managerialism which is currently plaguing Anglo-American policy-making. Turkish criminal policy-making remains, to a large extent, pre-ideological.

> "It is a whole system of packages and the penal code is just a part—criminal procedure will follow and then punishment, and then ways of dealing with petty crime. The idea of another system of prosecution should also come into force—it is a whole system which is being revised—the idea of it being a system is new for Turkey, if you change a little in the way of prosecution it shows itself in other areas of criminal justice. The draft is a system and if they change it too much it will lose its complexity and I hope they [the parliament] don't change it too much" (Feridun Yenisey).[32]

Punishment within the new code has, it is claimed by the Commission, been generally reduced. There is, however, little evidence to substantiate this claim. The conditional discharge (while often a politically corrupt instrument in the hands of the Turkish state) may nonetheless have played a role in weakening the generalised power of the penal process in the public consciousness.

The conditional discharge has been recognised by the Commission as inconsistent with having sentencing principles and a consistent policy of criminal justice. As Kirchheimer has suggested, it represents the discretionary and arbitrary power of the administrative agency. This is, of course, true but its use had the very tangible effect of reducing prison populations in a way which the

[30] I use the term to refer to the conservative and liberal reformists, usually law professors or legal practitioners who are keen to modernise Turkish criminal justice along democratic, continental lines—see particularly members of the Penal Code Reform Commisssion.

[31] While no executions have been carried out since 1984, significant numbers of defendents continue to be sentenced for capital offences—in the last five months of 1997, 43 people were given the death penalty (Human Rights Foundation of Turkey, 1998: 12). The capture, trial and sentencing to death of PKK leader Abdullah Öcalan in June 1999 has provided a celebrated case by which Turkey will be judged on this issue.

[32] Professor Feridun Yenisey, Penal Code Reform Commission member, March 1998.

consistencies and efficiencies of modern Western criminal policies are unable to entertain.

Now, instead, the new policy-makers,

> ". . . are setting sentence tariffs with judicial discretion. In this way we are thinking about policy—finding balance between fault, human rights and the protection of private life (for example there are new crimes relating to the taping of an individual's conversations without their permission). So the protection of individual rights and personal privacy; and the protection of the justice system have all been improved" (ibid.).

More, and increasingly punitive, reforms are also being planned within the Ministry. According to former Director of Penal Affairs, and now Deputy Under Secretary, Yildirim Türkmen, Turkish sentencing practices are currently far too lenient,

> "Inmates serve half their sentence and then they are conditionally discharged. In addition if a prisoner is well-behaved then they can gain six days per month, that is 72 days per year. In this way an inmate may serve only 42 per cent of their sentence. But this is not good. We have now a new project to ensure that inmates will serve two thirds of their sentence. In this way Turks from foreign jurisdictions may be repatriated to serve the remainder of their sentences."[33]

There are considerable tensions between the police and the prosecution and, rather than work co-operatively, they have developed two separate columns of operation—both police and prosecution conduct investigations independently of each other. According to Feridun Yenisey, ". . . it functions like this because we don't have police officers who assist the prosecution. In Germany there are middle-ranked police whose job it is to assist the prosecution. Through these individuals the prosecution has direct contact with the police, but the prosecutor never comes to a police station and issues orders to the police."[34]

Feridun Yenisey and other members of the commission to reform the Criminal Procedure Code will be arguing for the introduction of this system, linking police to prosecution.

For all reformers the police occupy one of the most intractable positions. Corrupt, uneducated, violent in their methods of investigation, the chief perpetrators of torture and a power unto themselves, Turkish police appear to be out of control. For Osman Dogru the problem lies centrally with an absence of formal mechanisms of control:

> ". . . if you give all this power to the police and to public officials but you don't control them of course they will be corrupt. The problem is this—there are no strict controls from the Minister of Justice over the activities of the police. Police officers are

[33] Yildirim Türkmen, Deputy Under Secretary, Ministry of Justice, personal communication, Ankara, December 1997.

[34] Professor Feridun Yenisey, Marmara University and member of the commission to reform the Penal Code, personal communication, 31 March 1998.

always acquitted, judges and public prosecutors don't treat the police harshly, instead they are sympathetic."[35]

Efforts are currently underway by human rights academics to improve the human rights practices of the police. Seminars and conferences are being held for senior police officers but, as the testimonies of those prisoners who have been tortured reveal, it is the nature of the policing mission which lies at the heart of police abuses. Osman Dogru has reported his experience of running police seminars, "I give lectures to the police chiefs of police stations at week-ends . . . they say 'I haven't come to such courses for many years because I'm working so hard . . .' 'well' I say, 'torture has no excuse—ill treatment has no excuse—you cannot justify torture and ill-treatment with your workload'."[36]

Feridun Yenisey's research (in collaboration with Ord. Professor Sulhi Dönmezer[37]) suggests to him that a more administrative strategy, and an increase in resources is necessary to eliminate torture. Their examination of 1,105 criminal case files revealed that, in terms of criminal investigations, police were preoccupied with interviewing the suspect (with the purpose of extracting a confession), rather than devoting resources to crime scene investigations and the interviewing of victims. "The preliminary investigation carried out by police is very brief, just an average of ten days, then the court phase averages 300 days—it should be just the contrary . . . and the reason for this is that the Turkish police haven't enough knowledge of how to conduct crime scene investigations, they focus on witnesses and the accused, thus interrogation plays a big role and this is where problems of torture arise."[38] As Douglas Johnson has observed, "When your only tool is a hammer every problem looks like a nail."[39]

THE DYNAMICS OF CHANGE

Political suppression, terrorism, state terror and martial law have all been central in shaping public perceptions of the institutions of criminal justice in Turkey, particularly those of the prison system and the police. It is rare in Turkey to find a person who has not known, either personally or through family, friends, colleagues or neighbours, the experience of imprisonment, torture or exile. Political dissidence and the state's response to it has been central both in shaping criminal and penal policy, and in shaping public perceptions of the agencies of criminal justice.

It is clear from discussions at the Ministry, and with its harshest critics, that it is the activity of political activists, both within the prisons and outside, which dictates the tenor of criminal policy in Turkey. It is, for example, the ability and

[35] Osman Doğru personal communication, Mormara Univeristy, April 1998.
[36] ibid.
[37] President of the Penal Code Reform Commission.
[38] Feridun Yenisey op.cit.
[39] Douglas Johnson, 20 November 1998, ibid.

success of political prisoners in organising themselves within prison which is currently driving the penal debate on dormitory reform (see above).[40] Interviews with the Minister of Justice and academic critics of the government reveal that, while the state is apparently in control of all prisons "from the outside", there is now a sense in which they have no control over the activities of prisoners on the inside.

> "For the time being most of the issues which occupy us relate to prison administration—we have troubles with regard to the terrorist and organised crime offenders—even in the prisons" (Oltan Sungur, 1997, Minister of Justice).[41]

Outside the prison walls, it is the activity of political activists, and particularly those who are seen to threaten the "indivisibility of the Turkish state", i.e. Kurdish and pro-Kurdish separatists, which has been most influential in shaping the nature of social control. In her historical review of political protest and the state in Italy and Germany, Donatella della Porta has argued that social and political movements can play an important role in influencing "even the more stable institutions and deep-rooted political cultures" (della Porta, 1995). By contrast, crime rates appear to play only a very minor role in the dynamics of Turkish penal policy. As Osman Doğru, Director of Marmara University's Institute of Human Rights confirmed,

> "In Turkey, political crimes drive policy more than ordinary crimes. Criminal policy is focused on the indivisibility of the state or on political crimes which are covered by the Anti-Terror law and articles from the general criminal court . . . there are many articles included in the penal code so I think they did not need to change the basic rules relating to ordinary crimes—but political crimes, yes."[42]

A related and striking contrast between the dynamics of criminal justice in Turkey and most Western liberal democracies is the absence of the concept of "fear of crime"– even more striking given the socio-economic and demographic conditions outlined in the previous section. Street crime in Turkey is publicly regarded as a relatively minor problem. This is true even in Istanbul, a city of some 12 million inhabitants—many of them impoverished immigrants from eastern Anatolia, drawn by hopes of employment in Turkey's largest city. Nor is fear of crime an expression in the popular idiom. There is no pressure from either the public or from the mass media to confront the street crime issues which so exercise the minds of Western politicians. Crime control, thus, does not drive party politics in Turkey and crime as a social problem has little political resonance when set against the continuing war against the Kurds, the economic crisis (not unrelated to the war, given that 20 per cent of the Turkish

[40] Personal communication with Doç Dr Şeref Unal, Adelet Bakanligi, Ministry of Justice, December 1997, Ankara.

[41] Personal communication, Ministry of Justice, December 1997, Ankara.

[42] Osman Doğru, op.cit.

budget is devoted to defence), endemic political corruption,[43] the perceived rise in Islamic fundamentalism and the activities of the "deep state" (*derin devlet*).[44]

> "The crime which touches ordinary individuals in Turkey is white collar crime. Occasionally there will be a drug-related mugging in a particular area but it's not common . . . there is some pick-pocketing on buses and some bag snatching (which is worse in winter when need is greater . . . there is very little car theft. The only crimes which are generally reported, apart from corruption, are sensational stories, crimes of passion, violent crime and the mafiosi."[45]

In Turkey, then, crime control does appear to exist without a formalised and coherent criminal policy and without the ideological framework of fear of crime. Criminal justice questions and penal reforms are not ideologically driven in the way of British criminal justice, rather they are determined pragmatically, as and when they arise.

This chapter can only tentatively suggest why crime control operates in Turkey without any formal notion of criminal policy. The social structure plays an important role. The vast majority of people, and certainly those with property, live in apartment blocks protected by "kapaci" or caretakers. Because the livelihood (in the form of tips and bonuses) of the kapaci is dependent upon the trust they build with those residing in their buildings, protection of residents is guaranteed.

The family is also a central element in social control. Despite the absorption by Turkish youth of certain aspects of Western culture, the family, and a responsibility towards it, continues to maintain a powerful restraining influence over the young. The influence of Islam is more contentious, with some commentators claiming it has no role and others arguing that it offers an important framework of social control (see below). There are no specifically tailored criminal justice lobby groups in Turkey. Pressure for prison and criminal law and procedure reform comes largely from the Bar Association, distinguished academics, political activists, human rights groups, such as the Human Rights Foundation of Turkey, and the media. There are, of course, more general pressures for reform and they are also discussed below.

[43] A number of parliamentary inquiries are currently underway investigating the involvement of senior politicians in cases of suspected embezzlement. In August 1997 a major judicial investigation was launched into the irregular tendering procedures of dozens of former civil servants, mayors and politicians. Low public sector pay and lack of public funding for political parties contributes to the widescale existence of official corruption.

[44] The "Susurluk" case has exposed the depths of Turkish state corruption. As a result of a motor accident in Susurluk—involving a Mercedes carrying, Hüseyin Kocadag, Commander of Special Teams and Director of State Security, Sedat Bucak, head of the Village Guards, a DYP Deputy from Urfa and Abdullah Çatli, a long-wanted murder suspect sought by Interpol—alliances between state and organised crime have been exposed. In addition to this, weapons and silencers, believed to have been used in a range of murders, were also found in the Mercedes.

[45] Martin Fryer, Cultural Consul, British Council, Istanbul, personal communication December 1997.

EUROPE

On 18 May 1984, Turkey ratified the European Convention on Human Rights; in 1988 it ratified the United Nations Convention Against Torture and the European Convention for the Prevention of Torture and Inhuman or Degrading Treatment or Punishment. And on 22 January 1990, it recognised the compulsory jurisdiction of the European Court of Human Rights (ECHR). Both the European Commission and the ECHR have found Turkey to be in violation of the European Convention on Human Rights in several cases. Since 1990, the Turkish government has been forced to pay over US $800,000 in compensation to victims of abuse who took their cases to the Court or Commission. There are currently over 1000 applications pending against Turkey (Human Rights Watch, 1999).

While all commercial law in Turkey is currently being harmonised to fit with Turkey's recent membership of the EU Customs Union, criminal law and criminal justice will, according to the Ministry of Justice, remain entirely domestic. That is not to say, however, that the Turkish authorities have been entirely immune to European and American pressure for reform, particularly in the realm of drug control. One member of the Penal Code Reform Commission, Professor Köksal Bayraktar, described the situation thus:

> "There is currently no interface. Turkey wants to join the EU—70 years ago we turned our face to the west—but the reforms that we want to make are not connected, our criminal codes are very old and not answering modern concerns. Our criminal codes need to be integrated into today's life and this includes human rights, but we don't want to reform it for EU reasons, we want to reform it because we need to."[46]

It does, however, seem likely that in the new punishment code, sentencing for the smuggling of contraband will be brought into line with European punishments, in order to conform with the requirements of the Customs Union. The removal of the death penalty and the outlawing of torture in the new penal code are seen as essential prerequisites for EU candidature. While torture is outlawed under the Penal Code the issue of the death penalty remains—a stumbling block which the EU has apparently postponed until the next stage of membership negotiations or until the Turkish state decides upon the fate of Abdullah Öcalan currently under sentence of death.

Despite subscribing to the international framework surrounding the protection of human rights, efforts to secure human rights for Turkish citizens are effectively sabotaged by Turkish domestic law and practice, which allow for incommunicado detention and special state security courts for those accused of security offences. The European Convention for the Prevention of Torture reported:

[46] Professor Köksal Bayraktar, Professor of Criminal Law, Istanbul University, member of the Penal Code Reform Commission, personal communication, December 1997.

> "It should be emphasised that the phenomenon of torture will not be eradicated by legislative fiat alone, it shall always be possible for the impact of legal provisions to be diminished by ever more expertly applied techniques of ill-treatment. Indeed, it can legitimately be advanced that attacking the root of the problem of torture and ill-treatment involves not so much changing laws as transforming mentalities. This process is required not simply amongst police officers but throughout the criminal justice system" (para. 36, cited in Medical Foundation, 1999: 15).

In late 1997 the European Union failed to include Turkey in its list of prospective members, citing the country's dismal human rights record as its main concern (*The Guardian*, 16 December 1997). Despite a recognition of continuing and widespread breaches of human rights, the EU in October 1999 noted "some encouraging signs of democratisation"[47]—encouraging enough, apparently, to override its human rights concerns. On 10 December 1999 the European Union invited Turkey to become a candidate for future membership, after 40 years of campaigning by the Turkish state. According to Human Rights Watch "if the EU holds Turkey to its commitments" membership discussions should provide a forum for genuine human rights reform.[48]

Each of the academic commentators interviewed agreed that, rather than the European Union and Turkey's desire for membership, it is the example of European law (particularly French and German), membership of the Council of Europe (which Turkey joined in 1950) and decisions handed down by the European Court of Human Rights that have made an impact on criminal justice reform.[49] According to Osman Dogru,

> ". . . the European Court of Human Rights will have a very strong impact on the penal code and criminal justice generally. There are still some articles in our codes which must be changed because in those articles the ECHR held that the application of this rule does not comply with European standards . . . From the human rights aspect Cyprus, democratisation and the Kurdish crisis form the central human rights package, so the constitution and the penal code should be changed in accordance with the judgements by the ECHR against Turkey on these issues."[50]

THE LEFT

Given the analysis presented here—that what criminal justice there is in Turkey is very largely driven by political offences—then it is logical that the left have been influential in fashioning the public consciousness about criminal justice. Professor Köksal Bayraktar from Istanbul University, and a member of the

[47] European Commission *Regular Report from the Commission on Progress towards Accession: Turkey*—October 13, 1999; http://europe.eu.int/comm/enlargement/turkey.

[48] Human Rights Watch "EU Membership Process Could Bring Human Rights Reform in Turkey" http://www.hrw.org/campaigns/turkey.

[49] The rebuff of Turkey's application for EU membership rides most significantly on satisfying conditions relating to parliamentary democracy, human rights and the reunification of Cyprus.

[50] Osman Doğru, op. cit.

Penal Code Revision Commission, argued that the political left have been instrumental in providing pressure for reform:

> "The second reason that Turkey started to improve the system was pressure from the left. Following demonstrations by the revolutionary left and their subsequent imprisonment, intellectuals were alerted to the politicisation of criminalisation. I think that as a result people now question much more the existing system. The activists received very harsh punishments and this led to a new consciousness which had not existed 10–20 years earlier".

ISLAMIC FUNDAMENTALISM

During the 1980s, the Islamic movement grew stronger than it had been since the founding of the republic in 1926. Amidst the corruption of local and national politics, the Islamic Welfare Party (Refah) offered an anti-corruption alternative to people (particularly the poor) tired of the self-seeking and untrustworthy politicians they were accustomed to.

In terms of criminal justice, the Refah Party was to provide an interesting dimension to the dynamic of change. Created in 1983, the party grew quietly under the hidden leadership of the ultra-conservative, charismatic Necmettin Erbakan until 1987 when he, along with other banned politicians, were permitted to return to political life. Younger members of the Party took up social work in the slum areas of Istanbul and won many over to the "welfare" intentions of the Islamic party.

To the shock and astonishment of the secularist political establishment and their supporters, in the March 1994 municipal elections the Refah Party succeeded in winning 327 mayoralties, 28 in major cities. Most shocking of all to the nationalists was Refah's success in Ankara and Istanbul. Then, in the December 1995 general elections, Refah moved closer to national government with its 21 per cent victory at the polls. Eventually, in June 1996, Erbakan was to form a coalition with Tansu Çiller's True Path Party. By 1997 the Military's National Security Council—custodians of the secular state—had intervened and declared the Refah Party unconstitutional and Erbakan was once more forced into the political wilderness.

But the rise of Refah had an important, somewhat paradoxical, impact upon criminal justice reform. During its period in office, the Islamic party consistently rejected the possibility of a reformed penal code. Rather, they wanted to see a return to Islamic or Shari'a law. In accordance, the Refah Minister of Justice, Şevkit Kazan, severed links with those groups lobbying for reform.[51] According to Köksal Bayraktar this galvanised the politicisation of criminal policy: "For the first time politicians argued for change—*law became an issue because it organised*

[51] Erlap Özgen, President of the Turkish Union of Bar Associations, personal communication, Ankara, December 1997.

the secularists . . . Refah made people think that the system needs reform—that decisions taken in court shouldn't result in such harsh penalties" (my emphasis). Thus, in order to counter the political impact of Refah, secular politicians and academics mooted changes to the existing penal system. Legal politics came from the perceived political threat the Islamicists presented to the Republic. According to Bayraktar, the reforming politicians were not interested in the details of criminal justice—these were subsumed within the wider political changes planned.

There is another important dimension of Islam which is central to understanding the practice of criminal justice in Turkey, and that is the generalised role it plays in social control. While secularisation aimed at the complete separation of state and religion (by transferring all public functions like law and education to the control of state agencies), it also recognised the cohesive importance of Islam to moral and social unity. The founders of the modern Turkish republic, while regarding religion as backward, superstitious and conservatising ". . . clearly recognised that Islam was a significant part of Turkish society, that religious faith was important for national unity and mobilization, and that it could contribute to moral and social welfare" (Ayata, 1996: 41).

For these reasons, among others, Islam was to some extent encouraged but outside the political sphere of control.

HUMAN RIGHTS AND CRIMINAL JUSTICE REFORM

The issue of human rights, principally the issue of torture in police and prison custody, is one which has long marred Turkey's reputation internationally and continues to distort any possibility of genuine penal reform. Successive governments continue to deny the systematic and widespread nature of police torture, attributing it to the acts of wayward officers and arguing that all cases of torture, where sufficient evidence is produced, are prosecuted. In April 1999, six police officers were sentenced to five and a half years each for torturing a suspect to death in 1993. But the majority of other cases have resulted in very lenient sentences, fines or acquittals.

There is, however, a growing number of parliamentarians, judges and state officials who have publicly condemned torture and human rights abuse. In 1997, the Minister of Foreign Affairs, Ismail Cem, referred to torture as "an agonising disgrace" in the country, and Prime Minister Yilmaz issued a circular to relevant ministries to prevent torture and abuse, as well as establishing a human rights minister (Human Rights Watch, 1999).

According to members of the Penal Code Revision Commission, the issue of human rights has formed a central thread in determining the nature and content of the code: ". . . the principle underlying every single article which came into the new code has been checked from the point of view of human rights and the principle of fault (*mens rea*)".[52]

[52] Feridun Yenisey, op.cit.

This is a claim contested by human rights academics, defenders and lawyers. According to Osman Dogru, human rights have played only a marginal role in the new reforms; "If human rights was such a consideration then the people who are interested in human rights law should have been called to work with the Commission. Human rights a driving force? Well they say so but I'm not sure . . . article 312 [this is the article under which Leyla Zana and the other DEP deputies were arrested and imprisoned] which protects the indivisibility of the Turkish state remains in the new code."[53]

Public debate around the issue of human rights has been vigorous in recent years and critics of the Turkish state's abuses are very unlikely to be satisfied by the reformulated penal code. Nonetheless, if prison sentences for civil servants and public officials found guilty of torture are increased substantially, as the reforms dictate (combined with the abolition of capital punishment), "the Turkish body of legislation will be brought considerably closer to European standards".[54] The role of civil society here is crucial. According to Human Rights Watch, the human rights community[55] is "one of the most active segments of civil society" (Human Rights Watch, 1999). Despite their legitimacy and credibility, both domestically and internationally, human rights organisations are frequently raided and their members harassed and subjected to criminal trials and arbitrary detention by police and security forces.

There are a significant number of reforms that the Bar Associations and Human Rights organisations are campaigning around. Among the largest and most active Bar Associations, central issues of concern are, "the independence of the judiciary, the respect of human rights, fair trials, the organisation of justice, and to inform the public about these issues and to inform the public about some very important trials—in particular those relating to the Susurluk affair".[56]

The 1992 amendments to criminal procedural law which fortified the rights of a defendant during police interrogation (by allowing for the presence of a defence lawyer), were not extended to those charged with political offences. The Bar Associations are now campaigning for those same rights to apply to the State Security Courts.

Despite its radical credentials, the Istanbul Bar (the biggest of all the Turkish Bar Associations) is considered the most important of the Bar Associations by the Ministry of Justice. According to its president Yücel Sayman this does not, however, imply that the Ministry is prepared to countenance any of the reforms advocated and the relationship between the Istanbul Bar and the Ministry is politically hostile.

[53] Osman Doğru, op.cit.

[54] European Commission, *Regular Report from the Commission on Turkey's Progress Toward Accession*, November 1998.

[55] Including, most importantly, the Human Rights Foundation of Turkey, the Human Rights Association, the Mazlum-Der and the Helsinki Citizens' Assembly Initiative.

[56] Yücel Sayman, President, Istanbul Bar Association, personal communication, March 1998.

The Bar has established its own commission to investigate the situation of prisoner rights and living conditions. In addition it is organising a public tribunal to review the cases of the many journalists murdered by the state security forces. According to its president, "We send the reports to the Ministry and to the police but we don't expect anything to happen as a result. It is, however, important that they know we are here, monitoring things."[57]

CONCLUSION

This chapter has focused on urban Turkey. Much of Turkish conflict resolution takes place outside the formal mechanisms of the state. The blood feud, for example, still exists in some rural areas (Içli, 1994: 69). But Turkey is becoming increasingly urbanised, and the process of law and criminal justice is centrally determined and applied nationally. A study conducted by Tülin Günsen Içli of 2,934 prisoners throughout Turkey found that 40 per cent were from rural areas (indicating the extent to which criminal justice operates beyond the urban centres) (1992, 159).

Turkey remains a strong state—it has a long tradition of what political scientists call statecraft. Respect for the state is paramount in political terms and the state has been the defining instrument in the history of the Turkish Republic.

The momentum for increased democracy is accelerating –driven in significant part by Turkey's desire to fully enter the European Union and by its more recent acquisition of candidacy status—but this pressure for increased democratisation may not lead to particularly liberal outcomes for Turkish criminal justice. What this analysis suggests is that with the process of democratisation will come the increasing formalisation of criminal policy, and with it a process of policy-making which will exclude the administrative measures like amnesties and the widespread use of the conditional discharge, which while politically corrupt, also have the effect of undermining the official process of punishment.

If criminal policy is evolving in the Turkish polity, then the consequences may not necessarily be towards liberalisation of punishment. A coherent and formalised process of criminal justice policy-making may be a distant vision for those administrative reformists working actively towards that end. But distant or otherwise it may not produce the liberal outcomes suggested by democratisation. The examples from Western Europe (see Faulkner, van Swaanigen, Chapters 5 and 6) and more specifically from America (see Beckett and Western, Chapter 2) in no way encourage optimism if Turkey is to follow this path. And as Beckett and Western make clear, US officials are particularly active in inducing democratising countries to adopt punitive criminal justice practices, particularly in relation to international drug control.

The absence of criminal policy-making in Turkey may have a more benign outcome for offenders than the presence of formalised policy would entertain.

[57] ibid.

We have seen that the Turkish state has "public enemies" far more effective than "crime" in coalescing public opinion (and in driving the dynamic of criminal justice). It seems clear that, for the present, crime and "fear of crime" will remain lesser concerns for legislators and code drafters while the darker elements of Turkish political life continue to direct the shape of state practices and criminal justice.

But there is a limited momentum—driven by international and domestic demands for an end to human rights abuses, and by the ruling elite's desire to enter the European Union –for a more democratic system of criminal justice. The development of a formal criminal justice policy-making process (based on defined legal principles and managerial efficiency), is seen by the new reformers as central to increasing democratisation, as part of the process of increased international acceptability. And while there may be significant progressive outcomes (e.g. community-based punishments, fairer trials, a reduction in torture), there will almost certainly be regressive outcomes if Western models are pursued without critique. Democratisation may, ironically, lead to more systematic and entrenched punitive practices, extending to fields of activity currently ignored by the Turkish state.

In many ways Turkey presents a picture of criminal policy in the developing world—an authoritarian/democratic state, pushed and stumbling into European institutional practices without a set of clearly enunciated and organic objectives.

To imagine that criminal policy in Turkey can be isolated from wider political processes, and reformed along Western lines, is to ignore the centrality of the political dynamic currently shaping Turkish criminal justice. Until that dynamic is addressed, until a political solution is found for the Kurdish crisis and the authoritarian responses it elicits, criminal policy reform will remain marginal to the actual practice of criminal justice. It is, perhaps, time to revisit Colin Sumner's remarks about comparative sociology, made in relation to criminal policy in post-colonial Africa: "Start to examine the use of criminal law and of crime by the colonialists and you are returned to the criminal economic system underpinning your own state" (Sumner, 1981: 2). Western penal entrepreneurs, bent on transposing democratic principles of criminal justice to the developing world, and the new policy reformers in Turkey, would do well to take note.

12

"Spain is Different": Beyond an Invisible Criminal Policy?

GEMA VARONA

"El horizonte sin luz está mordido de hogueras"[1]

THIS CHAPTER'S FOCUS is to locate currently debated issues in the field of Western criminology within the Spanish context. It begins with an analysis of the literature on Spanish criminal policy (juridical, sociological and criminological). This is followed by a brief review of criminal justice under Franco and its legacy, including current regional differences in autonomous communities such as the Basque Country. An analysis of the main issues currently capturing Western criminal policy and practice, managerialism and globalisation, is then offered. This leads to the application of the adjective *invisible* to the Spanish case as a metaphor for the lack of explicit penal agendas and for the routine enforcement of criminal law. It is suggested that this "invisible routine criminal policy" both underpins and subverts the principle of legality.

Spain offers a universe for those interested in criminology[2] as a standpoint for analysing unexplored "realities". A young democracy, it still, however, suffers the authoritarian legacy of Francoism. According to the United Nations Programme's scale of human development, Spain occupies eleventh place in relation to social tensions and change. Following a continued increase in official crime rates from the 1960s,[3] as the state became more flexible and "modern", crime rates have decreased and remained stable at the end of the 1990s. However, the decline is less the result of any specific criminal policy than a product of changes in statistical methods of recording crime, in the number of heroin addicts and in terms of demography. Obviously, there are other considerations. Although without definitive results, Stangeland's study of unemployment and

[1] "Horizon without light is bitten by bonfires" (from *¡Ay!* by Federico García Lorca. Among many events that will be detailed later, 1998 also meant remembering the 100th birthday of this Andalusian poet, who belonged to the 27 generation, and was killed in 1936).

[2] From the beginning, I should call the reader's attention to the fact that I see no problem in talking about *criminology*. The point of its racist, conservative and discriminatory origin and development is a point of departure and not taken as an essence. Authors like Bergalli prefer talking of sociology of social control, but the debate on naming is not the object of this chapter.

[3] On the deficiencies of crime statistics in Spain, cf. Stangeland (1997).

criminality between 1977 and 1996 concludes that, while there may be a correlation until 1985, criminality subsequently increased despite strong economic development until 1993 (Stangeland, 1997: 58–60).

In this chapter, I interpret these official data qualitatively and to extract general criminal policy implications. More theoretically I examine contemporary Spanish criminal policy against the symbolic historical background of 1898, a particularly significant moment in Spanish history. Having lost its remaining colonies, the 1898 generation of intellectuals reflecting on their country's future, promoted the idea of Spain's uniqueness in its resistance to modernisation and reform. Despite turbulent circumstances, the next generation, of 1927, brought with it a reorientation of thought and a hope for change by denouncing the misery of exploited social classes, repression and intolerance. Most of these ideas were, however, paralysed by the Civil War of 1936–9 and during the authoritarian Francoist regime which followed from 1939 to 1975. Nineteen ninety-eight was a significant year because it marked 20 years' experience of a democratic constitution, the oldest in force in Spanish history. In short, the tourist slogan, *Spain is different*, emerging remotely from the 1898 crisis and its literary conceptualisation of concrete idiosyncratic characteristics, may now be applied to criminal policy analysis.[4]

CRIMINAL POLICY IN SPAIN: ITS THEORETICAL LIFE BETWEEN CRIMINAL LAW AND CRIMINOLOGY

In Spanish academic discourse, criminal policy is regarded as the diffuse ground between criminal law and criminology. There are three interrelated concepts that occupy the introductory pages of penal handbooks: criminal policy, criminal law and criminology. *Criminal policy* encompasses the set of (political) criteria to deal with criminality, as understood by von Liszt at the end of the last century (Mir Puig, 1996: 16). A more realistic and explicitly non-value-free definition will be adopted in this chapter. Criminal policy within a social and democratic *Rechtsstaat* can be limited to the power of definition of criminal processes,[5] ideally within a state based on equality and liberty (social justice in the terms of van Swaaningen). This state power, because of its intrinsic violence, has to be submitted to constant critical revision (Bustos, 1996). Criminal policy means not only ways of reducing the harm caused by crime, but also limiting the harm originating in penal and juridical control. Policy-making is, therefore, more complex than the identification of the three contemporary trends in criminal policy, suggested by Silva, namely abolitionism, rehabilitation and guaranteeism (Silva Sánchez, 1992).

[4] In the same way, taking Ortega y Gasset's words (1997), we cannot *save* criminal justice without *saving* its *surrounding life*, which means understanding it first, as a more modest task.

[5] Being the concept of *juridical good* (*Rechtsgut*) a political criminal concept. Cf. Delmas-Marty (1986) and Sola Dueñas(1983).

Taking the definition of criminal policy as the ideology and the plan for the organised acting out of discursively produced *control thoughts* (Henry and Milovanovic, 1994: 126),[6] I talk of the absence of an explicit, general, long-term policy in Spain (in a different sense from that used by Penny Green in Chapter 11).[7] Spain, of course, is not unique in any respect. In Canada, for example, the absence of a clearly enunciated criminal policy, as a set of well-defined objectives that can be found in other administrative domains, has been decried (Fattah, 1997: 179). But in Spain there is not even a declared set of confusing objectives.

Criminology in Spain expanded at the end of the nineteenth century in response to the development of positivism and was taught in a specific School, created by Decree in 1903, with the aim of educating prison officials. However, the Civil War interrupted and thwarted its development into the more sociological or administrative knowledge which took place after 1945 in the rest of Europe (Marcó del Pont, 1986). When criminologists arrived in Madrid for the sixth International Congress of Criminology in 1970, they were taken to view the Lombrosian skulls in the old museum created by the positivist School of Criminology. The social protests of 1968 had virtually no impact on Spanish criminological discourse during Franco's dictatorship. However, today we can observe the difficult re-birth of a "Spanish" criminology—a criminology that has the considerable task of reflecting on the current situation and past periods (including dictatorship and the democratic transition). Criminology is taught as an optional subject in some Law Faculties and is available at graduate level in several Institutes of Criminology. Most research is reported in the unrelated literature of anthropology, sociology, political theory, social work, medicine, psychology, philosophy and economics. As a consequence, there is an absence not only of studies on criminal policy, but also of self-reflection on the discipline. Certainly, nobody talks of a crisis.[8]

A deeper question arises as to whether it is appropriate to apply to Spain the existing non-Spanish literature on criminal policy analysis. It is true that this approach is of great value for theories on criminalisation and comparative work.[9] However, sometimes the obvious is forgotten. History and culture show different developments in the process of democracy and criminalisation. In examining, for example, crime and imprisonment rates, Jock Young has

[6] We may also consider that: ". . . political decisions are not grounded in rational considerations or scientific research, but in sentiments, partly ideology and political expediency" (van Swaaningen 1997: 248).

[7] And yet there is a well-known Spanish review called *Cuadernos de Política Criminal* and even the development of a "criminal policy handbook" by scholars based at the Higher School of Criminological Sciences in Las Palmas, the only centre in Spain delivering criminological studies as a bachelor degree, where "criminal policy" is a mandatory subject.

[8] Cf., regarding English language criminology, Nelken (1994).

[9] An example could be the research carried out from 1994–7, within the UK's Economic & Social Research Council, on crime and social change in England and Spain, 1840–1970, relating trends in crime and modernisation in Liverpool, Blackpool, Bilbao and San Sebastián.

underlined the dangers of transplanting American criminology to Europe.[10] It is important that we learn to *transpose rather than transplant*, and that cognisance is taken of the specific social, political and cultural context in which generalisations about crime are evaluated and the qualitative differences between societies (Young, 1997b: ix–xi). For similar reasons, we should notice different realities within Europe.[11]

CRIMINAL POLICY UNDER FRANCOISM AND ITS LEGACY

The legacy of Francoism is alive in many areas of Spanish life.[12] Starting with the economic arena, the high unemployment which existed at the end of the 1990s can be explained not only in terms of the rigidity of the labour market or excessive welfare development, but also because of an archaic economic structure, inherited from Francoism, which has generated greater employment demands from the agricultural and female sectors, as well as from the shortage of migration opportunities. If we look for the remnants of an authoritarian past in current criminal policy, we find them most strikingly in the form of hierarchical penal institutions and ideologies. A quarter of a century after the end of dictatorship, authoritarianism is alive in the design and implementation of criminal policy by the army, police, judiciary[13] and in the rehabilitation ideologies within prisons.[14] Arguably, the worst legacy is that of terrorist violence.

Unfortunately, there are very few studies of criminal policy under Francoism. This task remains for social historians and scholars in criminology and penal law.[15] J.J. Linz defined Franco's government as an authoritarian regime of very limited pluralism, non-democratic and characterised by a certain mentality (with a strong Catholic and anti-communist sentiment), rather than a dominant ideology;[16] as well as by a passive social acceptance rather than an active mobilisation (Powell, 1998: 315). Five periods within the duration of the regime can be differentiated.[17]

[10] Spain is among the European countries with the lowest criminality indexes, but among those with the highest imprisonment rates. Assuming the critique that statistics reinforce stereotypes, see *Revista de Derecho Penal y Criminología* (1998), 1, 333–46.

[11] Bergalli (1995; 1997).

[12] Not only in the form of demands for the destruction of Francoism archives on "dangerous individuals", including homosexuals; or of apologies by the Catholic Church for its role under that regime; or of compensation for losses to political parties abolished in that period (see the Act 43/1998 on restitution or compensation to the political parties of goods and rights seized with the enforcement of the normative about political responsibilities during 1936–9).

[13] Areas sacrificed in the political consensus during the transition to democracy (Jaime-Jiménez, 1997: 75). On judicial power during Francoism, see Bastida (1986).

[14] Cf., in general, Miguel (1976).

[15] On the transition period, see Bergalli (1985).

[16] Of the same opinion, Hobsbawn (1995, 120), even though its fascist component should not be overlooked.

[17] See Biescas and Tuñón de Lara (1980).

1. 1939–45: The proclamation of Franco as undisputed head of government, the state and the military (*generalísimo*) was followed by a friendly relationship with the Axis powers during World War II, even though Spain remained neutral. The disaster of the Civil War had resulted in the death of around one million people and for the survivors life remained repressively precarious.
2. 1945–53 was the phase of ostracism and autarchy, despite attempts to give the regime a façade of "organic democracy".
3. 1953–9 represented the beginning of greater openness, with covenants with the Vatican and the US (in compensation for economic agreements, military bases were allowed in Spanish territory). In 1955, Spain joined the United Nations.
4. 1959–69: international contacts increased with economic liberalisation measures.
5. 1969–75 represented the crisis of Francoism. During the final period of dictatorship and transition, the ratification of human rights instruments (in 1977, the two UN Covenants) symbolised the real end of the autarchy and international isolation.

PENAL LEGISLATION

Franco's dictatorship made Spain's 1932 Penal Code more punitive. The 1932 Code had abolished the death penalty, except for military crimes. However, an Act of 1934 restored it for certain behaviour related to public order and in 1936 military jurisdiction over capital cases was extended. A Decree Act of 1938 reintroduced the death penalty into the penal code, because, according to its preamble, a "strong and righteous state" was needed. Garrotting and the firing squad were the techniques used for the execution of up to 300,000 people (according to political opponents) or about 20,000 (according to other sources), in the period after the Civil War.

After 1944, terrorist crimes were included in the Code, and prison remission through work was introduced. This practice was borrowed from military penal law, an expedient policy taking into account the large numbers of political prisoners and the needs of the labour market. Other punitive legal instruments used by Franco's regime included the Act on political responsibilities (1939), the Act on the repression of masonry and communism (1940), and the Act on state security (1941)—all were applied without a statute of limitations. Also, the Act of 1933 on "tramps and villains/criminals" (this was also applied to terrorists) was substituted by the Act 16/1970, on dangerousness and social rehabilitation. The Penal Code was further reformed in 1963 and 1971 and was finally adapted in 1973 (Serrano Buttragueño, 1994).

CRIME AND CRIMINAL JUSTICE UNDER FRANCO

Notwithstanding political crimes and the absence of reliable statistics, crime rates during Francoism were relatively low. At the beginning of the 1970s, a new focus on crime and delinquency was articulated (Landecho, 1971): internal and external migration, international crime, working women, drugs and consumer society, white collar crime[18] and anomie produced by a climate of a "happy and trusting society", along with economic growth were now enumerated as important concerns. In the previous two decades, one-third of the population migrated to urban centres to work in the industrial and service sectors. Although from 1963–73 the Institute for Migration assisted more than one million Spanish migrants to move to other European countries, increasing numbers of tourists started to visit Spain. The opening up of Spain facilitated international crime and exposed the inability of the Spanish police to deal with it. Police statistics of the 1970s also incorporate to around 1,000 drug-addicts and one and a half million alcoholics.

As with every totalitarian state, Franco's regime had an unquestionable concept of public order which required the policing of society with the purpose of eliminating every adversary. Towards the end of the Civil War, in 1938, the Public Order Ministry was created. The Act of Police of 1941 commanded this force to "defend the state, to carry out a rigorous and close vigilance of all enemies".[19] All security forces were considered to be within the armed forces (Villagómez: 1997, 52–6).

Initially, penal policy was developed by military authorities with the aim of achieving complete political control through the use of prison and the death penalty. A tribunal of public order dealt with the prosecution of offences against the state. In the early 1940s more than 300,000 prisoners were sentenced for political offences. From 1937, Franco's National Front created concentration camps and so-called militarised penitentiary colonies for prisoners, including foreigners, to work during the armed conflict and for reconstruction after it. They were located in Medina de Rioseco, Santa Espina, Salamanca, Miranda del Castañar, San Pedro de Cardeña, La Línea, Miranda de Ebro and Nanclares de la Oca.[20]

Franco's regime reported prison rates which were among the lowest in the world. The validity of these figures is open to question but there was a policy of granting amnesties and general pardons from time to time, mainly coinciding

[18] Cf. Sainz Cantero (1971).

[19] Including one particular Spanish ethnic minority arriving in Spain in the fifteenth century: the gypsies. Arts 4, 5 and 6 of the 1943 Regulations on the *Guardia Civil* pointed out its special function of watching gypsy people.

[20] Despite the sparsity of literature on this subject, see Bartolí (1944), Llarch Roig (1978) and the recent work by Monago Escobedo on the camp of Nanclares de la Oca (1998).

with political or religious commemorations.[21] During Francoism, at least 12 general pardons to political and common inmates and two amnesties for fiscal crimes were granted.

PENAL LEGISLATION AND THE CRIMINAL JUSTICE PROCESS SINCE 1975

Since Franco's death in 1975, the Penal Code has been modified more than 40 times. There is one aspect that deserves further attention when considering the relationship of morality and crime. From the end of the 1970s to the end of the next decade, significant reforms were introduced which changed the object of penal protection from collective sexual morals (or rather male morals) to individual sexual freedom. Adultery, cohabitation, under-age sex, expressing views against public morals, public scandal and indecent behaviour were all decriminalised.[22] Since the mid-1980s some cases of abortion have also been decriminalised in a limited form.

Within penal legislation, we should also consider changes in police and penitentiary legislation. The pre-constitutional Act of 1978 on National Police introduced a conceptual change which favoured "safety" instead of "public order", while nonetheless retaining the military character of the police. Only with regard to the Constitution and the Autonomy Statutes, has the military element of police forces been reduced, despite a lack of definition of the *Guardia Civil*. According to Art. 104(1) of the Constitution, all police corps serve the government and have the mission of "protecting the free exercise of rights and liberties and guaranteeing citizen safety".[23]

The regional structure of the state determines the coexistence of state, regional and local police forces. The national police (*Policía Nacional)* is an armed civilian institution and the civil guard *(Guardia Civil)* is an armed military institution; both are located within the Interior Ministry. At the regional level, the Basque Autonomous Police force has considerable powers, including specific powers to combat terrorism.[24] Social and political history explains the higher rate of police per inhabitant in the southern countries of the European Union[25]—according to the *Proyecto Policía 2000* Spain has the highest rate. The Police Plan 2000 has the goals of ending centralism, promoting the development

[21] Art. 62(i) of the 1978 Spanish Constitution forbids this kind of pardon.

[22] Recent proposals to modify the 1995 Penal Code have been criticised for being regressive and bringing back Franco's policy.

[23] The Spanish Constitutional Court (STC 55/1990) considered that this article followed article 12 of the French Declaration of the Rights of Man and Citizen. Also recognised in the Organic Act of State's Security Forces and Corps of 1986.

[24] Recently British authorities paid a visit to the Basque Police Academy to gather information in relation to the design of a new service for Northern Ireland.

[25] Cf. Ebbe (1996). In concrete terms today, the police rate per 1,000 inhabitants in Euskadi (Basque Country) is the highest in Europe and autonomous authorities demand a better rationalisation, with a withdrawal of national police and civil guard. The only two other communities with their own police are Catalonia and Navare.

of community police (*policía de proximidad* or *de barrio*) and implementing the *six per six programme*, which concentrates on the six cities with the highest crime rates for the most common crimes: vehicle thefts, thefts from vehicles, street thefts, domestic robberies, small-scale drug trafficking and vandalism.

Regarding human rights abuses by police, following a 1994 visit by the European Committee on the Prevention of Torture, the State General Prosecutor's Office reported that, between 1992 and 1994, 54 penal cases were instructed for ill-treatment. However, unofficial data collected by NGOs suggest there were 765 new cases for that period and 248 in 1995; the majority pertaining to the national police, civil guard and autonomous police,[26] in that order.

On prison policy, the Constitution of 1978 accepted the rehabilitation paradigm, which was endorsed by the Penitentiary Act of 1979. Amnesties and pardons are a clear instrument of political criminal policy, and after Franco's death many pro-amnesty demonstrations were organised in San Sebastián by Basque lawyers. The Royal Decree Act of 1976 and the Act of 1977 were acts of national reconciliation and issued amnesties for political prisoners (Rivera Beiras, 1997; Sobremonte Martinez, 1980: 98, 102, 236). Serious violent crimes were excluded. A further Royal Decree Act of 1977 allowed the 1976 amnesty to be enforced by the government, instead of by the courts.[27] General pardons were given to both political and common prisoners in 1971 (the thirty-fifth anniversary of Franco's rule), in 1975 (the proclamation of King Juan Carlos I, when six hundred and eighty-eight people were released and eighty-five were granted a reduction of their penalty, including the commutation of all capital punishments imposed or to be imposed);[28] and in 1977 (for pacification reasons). A number of ETA prisoners were expelled from Spain as an alternative to prison (Escrivá, 1998: 56–69).

Amnesties were discretionary with respect to non-political prisoners. The Spanish Prisoners in Struggle Co-ordinating Committee (Coordinadora de Presos Españoles en Lucha, COPEL) was created in 1977 by three "common" prisoners and one political prisoner in the *Modelo* prison of Barcelona. Later COPEL was largely composed of common prisoners demanding the cessation of ill-treatment and exploitative work, the total respect for human rights, significant penitentiary reforms and further amnesties or pardons. COPEL received the support of other social movements. A period of violent prison protests, including self-injury, uprisings, hunger strikes, escape attempts, fires and van-

[26] At the end of 1998 the CPT visited some detention centres run by the Basque police, and were particularly worried by ill-treatment of foreigners in certain poor neighbourhoods of Bilbao. According to the detainees' register, in 1998 in the Basque Country foreigners represented about 15.7 per cent (30 per cent in the province of Bizkaia, reaching 50 per cent in the neighbourhood of San Francisco in Bilbao). Cf. Díaz and Fantova (1998).

[27] For critical comments on the 1976 amnesty, coming from a Basque separatist point of view, see Castells (1977, 207–15). Cf. Portell (1977), Landrove Diaz (1976).

[28] Art. 15 of the 1978 Constitution will abolish the death penalty (Amnistía Internacional 1995). Recently, the Organic Act 11/1995 abolished the death penalty in wartime.

dalism followed, under the premise that prisoners' rights had to be "won", not just recognised by those in power.

In March 1978 the General Director of Penitentiary Institutions was murdered and a young reformist penal law professor, García Valdés, replaced him. In May 1978 a committee charged with the task of inquiring into the prison situation presented its damning conclusions to the Senate. It reported that prisons suffered from over-population; the mixing of remand and sentenced prisoners, primary and repeat offenders, minors and adults; excessive censorship of news and literature; lack of education and professional training; a deficient health system; absence of judicial assistance; excessive detention on remand; lack of penitentiary staff (their paramilitary character was also criticised), poor working conditions; ill-treatment practices and harsh disciplinary systems. At a time when Spain was looking for external legitimation, reforms were urgently required to guarantee respect for prisoners' human rights according to international standards.

The Prison Act 1/1979 (*Ley Orgánica General Penitenciaria*), currently in force, contains a progressive policy based on "scientific individualisation", with work defined as a right and a duty, and as transforming and redeeming.[29] The Act encourages the protection of prisoners' human rights, including the provision of a supervising judge (*juez de vigilancia penitenciaria*) who decides on rights, complaints and appeals against disciplinary penalties imposed on inmates. However, once again, there is a gap between the written law and the law in action.[30]

Decentralisation, as carried out in some other spheres of criminal policy, has been constitutionally sanctioned in the penitentiary sphere (Art. 149(1)(6)). However, only Catalonia has been given real competence on the execution of penitentiary legislation (Royal Decree 3462/1983), although, in the near future this may be extended to the Basque Country.[31]

CURRENT CRIMINAL POLICY: REGIONAL DIFFERENCES

Regional differences in criminal justice arise from the autonomous communities into which the state was divided under the 1978 Constitution. Despite the existence of centralised authorities, there are many aspects which are under the

[29] For a review of this Act, see Vogler (1989, 84–123).

[30] In the prison system there were, as of November 1998 45,319 inmates (of these: 25 per cent were awaiting trial, nine per cent were women and 17 per cent foreigners, mainly from the Maghreb countries). Using 1997 data, the Penitentiary Administration draws the following prisoner profile: a young male, average age 29 years, with incomplete primary school studies, (ten per cent totally illiterate and 19 per cent functionally illiterate), unemployed (50 per cent were working when entering prison), with family (84 per cent lived with their partner or relatives) and with a family income higher than the minimum salary (30 per cent with a lower one). In addition, recent unofficial sources indicate that 58 per cent of prisoners were affected by AIDS.

[31] On the prisons of the Basque Country, see Ararteko (1996) and Manzanos Bilbao (1987)

control of regional, provincial and local authorities. This is also the case for the measures relating to juvenile justice and alternative and pilot experiments for adults. In this respect Catalonia is noted for its personnel and material resources; Valencia carries out victim-offender adult mediation under the auspices of its crime victim office; and the Basque Country is known for progressive alternatives for drug-addicts and their favourable acceptance by the judiciary. Attention in this chapter is addressed to terrorism and the Basque Country because of its considerable influence on overall criminal policy.

The Basque Country and terrorism

ETA, the Basque separatist terrorist organisation, was created in 1959, in the confluence of anti-Francoism and Basque nationalism.[32] After Franco's death and the post-Franco amnesties, it was widely believed that ETA would be transformed into a political party, but this was true only of the political branch, Herri Batasuna (HB). Why was ETA less aggressive during Francoism than under democratic conditions, despite the existence of a high degree of autonomy for the Basque country with its own political institutions? ETA demands complete political autonomy, a unified and independent Basque Country,[33] which is socialist and Basque-speaking. The difficulty of this objective, even within a democracy, has led to the continuation of ETA in order to guarantee its own existence (Unzueta, 1997: 34).

ETA obtained legitimation when counter-terrorism measures were adopted by Spanish police and the *Guardia Civil* in what was called GAL (*Grupos Antiterroristas de Liberación*, Anti-terrorist Groups for Liberation). These groups were active between 1983 and 1987 and were responsible for the murders of 27 people. Mercenaries were hired to act mainly on French territory when the French government was not collaborating with Spain.[34] Corruption was rife, with money from the reserve funds of the state used to buy silence and to pay for illegal activities.[35] At the end of the 1990s, as Unzueta has argued (1997, 43), there was a media exposé of the issue through the trials of several mercenaries, secret agents, police members and senior politicians involved in actions carried out during this period. Trials in the Supreme Court, which began at the end of May 1998, resulted in the imprisonment of a former socialist Interior Minister and several senior officials of the state security service and police. Mercenaries

[32] For a critical interpretation of nationalist myths, see Aranzadi, Juaristi and Unzueta (1994); on its origin and evolution, see Jauregui Bereciartu (1981; 1997).

[33] Including Navarra, where non-nationalist voters are in the majority, and three provinces in French territory (where there are no elected deputies of Basque nationalist parties).

[34] As happened in the transition years: between 1978 and 1980, 14 people connected with ETA were killed by mercenaries of the *Batallón Vasco-Español* or other parapolice activists.

[35] Since the 1980s, political and economical corruption in Spain is the result of a mixture of old and new forms of abuse of power (Andrés Ibáñez, 1996; Laporta and Álvarez, 1997; García Nieto, 1997).

and members of the CESID (Superior Centre for Defence Information, a military intelligence service set up within the Defence Ministry in 1977[36]) were also involved. The CESID attracted criticism when it refused to provide the courts with documents relating to counter-terrorism in the cases of Oñaederra, Lasa-Zabala and Lucía Urigoitia. This conflict was resolved by the Supreme Court's decision to give priority to the judicial protection of individuals over the demands of state secrecy in April 1997 (Lozano Cutanda, 1998).[37]

The post-Franco anti-terrorist policy was based on reintegration for ETA members, and a quest for international police co-operation. But, unofficially, an inclination to negotiate has always existed. In any case, according to Sánchez, a well-planned anti-terrorist policy never existed:

> "Instead, anti-terrorist action has been taken reluctantly, following attacks, kidnappings and other outrages. No single, clear and constant line of action has been pursued. Contradictions have occurred and there have been abrupt changes in certain fields of action such as, for example, the issue of whether to keep ETA prisoners together in the same jails or to separate them. But of most concern is that a large number of rules and constitutional principles have been broken such as separation of powers, jurisdictional unity and equality, while human rights have been violated" (1997, 43).

In 1983, police inefficiency and lack of co-ordination in this area was tackled with further political involvement and the design of the so-called ZEN (Special Northern Zone) plan, involving police, political and social measures. The following year, however, a new anti-terrorist Act introduced more repressive measures. Following the traditional repression of insurgent movements, most anti-terrorist policy has been based on police analysis. As a result, the police were granted special powers but without achieving more efficacy (Jaime-Jiménez, 1996: 592).

By the end of 1998, a new landscape had been drawn as a result of an ETA ceasefire. The ceasefire was motivated by several factors: police[38] and judicial actions (including French and international collaboration); internal

[36] Some of its members were involved in the coup d'état of 1981.

[37] In 1995, *El Mundo* newspaper published details of how, for a decade, this Centre intercepted and taped private conversations of entrepreneurs, journalists, politicians and even the King. In May 1999, all accused officials, including the Director of the Centre, were sentenced by the Provincial Court of Madrid. See Rueda and Pradas (1997), Urbano (1997) and Rueda (1993). Recently it has been discovered that the Centre was taping the offices of Herri Batasuna. All this has provoked several political initiatives to regulate the Centre, especially its preventive activities. In January 1998 new political contacts started to discuss the Bill that would regulate its administrative, parliamentary and judicial control. The Bill proposes a judicial control *a posteriori* when investigation is carried out in relation to terrorist groups.

[38] In the case of the Basque autonomous police, denounced by several victims and police trade unions, in several occasions it showed a policy based on tolerance. Cf. Fernández Aúz (1998) who, in relation to the discourse of plural democracy, highlights the clash between central government and the Basque government in viewing terrorist attacks and its less serious manifestations as common crimes or political ones, respectively. The current situation in the Basque Country is so complex that predictable analysis should be rejected (the terrorist as hero or demon). See Arteta, Velasco and Zubero (1998).

disagreements; and the social rejection expressed through mass demonstrations[39] following a high profile murder and kidnapping. Influenced by the Northern Ireland peace process, the growth of the Basque pacifist movement and the dire economic situation in the north also contributed to this new situation.

In November 1998, Congress unanimously passed a proposal calling for a more open dialogue among all political forces in the development of a new way forward; a policy which would be more dynamic and flexible, and which would promote peace, together with actions of solidarity with the victims of terrorism and the respect of democratic principles. The terms employed were ambiguous and euphemistic, but suggested a new criminal policy designed to end terrorism. By December 1998, all ETA prisoners had been brought to the Peninsula, but this was only a limited manifestation of the gradual end of the dispersal penitentiary policy. We have yet to see the consequences of the partial pardon to the politicians and officials involved in the GAL scandal and the outcome of a Constitutional Court review of the HB politicians incarcerated.

As for the victims of terrorism (including at least 800 deaths), some have benefited from recently expanded schemes which have been extended to the victims of non-political offences.[40] With the Royal Decree 1211/1997, a more "direct and personal" relationship between the central Administration and terrorism victims (including relatives) has been promoted. However, victims do not constitute a meaningful pressure group in the political discussions for pacification.

Since the end of 1998, and contrary to the traditional agreement with the Socialist Party, the Basque government has been comprised of an alliance of nationalist parties, with the support of HB. This alliance, which represents about half the Basque population, considers the Statute of Autonomy for the Basque Country, adopted by its Parliament in 1979, to be insufficient to protect Basque autonomy. It argues that the Spanish Constitution should be amended to allow for Basque self-government. The Basque Country has reached very high levels of autonomy: it has its own police, it is recognised as a nation, Basque is the co-official language, it has its own political institutions and powers to raise taxes. For many years, the most striking feature of the Basque problem centred on the refusal of ETA and the other Basque nationalists to acquiesce to the Spanish state. Today the problem is more one of governability: there is no consensus in a very plural society of what a Basque identity means, or of the kind of political agreements (in terms of both content and process) which need to be reached for pacification. Future criminal policy will be only a partial, albeit important, instrument of that pacification.

[39] See, in English, Tejerina (1997).

[40] For those, see the Act 35/1995 on the creation of public offices for their assistance and public compensation for violent and sex crimes.

SPAIN'S "INVISIBLE" CRIMINAL POLICY AND RECENT REFORMS

At first glance, Spanish criminal justice operates without a formal criminal policy (see Green, Chapter 11). But it is clear that some decisions are taken and implemented, with mixed results, allowing us to distinguish between a *visible general* criminal policy and an *invisible routine* one. The *invisible routine criminal policy* attracts little public interest and is therefore difficult to control but the managerial trend, discussed by several contributors to this Volume, can nonetheless be observed. Invisible criminal policy responds specifically to administrative regulations and internal instructions by senior officials and politicians, with an informality presiding over practical enforcement.

For a *visible general criminal policy*, one should first consider the formal criminal justice programme of Spanish democracy, basically contained in the 1978 Constitution (Cantarero Bandrés, 1990). There we find guarantees translated into principles and subjective fundamental rights, despite their devaluation in everyday life (Rivera Beiras, 1997). Beyond the Constitution, criminal policy should be sought in the pre-election agendas of political parties, in concrete administrative structures and agencies, and in law-making. The party in government at the end of the 1990s, the conservative Popular Party, based part of its electoral programme on reforming the penal code to correct the "disproportionate reduction in prison sentences for the most serious crimes (murder, rape, corruption), guaranteeing that the drug-dealers and terrorists will serve their entire penalties and that there will be a real application of the rest of the prison sentence . . ." Regarding the penitentiary administration, there would be "an active fight against drugs in prisons".[41] The Socialist Party (PSOE), in a review of the 1996–8 public safety policy, highlighted the lack of direction and motivation of the police, the promotion of proactive controls and the increasing use of private police.

In practical terms, the current basic organic administration for criminal policy was established by the Royal Decree 1885/1996, ending with the unified structure of the Justice and Interior Ministries created in 1994. According to its Preamble, it is aimed at rationalisation, maximum efficacy and the reduction of public expenditure. For more concrete criminal policy attention should be directed to recent legislation. At the close of the socialist mandate, very important acts and regulations in the penal field were approved in a hasty way as "symbols of democracy" in Spain: the new Penal Code (Organic Act 10/1995, in

[41] The only original and never discussed project during the 1996 elections, in what can be observed as an influence of left realist ideology, was the Citizen Safety Councils proposed by Unified Left (IU). They were conceived to take into account neighbours' participation in the design of safety policies (*El País*, 18 January 1996, 26).

force from 26 May 1996),[42] the Jury Act (5/1995),[43] the reform of the penitentiary regulations (Royal Decree 190/1996), and of the immigration regulations (Royal Decree 155/1996).

As indicated earlier, Spanish criminal policy is not influenced by any criminological trend (theoretical or practical),[44] but is shaped by wider forces, translated in diverse ways into social concerns which affect other countries too.[45] By contrast, penal jurisprudence influences, with varying impact, some aspects of policy-making, and monopolises the scientific discourse on criminal policy. Thus, within the academic sphere of knowledge, three "concentric circles of consent in criminal policy" have been signalled. As far as the Penal Code of 1995 is concerned, this consent was manifested in:

(i) The need for a new Code as a penal adaptation to the 1978 Constitution;
(ii) Explicit recognition of the four constitutional pillars: the principles of legality, proportionality, subsidiarity and social reintegration; and,
(iii) Adaptation to reflect social transformations affecting freedom of expression and sexuality, socio-economic crimes, workers' rights, equality, social reintegration, subsidiary responsibility of the state, crimes against the environment and corruption.

The research results on how the Code is functioning are awaited, including its implications for imprisonment rates (López Garrido and García Aran, 1996). This goes beyond criminal policy into everyday judicial practice as an independent power of the state.[46]

According to its preamble, the objectives of the Penal Code were to introduce a penalty structure to attain the constitutional aim of resocialisation of offenders, to balance the principle of minimal intervention in penal provisions and the need to protect new interests in an ever more complex society, and to provide better protection of human rights, especially against increasing abuses by civil servants, while contributing to the achievement of a higher level of true equality among citizens.[47] Some innovations included in the new Code are: the age for full criminal responsibility is raised to 18; racial, ethnic and nationalist motiva-

[42] For a descriptive English summary of the content of the 1995 Penal Code together with the Spanish procedural system, see Martín-Canivell (1998). See also his contribution to the *World Factbook of Criminal Justice Systems* prepared by the School of Criminal Justice of the State University of New York at Albany, in http://www.ojp.usdoj.gov/bjs/.

[43] For its relation to a more adversarial system in criminal procedure reform, see Thaman (1998).

[44] Here I mean that, when they exist, their research conclusions (the facts they offer about criminalisation) are not taken into account when deciding what is to be done about crime, which implies ethical questions. Cf. Wilson (1974, 53), Stangeland (1998) and Bridges et al. (1997).

[45] Such as the withdrawal of the welfare state.

[46] Of course, one should also study the public prosecutor's role, according to the instructions given by the State General Prosecutor who is nominated by the government (art. 124.4 Constitution).

[47] It was argued that a tendency of reduction in the use of imprisonment could be observed, but this seems not to be true regarding the penalties for common crimes in Spain: those against property (mainly thefts from vehicles) related with drugs.

tions for offences are considered aggravating circumstances; the maximum prison penalty is reduced to 20 years (with a few exceptions of 25 and 30 for particularly serious offences including terrorism); weekend custody is introduced as a penalty; fines are calculated in days, and are to be based on the financial circumstances of the convicted person; the length of sentences of imprisonment that can be suspended is increased to two years (up to three years for drug addicts); the possibility of substituting prison penalties of one year or less for weekend custody or fines is introduced; the possibility of submission to socio-medical treatment is foreseen; greater penal protection of land, historic landmarks and natural resources is developed (a specific offence of intentional forest arson is included); sexual harassment becomes a separate criminal offence; nuclear energy and ionic radiation spilling are also separate criminal offences; failure to comply with the social service alternative to military service for objectors is defined as an offence; offences committed by civil servants against human rights are defined more clearly; and genocide is included among the offences against international law.

As we will see, the Popular Party (PP), with the consent of other parties, has promoted the reform of laws dealing with certain crimes and procedures regarding terrorism (López Garrido and García Aran, 1997). It has also proposed a Bill on crimes against sexual freedom and domestic violence.[48] These proposals have been severely criticised by the Study Group on Criminal Policy because of their symbolic function and lack of guarantees. There is also a public debate around the issues of euthanasia and conscription to military service. Because of public opinion and the future professionalisation of the military forces, the Organic Act 7/1998 has modified the 1995 Penal Code so that prison penalties and fines for persons refusing to do military service and its substitute (community service) have been abolished.

The Penal Code foresees a new juvenile justice system. The Act on Courts for Minors of June 1948 was amended in 1992, after the Constitutional Court considered some provisions unconstitutional with respect to procedural guarantees for minors. Only with future legislation regulating penal responsibility for minors (several drafts have been prepared by the Ministry of Justice, some with a repressive character regarding terrorism), will the provision foreseen in the Penal Code of raising the maximum age limit to 18 years be achieved (the minimum age remains 12 years). Juvenile justice is the only sphere where discretion is legally recognised, following *no intervention* international standards to avoid stigmatisation. Diversion and alternatives, such as mediation and community service may be used, but their implementation depends on the actual agreements with regional or local social services in order to provide infrastructure to develop programmes.

Other fields of recent reform in criminal policy are the jury and prison regulations. The Organic Act 5/1995 reintroduced trial by jury for certain criminal

[48] See the Organic Acts 11/1999 and 14/1999 that have modified the Penal Code on these subjects.

behaviour: offences against human life, offences by public servants, offences against one's honour, neglect to fulfil a duty to help others and offences against privacy and sanctity of the home, against freedom and against the environment. Juries are composed of nine lay members and a professional judge. Lay members will give their verdict on whether or not the facts have been proven, and on the guilt or innocence. The rhetorical aim of having a more democratic penal policy with the reintroduction of the jury in Spain has faced widespread refusal by citizens to participate as jury members,[49] even though most defendants want to be tried by jury.[50]

Another fruit of the socialist government was the Royal Decree 190/1996 on Penitentiary Regulations (which substituted those of 1981). Among the changes introduced were: the development of mothers' units and mixed gender institutions, the creation of centres for social reintegration and the abolition of the system of prison remission through work, so that the penalty decided by the judge matches that actually served in prison. The Royal Decree 758/1996 also transferred the General Directorate of Penitentiary Institutions from the control of the Department of Justice to the Interior Ministry. The Minister for the Interior is now responsible for the development of prison policy. The reasons for this change can be explained in general criminal policy terms by understanding the importance of terrorism in developing policy, but also to achieve some coherence between the police, criminal and penitentiary policies (RiveraBeiras, 1997: 200).

A key question continues to be human rights in prison,[51] today under investigation by the Spanish General Council of the Judiciary, following demands from several NGOs.[52] Even though real abuses are present, the relatively open character of Spanish prisons (allowing more social life) should be taken into account in explaining why some foreign prisoners do not apply for transfer to their own countries, despite the European Covenant and bilateral agreements providing for such transfers (see Green, Chapter 11).

Apart from this, there is neither a political nor a public consciousness about the so-called *prison crisis*. The Penal Code lacks real alternatives to prison. Schemes requiring flexible legal interpretation, such as victim-offender media-

[49] According to empirical studies, there are various reasons for refusal: some people do not want an additional task in their everyday lives, others do not feel comfortable about judging a defendant as they do not consider themselves sufficiently prepared or do not want to assume that responsibility, some are afraid of reprisals and/or manipulation and others do not have a positive opinion of the justice administration and do not wish to be part of it.

[50] Despite being discredited in the Otegi case (a young man connected to HB who killed two officials of the Basque police in 1996), and who was acquitted and later escaped from the country when the case was going to be revised under the suspicion of pressure on and prejudice by jury members.

[51] An increase in the number of foreign and women prisoners is observed. Today women represent almost ten per cent of prison population, mainly for crimes against public health (in relation to drugs).

[52] Their strategy is very interesting: this judicial investigation cannot review the facts of ill-treatment or death, but it can control the judicial response (unjustified delay, unmotivated decisions or no decision at all).

tion projects, are rare. But these are radical innovations at the margins of the criminal justice system, which if allowed to develop, could imply an important break with the modern penal structures (Garland, 1995: 206, note 10).[53] One might even talk of marginal criminal policy directed by regional governments promoting victim-offender mediation, such as in the Basque Country. The Directorate of Human Rights of the Basque Country organised training in victim-offender mediation for the technical teams assisting juvenile courts (in 1997), and for workers in the offices for crime victims and detainees (in 1998). With adults, where the legality principle is an obstacle to these projects, informal agreements with certain judges and prosecutors exist and future developments will depend on the interest and political support within the Directorate. These schemes, which involve a very small number of cases, await external evaluation.

Even without that consciousness, the general public plays a very significant role in driving contemporary criminal policy (especially with regard to terrorism, corruption, sexual crimes, domestic violence and racism) *a golpe de titular* (at the rhythm of newspaper headlines) within a culture of political opportunism prompting policy-makers to create new criminal offences, to give the public the impression that something is being done. Sartori (1998) has argued that the operation of the visual leads to mind colonisation when the complexity of problems cannot be grasped (see Mathiesen, Chapter 10). Media changes the nature of human beings into *homo videns* (and *ludens*),[54] for whom the written word is almost forgotten. Criminal policy exists as long as it is *seen* rather than critically read or reflected upon; thus one might talk of a "video criminal policy".[55]

PUBLIC ORDER POLICY REVISITED: TERRORISM, MIGRATION AND CITIZEN SAFETY LINKED TO THE DRUG ISSUE

The model of "public order criminal policy", in contrast to a liberal guarantee model, is most evident in three domains of the Spanish criminal justice system: terrorism, immigration and public safety related to drugs. In these three areas efficacy is the legitimation for state action promoted by the main political parties and the mass media (Ferrajoli, 1989; Gómez Benítez, 1982; Serrano-Piedecasas, 1988). In these spheres public alarms and fears are socially constructed and translated into emergency legislation, which some authors connect to the building of identities in post-welfare states (Bergalli, 1995). They can also be linked to legacies of the past.

[53] See a polemic proposal, under a model based on proportionality, linked to the issue of principles and safeguards, in Cid Moliné and Larrauri Pijoau (1997).

[54] Cf. Postman (1985). For a metaphor on becoming blind as consequence of the visual colonisation, see the Portuguese writer Saramago (1997). The decline of the literacy and the dominance of the visual was suggested by Ortega y Gasset as one manifestation of the process of mass societies (quoted in Manning, 1988: xvi).

[55] On media and power in contemporary Spain, see Reig (1998).

This hierarchy of social fears in Spain today starts with the economy. In 1996, the unemployment rate was 1.6 times greater than that of the United Kingdom. At the same time, public welfare expenditure was lower in Spain. However, the quality of life was much the same, due perhaps to the cultural configuration of Spanish families where young people, with or without work, remain for much longer with their parents, who provide them with enough money for their higher education, professional training and personal expenses.[56] Others have also accounted for the low level of crime, especially violent offences, in terms of this family structure, together with a more controlled social use of alcohol and tight gun control legislation.

The ridiculed political slogan "Spain goes well" corresponds to Spain's fulfilment of macro-economic requirements for entry into European Monetary Union and to some decline in unemployment. But macro-economic indicators do not explain the sense of pessimism and lack of well-being of many citizens, especially the young and excluded. This is because fiscal and economic policies are enhancing social inequalities. Moreover, consideration of social indicators such as health and education do not lead to such an optimistic conclusion (Navarro, 1998).

A second social preoccupation is terrorism. As noted earlier, its influence on criminal and procedural law reform and public penitentiary policy continues to be enormous.[57] According to Jaime-Jiménez (1996), four periods in anti-terrorism legislation can be distinguished: Francoism (1960–75), the democratisation process (1976–84), the unification of anti-terrorism legislation (1985–8) and normalisation of the legislation (1988–96). In each period political and penal responses to terrorism have been central in shaping Spanish criminal policy.

A third social fear is immigration, linked to the social construction of the "criminal other" and the black market economy. Since 1992, Spain has become a country of immigration (Varona Martinez, 1994), with non-European Community migrants mainly coming from Morocco and Latin America. Although the foreign population represents less than two per cent of the total, they are over-represented in all penal institutions. The Organic Act 7/1985, on foreigners' rights and duties brings into play the ideology of safety and, contrary to its name, establishes a system by which foreigners, usually immigrants from impoverished countries, are treated as objects without substantive rights. This ideology reflects the European Union policy on *extracommunitarian* citizens, marked by the concept of "Fortress Europe" (see Chapters 9, 10, and 13) as a compensatory measure for the free market, despite the attempts at judicial and parliamentary controls under the Amsterdam Treaty, and despite the reform

[56] In 1997, Spain had the highest unemployment rate for young people in the EU, considering the total active population (22.1 per cent), followed by Finland (15.7 per cent), France (12.4 per cent) and Italy (12 per cent). The percentage for the UK was 8.2 (*Anuario El País 1998*, 72).

[57] Even its term is taken to signify the gravity of offences like domestic violence (domestic terrorism?) by some feminist groups.

brought by the Spanish 1996 Regulations on Foreigners. In principle, these measures aim at granting more general protection for regular migrants, but leave unaddressed the lack of guarantees for detention conditions of persons who are to be expelled or denied entry into the country, along with other devaluations of human rights.

The "drug problem" follows unemployment and terrorism, in terms of public safety, as being of greatest concern to the general public. The Organic Act 8/1983 softened the penalties for drugs and property crimes, together with procedural reform of detention pending trial. Political and public reaction was very negative and some scholars contended that, after these reforms, property crimes grew by more than 50 per cent in two years (Rodríguez and Serrano: 1993, 139). These concerns led to narcotic offences being punished more severely. In 1988 and 1992 respectively, the possession or use of goods or property, knowing that they have been obtained through drug trafficking, and all types of assistance to traffickers in money-laundering, were criminalised, and in the 1995 Criminal Code, penalties were once again made harsher.

To understand recent policy on drugs and public order, the polemic Organic Act 1/1992, of Citizen Safety Protection,[58] must be considered. It was promoted to give normative cover to policing strategies regarding crime prevention, particularly drug-related activity.[59] Nineteen ninety-two was the year of the Expo, the cultural European capital and the Olympics, as well as being the year in which negotiations on the social costs of restructuring the metal industry and the announcement of the reduction of medications to be financed by the Department of Social Security took place (Muñagorri Laguia, 1995: 333). The Preamble to this Act conceives as a continuum the protection of public safety and the exercise of public liberties. However, the report of the General Council of the Judiciary Power, prior to the Act's approval, made it clear that public safety is not as fundamental as individual freedom. Later, the Constitutional Court (s. 341/1993) declared unconstitutional and nullified some parts of the Act and restricted the interpretation of a key article.[60] However, the Act constructs "dangerous categories" of subjects, and gives the police extended powers on the

[58] Citizen safety protection may be defined as an "omni comprehensive concept of police activity against all kinds of dangers" (Agirreazkuenaga Zigorraga, 1995: 22). The term began to be used in the mass media in the 1980s. The Act 3/1979 was already addressed to the "protection of citizen security" and by a Ministerial Order of 1980 the Centre for the Studies on Citizen Safety Protection was created within the Interior Ministry, signalling the increasing juvenile and drug-related delinquency. During the 1980s conventional delinquency grew strongly, associated largely with the consumption of heroin. Within a risk reduction policy, today methadone, and even heroin, is being supplied by authorities (Díez Ripollés, 1998a).

[59] For a comparison of penal policies on drugs, see Díez Ripollés and Copello (1993).

[60] This article (20(2)) allows the gathering of personal data by the police to be treated as part of computer databases, without consent by the affected persons. This is limited to those cases where it is necessary for the "prevention of a real danger to public health" (drugs) or for the repression of crimes. Exceptionally, Art. 20(3) makes it possible to gather and deal with data related to ideology, religion, beliefs, ethnic origin, health and sexual life if it is "absolutely necessary for the purposes of a concrete investigation".

exact meaning of certain vague terms, resulting in a "calculated ambiguity" that favours the role of the police.

Thus, in each of these three spheres, the *function* of crime prevention is clearly specified, without precisely specifying the concrete police *powers* to carry it out, i.e., without strict judicial control. The legislation creates a kind of *infra-* or sub-law, generating a process of administration or dejudicialisation of repressive social control (Calvo, 1995: 97, 104, 121).[61] Aspects of the 1/1992 Act are comparable to the British Crime and Disorder Act 1998 (see Rutherford, Chapter 3).

NEAR FUTURES FOR THE SPANISH CRIMINAL POLICY

Despite its *invisible* character, and reflecting on the introductory quotation from Lorca, small bonfires enlighten an analysis of Spanish criminal policy. During Francoism there was a repressive interpretation of public order. In order to achieve a peaceful transition to democracy, the amnesties and pardons were pursued together with a progressive depenalisation in certain fields affecting public morals. However, a fundamental reform of crime control agencies and "the Basque question" remained unresolved. The search for democratic legitimation continues, as evidenced by attempts to reform the police, the reintroduction of the jury and the adoption of a "penal code of democracy".

Although crime has increased, explained, in part, by modernisation theories, crime itself does not constitute the main concern of the plural Spanish society and criminal policy is not an important element of electoral programmes. However, criminal policy can no longer be studied separately from economic and social policies. At present, contradictory directions can be observed. For terrorism, informal negotiation and rewards for persons collaborating in the "fight" against it, coexist with repressive and exceptional penal and procedural laws. This emergency policy (with limited juridical guarantees) is also found in the arenas of migration and narcotics. But here there are certain elements, even if minimal, which make such a policy less one-dimensional. These elements are more visible in the area of social services (for example, basic social protection for irregular migrants and harm reduction policy for drug-addicts, providing them with methadone and heroin). In addition, more and more emergency legislation is related to public alarm, for example, in the case of domestic violence, genetic engineering and hate-crimes as well as measures aimed at enhancing the victim's status. The result is that criminal policy becomes a part of education policy or social pedagogy. The absence of a social ethic, in a soci-

[61] At this point it is clear that the political level is distinct from everyday police activity. Despite real abuses and prejudices that must be constantly denounced, the simple demonisation of the police brings only foretold criminological analysis, overlooking constructive strategies adopted by at least some police officials, when they have to deal with problematic cases.

ety becoming less and less religious, has driven some public opinion and social movements to invest morality in the content of the Penal Code. Erroneously, penal law is required to give answers to social problems beyond its limited opportunities. A *penal inflation* is produced to deal with euthanasia, denial of blood transfusion for religious reasons, protest hunger strikes, abortion and genetic engineering. Symbolic gestures to induce a sense of public safety and social education are also to be found in tackling crimes that are very complex to prosecute, such as offences of corruption by public officials (Díez Ripollés, 1998b: 48–51).

This chapter has sought to distinguish aspects of Spain's developing criminal policy, but these differences compared to elsewhere in Europe have not impeded the development in Spain of a managerialist trend in the public sphere. Although there is no administrative criminology to promote managerialism, actuarial justice is part of the broader political discourse in Spain, as a reflection of global politics. Spain "is different" because it "is" a young democracy, albeit processes have been accelerated by immersion into the European Union. The distinctive features are: structural (unemployment related to families' role "supporting" youth); political (terrorism) and social (new country of immigration, guardian of the southern border of Fortress Europe, women's emancipation, very low birth rate). In any case, in the future, much of what will drive general criminal policy will be defined at the European level (drugs, organised crime, issues affecting immigration). Only if the European obsession with internal security is replaced by a democratic obsession, may optimistic conclusions be drawn.

The difficult task remains in Spain of transforming not only mentalities and institutions, but organisational cultures such as police, judiciary and penitentiary systems, all heirs of Francoism in varied but persistent degrees. This is the last "sense" of promoting the criminological endeavour to provoke a discourse on crime, victimisation and crime control ". . . in such a way that it alerts us to aspects of the human condition otherwise suppressed in the name of normalcy" (Morrison, 1995: 151). At present, some scholars look for its "sense" by denouncing the lack of principles and procedural safeguards of actuarial and dual justice (see Carlen, Chapter 3 and van Swaaningen, Chapter 6). In Spain this belongs, traditionally, to the vocabulary of criminal jurisprudence, albeit never translated into everyday life. The rule of law is supposed to signify legality and due process, but at the dawn of a new century we face wider administrative discretion in the concrete definition of imprecise terms and clauses in what has been called a "calculated ambiguity" (Calvo Garcia, 1995: 106). As a reaction, criminology may be able to rediscover the modest value of guarantees and continue exposing their violations and biased interpretations. This makes pertinent Jhering's struggle for law (1881), but now mainly because rights are understood as real opportunities for the exercise of civil, political, social and economical rights (Lucas Verdú, 1997). At the end of the second millennium, the requirement is not the maintenance of the welfare state, but the reaffirmation of a social justice state which is truly democratic, providing for the realisation of basic rights and the foundations of a critical public opinion in the penal sphere.[62]

[62] In Rawls's words, adopted by Baratta following Kant's description of the Enlightenment, of a public use of reason (Cortina, 1997: 87, 167–8). Cf. Deflem (1998).

13

Three Trends into the New Millennium: The Managerial, the Populist and the Road Towards Global Justice

SEBASTIAN SCHEERER

SPELLBOUND BY THE PAST?

WHAT WILL THE future bring in terms of criminal policy? Will it be soft or tough on crime (and what will crime be like)? Can we be optimistic—or is there more reason to have the "New Millennium Blues" (Francis, Davies and Jupp, 1997)? Authors agree about the "significance of learning from the past in preparing for the future of the criminal justice system", but quite rightly never forget to add that there is little agreement "as to what the past exactly is and how it shapes both the present and the future" (Stojkovic and Klofas, 1995: xi). Knowing the past might be as difficult as knowing the future. Everything is intricately and inescapably linked—"after-images of the past, metaphors of the present and visions of the future" (Cohen, 1985: 211).

There are "past futures" (Hess, 1998), though, in the form of past predictions published by criminologists and (other) fiction writers, which are easily accessible in archives and libraries. There are books on the future of imprisonment (for example, Morris, 1974), the future of policing (for example, Hoogenboom et al., 1997), and of crime and justice (for example, Klofas and Stojkovic, 1995), not to mention the more elaborate vision of social control in general (for example, Cohen, 1985). The first thing to notice is that real optimism is rare. Not that there is a shortage of writers who have an idea of how things *could* and *should* improve, but few dare say that they *will*. Norval Morris, for instance, devoted much of his book to arguing that societies should start with what he calls a "deep-end" approach to prison reform, i.e. with building adequate prisons for repetitively violent criminals first, and then hoping that this would "set free resources of intelligence, decency, and efficiency for the correctional treatment of all convicted criminals" (Morris, 1974: 89). What he did not do, though, was to say that things *would* indeed happen that way.

Those who dare say what *might* or *will* happen normally adopt a more cautious, fearful, and warning pose. Leslie Wilkins, for instance, has never overestimated the role of enlightened reason in criminal policy. He assumed some time ago that people would continue to seek solutions by doing more of the same, and that the public would continue with the erroneous belief that because nobody liked crime, what one did about it would decrease it. As a consequence, he predicted a total breakdown of the criminal justice system some time before the year 2000 (cf. Wilkins, 1973). A few years later, Gresham Sykes (1980, 7) thought it quite possible to envision either "a society marked by increasing violence and attacks on private property, by intolerance of any deviation from an obsessive morality, and by far-reaching police surveillance, coupled with a loss of civil liberties in a totalitarian social order"—or one "with widespread acceptance of and conformity to the criminal law, a modest view of the proper reach of the State, and methods of law enforcement that are just, humane and effective", the latter vision being "admittedly more difficult" to credit with some plausibility.

Why are there not more strongly optimistic predictions about the future of criminal justice? At first glance this absence of optimism does not seem to make much sense. At least not in terms of long-term developments. As is well known, in early modernity the general nature of punishment was deliberately brutal:

> "Those who were not put to death could be blinded, branded or subjected to various forms of frightful amputation. Methods of capital punishment likewise provided images that were fearful. For the common criminal, hanging was an excruciatingly painful death which was publicly degrading. For this reason the nobility were permitted the luxury of decapitation, the axe being a symbolic representation of the knightly sword. (. . .) Yet hanging and decapitation were as nothing compared with the process of being half-hanged then emasculated and disembowelled whilst alive—the fate of traitors. Women judged to be witches were either strangled, drowned or burned alive, though the last two to die in England—a woman and her nine-year-old daughter—were hanged in 1716" (Morris, 1999: 7).

Since then criminal justice has lost many of its terrorist features. It has become, in our understanding at least, more humane by respecting the offender and regularly giving him or her another chance in life. Moreover, there are strong indications that, at least as far as long-term historical trends in Europe are concerned, there has been a fairly continuous decrease of individual violence since the ascension of the modern state (Eisner, 1998; Thome, 1998). To an extent one can say that things have worked out, that things have become better both in terms of decreasing violent crime and the increasing humanisation of criminal justice. Thus far, modernity has kept its promise. So why is there not more optimism with regard to the new millennium? Why is the *leitmotiv* of practically all that is being written about the future of criminal justice that things will go from bad to worse, that incarceration rates will go up, the net of social control will get wider, civil rights will erode and social life at large will be comparable to conditions in a minimum security, if not even a maximum security, prison? Why does everyone speak of Michel Foucault's idea of society becoming a *carcéral*? Why this dystopian pessimism if modernity can claim to have achieved what it had set out to do half a millennium ago?

The answer to this question is that modernity has indeed achieved relative internal pacification and a relatively humane criminal justice system, but that it has done so at exorbitant costs. These costs have to do with the disillusioning performance of the state. Hailed as the incarnation of Reason, Liberty and Objectivity by early-modern philosophers, late modernity had to adapt to the fact that the state itself could easily turn into a source of evil that was many times more terrible than the dangers it was supposed to defend us against. The experience of the Holocaust has shaken modern thinking to the bones, and the modern state of depression was only deepened by the additional awareness of humanity's increased likelihood of one day annihilating itself by either the atomic bomb or the destruction of its natural environment. So, evidently, something has gone quite wrong with modernity, and this is what makes it so unpopular in contemporary discourse. There is a deep-rooted sentiment of broken promises and terrible betrayal, a general disillusionment and a loss of faith in the modern world (Bauman, 1989; Miller and Soeffner, 1996).

Quite rightly, the state has undergone a status transformation. Once seen as having potential to control individual violence, it is now regarded as a source of massive and sometimes uncontrollable violence in itself. Over the centuries the modern state has relentlessly become stronger, but it has not become easier to control—in spite of the invention of modern mass democracy. and where checks and balances are still functioning, history has taught us not to be too sure that these will remain intact. This is why, while we are in a phase of deconstructing the notion of the *dangerous individual* (Foucault, 1978), we are at the same time fortifying the notion of *dangerous states* (Christie, 1999). This distrust towards the state is basically why it would be hard to find a single glimpse into the future by a criminologist which does not share the general apprehension about a process that might be termed the *totalisation of control*—be it by means of increased manipulation (reminiscent of Huxley's *soma* as well as of Marcuse's *one-dimensional man*), surveillance (*pace* Orwell's *1984*), or incarceration (a renewal of *GULAGs* and *concentration camps*).

But again, things may differ from what we imagine them to be. While the late-modern state might still be unpredictable, another long-term trend might have come to a standstill or might even be in the process of reversal. The assumption here is that we are living in an age of an ever-stronger state. The dominant visions of the future of social control are obsessed with the idea that the future will be shaped by a strong state with an ever increasing capacity to control our lives. The assumption of such increasing state power is the result of historical processes, and of the experience of generations, with the state's relentless expansion ever since its emergence from pre-modern times. To that extent the current visions of social control have a very sound basis. But what if a long-standing trend suddenly changes, is reversed or brought to a standstill, leaving the door to the future wide open? This thesis has been recently advanced by Henner Hess (1998) who argued that the "past futures of social control" have been made obsolete by recent economic and demographic developments. According to Hess, the political system is on the horns of a dilemma between rising economic and regulatory expectations on the one hand, and rapidly decreasing financial resources and legal competencies on the other. Dwarfed in its problem-solving capacity, the state is facing unprecedented pressures concerning health, education and welfare for an ageing population, the integration of ethnic and religious diversity, the channelling of international migration, and the conflicts around social exclusion (urban underclass). Given the reduced capacity of the state to preventively deal with social conflicts, or to pacify them by relatively simple measures of material redistribution, tensions along the socio-structural and cultural fault lines might increase to a point where the most important problem of the next century might not so much be the ascension of the state to a Big Brother, but rather an uncontrollable rise in crime. If organised state violence has left its mark on the twentieth century, an increasingly disorganised state violence and a concomitant rise of non-institutional social violence might become the signature of the twenty-first.

Maybe we are only clinging to the old futures of social control because of the in-built inertia of utopian visions, which, for some reason or another, are harder to invalidate and to surpass than the descriptions and analyses of normal science. Once established they tend to outlive reality to a surprising degree. One of the reasons for their longevity might be precisely that they are not (directly) based on facts, but need to be understood within a broad *cultural stream*, an axiomatic undercurrent of everyday life that changes as slowly as mentalities. They owe as much to those background beliefs as they owe to the observation of the phenomenal world, of crime bills and sentencing practices, of changes in policing and in the treatment of young offenders. And when the phenomenal world changes, we interpret these changes as short-term exceptions to the rule for as long as we can. While most criminologists seem to cling to the idea that basically nothing has changed, and that the most probable developments will be either very similar to the present, or at least to the classical visions of a future determined by a system of total control, Hess (1998) and Thome (1998) have argued that it is entirely possible to interpret present trends as expressions of a more fundamental shift in the frame of reference. Orwell's model for his utopian novel *1984*—the Soviet Union—has collapsed. Huxley's *Brave New World* was based on the assumption that middle-class affluence would be generalised to the point of total manipulation through the ephemeral pleasures of consumption. This vision is almost as outdated as the Stalinist one, though, since the world has changed so drastically from a few decades ago, control by affluence has ceased to be a realistic option. At the time Huxley lived his Californian experience (from which he derived *Brave New World*), there were some two billion people on the face of the earth. In the late 1950s, there were three billion. In the year 2000 there will be more than six billion, and between

2030 and 2050 there will be somewhere between seven and 11 billion, depending on birth control, life expectancy and many other influences. All these new inhabitants of the earth will require space, food, housing, health services, education, and some material and non-material welfare. It is one thing to know that most of this population increase will take place in Asia (already the home of more than half of the world's population), it is another to recognise that the vast majority of the additional population will be born in areas with an average daily income of less than two US dollars. In former times, population explosions of a lesser degree could be dissipated by emigration—but today there are many more people and fewer places to go. There are no continents to be discovered, but states with sealed borders—and immigrants who do cross the borders are not coming to live in the wilderness somewhere at the frontier, but they are coming with specific aspirations in terms of health and welfare, and with the same internalised symbols of success as the resident citizens. As migration takes on gigantic proportions, border questions, dealing with illegal immigrants, conflicts between residents and both legal and illegal newcomers and the delinquency of foreigners are approaching the top of the political agenda and that of criminal justice policies (see Albrecht, Chapter 8; Melossi, Chapter 9).

Even with immigration restrictions and border controls along the Rio Grande or around *Fortress Europe,* it is highly unlikely that billions of people will stay where they are when that place does not even feed them with the hope of ever getting what they believe they deserve. While economic globalisation increases productivity by technological innovation, it creates a rather abstract wealth for some, but real misery for the majority. With a few winners and masses of losers, there is trouble ahead.

The age pyramid will change. On a global scale, the earth has already become "younger", necessitating more investment in education than ever before (presently, 50 per cent of the world's population is below 20 years of age). Only in Europe will things look different. Here, the populations will not grow, but there will be an increase in old people. If the world comprises 390 million pensioners (above 65) today, it will accommodate some 800 million by the year 2025, when life expectancy will be around 80 years in Europe and North America. For a country like France, this means that instead of having 200 inhabitants older than a century, there will be 150,000 by 2050. Financial demands on the state will multiply in Europe, but state income is dramatically decreasing at the same time; the asymmetry between centre and periphery, so accentuated by economic globalisation, will be replicated within the centre, where the rich will get richer, and the poor will increasingly . . . go to prison.

Traditional visions of the future of social control involved extrapolating trends that were real and expanding in their times. Their appeal was their kernel of real-life experiences. In the contemporary world, our old visions of the future are rapidly losing their power to fascinate and to mobilise. They are losing their grip on our imagination because what they reflect and dwell upon is not our present-day experience, but that of half a century ago. Having grown ever-stronger for centuries, the nation states are now in decline. They are losing their ability to control industry and capital, and to a much greater extent they are losing their capability to control their borders in terms of human migrations. But they are losing on both levels, and while states were once continuously claiming more tasks and competencies, they are now selling their property, outsourcing their services and losing ground due to the strong and conflicting pulls of tribalism, on the one hand, and globalisation, on the other.

This is why tomorrow's criminal justice systems will not only be different from what they are today, but also different from what we used to imagine they would be like in the future. As Bill Gates of Microsoft has said, people tend to overestimate the changes that will take place in the next two years, but they also tend to underestimate the changes that will take place within the next ten years. In a way, though, it might already look different today from the way in which we think it does—due to the influence our obedience to obsolescent images of the future has on the way we see the present. In the remainder of this chapter I shall, therefore, try to outline three major trends which might dominate an ever-growing part of the criminal justice systems and their philosophies—and which are partly complementary, partly contradictory, but which share as one of their features the fact that they had not been at the centre of the futurologist discourse of the past.

The first of these trends, "managerialism", is the tendency to strip the criminal justice system of moral components and idealistic purposes, and to see criminal justice as a problem of book-keeping and "actuarialism". The second is "populism", i.e. the tendency to let criminal policy be governed by the general audience's affective needs and often erroneous fears, while renouncing a solid assessment of the situation and development of instruments—as long as such a turn to legitimation by acclamation can further the power interests of those who propagate it. The last, but not least, is what I would term the thorny and ambivalent "road to global justice", i.e. the tendency to reduce national criminal justice systems to "local" issues with a reduced moral weight, while moralising macro-offenders and macro-damages, and thereby paving the way towards the establishment of a (new) criminal justice system of global dimensions.

TREND ONE: MANAGERIALISM

As René van Swaaningen (Chapter 6) states, both the vocabulary and the practice of criminal justice and penal policy today differ markedly from what we have been used to: "The traditional legal questions of legality or guilt, or the traditional criminological ones of stigma or rehabilitation, or indeed the visions behind a certain criminal justice policy, seem to have lost their meaning. Nowadays, officials mainly speak about criminal justice in terms of business management." What van Swaaningen points to is the phenomenon of *manage-*

rialism, now a pervasive trend in criminal justice systems—and, by the way, one whose advent had not been anticipated by criminological futurology. It emerged without their help. Neither is managerialism a fruit of the "social criminologists" (O'Malley, 1996). Managerialism only had a chance to blossom after the decline of the welfare state and its rehabilitative ideal; only after one had come to believe that "nothing works", could there appear an attitude, a practice and a terminology that saw it as irrelevant if the offenders were anti-social or kleptomaniacs, bad or mad or whatever else—an attitude which reflected the wish to simply manage the practical problems of tracing people, of locking them up and of ensuring, to a sufficient degree, they would not do it again. Managerialism in prisons today is not that which characterised the founders of Walnut Street Prison at the end of the eighteenth century. Managers of today do not see prison as a place where sinners will become saints, or anti-social individuals will get cured. But they are willing to support prison expansion as long as it gives them the feeling that it incapacitates some stubborn offenders and keeps them away from the community. With the privatisation of prisons there is an additional reinforcement of the trend of warehousing (Christie, 1993). As Jock Young (1988, 14) expressed it: "*You want above all to avoid trouble rather than to understand it*. You want to minimise risk rather than morally condemn behaviour." That is the basic message Malcolm Feeley and Jonathan Simon (1994) have named *actuarial justice*. Crime should not get out of hand, controls should contain it, and both the institutions and the population at large should learn how to live with it, instead of trying to somehow eradicate it. At one time, for example, car accidents used to be a source of moral outrage and bitter conflicts about guilt and negligence. With the advent of the insurance business and the massive number of such incidents, accidents ceased to be a source of such conflicts. What used to be a regular sight in the inner cities—exasperated drivers standing in the middle of the street beside their awkwardly traffic-jamming cars—has become near to unthinkable. Things are done swiftly, cars are pulled to the side, facial expressions hardly altered. What used to be set in scene as a public morality play has been routinised and stripped of moral significance. This de-moralisation is happening in many areas that once used to arouse strong emotions. Thieves, once hanged, are now subjected to a routine process which maybe does not even involve a court appearance, let alone any visible and serious moral exhortation. Homosexuality, once a highly moralistic drama of sin and virtue, jail and defamation, has become a morally neutral lifestyle.

The same is true, to a large extent, with respect to drug use. Of course, it is still punishable, and urine analysis is widespread and consequential—but the moral dilemma has largely evaporated. In Frankfurt, bankers and residents have long given up hope of finding a solution to the inner city nuisance of drug users openly injecting—but out of a sense of decorum, they and many of their counterparts in other larger cities, now favour state-subsidised heroin rooms, where users can safely inject their drug before returning to another low-threshold counselling centre where they are provided with free food and with washing machines which clean their worn-out streetwear free of charge. The morality play is over. They must know what they want—and if they want this, we give it to them as long as they stop bothering us. Rather than being defined as deviant malefactors, drug users are becoming "the self-selected occupant(s) of a high-risk category that is channelled away from employment and the greater access it brings" (Simon, 1987: 85). On the one hand, this ends a hard-to-bear hypocrisy and intolerance towards difference, but the stripping of actions of their moral properties closely resembles what Zygmunt Bauman (1996, 48) called *adiaphorisation*—a separation of acts and moral evaluation of their meaning that he found to be conducive to individuals' participation in the Holocaust. At a closer look, though, the dissociation of acts and meanings in the Holocaust was a basically modern phenomenon, linked to the division of labour (Jäger, 1988). Actuarialism and managerialism do not separate action and morality for *modern* reasons of long chains of production, but because of a *post-modern* loss of faith in the *telos* of history. This may be why actuarialism and managerialism were not predicted in our traditional visions of the future, but why it had to develop before it was recognised, named and explained. It had been impossible to predict because it arose as a consequence, not of modern thinking—which in their way even Huxleyan and Orwellian dystopias adhered to—but of a post-modern loss of faith in the direction of history. While modernity was convinced that, for better or for worse, modernity would increase our knowledge about the social and natural environments, which in turn could not fail to bring about more health and wealth for an increasing number of people, post-modernity is characterised by a loss of such quasi-metaphysical orientation. Post-modernity has lost faith in destiny and progress, and it sees little sense in getting outraged at deviance, at a time when our knowledge of absolute values has gone with the wind. In a post-modern reflexive turn, some of the best criminologists tend to see their discipline's most important challenge not in finding the causes of crime, but in the analysis of why some acts are being called criminal and others not.

As Nils Christie (1998, 130) has said, "One of the challenges for criminology is to analyse the social conditions giving unwanted acts their particular meaning." Moral condemnation and juridical criminalisation are becoming increasingly questionable. Another sign of *adiaphorisation*? Acts and their evaluations have to be separated, scrutinised. Morality is put under as much suspicion as is crime—or even more. Does this announce the death of morality? It might seem so. But as we shall later see, the loss of moral outrage is really less a death and disappearance than a migration of morality. Morality is leaving one field, because its force is needed elsewhere. As far as managerialism is concerned, though, the disappearance of morality is a fact. A fact which certainly responds to the general spread of *theories of management*, the popularity of *law and economics*, and the fiscal crisis's emphasis on *rationalisation* (see Faulkner, Chapter 5), as well as to the *rising level of crime* and also the awareness by the public that it is cohabitation with incivilities and crimes rather than their defeat (Garland, 2001) which is on the agenda. It is also an awareness that risk societies' basic response to the *post-modern* condition is that we live in a world of no manifest destiny, of no absolute standards, but of constantly changing possibilities and dangers (Young, 1988). A case in point is AIDS. Once illicit sexual relations gave reason enough for the moral death penalty of a scarlet letter—but in a society that is aware of the inevitability of infidelity, adultery and promiscuity, and that has grown to value the minimisation of risks more highly than the gratifying sentiment of moral outrage, esteem for safer sex technicians is much higher than that for relentless preachers of fidelity. Where the *calculative attitude* inherent in managerialism leads the way, theories of rational choice will thrive, but also those that show their limitations; insurance business will grow at the same rate as risk awareness does—and it will take the lead over old-fashioned criminal condemnation. Where drama was, shall routine be—and to the extent that routine spreads, it reflects in *the new criminologies of everyday life* (Garland, 2000a).

Furthermore, it will become of paramount importance to collect knowledge and to be able to pinpoint persons and things—and it will become less imperative to catch every offender at the earliest possible time, since that could prevent the collection of further knowledge about his contacts, his plans and possible criminal organisations. So police will want to accumulate knowledge more than to react to single offences. Police will learn from secret services, they will learn to build archives and to follow suspects for a long time and over large distances—they will let people continue to commit crimes, and they will continue to watch; they will bring in undercover agents and they will let these undercover agents participate in crimes in order to keep the secret. They will use techniques of surveillance and control, like a secret police (Marx, 1988). This trend is a managerial trend, and it is strong and unbroken, it puts civil liberties at risk much more than we used to know (see Mathiesen, Chapter 10). But while it might seem to fit into the old Orwellian mould, the objects of control are not necessarily remaining as passive and static as modernity saw them. Many left and liberal analyses are missing that point because they see control, not human action, as the *primum movens* of history. With all laws changed and all surveillance in place, with wire-tapping and eavesdropping, with videos and microphones, with *1984* surpassed—efficiency of control has probably decreased over the last decades rather than increased (Thome, 1998). While surveillance becomes more sophisticated, the targets of control disappear into a smartness that outsmarts and an elusiveness which is hard to perceive.

What remains is a change of forms and an erosion of rights. Managerialism gives a boon to technical controls that display some kind of elective affinity to it. There is, for instance, such an elective affinity between managerialism and electronic monitoring, but also any other kind of pragmatism (such as that reigning in youth justice). On the other hand, managerialism certainly does not favour a policy guided by higher-than-technical principles and democratic justification (see Carlen, Chapter 4; Faulkner, Chapter 5). Modernity was obsessed with the conflict between justice and truth, on the one hand, and mere interests and technical rationality on the other side. Managerialism is the result of the victory of technical rationality. It is a defeat of modern ideals. But there might be reason to suspect that technical rationality's victory could be—or that it could be turned into—a pyrrhic victory, that it could be made to serve new principles. Technical rationality and managerialism in themselves are neither bad nor good. They de-emphasise hypocritical moral outrage as well as true compassion. They can degrade and respect. Under the given circumstances, there is certainly ample reason to stress the risks. As Julia Fionda (Chapter 7) correctly states,

> "We are in danger of losing sight of the fact that imposing punishment on others is more than a technical process (. . .). The penalties being inflicted reflect the lack of emotion in the 'ideology' behind them. Community penalties become less compassionate and empathetic and custodial penalties more basic and security oriented. Whereas the demise of the rehabilitation model has, in the past, been hostage to the rise and fall of the 'nothing works' philosophy, it would now appear that it has fallen prey to the 'nobody cares' outlook."

At present, this is what we are experiencing. It might be superfluous to add (but I wish to add it for the sake of ambiguity) that, in the end, it will be much larger developments which will decide whether managerialism develops into a widespread de-sensibilisation towards the sufferings of punishment and victimisation, or if it might be useful in banishing moralistic hypocrisy and the readiness to sacrifice human lives to it.

Managerialism is the perfect expression of what French philosopher Gilles Deleuze (1990) called *control society*. The society that does not care to punish, but to control. The society that does not care to improve, but to cope; not to moralise, but to influence; not to steer the individual, but the situation; not to think in terms of guilt, but in terms of risk. While I am writing this—there is still snow in the streets and it is still the year 1999—people are nervous about what will happen to their computers when 1999 turns to 2000. Will "the bug" destroy their PCs and those of electricity companies, banks and merchants, will it lead to general chaos? If the world should continue after New Year's Eve, it will be to the credit of *managerialism*. In the case of a general breakdown of law and order, of economy and loyalty, though, people will not turn towards philosophers and prophets, not towards priests or sociologists, but to those who have a credible claim to be able to *manage* it. It might dare to be liberal, and if it plays safe it will be authoritarian, but risk society will always hold managers of crime and risk control in high esteem.

TREND TWO: POPULISM

Populism is anti-élitist and anti-intellectual, but primarily anti-élitist. It distrusts interest groups, but it does trust the *common man*. It dislikes lawyers and their jurisprudence, but it does know right from wrong. It hates paperwork and bureaucracy, banks and brokers, but it wants low interest rates and grass-roots democracy. Once used by members of a broad movement, and even a political party in the USA (which lost both the elections of 1892 and 1896), to describe themselves, the word carries so many negative connotations today (Puhle, 1983) that neither Le Pen in France nor Hugo Chávez in Venezuela would be glad to hear it applied to them. On the other hand, it cannot be denied that criminal justice is becoming a popular topic and a politicised one:

> "Policy measures are constructed in ways that elevate public opinion over the view of experts and elitists. The professional groups—criminologists, probation and parole officers, social workers, prison officials, the judiciary, government research staff—who until recently formed the policy-making community are now increasingly disenfranchised. Policy is formulated by political action committees and political advisers—not by researchers and civil servants. Policy initiatives are announced in political settings—the party convention, the party conference, the televised interview. They are encapsulated in sound-bite statements—'prison works', 'three-strikes and you're out', 'truth in sentencing', 'no frills prisons', 'tough on crime, tough on the causes of crime'. Typically such initiatives are under-researched—the primary concern being to resonate with public opinion and common sense, not to accord with empirical research findings or expert wisdom—and lack the elaborate costings and statistical projections that are a standard feature in other areas of policy" (Garland, 2000a: 7).

In a way, of course, populism defends the ideals of direct democracy and common sense, but its moral zeal makes it an easy prey for professional lobbies in the background and the self-interests of the tabloid press. While it pretends to please the public, it might rather be serving basic instincts. In the realm of criminal justice, these instincts spell anger, revenge and retaliation, exemplary punishments, and the death penalty. It smacks of populism if the California voters managed to drive up their State's expenditure for the prison system from below five per cent of the budget in 1990 to almost ten per cent in 1996, and to drive down expenditure for the university system from above 12 per cent to eight per cent in the same period—knowing that a prisoner costs the state $34,000 per annum while a university student costs the state $6,000 (Hess, 1998: 156).

Populism is managerialist only to the extent that it does not care, but it despises managerialism to the extent that it cannot project its own strong values in its visible outcome. Managerialism is not principally opposed to incarceration, and as long as prisons are at least able to serve as a symbol for the expressive needs of populism, both will get along. A single reality can serve both functions: to be an instrument for some, and an expression for others. On the other hand, populism and managerialism will never coincide. Populism will want impunity where the managers see no reason to make an exception. It will want the spectacle of the death penalty where managers will see a senseless waste of a single life and a lot of resources for a more than questionable effect.

Managerialism does not care about guilt. When it establishes "shooting galleries" for junkies it does not even care about responsibilities. It does not punish and it does not sanction, but it does not attribute nor assume responsibility. It merely copes. Populism, in turn, while shunning reflexivity, does not hesitate to push a policy of responsibilisation (Garland, 2000a: 4). It needs icons to represent the Good and the Bad, and it does not like the ambivalence of an innocent Ugliness. So it will try to attribute disorder and incivilities to one of the two moral camps. Populism polarises in moral terms. A paedophile is a sex fiend and a sex fiend should have no place in society. Populism is highly appealing in times of blurring moral boundaries and growing social distance between the re-emerging "dangerous classes" on the one hand, and the threatened middle and far-out upper classes on the other hand (Steinert and Cremer-Schäfer, 1998). As the Willie Horton case showed, populism has an affinity to archaic fears and a revengeful criminal policy—and the way things are going populism will be going strong for quite some time to come.

It is an ambivalent trend, though, and it should not be met with general resistance, but rather with a readiness to differentiate. A case in point is the image of the victim within present policy trends. For centuries, the criminal justice system did its best to exclude the crime victim—until just two or three decades ago, when the victim began to reappear. Today, the

> "interests and feelings of victims—actual victims, victims' families, potential victims, the projected figure of 'the victim'—are now routinely invoked in support of measures of punitive segregation. (. . .) Measures are named for victims (Megan's law; Jenna's law, the Brady bill). The rhetoric of penal debate routinely invokes the figure of the victim—typically a child or a woman or a senior citizen—as a righteous figure whose suffering must be expressed and whose security must henceforth be guaranteed. (. . .) This vision of the victim as 'Everyman' (and, above all 'Everywoman') has undermined the older notion of 'the public', and has helped redefine and disaggregate that collective entity. It is no longer sufficient to subsume the individual victim's experience in the notion of the public good: the public good must be individuated—broken down into individual component parts. (. . .) If the centre-piece of penal-welfarism was the [expert projection of the] individual offender and his or her needs, the centre of contemporary penal discourse is [a political projection of] the individual victim and his or her feelings" (Garland, 2000a: 7; also cf. Simon, 1997).

While there are stereotyped tendencies to exploit "victimism" (Steinert and Cremer-Schäfer, 1998: 23) to invoke tougher laws and sentences, there cannot be the shade of a doubt that a more differentiated look at the victim is badly needed, and could produce positive influences on how criminal justice will be understood in the future.

TREND THREE: THE ROAD TOWARDS GLOBALISM

The third trend might be an even more lasting one. It is the trend of extending the reach of both the concept and the reality of criminal justice to dimensions once thought to be exempt from criminalisation. Until the execution of King

Charles I and later the events of the French Revolution, it had been unthinkable to drag rulers before a criminal court, and even afterwards, the old principle that rulers were above the law *(princeps legibus solutus)*—a principle forcefully defended by German philosopher Immanuel Kant—*de facto* stayed in effect. What we are witnessing today, though, is a turnaround. There is a growing belief in the necessity of a global recognition of some basic values and a global effort to prevent their violation and punish offenders.

There is a change in the prevailing idea of what deserves to be defined as a legally protected good—and what does not. The classical claim of the criminal law was to deal with severe violations of national security (treason, insurrection) and of life, liberty and the property of citizens. Pre-democratic societies were openly class- and race-biased. Democratic societies still practised *class justice*, albeit with a guilty conscience, which gave rise to several attempts to end the impunity of white-collar offenders. In a way, of course, it was by mere coincidence that Edwin H. Sutherland's study of white-collar crime (Sutherland, 1949) appeared the same year that the Nuremberg Trials demonstrated the claim of the world's leading nations to deal with offences against the vital interests and values of humanity not by the means of war, but through the courts.

The Cold War which followed did not prevent the further elaboration of this topic, but certainly halted any progress in terms of its materialisation. Nevertheless, the theoretical work done during that time shaped much of what is gaining real life today. Karl Jaspers's *world philosophy*, for example, which emerged as the result of the philosopher's total revision of his thinking following his realisation (in 1948) that modern technology in the sphere of communication and warfare had made it imperative for mankind to strive for world unity, projected a *world state* with just one government and with something like the UN plenary as a world parliament. Such a world state, the main objective of which would consist, according to Jaspers, of preventing wars (which would all be considered civil wars) and securing freedom and equality on the whole globe. In *The Future of Mankind* (1961), Jaspers explained that the aim of this political world union would not be absolute sovereignty but rather world confederation, in which the various entities could live and communicate in freedom and peace. and while the philosopher developed the concept of *cipher*, in an attempt to show how thoughts and beliefs of different cultures and times could become communicable, creating the possibility of a far greater tolerance than had ever before been possible, the UN was drafting both a Code of Offences against the Peace and Security of Mankind in 1951, and a Statute for an International Criminal Court in 1953. Later, during the Cold War, the political left in the Western countries tried to extend the limits of the concept of crime to incorporate "crimes of the powerful" and "repressive crimes" into the criminological discourse, thus significantly revising its traditional focus on delinquent youth, petty property offences and violent acts among the lower classes. In 1988, when the term "macro-criminality" was invented to designate politically motivated collective crimes, such as genocide and mass destruction (Jäger, 1988), the UN changed the name of its Draft Code of *Offences* . . . into Draft Code of *Crimes* . . . in order to stress the gravity of those acts (Triffterer, 1998: 274). Since the end of the Cold War, both the semantics and the practice of a global criminal justice policy have gathered momentum. It is not completely uncommon to refer to the President of the United States as The World's Leader (Broder, 1999), and to openly prepare criminal prosecution of national leaders and other politicians, not only after their term in office (like Pinochet/Chile), but even while they are in the exercise of power (Milosevic/Yugoslavia). To be the acting president of a country does not prevent one from being referred to as a criminal, a terrorist, and/or to be threatened by criminal prosecution before an international court—and the general feeling is that it should not be able to, either (Jäger, 1995). This change in rhetoric goes hand in hand with the increasing possibility of—and it helps create an increasing climate of legitimacy for—the establishment of a permanent international criminal court. As a matter of fact, the signature of the Rome Statute for the International Criminal Court on 17 July 1998 means that it will indeed be created after ratification of the statute by 60 member states of the UN (Triffterer, 1998: 273).

Correspondingly, the UN criminal policy machinery has undergone substantial changes. While originally centring very much on the drafting of minimum standards for the treatment of offenders and other segments of the criminal process, a major shake-up in 1991 brought not only the upgrading of the *Committee* on Crime Prevention and Control to the rank of a *Commission*, but also its purge of all non-governmental members and their relegation to a rather powerless separate body. Since 1991, the emphasis has changed from concerns about human rights to the fight against international organised crime. On the other hand, a number of Nongovernmental Organisations such as Amnesty International, Human Rights Watch and the Association for the Prevention of Torture have entered the international arena—initially in order to help safeguard human rights, but now certainly also with an eye towards the collection of evidence for future trials before the International Criminal Court (Feest, 1998).

In a way, we are witnessing a repetition of a state building processes on a higher level. Instead of the emergence of many nation states out of regional concentrations of power, we see the emergence of a single world state out of a global concentration of single, national power systems which will finally reduce national politics to a matter of rather provincial importance. If criminal justice on a global level does not only emerge as a result of this process, but is in itself instrumental in the making of a global government, this, too, would only repeat historic precedents. In the global village, there will be as much attention given to the containment of "dangerous states" as the nation state accorded to the "dangerous individual". Since the end of the Cold War, there is a strong discursive trend to relativise the once high-held value of national sovereignty. Sovereign states are helpless when it comes to finding a response to simultaneous occupations of embassies and consulates by ethnic minorities in a dozen countries, to the ozone hole, the greenhouse effect, or to the questions pertaining to nuclear reactor safety in Eastern Europe. Single states cannot prevent global stock exchange disasters, nor can they find solutions to international migratory movements, the population explosion or transnational crime. Informed observers of the state of the globe have come to believe that "crime becomes, perhaps, the greatest danger of the next century" (Kaplan, 1997: 14), and it is small wonder, therefore, that the main argument for, and the main means of, establishing a single global power will be the hope for progressive global pacification. The World State, then, is the New Leviathan, with all its promises and all its dangers, gone global. Just as the flag followed the trade in earlier times, rampant global capitalism will not be able to develop much further without support by adequate political structures. As George Soros (1998, 24) has said, the most pressing problems today are not the deficiencies inherent in the global economy—like the instability of financial markets, the asymmetry between centre and periphery, and the difficulty in taxing capital—but those pertaining to the political system: "The development of global society has lagged behind the growth of a global economy. Unless the gap is closed, the global capitalist system will not survive."

While history is contingent and without an in-built destiny, while there are always other options—including a return to the Middle Ages or a post-modern *tribalism* (Maffesoli, 1988), a *clash of civilisations* (Huntington, 1993), none of the above, or a mixture of all of the above—it is more likely than not that things are steering towards some central hyper-structure. Will it be despotic or democratic, federalist or centralist, effective or ineffective in its efforts to create and implement a universal order? Nobody knows. One fact should demand our attention, though. The technical potential for world rule certainly precedes its democratic legitimation. In terms of weaponry, the United States can already be seen as the new world government. Its reconnaissance reaches to the most remote Asian villages. Today, there is not a single phone conversation, not a single fax, e-mail, internet connection, or other kind of data transmission which cannot be automatically recorded and later evaluated (first by machine, then by human brains) by the US National Reconnaissance Office (NRO) and the National Security Agency (NSA)—at least in theory, but also in praxis. According to the Federation of American Scientists (FAS) they do. By 1992, NSA was capable of automatically intercepting and checking two million messages per hour worldwide; computer evaluation would screen them and sort out some 13,000 for further analysis, later reducing them to 2,000 which would undergo manual screening. Since NSA employs more than 20,000 people around the world, that job can be done. Out of the 2,000 messages, 20 would be of significance and two of them would land on the desk of "The World's Leader" (Ulfkotte, 1998). When a globally operating "top-terrorist", like Osama bin Laden, suspected of being responsible for the bombing of two US embassies in Africa, is thought to be hiding in a certain part of Afghanistan, this leader can proceed to drop some bombs on his headquarters (as he had done in Tripoli some years before). How does he know where bin Laden is? He simply does.

And he also knows when bin Laden, at the verge of being expelled by his host country (afraid of US pressures), secretly meets with a high-ranking Iraqi official in the mountains near Kandahar, at that time certainly a no-go area for any Westerner.

Of course, there are objections to the idea that the US can be seen as something of a global ruler. It might be argued, for example, that the US is still far from being able to control effectively everything and everybody on the face of the earth. This is certainly the case; but many a country's government is facing more severe problems with respect to the administration of its own remote areas, without being denied recognition as the country's ruler. Given the discrepancy between an arsenal of arms already able to attack anyone at any time and place on the globe on the one hand, and the lack of a single global space and language of communication on the other, the first thing to see is a democratic deficit. While the US can rule the world, it certainly cannot globalise its internal system of democratic legitimation. There are too many radically different cultures, too many radically different spheres and means of discourse to extend the American election laws to the globe. Given the deep and tense fault lines between the different great civilisations of the earth, the Western, the Islamic, the Slavic-Orthodox and a few more, it is unlikely that the new world state will be structured like a nineteenth- or twentieth-century nation state. It is not unlikely that the coming global empire will resemble less the political system of the US, than that of the Roman or the Ottoman Empire. In Islamic regions, the Shariá will be the regional law of the land, and there will not even be a general acceptance of Western-style representative democracy. Turkey, for instance, might well remain a borderline case in terms of criminal justice for the next century (see Green, Chapter 11). In the Arab world, there is no trace of a political Westernisation process, as the burial of King Hussein of Jordan, at the threshold to the third millennium, demonstrated—while the Western world sent almost exclusively elected representatives to attend the funeral and to greet the new king, Hussein's son Abdullah, the Arab world was represented almost entirely by fathers and sons, i.e. either kings and their sons or coup leaders and their sons (both Moammar Gadhafi and King Hassan of Morocco sent their sons and heirs apparent; Hafez Assad and Hosni Mubarak could have sent their sons and heirs apparent, but appeared themselves; if Iraq had been invited, Saddam Hussein could also either have come himself or sent his son and heir apparent, Uday; cf. Friedman, 1999).

However, the difference of civilisations would not prevent the building of a post-modern empire. Historical empires were not conceptualised as being made up of single citizens *(one man, one vote)*, but rather as being a conglomerate of diverse cultural, ethnic, religious, regional, and corporate entities with a high degree of internal autonomy, but a single focus for their transcending common belief system.

Perhaps an eventual post-modern global empire will organise peaceful coexistence in the global village, with attention to its vulnerable ecology, its climate, its rainforests, its water and its atmosphere, if it just had a mandate to deal with truly global problems, and nothing more. Instead of homogenising global cultures, it would protect diversity and difference while, at the same time, developing the preconditions for both free communication and a free world order. It would be self-defeating to bestow the global empire with the metaphysical hope of having to embody objectivity, justice, freedom, reason and progress all at one time. Rather, nation states, civilisations, and civil societies of limited geographical outreach should jealously guard their autonomy, while the empire itself should be restricted to guarding the principles of international justice, preventing genocide and wars of aggression, torture and "ethnic cleansing", all of which are so strangely familiar to our supposedly so illuminated times.

Bibliography

Abel, R. (1995) "Contested Communities", *Journal of Law and Society*, 22, 113–26.

Aftenposten (1999) 31 May.

Agirreazkuenaga Zigorraga, Iñaki (1995) "Contexto de la Ley de Seguridad Ciudadana. Análisis Jurídico de los Controles de Identidad: Voluntas Legis e Interpretación Jurisprudencial del T.C", in I. Muñagorri, *(ed.)*, *La protección de la Seguridad Ciudadana*. Oñati: IISJ.

Ahmad, F. (1993) *The Making of Modern Turkey*. London: Routledge.

Albrecht, H.-J. (1987) "Foreign Minorities and the Criminal Justice System in the Federal Republic of Germany", *The Howard Journal of Criminal Justice*, 26, 272–88.

—— (1991) "Ethnic Minorities: Crime and Criminal Justice in Europe", in F. Heidensohn and M. Farrell, (eds), *Crime in Europe*. London, New York: Routledge, 84–102.

—— (1997) "Ethnic Minorities, Crime and Criminal Justice in Germany", in M. Tonry, (ed.), *Ethnicity, Crime and Immigration. Comparative and Cross National Perspectives*. Chicago, London:University of Chicago Press, 31–99.

Albrecht, H.-J. and van Kalmthout, A., (eds), (2000) *Illegal Immigration and Detention in Europe*. Freiburg: edition in ???

Allen, Francis (1996) *Habits of Legality*. Chicago: University of Chicago Press.

Amnistía Internacional (1995) *La Pena de Muerte y su Abolición en España*. Madrid: Los Libros de la Catarata.

Amnesty International (1998) *Annual Report*. London: Amnesty International.

Anderson, Paul and Mann, Nyta (1997) *Safety First, The Making of New Labour*. London: Eranta.

Andrés Ibáñez, Prefecto, (ed.) (1996) *Corrupción y Estado de Derecho. El Papel de la Jurisdicción*. Madrid: Trotta.

Aranzadi, Juan, Juaristi, Jon and Unzueta, Paxto (1994) *Auto de Terminación*. Madrid: El País Aguilar.

Ararteko (1996) *Situación de las Cárceles en el País Vasco*. Vitoria-Gasteiz: Ararteko.

Arteta, Aurelio, Velasco, Demetrio and Zubero, Imanol (1998) *Razones Contra la Violencia. Por la Convivencia Democrática en el País Vasco, vol. II*. Bilbao: Bakeaz.

Ashworth, Andrew (1983) *Sentencing and Penal Policy*. London: Weidenfeld and Nicolson.

—— 1988) "Criminal Justice and the Criminal Process", *British Journal of Criminology*, 28, 111–23.

—— (1995a) *Sentencing and Criminal Justice*. London: Butterworths.

—— (1995b) *Principles of Criminal Law*. Oxford: Clarendon Press.

—— (1997) *Criminal Law Review*, November, 769–70.

Ashworth, Andrew, Gardner, John, Morgan, R., Smith, A.J.H., von Hirsh, A., and Wasik, M., (1998) "Neighbouring on the Oppressive: The Government's Anti-Social Behaviour Order Proposals", *Criminal Justice*, 16/1, 7–14.

Ashworth, Andrew and von Hirsch, Andrew, (eds) (1992) *Principled Sentencing*. Edinburgh: Edinburgh University Press.

Atkinson, A. (1998) "Whither Welfare?", *Oxford Today*, 10, 10–12.

Audit Commission (1996) *Misspent Youth: Young People and Crime*. London: Audit Commission.

Ayata, S. (1996) "Patronage, Party and State: The Politicization of Islam in Turkey", *Middle East Journal*, 50:1, (Winter).

Baldwin, John and McConville, Michael (1977) *Negotiated Justice*. Oxford: Martin Robertson.

Bartolí, Josep (1944) *Campos de Concentración*. México: Iberia.

Bastida Freijedo, Francisco Javier (1986) *Jueces y Franquismo*. Barcelona: Ariel.

Bauman, Zygmunt (1989) *Modernity and the Holocaust*. Oxford: Blackwell.

—— (1995) "The Strangers of Consumer Era; from the Welfare State to Prison", *Tijdschrift voor Criminologie*, 37:3, 210–18.

—— (1996) "Gewalt—Modern und Postmodern", in M. Miller and H.-G. Soeffner, (eds), *Modernität und Barbarei. Soziologische Zeitdiagnosen am Ende des Jahrhunderts*. Frankfurt: Suhrkamp, 36–67.

—— (1997) *Postmodernity and its Discontents*. Cambridge: Polity Press.

Beck, Ulrich (1992) *Risk Society; Towards a New Modernity*. London: Sage.

Becker, H. (1964) *Outsiders*. New York: The Free Press.

Beckett, Katherine (1994) "Setting the Public Agenda: Street Crime and Drug Use in Contemporary American Politics", *Social Problems* 41: 3, 425–47.

—— (1995) "Media Depictions of Drug Abuse: The Impact of Official Sources", *Research in Political Sociology*, 7, 161–82.

—— (1997) *Making Crime Pay: Law and Order in Contemporary American Politics*. New York: Oxford University Press.

Beckett, Katherine and Sasson, Theodore (2000) *The Politics of Injustice: Crime and Punishment in America*. Thousand Oaks, Ca. and London: Pine Forge Press.

Beer, Ad P.G. de and Ploeg, Gerhard J. (1994) "Een Reclassering op Vernieuwde Leest", *Justitiële Verkenningen*, 20: 4, 9–20.

Belgian SIRENE Office Brussels, Belgium, (1994) *The Schengen Information System and its Implementation in Belgium*. December.

Bennett, Mike (1993) Unpublished Speech to the Metropolitan Police Federation, 27 October.

Benoist, A. de (1991) "The Idea of Empire", *Telos*, 1998–99, 81–98, 1993–1994.

Bergalli, Roberto (1985) "Transición Política y Justicia Penal en España", *Sistema* 67, 57–96.

—— (1995) "The Spanish Attempt to Build a Democratic Criminal Justice System", in V. Ruggiero, M. Ryan and J. Sim, (eds), *Western European Penal Systems. A Critical Anatomy*. London: Sage.

—— (1997) "The New Order in Spain and an Hispanic Perspective on the History and Meaning of Social Control", in R. Bergalli and C. Sumner. (eds), *Social Control and Political Order. European Perspectives at the End of the Century*. Thousand Oaks, Ca.: Sage.

Bergalli, R. and Sumner, C. (1997) *Social Control and Political Order: European Perspectives at the End of the Century*. London: Sage.

Berman, M. (1982) *All That is Solid Melts into Air*. New York: Verso.

Biçak, V. (1996) *Improperly Obtained Evidence: A Comparison of Turkish and English Laws*. Ankara: (unpublished monograph).

Biescas, J. A. and Tuñón de Lara, M. (1980) *España Bajo la Dictadura Franquista (1939–1975)*. Barcelona: Labor.

Blagg, H. (1997) "Aboriginal Youth and Conferencing in Australia", *British Journal of Criminology*, 37:4 (Autumn), 481–501.

Blair, Tony (1998) *The Third Way: New Politics for the New Century*. London: Fabian Society.

Blauwdruk ("Blueprint") (1993) *De Reclassering in Breder Perspectief*. (unpublished government paper).

Blume, Peter (1992) "Schengen og personaldatabeskyttelsen" (Schengen and the Data Protection) *Social Kritik*, 22/23, 64–71.

Blumstein, Alfred (1988) "Coherence, Coordination and Integration in the Administration of Criminal Justice", in J.J. van Dijk, (ed.), *Criminal Law in Action: An Overview of Current Issues in Western Societies*. Deventer: Kluwer.

Bohlander, M. (1994) "Expediency over Due Process", *Legal Action*, March, 9.

Boswell, G. (1995) *Violent Victims: The Prevalence of Abuse and Loss in the Lives of Section 53 Offenders*. London: Princes Trust.

Bottoms, A. (1994) "Avoiding Injustice, Promoting Legitimacy and Relationships" in J. Burnside and N. Baker, (eds), *Relational Justice*. Winchester: Waterside Press, 53–68.

—— (1995) "The Philosophy of Punishment and Sentencing" in C. Clarkson and R. Morgan, (eds), *The Politics of Sentencing Reform*. Oxford: Clarendon Press, 17–49.

Bottoms, Anthony E. (1990) "Crime Prevention Facing the 1990s", *Policing and Society*, 1, 3–22.

Bourgois, P. (1995) *In Search of Respect: Selling Crack in El Barrio*. Cambridge: Cambridge University Press.

Box, S. "Recession, Crime and Punishment". London: Macmillan.

Braithwaite, John (1989) *Crime, Shame and Reintegration*. Cambridge: Cambridge University Press.

Brake, M. and Hale, C. (1992) *Public Order and Private Lives: The Politics of Law and Order*. London: Routledge.

Brantingham P. J. and Faust, F. L. (1988) "A Conceptual Model of Crime Prevention", *Crime and Delinquency*, 22, 130–46.

Bratton, William J. (1997) "Crime is down in New York City: Blame the Police", in Norman Dennis, (ed.), *Zero Tolerance Policing in a Free Society*. London: IEA Health and Welfare Unit, 29–42.

Bratton, William J. with Peter Knobler (1998) *Turnaround: How America's Top Cop Reversed the Crime Epidemic*. New York: Random House.

Brewin, C. (1996) "Turkey and the European Union", *Cambridge Review of International Affairs*, x, 1.

Bridges, L. J. Hodgson, McConville, M. and Pavlovic, A. (1997) "Can Critical Research Influence Policy? A Response to Max Travers", *British Journal of Criminology* 37:3, 378–82.

Brion, F. (1996) "Chiffrer, Déchiffrer. Incarcération des Étrangers et Construction Sociale de la Criminalité des Immigrés en Belgique", in S. Palidda, (ed.), *Délit d'immigration* (Immigrant Delinquency). Bruxelles: Communauté Européenne, 163–224, 166.

Broder, Daniel S. (1999) "The World's Leader Has a Credibility Problem", *International Herald Tribune*, 15 February, 8.

Brown, S. (1995) "Adult Pasts and Youthful Presence: 'Community Safety', Age and the Politics of Representation". Paper presented at the British Criminology Conference, Loughborough University, July.

Brown D. and Ellis T. (1994) *Policing Low–Level Disorder: Police Use of Section 5 of the Public Order Act 1986*. Home Office Research Study No. 135, London: HMSO.

Bruggeman, W. (1998) "Data Protection Issues in Interinstitutional Information Exchange:

The Case of Criminal and Administrative Intelligence". Paper delivered at the *Sixth Schengen Colloquium: Schengen's Final Days?* European Institute of Public Administration, Maastricht.

Bunyan, Tony (1995) *The Europol Convention*. A *Statewatch* Publication.

Bureau of the Census (1995) *Statistical Abstract of the United States, 1992*. Washington DC: US Government Printing Office.

Bureau of Justice Statistics (BJS) (1995a) *Sourcebook of Criminal Justice Statistics, 1994*. Washington DC: Bureau of Justice Statistics.

—— (1995b) *Census of Federal and State Correctional Facilities*. Washington DC: Department of Justice.

—— (1998) *Sourcebook of Criminal Justice Statistics, 1997*. Washington DC: Bureau of Justice Statistics.

—— (1999) *Prison and Jail Inmates at Midyear 1998*. Washington DC: Bureau of Justice Statistics.

Burney, Elizabeth (1999) *Crime and Banishment, Nuisance and Exclusion in Social Housing*. Winchester: Waterside.

Burtless, Gary (1994) "Public Spending on the Poor: Historical Trends and Economic Limits" in Sheldon H. Danziger, Gary D. Sandefur and Daniel H. Weinberg, (eds), *Confronting Poverty: Prescriptions for Change*. New York: Russell Sage Foundation, 51–84

Bush, George (1989) "Address to Students on Drug Abuse", *Public Papers of the Presidents*, Vol. I, Washington DC: Government Printing Office, 746–9.

Bustos Ramírez, Juan (1996) "Política Criminal y Estado", *Ciencias Penales*, 12, 3–9.

Bustos Ramírez, Juan and Hormazábal Malarée, Hernán (1997) *Lecciones de Derecho Penal Vol. I*. Madrid: Trotta.

Butterfield, Fox (1998) "Inmates Serving More TIme, Jistice Department Reports". New York Times, 11 January.

Calvo García, Manuel (1995) "Políticas de Seguridad y Transformaciones del Derecho", in I. Muñagorri, (ed.), *La Protección de la Seguridad Ciudadana*. Oñati: IISJ.

Campbell, Duncan (1998) "ENFOPOL Plans Provoke Strong Opposition", *Telepolis* 31 December (http://www.de/deutsch/special/enfo/6329/.html).

Cantarero Bandrés, Rocio (1990) "Seguridad Ciudadana. Constitución. Derecho Penal", *Cuadernos de Polítca Criminal*, 42, 521–36.

Carlen, P. (1983) "On Rights and Powers in Penal Politics" in D. Garland and P. Young, (eds), *The Power To Punish*. London: Heinemann, 202–16.

—— (1988) *Women, Crime and Poverty*. Buckingham: Open University Press.

—— (1989) "Crime, Sentencing and Inequality" in P. Carlen and D. Cook, (eds), *Paying For Crime*. Buckingham: Open University Press, 8–28.

—— (1990) *Alternatives to Women's Imprisonment*. Buckingham: Open University Press.

—— (1996) *Jigsaw—A Political Criminology of Youth Homelessness*. Buckingham: Open University Press.

—— (1998) *Sledgehammer—Women's Imprisonment at the Millennium*. London: Macmillan.

Castells, Miguel (1977) *Los Procesos Políticos (De la Cárcel a la Amnistía).* Madrid: Fundamentos.

Cavadino, Michael and Dignan, James (1997) *The Penal System: An Introduction.* London: Sage.

Central Group in Schengen (1996) *Annual Report on the Implementation of the Schengen Convention: 26 March 1995–25 March 1996.* 26 March. SCH/C (96) 17 rev. (German).

Central Group in Schengen (1997) *Annual Report on the State of Affairs at the External Border 1 January 1996 to 31 December 1996 of the States in which the Schengen Convention has been enforced.* 20 March. (German).

Christie, Nils (1977) "Conflicts as Property", *British Journal of Criminology*, 17, 1–15.

—— (1982) *Limits to Pain.* Oxford: Martin Robertson.

—— (1984) "Suitable Enemies". Paper presented to the Conference of the Howard League, *The Impact of Criminal Justice*, Oxford.

—— (1993) *Crime Control as Industry. Towards Gulags, Western Style?* London: Routledge.

—— (1998) "Roots of a Perspective", in S. Holdaway and P. Rock, (eds), *Thinking about Criminology.* London: UCL, 121–31.

—— (1999) "Dangerous States". Oslo (unpublished manuscript).

Cid Moliné, José and Larrauri Pijoan, Elena (1997) "Introducción", in J. Cid and E. Larrauri, (eds), *Penas Alternativas a la Prisión.* Barcelona: Bosch.

Clarke, J., Cochrane A. and Smart, C. (1987) *Ideologies of Welfare.* London: Routledge.

Cohen, Stanley (1972) *Folk Devils and Moral Panics.* London: Macgibbon and Kee.

—— (1985) *Visions of Social Control. Crime, Punishment, and Classification.* Cambridge: Polity Press.

—— (1987) *Visions of Social Control.* Cambridge: Polity Press.

—— (1994) "Social Control and the Politics of Reconstruction", in David Nelken (ed.), *The Futures of Criminology.* London: Sage, 63–88.

Cohn, Steven Barkan and Halteman, William (1991) "Punitive Attitudes Toward Criminals: Racial Consensus or Racial Conflict?", *Social Problems* 38, 287–96.

Collins, Simon and O'Carroll, P. (1997) *Anti-Social Behaviour and Housing: The Law.* Edinburgh: Chartered Institute of Housing.

Collison, M. (1995) *Police, Drugs and Community.* London: Free Association Books.

Cook, D. (1997) *Poverty, Crime and Punishment.* London: Child Poverty Action Group.

Cortina, Adela (1997) *Ciudadanos del Mundo. Hacia una Teoría de la Ciudadanía.* Madrid: Alianza.

Council of Europe *Convention on Data Protection*, Strasbourg, 1981.

Cragg, Wesley (1992) *The Practice of Punishment: Towards a Theory of Restorative Justice.* London: Routledge.

Crawford, Adam (1997) *The Local Governance of Crime.* Oxford: Clarendon Press.

Crown Prosecution Service (1994) "Code for Crown Prosecutors", London: Crown Prosecution Service.

Cullen, Francis T., Clark, Gregory A. and Wozniak, John F. (1985) "Explaining the Get-Tough Movement: Can the Public Be Blamed?", *Federal Probation* 45:2, 16–24.

Cullen, Francis T., Evans Skovron, Sandra, Scott, Joseph E. and Burton Jr., Velmer S. (1990) "Public Support for Correctional Treatment", *Criminal Justice and Behavior* 17:1, 2–18.

Cullen, F. and Gilbert, K. (1982) *Reaffirming Rehabilitation.* Ohio: Anderson Publishing.

Currie, Elliott (1998) *Crime and Punishment in America*. New York: Henry Hold and Co. Inc.

Dagi, I.D. (1996) "Democratic Transition in Turkey, 1980–83: the Impact of European Diplomacy", *Middle Eastern Studies*, 32:2.

Dahrendorf, R. (1985) *Law and Order*. London: Stevens.

Danziger, Sheldon and Gottschalk, Peter (1995) *America Unequal*. New York: Russell Sage Foundation.

Danziger, Sheldon H. and Weinberg, Daniel H. (1994) "The Historical Record: Trends in Family Income, Inequality, and Poverty", in Sheldon H. Danziger, Gary D. Sandefur and Daniel H. Weinberg, (eds), *Confronting Poverty: Prescriptions for Change*. New York: Russell Sage Foundation, 18–50.

Davies, R. (1997) "'Restorative Justice'—A Window of Opportunity", *Prison Service Journal*, November, 14, 27–33.

Deflem, Mathieu (1998) "The *Democratic Deficit* Revisited: Considering the Politics of Criminal Justice", in Y. Cartuyvels et al., (eds), *Politique, Police et Justice au Bord du Futur. Mélanges pour et avec Lode Van Outriv*. París: L'Harmattan.

D'Elia, A. (1997) "Devianza, Immigrazione e Mass Media: il Caso del Salento". Thesis in Criminal Sociology. Faculty of Law, Bologna, 1995–6.

Deleuze, Gilles (1990) "Das Elektronische Halsband. Innenansicht der Kontrollierten Gesellschaft", *Neue Rundschau*, 4, 5–10.

Della Porta, D. (1995) *Social Movements, Political Violence and the State: A Comparative Analysis of Italy and Germany*. Cambridge: Cambridge University Press.

Delmas-Marty, Mireille (1986) *Modelos Actuales de Política Criminal*. Madrid: Ministerio de Justicia.

Department of Social Security (1998) *New Ambitions for our Country—A New Contract for Welfare*. Cm. 3805. London: Stationery Office.

Díaz, Beatriz and Fantova, Javi (1998) *El Color de la Sospecha. El Maltrato Policial a Personas Inmigrantes en el Barrio de San Francisco (Bilbao)*. Bilbao: Imprenta Luna.

Díez Ripollés, José Luis (1998a) "La Administración Controlada de Heroína", *Boletín Criminológico*, 34.

—— (1998b) "Exigencias Sociales y Política Criminal", *Claves de la Razón Práctica*, 85, 48–53.

Díez Ripollés, José Luis and Copello, Patricia Laurenzo, (eds), (1993) *La Actual Política Criminal Sobre Drogas. Una Perspectiva Comparada*. Valencia: Tirant lo Blanch.

Dijk, Jan J.M. van, Mayhew, Pat and Killias, Martin (1991) *Experiences of Crime Across the World: Key Findings of the 1989 International Crime Survey*. Boston: Kluwer.

Dijk, T.A. van (1993) *Elite Discourse and Racism*. London: Sage.

Dodd, C.H. (1990) *The Crisis of Turkish Democracy*. Huntingdon: Eothen Press.

Donziger, Steven R., (ed.) (1996) *The Real War on Crime: The Report of the National Criminal Justice Commission*. New York: Harper Perennial.

Doyal, L. and Gough, I. (1991) *A Theory of Human Need*. London: Macmillan.

Downes, D. (1997) "What the Government Should Do About Crime", *The Howard Journal of Criminal Justice*, 36/1, 1–13.

Driver, Stephen and Martell, Luke (1997) "New Labour's Communitarianisms", *Critical Social Policy*, 17, 27–46.

Duff, Peter (1993) "The Prosecutor Fine and Social Control: The Introduction of the Procurator Fiscal Fine in Scotland", *British Journal of Criminology* 33, 481–503.

Dumm, T. (1987) *Democracy and Punishment: Disciplinary Origins of the United States*. Wisconsin: University of Wisconsin Press.

Dworkin, Ronald (1987) *Taking Rights Seriously*, London: Duckworth.

Ebbe, Obi N. Ignatius, (ed.) (1996) *Comparative and International Criminal Justice Systems: Policing Judiciary and Corrections*. Boston: Butterworth-Heinemann.

Edsall, Thomas B. and Edsall, Mary (1991) *Chain Reaction: The Impact of Rights, Race and Taxes on American Politics*. New York: Norton and Co.

Eisner, Michael (1998) "Modernization, Self-control and Violence: The Long-term Dynamics of European Homicide Rates in Theoretical Perspective". Paper presented at the session on *The Use of Criminological Theory in Historical Research*, Amsterdam, ESSH-Conference.

Elliott, L. and Atkinson, D. (1998) *The Age of Insecurity*. London: Verso.

Erikson, K. (1966) *Wayward Puritans*. New York: John Wiley.

Escrivá, María Angeles (1998) *El Camrno de Vivelta—La Larga Marcha de las Reinsertades de ETA*. Madrid: El Pais-Aguilas.

Eskeland, Ståle (1997) *Grunnloven og Schengensamarbeidet* (The Constitution and Schengen). Oslo: Gyldendal Publishers.

Etzioni, Amitae (1993) *The Spirit of Community*. New York: Crown Publishers.

European Commission (1994), *Communication from the Commission to the Council and the European Parliament on a European Action Plan to Combat Drugs, 1995–1999* COM(94)234 Final, Brussels.

—— (1998) *Regular Report from the Commission on Turkey's Progress Towards Accession*. Brussels. November.

European Information System (1995) *Brussels Draft Convention of the European Information System*. 10 November 1993/1, December. Draft Council legal document 12029/94–9277/1/95–C4–0249/95.

European Union (1995) *Brussels Directive on Data Protection*, 95/46EF.

—— (1997) *Draft Convention on Mutual Legal Assistance in Criminal Matters*.

Fattah, Ezzat A. (1997) *Criminology: Past, Present and Future. A Critical Overview*. London: Macmillan.

Faulkner, David (1998) "A Principled Response", *Criminal Justice Matters*, 31, Spring, 4–5.

Favell, A. (1997) "The Europeanisation of Immigration Politics: Some Comments". Paper presented at the International Conference on *Migrations, Interactions and Conflicts in the Making of a European Democracy*. Bologna and Reggio Emilia, 16–19 December.

Feeley, Malcolm and Simon, Jonathon (1992) "The New Penology: Notes on the Emerging Strategy of Correction and its Implications", *Criminology*, 30(4) 449–74.

—— (1994) "Actuarial Justice; the Emerging New Criminal Law", in David Nelkin, (ed.), *The Futures of Criminology*. London: Sage, 173–201.

Feest, Johannes (1998) "International Criminal Policy". Paper delivered to IISL workshop *Criminal Policy in Transition: Criminal Policy Trends into the New Millennium*, 15–16 May, Onati.

Fernández Aúz, Tomás (1998) "Delito, Castigo y Conciencia Colectiva", *El Mundo*, 24 April, 2.

Fernández López, Javier (1998) *El Rey y Otros Militares. Los Militares en el Cambio de Régimen Político en España (1969—1982)*. Madrid: Trotta.

Ferracuti, F. (1968) "European Migration and Crime", in M.E. Wolfgang, (ed.), *Crime and Culture: Essays in Honour of Thorsten Sellin*. New York: Wiley, 189–219.

Ferrajoli, Luigi (1989) *Diritto e Ragione. Teoria del Garantismo Penale*. Bari: Laterza.

Field, Stewart and Thomas, Philip (1994) *Justice and Efficiency? The Royal Commission on Criminal Justice*. Oxford: Blackwell Publishers.

Fijnaut, C. (1990) "Organized Crime: The Forms it Takes, Background and Methods Used to Control it in Western Europe and the United States", in G. Kaiser and H.-J. Albrecht, (eds), *Crime and Criminal Policy in Europe*. Freiburg: Max Planck Institute, 53–98.

—— Goethals, J., Peters, T. and Walgrave, L. (eds), (1995) *Changes in Society, Crime and Criminal Justice in Europe*. Volume II. *International Organised and Corporate Crime*. Antwerp: Kluwer.

Fionda, Julia (1995) *Public Prosecutors and Discretion: A Comparative Study*. Oxford: Oxford University Press.

—— (1998) "The Age of Innocence? The Concept of Childhood in the Punishment of Young Offenders", *Child and Family Law Quarterly*, 10, 77–87.

—— (1999) "New Labour, Old Hat: Youth Justice and the Crime and Disorder Act 1998", *Criminal Law Review*, 36–47.

Fionda, Julia and Cowan, David (1998) " 'He asked for it': Paedophiles and the Homelessness Legislation", *Child and Family Law Quarterly* 10, 321–7.

Fitzgerald, Marion (1993) *Ethnic Minorities and the Criminal Justice System*. Royal Commission on Criminal Justice Research Study No. 20. London: HMSO.

Fortress Europe, Fortress Europe?, Falun, Sweden, several issues.

Foster, C. and Plowden, F. (1996) *The State Under Stress*. Buckingham: Open University Press.

Foucault, Michel (1977) *Discipline and Punish*. Harmondsworth: Peregrine.

—— (1978) "About the Concept of the 'Dangerous Individual' in 19th-Century Legal Psychiatry", *International Journal of Law and Psychiatry*, 1, 1–18.

—— (1979) *Discipline and Punish, The Birth of the Prison*. New York: Vintage Books.

Fox Piven, Francis (1998) "Politics and Public Opinion", *Contemporary Sociology*, 27:5, 457–60.

Francis, Peter, Davies, Pamela and Jupp, Victor (1997) "New Millenium Blues? Policing Past and Policing Futures", in P. Francis, P. Davies and V. Jupp, (eds), *Policing Futures. The Police, Law Enforcement and the Twenty-First Century*. Basingstoke: Macmillan, 1–19.

Franklin, Bob and Petley, Julian (1996) "Killing the Age of Innocence: Newspaper Reporting of the Death of James Bulger", in J. Pilcher and S. Wagg, (eds), *Thatcher's Children?: Politics, Childhood and Society in the 1980s and 1990s*. London: Falmer Press.

Frankfurter Rundschau, 25 October 1997.

Freeden, Michael (1978) *The New Liberalism, An Ideology of Social Reform*. Oxford: Clarendon Press.

—— (1999) "The Ideology of New Labour", *Political Quarterly*, 42–51.

Freedland, M. (1994) "Government by Contract and Public Law", *Public Law*, 86–104.

—— (1998a) "Public Service, the State and Citizenship: A Case for a Public Service Act". Paper given at a seminar in St. John's College, Oxford: 10 October 1997. Oxford: St. John's College.

—— (1998b) "Law, Public Services, and Citizenship—Domains, New Regimes?" in M. Freedland and S. Sciarra, (eds), *Public Services and Citizenship in European Law*. Oxford: Clarendon Press.

French, Thomas C. (1988) "Is it Punitive or Regulatory? United States v. Salerno", *University of Toledo L.Rev.* 20, 189.

Friedman, Thomas L. (1999) "The Arab World Needs More Than Fathers and Sons", *International Herald Tribune*, 15 February, 8.

Frigaard, Iver (1996) "Police Cooperation: Current Problems and Suggestions for Solutions in Interstate Co-operation in Europe". Paper delivered at the *Fourth Schengen Colloquium: Schengen and the Third Pillar of Maastricht*, European Institute of Public Administration: Maastricht.

Galbraith, John Kenneth (1992) *The Culture of Contentment*. Harmondsworth: Penguin.

García Nieto, Alejandro (1997) *Corrupción en la España Democrática*. Barcelona: Ariel.

Gardner, John, Hirsh, Andrew von, Smith, A.T.H., Morgan, Rod, Ashworth, Andrew and Wasik, Martin (1998) "Clause 1—The Hybrid from Hell?", *Criminal Justice Matters*, 31, 25–7.

Garland, David (1990) *Punishment and Modern Society*. Oxford: Oxford University Press.

—— (1995) "Penal Modernism and Postmodernism", in T. G. Blomberg and S. Cohen, (eds), *Punishment and Social Control. Essays in Honor of Sheldon L. Messinger*. New York: Aldine de Gruyter.

—— (1996) "The Limits of the Sovereign State: Strategies of Crime Control in Contemporary Society", *British Journal of Criminology*, 36:4, 445–71.

—— (2000a) "Prosaic Naturalism: The New Criminologies of Everyday Life", (forthcoming).

—— (2000b) "The Culture of High Crime Societies: Some Preconditions of Recent 'Law and Order' Policies", *British Journal of Criminology*, 40, 3, 347–75.

—— (2001) *The New Culture of Crime Control*, Oxford: Oxford Univeristy Press.

German Ministry of the Interior (1995) *Continuation of Information on Experience to date on the use of the Schengen Implementing Convention Report*. Fall 1995. (German).

German Ministry of the Interior (1997a) *Report about the Schengen Cooperation in 1996*. Delivered to the Federal States 5–6 June 1997. (German).

German Ministry of the Interior (1997b) *Information News Letter: Information for People Working in the Ministry of the Interior*. Bonn. 1 September. (German).

Giddens, Anthony (1998) *The Third Way*. Cambridge: Polity Press.

Gilliard, Darrell K. and Beck, Allen J. (1997) "Prison and Jail Inmates at Midyear 1996", *Bureau of Justice Statistics Bulletin*, Washignton DC: Department of Justice.

Gómez Benítez, José Manuel (1982) "Crítica de la Política Penal del Orden Público", *Cuadernos de Política Criminal*, 16, 49–92.

Goode, Erich and Ben-Yehuda, Nachman (1994) *Moral Panics: The Social Construction of Deviance*. Oxford: Blackwells.

Gould, Philip (1998) *The Unfinished Revolution, How the Modernisers Saved the Labour Party*. London: Little Brown.

Great Britain (1991) *The Citizen's Charter: Raising the Standard*. Cm. 1599. London: HMSO.

Green, Penny J. (1998) *Drugs Trafficking and Criminal Policy: The Scapegoat Strategy*. Winchester: Waterside.

Greenberg, Stanley B. (1995) *Middle-Class Dreams: The Politics and Power of the New American Majority*. New Haven and London: Yale University Press.

Gross, Bertram (1982) "Reagan's Criminal Anti-Crime Fix", in Alan Gartner, Colin Greer and Frank Riessman, (eds), *What Reagan Is Doing To Us*. New York: Harper and Row.

Haan, Willem de (1990) *The Politics of Redress: Crime Punishment and Penal Abolition*. London: Unwin Hyman.

Habermas, Jürgen (1962) *Strukturwandel der Öffentlichkeit. Untersuchungen zu einer Kategorie der Bürgerlichen Gesellschaft*. Neuwied: Luchterhand.

—— (1992) "Citizenship and National Identity", in B. van Steenbergen, (ed.), *The Condition of Citizenship*. London: Sage.

Hager, Nicky (1996) *Secret Power. New Zealand's Role in the International Spy Network*. Nelson, New Zealand: Craig Potton Publishing.

—— (1996–7) "Exposing the Global Surveillance System", *Covert Action Quarterly*, 59, Winter.

Hale, C. (1998) "The Labour Market and Post-War Crime Trends in England and Wales", in P. Carlen and R. Morgan, (eds), *Crime Unlimited? Questions for The Twenty-First Century*. London: Macmillan.

Haln, P. (1998) *Emerging Criminal Justice*. London: Sage.

Hannemyr, Gisle (1998) "Fantastiske Fortellinger om Teknologi" (Fantastic Tales about Technology) *Aftenposten*, 18 March.

Harden, I. (1992) *The Contracting State*. Buckingham: Open University Press.

Harlow, Carol and Rawlings, Richard (1997) *Law and Administration*. London: Butterworths.

Hart, August C. 't (1988) "Criminal Law Policy in The Netherlands" in Jan van Dijk, Charles Haffmans, Frits Rüter, Julian Schutte and Simon Stolwijk (eds), *Criminal Law in Action. An Overview of Current Issues in Western Societies*. Deventer: Kluwer Publishers, 73–99.

—— (1999) *Criminal Law Enforcement and Legal Protection*. London: Howard League for Penal Reform.

Heclo, Hugh (1994) "Poverty Politics", in Sheldon H. Danziger, Gary D. Sandefur, and Daniel H. Weinberg, (eds), *Confronting Poverty: Prescriptions for Change*. New York: Russell Sage Foundation, 396–437.

Heine-Wiedenmann, D. and Ackermann, L. (1992) *Umfeld und Ausmaß des Menschenhandels mit Ausländischen Mädchen und Frauen*. Stuttgart, Berlin, Köln: Kohlhammer.

Heinrich, Jean-Paul (1995) *Particuliere Reclassering en Overheid in Nederland sinds 1823*. Arnhem: Gouda Quint.

Henry, Stuart and Milovanovic, Dragan (1994) "The Constitution of Constitutive Criminology. A Postmodern Approach to Criminological Theory" in D Nelken, (ed.), *The Futures of Criminology*. London: Sage.

Heper, M. (1985) *The State Tradition in Turkey*. Hull: Eothen Press.

—— (1992) "The Strong State as a Problem for the Consolidation of Democracy: Turkey and Germany Compared", *Comparative Political Studies*, 25:2, July, 169–93.

Hess, Henner (1998) "Die Zukunft des Verbrechens", *Kritische Justiz*, 145–61.

Hirsh, Andrew von, Ashworth, Andrew, Wasik, Martin, Smith A.T.H., Morgan, Rod and Gardner, John (1995) "Overtaking on the Right", *New Law Journal*, 13 October, 1501–2, 1516.

HM Treasury (1998) *Public Services for the Future: Modernisation, Reform, Accountability*. Cm. 4181. London: The Stationery Office.

Hobsbawn, Eric (1995) *Historia del Siglo XX. 1914–1991*. Barcelona: Crítica.
Holdaway, S. (1997) "Some Recent Approaches to the Study of Race in Criminological Research", *British Journal of Criminology*, 37, 383–400.
Hollway, W. and Jefferson, T. (1997) "The Risk Society in an Age of Anxiety: Situating Fear of Crime", *British Journal of Sociology*, 48:2, 255–66.
Home Office (1977) *A Review of Criminal Justice Policy*. London: Home Office.
—— (1985) Circular 14/1985.
—— (1988) *Punishment, Custody and the Community*. Cm. 424. London: HMSO.
—— (1990) Circular 59/1990.
—— (1990) *Crime, Justice and Protecting the Public*. Cm. 965. London: HMSO.
—— (1991) *Report of the Standing Committee on Crime Prevention*. London: Home Office.
—— (1994) Circular 18/1994.
—— (1996a) *Protecting the Public*. Cm. 3190. London: HMSO.
—— (1996b) *Stalking—The Solutions: A Consultation Paper*. London: Home Office.
—— (1997a) *Community Safety Orders: A Consultation Paper*. London: Home Office.
—— (1997b) *Tackling Youth Crime: A Consultation Paper*. London: Home Office.
—— (1997c) *No More Excuses—A New Approach to Tackling Youth Crime in England and Wales*. Cm. 3809. London: Stationery Office.
—— (1998a) "Revised Projections of Long Term Trends in the Prison Population to 2005", Statistical Bulletin No. 2/98. London: Home Office.
—— (1998b) *Joining Forces to Protect the Public: Prisons—Probation. A Consultation Document*. London: Home Office.
—— (1998c) *Reducing Offending*. Home Office Research Study No.187. London: Home Office.
—— (1998d) *British Crime Survey*. London: Stationery Office.
—— (1998e) *Sex Offender Orders: Guidance*.
—— (1999) *Anti-social Behaviour Orders: Guidance*.
Home Office and Department of Health (1999) *Managing Dangerous People with Severe Personality Order, Proposals for Policy Development*. London: Home Office and Department of Health.
Honderich, Ted (1969) *Punishment: Its Supposed Justifications*. London: Hutchinson.
Hood, C. (1991) "A Public Management for All Services", *Public Administration*, 69/1 3–11.
Hoogenboom, A.B., Meiboom, M.J., Schoneveld, D.C.M. and Stoop, J.W.M. (eds) (1997) *Policing the Future*. The Hague: Kluwer Law International.
Hough, Michael and Roberts, Julian (1997) *Attitudes to Punishment: Findings from the British Crime Survey*. Home Office Research Study 179. London: Home Office.
Howard League (1988) *The Community, Punishment and Custody: The Response of the Howard League for Penal Reform to the Green Paper "Punishment, Custody and the Community"*. London: Howard League.
—— (1997) *Lost Inside—the Imprisonment of Teenage Girls*. London: Howard League.
Hughes, Gordon (1996) "Communitariarism and Law and Order", *Critical Social Policy*, 44: 16, 17–41.
Hulsman, Louk (1971) "Reclassering en Strafrecht", in F. van Rossen, (ed.), *Menswetenschappen*. Amsterdam: Psychiatrisch Juridisch Gezelschap, 64–79.
—— (1986) "Critical Criminology and the Concept of Crime", *Contemporary Crises*, 10, 63–80.

Human Rights Foundation of Turkey (1997) *1995 Turkey: Human Rights Report*. Ankara: Human Rights Foundation of Turkey.

—— (1998) *Treatment and Rehabilitation Centres Report 1997*. Ankara: Human Rights Foundation of Turkey.

Human Rights Watch (1999) *World Report 1999*. London: Human Rights Watch.

Huntington, Samuel P. (1993) "The Clash of Civilizations?", *Foreign Affairs*, Summer, 22–49.

Hutton, W. (1995) *The State We're In*. London: Jonathan Cape.

Içli, T.G. (1994) "Blood Feud in Turkey: A Sociological Analysis", *British Journal Of Criminology*, 4:1, (Winter).

Independent Delegation (1991) "An Investigation of Ten Killings by Turkish Security Forces on 12 July 1991". A Report by an Independent Delegation, 22–7 August.

Information (Danish daily) 3 December 1997.

Irwin, John and Austin, James (1994) *It's About Time: America's Imprisonment Binge*. Belmont, Ca.: Wadsworth.

Jäger, Herbert (1988) "Versuch über Makrokriminalität", *Strafverteidiger*, 172–9.

—— (1995) "Makroverbrechen als Gegenstand des Völkerstrafrechts. Kriminalpolitisch-kriminologische Aspekte", in Georg Hankel and Günther Stuby, (eds), *Strafgerichte gegen Menschheitsverbrechen. Zum Völkerstrafrecht 50 Jahre nach den Nürnberger Prozessen*. Hamburg: Hamburger Edition, 325–54.

Jaime-Jiménez, Óscar (1996) "Legislación Antiterrorista y Agencias Estatales de Seguridad: Un Análisis Preliminar de la Experiencia Española, 1960–1996", *Revista de Derecho Penal y Criminología, 6, 569–97.*

—— (1997) "Avatares Políticos y Organizativos de la Respuesta Policial al Terrorismo en España (1976–1996)", in Fernando Reinares, (ed.), *State and Societal Reactions to Terrorism*. Oñati: IISJ.

James, Ann and Raine, John (1998) *The New Politics of Criminal Justice*. London: Longman.

Janse de Jonge, Han A. (1991) *Om de Persoon van de Dader; Over Straftheorieën en Voorlichting Door de Reclassering*. Arnhem: Gouda Quint Pompe Reeks no.4.

Jareborg, Nils (1995) "What Kind of Criminal Law Do We Want", in Annika Snare, (ed.), *Beware of Punishment. On the Utility and Futility of Criminal Law*. Oslo: Pax Forlag, 17–36.

Jaspers, K. (1961) *The Future of Mankind*. Translated E.B. Ashton, Chicago: University of Chicago Press.

Jáuregui Bereciartu, Gurutz (1981) *Ideología y Estrategia Política de ETA. Análisis de su Evolución Entre 1959 y 1968*. Madrid: Siglo XXI.

Jhering, Rudolf von (1881) *La Lucha por el Derecho*. Madrid: Vitoriano Suárez.

Joint Supervisory Body of Europol (1997) *Draft Rules of Procedure*. 13 October.

Jones, Carol (1993) "Auditing Criminal Justice", *British Journal of Criminology*, 33:2, 187–202.

Jones, T. and Newburn, T. (1998) *Private Security and Public Policing*. Oxford: Clarendon Press.

JUSTICE (1997) *Under Surveillance*. Report of the JUSTICE Working Party on Proactive Policing Methods. London: JUSTICE.

Justice and Home Affairs Council (JHA) (1996) *Draft Convention on EURODAC*. 17 April (Danish); third revision 24 November 1997.

Kadish, Sandford H. (1962) "Legal Norms and Discretion in the Police and Sentencing Process", *Harvard Law Review*, 75, 904.

Kaplan, Robert D. (1997) *The Ends of the Earth. From Togo to Turkmenistan, from Iran to Cambodia—A Journey to the Frontiers of Anarchy*. New York: Knopf.

Katz, Michael B. (1993) "The Urban Underclass as a Metaphor of Social Transformation", in Michael B. Katz, (ed.), *The Underclass Debate*. Princeton: Princeton University Press.

Kay, J. (1996) *The Business of Economics*. Oxford: Oxford University Press.

Kelling, George L. and Coles, Catherine M. (1996) *Replacing Broken Windows: Restoring Order and Reducing Crime in our Communities*. New York: Free Press.

Kelly, R.J., Chin, K-L. and Fagan, J.A. (1993) "The Dragon Breathes Fire: Chinese Organized Crime in New York City", *Crime, Law and Social Change*, 19, 245–69.

Killias, M. (1997) "Immigrants, Crime, and Criminal Justice in Switzerland", in M. Tonry, (ed.), *Ethnicity, Crime, And Immigration. Comparative and Cross-National Perspectives*. Chicago: University of Chicago Press, 375–405, 381.

Kirchheimer, O. (1940) "Criminal Law in National-Socialist Germany", *Studies in Philosophy and Social Science*, 8, 444–63.

Klaauw, Johannes van der (1998) "The Dublin Convention: A Difficult Start". Paper delivered at the *Sixth Schengen Colloquium: Schengen's Final Days?* European Institute of Public Administration, Maastricht.

Klofas, John and Stojkovic, Stan, (eds), (1995) *Crime and Justice in the Year 2010*. Belmont: Wadsworth.

Krevert, P. and Kohl, A. (1996) Europa und die innere Sicherheit, Bundeskriminalant, Wiesbaden.

Labour Party (1994) *Partners Against Crime*. London: Labour Party.

—— (1995) *A Quiet Life, Tough Action on Criminal Neighbours*. London: Labour Party.

—— (1996a) *Protecting our Communities. Labour's Plans for Tackling Criminal and Anti-social Behaviour*. London: Labour Party.

—— (1996b) *Tackling Youth Crime, Reforming Youth Justice*. London: Labour Party.

Lacey, N. (1986) *State Punishment: Political Principles and Community Values*. London: Routledge.

Lacey, N., Wells, Celia and Meure, Dirk (1989) *Reconstructing Criminal Law*. London: Butterworths.

Lacey, N. and Wells, Celia (1998) *Reconstructing Criminal Law*. London: Butterworths.

Lacey, N. and Zedner, L. (1995) "Discourses of Community in Criminal Justice", *Journal of Law and Society*, 22/3.

Landecho, Carlos María (1971) "Tendencias de la Delincuencia en la Sociedad Española", *Cuadernos para el Diálogo* 28 extr., 7–12.

Landrove Díaz, Gerardo (1976) *La Amnistía en España*. Madrid: Cuadernos Diálogo.

Laporta, Francisco J. and Álvarez, Silvina, (eds) (1997) *La Corrupción Política*. Madrid: Alianza.

Lea, John and Young, Jock (1984) *What is to be Done about Law and Order?* Harmondsworth: Penguin.

Leadbeater, Charles (1996) *The Self-Policing Society*. London: DEMOS.

Lehmann, B. (1998) "Bekämpfung Vietnamesischer Straftätergruppierungen in Berlin", *Der Kriminalist*, 30, 50–8.

Leng, Roger, Taylor, Richard and Wasik, Martin (1998) *Blackstone's Guide to the Crime and Disorder Act 1998*. London: Blackstone.

Llarch Roig, Juan (1978) *Campos de Concentración en la España de Franco*. Barcelona: Producciones (ed.) J. J. Fernández Ribera.

Loader, I. (1996) *Youth, Policing and Democracy*. Basingstoke: Macmillan.

López Garrido, Diego and Aran, Mercedes Garcia (1996) *El Código Penal de 1995 y la Voluntad del Legislador. Comentario al Texto y al Debate Parlamentario*. Madrid: Eurojuris.

Lozano Cutanda, Blanca (1998) *La Descalificación de los Secretos de Estado*. Madrid: Civitas.

Lucas Verdú, Pablo (1997) *Teoría de la Constitución Como Ciencia Cultural*. Madrid: Dykinson.

Lustgarten, Laurence and Leigh, Ian (1994) *In From the Cold. National Security and Parliamentary Democracy*. Oxford: Clarendon Press.

Lynch, James (1995) "Crime in International Perspective", in James Q. Wilson and Joan Petersilia, (eds), *Crime*. San Francisco, CA.: Institute for Contemporary Studies, 11–33.

Maffesoli, Michel (1988) *Le Temps des Tribus*. Paris: Klinksieck.

Mandleson, Peter and Liddle, Roger (1996) *The Blair Revolution—Can New Labour Deliver?* London: Faber.

Manning, Peter K. (1988) *Symbolic Communication. Signifying Calls and the Police Response*. London: MIT Press.

Manzanos Bilbao, César (1987) *Prisión y Sociedad en Euskadi*. Oñati: Instituto Vasco de Administración Pública.

Marcó del Pont, Luis (1986) *Criminólogos Españoles del Exilio*. Madrid: Ministerio de Justicia.

Marion, Nancy E. (1994) *A History of Federal Crime Control Initiatives, 1960–1993*. Westport, CT: Praeger.

Marquand, David (1998) *The Guardian*, 2 May, 14.

Marshall, I.H., (ed.) (1997) *Minorities, Migrants, and Crime*. London: Sage.

Marshall, T.H. (1977) *Class, Citizenship and Social Development*. Westport: Greenwood Publishing.

Martín-Canivell, Joaquín (1998) *Spain. Criminal Justice Systems in Europe and North America*. Helsinki: Heuni.

Marx, Gary T. (1988) "The New Surveillance", in Gary T. Marx, (ed.), *Undercover. Police Surveillance in America*. Berkeley: University of California, 206–33.

Mathiesen, Thomas (1982) *Makt og Motmakt* (Power and Counter-Power). Oslo: Pax. Also available in German, (1986) *Macht und Gegenmacht Überlegungen zu Wirkungsvollem Widerstand*. München: AG Spak Publikationen.

—— (1990) *Prison on Trial*. London: Sage.

—— (1992) "Contemporary Penal Policy: A Study in Moral Panics". Unpublished lecture to Howard League AGM, 25 November 1992.

—— (1996) "Driving Forces Behind Prison Growth: The Mass Media", *Nordisk Tidsskrift for Kriminalvidenskab*, 83:2, 133–43.

—— (1997a) *Schengen: Politisamarbeid, Overvåking og Rettssikkerhet i Europa* (Schengen: Police Cooperation, Surveillance and Legal Protection in Europe). Oslo: Spartacus Publishers.

—— (1997b) "The Viewer Society: Michel Foucault's "Panopticon" Revisited", *Theoretical Criminology*, 1:2, 215–34.

Matthews, Roger (1987) "Taking Realist Criminology Seriously", *Contemporary Crises*, 11, 371–401.

—— (1992) "Replacing 'Broken Windows': Crime, Incivilities and Urban Change" in Roger Matthews and Jock Young, (eds), *Issues in Realist Criminology*, London: Sage, 19–50.

Matusow, Allen J. (1984) *The Unraveling of America: A History of Liberalism in the 1960s*. New York: Harper Torchbooks.

Mauer, Marc (1994) *Americans Behind Bars: The International Use of Incarceration*. Washington, DC: Sentencing Project.

Maung, N. (1995) *Young People, Victiminization, and the Police: British Crime Survey Findings on Attitudes of 12 to 15 Year Olds*. Home Office Research Study 140. Home Office and Planning Unit Report. London: HMSO.

Mayhew, Pat and van Dijk, Jan (1997) *Criminal Victimization in Eleven Industrialized Countries: Key Findings from the 1996 International Crime Victims Survey*. The Hague: Dutch Ministry of Justice.

McElrea, F. (1994) "Justice in the Community: The New Zealand Experience" in J. Burnside and N. Baker, (eds), *Relational Justice: Repairing The Breach*. Winchester: Waterside Press.

McGarrell, Edmund and Sandys, Marla (1996) "The Misperception of Public Opinion Toward Capital Punishment", *American Behavioral Scientist*, 39:4, 500–13.

McRae, S. (1987) "Social and Political Perspectives Found Among Young Unemployed Men and Women" in M. White, (ed.), *The Social World of the Young Unemployed*. London: Policy Studies Institute, 61–86.

Medical Foundation for the Care of Victims of Torture (1999) *Staying Alive by Accident: Torture Survivors from Turkey in the UK*. London: Medical Foundation.

Medina, F. Xavier (1998) "Los Movimientos Migratorios en la Europa Occidental. El Caso de Cataluña", *Revista Catalana de Seguridad Pública*, 2, 87–95.

Medosch, Armin (1998) "The European Secret Service Union", *Telepolis*, 30 November. (http://www.de/deutsch/special/enfo/6329/.html).

Melossi, D. (1985) "Punishment and Social Action: Changing Vocabularies of Punitive within a Political Business Cycle. Current Perspectives in Social Theory", 6: 169–94.

—— (1990) *The State of Social Control: A Sociological Study of Concepts of State and Social Control in the Making of Democracy*. Cambridge. Polity Press.

—— (1997) "State and Social Control *à la Fin de Siècle:* from the New World to the Constitution of the New Europe", in R. Bergalli and C. Sumner, (eds), *Social Control and Political Order: European Perspectives at the End of the Century*. London: Sage.

—— (1999) *Multiculturalismo e Sicutezza in Emilia-Romagna: Prima Parte*. Bologna: Regione Emilia-Romagne.

Michael, A. (1998) "Themes for the Active Community: Building the Future Together". The 1998 Geraldine Aves Memorial Lecture. London: Royal Society of Arts.

Miguel, Amando de (1976) *La Herencia del Franquismo*. Madrid: Cambio, 16.

Miller, Max and Soeffner, Hans-Georg, (eds) (1996) *Modernität und Barbarei. Soziologische Zeitdiagnosen am Ende des 20. Jahrhunderts*. Frankfurt: Suhrkamp.

Mir Puig, Santiago (1996) *Derecho Penal. Parte General*. Barcelona: PPU.

Monago Escobedo, Juan José (1998) *El Campo de Concentración de Nanclares de la Oca 1940 –1947*. Vitoria-Gasteiz: Gobierno Vasco.

Morgan, R. and Carlen, P. (1998) "Regulating Crime Control", in P. Carlen and R. Morgan, (eds), *Crime Unlimited? Questions for the Twenty-First Century*. London: Macmillan.

Morris, Norval (1974) *The Future of Imprisonment*. Chicago: University of Chicago Press.

—— and Rothman, David, (eds) (1995) *The Oxford History of the Prison*. Oxford: Oxford University Press.

Morris, Terence (1999) "What's All This About Punishment?", *The Howard League Magazine,* 17:1, 6–8.

Morrison, Wayne (1995) *Theoretical Criminology: From Modernity to Postmodernism*. London: Cavendish.

Muñagorri Laguia, Ignacio, (ed.) (1995) *La Protección de la Seguridad Ciudadana*. Oñati Proceedings 18. Oñati: IISL.

Münch, R. (1995) "Elemente einer Theorie der Integration Moderner Gesellschaften. Eine Bestandsaufnahme", *Berliner Journal für Soziologie*, 5, 5–24.

Murray, Charles (1990) *The Emerging British Underclass*. London: Institute for Economic Affairs.

—— (1994) *The Underclass: The Crisis Deepens*. London: Institute for Economic Affairs.

NACRO (1997) *A New Three Rs For Young Offenders: Responsibility, Restoration and Reintegration—Towards A New Strategy for Children Who Offend*. London: National Association For the Care and Resettlement of Offenders.

Nadlenain, Ethan, A. (1993) "Cops Across Borders: The Internationalisation of U.S. Criminal Law Enforcement". Pennsylvania: Pennsylvania State University Press.

Navarro, Vicenç (1998) *Neoliberalismo y Estado del Bienestar*. Barcelona: Ariel.

Nelken, David, (ed.) (1994) *The Futures of Criminology*. London: Sage.

Netherlands Ministry of Justice (1985) *Samenleving en Criminaliteit: Een Beleidsplan voor de Kommende Jaren*. The Hague, Ministry of Justice.

—— (1990) *Law in Motion: A Policy Plan for Justice in the Years Ahead*. The Hague, Ministry of Justice.

—— (1993) *Effective Detention: Summary and Implementation Plan*. The Hague, Ministry of Justice.

Nikolopoulos, George (1998) "Security Arrangements at the External Borders of Schengen: A View from Greece". Paper presented at the *Sixth Schengen Colloquium: Schengen's Final Days*. European Institute of Public Administration, Maastricht.

Nolan, Lord (1995) *The Nolan Committee's First Report on Standards in Public Life*. Cm. 2850. London: Stationery Office.

Norris, C. and Armstrong, G. (1998) "CCTV and the Rise of Mass Surveillance Society" in P. Carlen and R. Morgan, (eds), *Crime Unlimited? Questions for the Twenty-First Century*. London: Macmillan.

Norwegian Parliament (1996) *Report to Parliament from the Commission appointed by Parliament to investigate allegations of illegal surveillance of Norwegian citizens (the Lund Report)*. Oslo: Norwegian Parliament, 28 March. (Norwegian).

Ohlemacher, T. and Pfeiffer, Ch. (1997) "In Konfrontation mit Schutzgelderpressung und Korruption? Eine Bundesweite Befragung von Deutschen und Ausländischen Gastronomiebetrieben", *Kriminalisitik*, 51, 470–4.

O'Malley, Pat (1996) "Post-Social Criminologies. Some Implications of Current Policy Trends for Criminological Theory and Practice", *Current Issues in Criminal Justice*, 8, 26–39.

Omi, Michael and Winant, Howard (1987) *Racial Formation in the United States*. New York: Routledge and Kegan Paul.

Ortega y Gasset, José (1997) *¿Qué es la filosofía?*. Madrid: Alianza.
Orwell, George (1982) *Nineteen Eighty-Four*. Harmondsworth: Penguin. (Original edition, 1948.)
Osborne, D. and Gaebler, T. (1992) *Reinventing Government*. Reading, MA.: Addison-Wesley.
Palidda, S. (1994) *Devianza e Criminalit à Tra Gli Immigrati*. Milano: Fondazione CARIPLO-ISMU.
Palidda, S., (ed.) (1996) *Délit d'immigration*. (Immigrant Delinquency). Bruxelles: Communauté Européenné.
Park, R.E. (1928) "Human Migration and the Marginal Man", in Robert E. Park, (ed.), *On Social Control and Collective Behaviour*. Chicago: University of Chicago Press, 194–206.
Pashukanis, E. (1978) *Law and Marxism: A General Theory*. London: Ink Links.
Patterson, James T. (1981) *America's Struggle Against Poverty*. Cambridge: MA.: Harvard University Press.
Pavarini, M. (1994) "The New Penology and Politics in Crisis. The Italian Case", *British Journal of Criminology*, 34, 49–61.
Pavlich, G. (1998) "Justice in Fragments", *The Critical Criminologist*, 8, 20–3.
Pease, Ken (1997) "Crime Prevention" in Mike Maguire, Rod Morgan and Robert Reiner, (eds), *The Oxford Handbook of Criminology*. Oxford: Clarendon Press, 963–95.
Penal Affairs Consortium (1996) *The Imprisonment of Women: Some Facts and Figures*. London: Penal Affairs Consortium.
Perryman, Mark, (ed.) (1996) *The Blair Agenda*. London: Lawrence Wishart.
Peters, Antonie A.G. (1988) "Main Currents of Criminal Law Theory" in Jan van Dijk et al., (eds), *Criminal Law in Action*. Deventer: Kluwer, 19–36.
Pitsela, A. (1986) *Straffälligkeit und Kriminelle Viktimisierung Ausländischer Minderheiten in der BRD*. Freiburg: Max-Planck-Institut.
Pitts, John (1992) "The End of an Era", *Howard Journal of Criminal Justice*, 31, 133–49.
Pope, H. and Pope, N. (1997) *Turkey Unveiled: Ataturk and After*. London: John Murray.
Portell, José María (1977) *Euskadi, Amnistía Total*. Dopesa: Barcelona.
Postman, Neil (1985) *Amusing Ourselves to Death*. New York: Viking Press.
Potter, G.W. (1994) *Criminal Organizations. Vice, Racketeering, and Politics in an American City*. Prospect Heights: Waveland Press.
Powell, Charles T. (1998) "Franquismo", in S. Giner, E. Lamo de Espinosa and C. Torres, (eds), *Diccionario de Sociología*. Madrid: Alianza.
Powell, G.B. (1981) "Party Systems and Political System Performance: Voting Participation, Government Stability and Mass Violence in Contemporary Democracies", *American Political Science Review*, 75, 861–79.
Puhle, Hans-Jürgen (1983) "Was ist Populismus?", *Politik und Kultur*, 10, 22–43.
Pusey, M. (1991) *Economic Rationalism in Canberra*. Cambridge: Cambridge University Press.
Putnam, R. (1993) *Making Democracy Work: Civic Traditions in Modern Italy*. Princeton: Princeton University Press.
Radzinowicz, Leon (1991) "Penal Regressions", *Cambridge Law Journal*, 50, 422–44.
Raine, J. and Willson, M. (1997) "Beyond Managerialism in Criminal Justice", *Howard Journal of Criminal Justice*, 36/1, 80–95.

Reagan, Ronald (1984a) "Remarks at the Conservative Political Action Conference Dinner", *Public Papers of the Presidents 1983, Volume I*. Washington DC: US Government Printing Office, 251–4.

—— (1984b) "Remarks at a Fundraising Dinner Honoring Former Representative John M. Ashbrook in Ashland, Ohio". *Public Papers of the Presidents 1983, Volume I*. Washington DC: US Government Printing Office, 670–3.

—— (1985) "Radio Address to the Nation on Proposed Crime Legislation". *Public Papers of the Presidents 1984*, Volume II. Washington DC: Government Printing Office, 1175–7.

Reclassering Nederland (1996) *Gemotiveerd Kiezen; Strategisch Meerjarenplan 1996–1999*. Den Bosch: SRN.

—— (1997a) *Jaarrekening 1996*. Den Bosch: SRN.

—— (1997b) *Handboek Planning and Control*. Den Bosch: SRN.

—— (1997c) *Fundamenten voor de Toekomst; Jaarverslag 1996*. Den Bosch: SRN.

Reid, Kiron (1998) "The Public Order (Amendment) Act 1996", *Criminal Law Review*, December, 864–9.

Reig, Ramón (1998) *Medios de Comunicación y Poder en España. Prensa, Radio y Mundo Editorial*. Barcelona: Paidós.

Reinarman, Craig and Levine, Harry G. (1997) *Crack in America: Demon Drugs and Social Justice*. Berkeley: University of California Press.

Rentoul, John (1997) *Tony Blair*. London: Warner Books.

Richards, Edward P. (1989) "The Jurisprudence of Prevention. The Right of Societal Self-Defence against Dangerous Individuals", *Hastings Constitutional L Q.*, 9.

Richelson, Jeffry T. (1995) *The US Intelligence Commmunity*. Boulder: Westview Press.

Ritzer, George (1996) *The McDonaldization of Society; An Investigation into the Changing Character of Contemporary Social Life*. Thousand Oaks, CA: Pine Forge.

Rivera Beiras, Iñaki (1997) *La Devaluación de los Derechos Fundamentales de los Reclusos. La Construcción Jurídica de un Ciudadano de Segunda Categoría*. Barcelona: Bosch.

Roberts, Julian V. (1992) "Public Opinion, Crime and Criminal Justice", in Michael Tonry, (ed.), *Crime and Justice: A Review of Research*. Volume 16. Chicago: University of Chicago Press.

Rodríguez Devesa, José María (1967) "Contribución Numérica a la Imagen de la Pena de Muerte en España", *Revista de Estudios Penitenciarios*, 178–9, 359–69.

Rodríguez, José María and Serrano, Alfonso (1993) *Derecho Penal Espanol. Parte General*. Madrid: Dykinson.

Rood-Pijpers, Elly and Combrink-Kuiters, Lia (1991) *Gelet op de Reclassering; Een Onderzoek Naar Beelden*. Arnhem: Gouda Quint.

Rose, D. (1996) *In the Name of the Law*. London: Jonathan Cape.

Royal Commission on Criminal Justice (1993) *Report*. Cm. 2263. London: HMSO.

Rubin, Sol (1971) *Civil Commitment of Special Categories of Offenders*. Rockville, Md.: National Institute of Mental Health.

Rueda, Fernando (1993) *La Casa: El CESID, Agentes, Operaciones Secretas y Actividades de los Espías Españoles*. Madrid: Temas de Hoy.

—— and Pradas, Elena (1997) *KA, Licencia para Matar: Qué Hacen y Cómo Son los Espías Más Peligrosos del CESID*. Madrid: Temas de Hoy.

Rutherford, Andrew (1986a) *Growing out of Crime*. Harmondsworth: Penguin.

—— (1986b) *Prisons and the Process of Justice*. Oxford: Oxford University Press.

—— (1992) *Growing Out of Crime: The New Era*. Winchester: Waterside.

—— (1993) *Criminal Justice and the Pursuit of Decency*. Winchester: Waterside.

—— (1996) *Transforming Criminal Policy*. Winchester: Waterside.

—— (1997a) "Criminal Policy and the Eliminative Ideal", *Social Policy and Administration*, 31/5, 116–35.

—— (ed.) (1997b) *Criminal Policy Making*. Aldershot: International Library of Criminology, Criminal Justice and Penology.

—— (1998) "Confiscation without Conviction", *New Law Journal*, 4, December 1820–1.

—— (forthcoming) *Tough and Smart: Criminal Policy and the New Progressives*.

Sainz Cantero, José A. (1971) "Delincuencia Económico-financiera", *Cuadernos para el Diálogo*, 28 extr., 8–13.

Sánchez, Santiago (1997) "Spain: Have We Learnt Anything from our Experience?", in Fernando Reinares, (ed.), *State and Societal Reactions to Terrorism*. Oñati: IISJ.

Sanders, Andrew (1988) "The Limits to Diversion from Prosecution", *British Journal of Criminology*, 28, 513–32.

Sandys, Marla and McGarrell, Edmund (1995) "Attitudes Toward Capital Punishment", *Journal of Research in Crime and Delinquency*, 32:2, 191–213.

Saramago, José (1997) *Ensayo Sobre la Ceguera*. Madrid: Alfaguara.

Sartori, Giovanni (1998) *Homo Videns. La Sociedad Teledirigida*. Madrid: Taurus.

Sasson, Theodore (1995) *Crime Talk: How Citizen's Construct a Social Problem*. New York: Aldine de Gruyter.

Savelsberg, Joachim (1999) "Cultures of State Punishment USA–Germany". Paper presented at the meetings of the Law and Society Assocation, Renaissance Hotel, Chicago, Illinois, May 27–30.

Sayad, A. (1996) "La Doppia Pena del Migrante. Riflessioni sul 'Ëpensiero di Statoí' ", *Aut Aut*, 275, 8–16.

Scarman, Lord (1981) *The Brixton Disorders, 10–12 April 1981*. Cm. 8427. London: HMSO.

Scheerer, Sebastian (1986) "Towards Abolitionism", *Contemporary Crises*, 10, 5–20.

—— (1996) "Zwei Thesen zur Zukunft des Gefängnisses—und Acht über die Zukunft der Sozialen Kontrolle", in Trutz von Trotha, (ed.), *Politischer Wandel, Gesellschaft und Kriminalitätsdiskurse; Beiträge zur interdisziplinären wissenschaftlichen Kriminologie—Festschrift für Fritz Sack zum 65. Geburtstag*. Baden Baden: Nomos.

Schengen Central Group (1997) *Work Programme of the Austrian Chairmanship in Schengen During the Second Half of 1997*. 16 June. Brussels SCH/C (97) 80. (German).

Schengen Executive Committee (1997a) Minutes of Meeting of 7 October.

—— (1997b) Information Newsletter: Information for people working in Ministry of Interior No. 1, Sept., p. 3.

Schengen Joint Supervisory Authority (1997) *Activity Report March 1995–March 1997*.

Schengen Joint Supervisory Authority (1998) *Annual Report March 1997–March 1998*.

Schengen Working Group I on Police and Security (1997) *Draft Schengen Manual on Police Cooperation in Maintaining Public Order and Security*. 11 June, SCH/1 36 rev. 5.

Schlesinger, P. (1992) "A Question of Identity", *New European*, 5(1), 10–14.

Schlesinger, Philip and Tumber, Howard (1994) *Reporting Crime: The Media Politics of Criminal Justice*. Oxford: Oxford University Press.

Schutz, A. (1944) "The Stranger: An Essay in Social Psychology", *American Journal of Sociology*, 499–507.

Scottish Office (1998) Edinburgh *Guidance on Anti-Social Behaviour Orders.*

Sellin, T. (1938) *Culture Conflict and Crime.* New York: Social Science Research Council.

Serrano Butragueño, I. (1994) "Legislación Penal y Penitenciaria Española entre 1936 y 1975", *Boletín de Información del Ministerio de Justicia e Interior,* 1, 694–5, 200.

Serrano-Piedecasas, Ramón (1988) *Emergencia y Crisis del Estado Social. Análisis de la Excepcionalidad Penal y Motivos de Perpetuación.* Barcelona: PPU.

Shearing, Clifford D. and Stenning, Philip C. (1985) "From Panopticon to Disney World; The Development of Discipline", in A. Doob and E. Grenspan, (eds), *Perspectives in Criminal Law.* Ontario: Canada Law Book Inc., 335–49.

Shelter (1992) *The Foyer Project: A Collection of Background Papers.* London: Shelter.

Silva Sánchez, Jesús M. (1992) *Aproximación al Derecho Penal Contemporáneo.* Barcelona: Bosch.

Simmel, G. (1908) "The Stranger", in G. Simmel, *On Individuality and Social Forms.* Chicago: University of Chicago Press, 1971.

Simon, Jonathan (1987) "The Emergence of a Risk Society: Insurance, Law and the State", *Socialist Review,* 95, 93–108.

—— (1997) "Gewalt, Rache und Risiko. Die Todesstrafe im Neoliberalen Staat", in Trutz von Trotha, (ed.), *Soziologie der Gewalt. Sonderheft 37 der Kölner Zeitschrift für Soziologie und Sozialpsychologie.* Opladen, 279–301.

SIRENE Manual (Danish) March 1994.

Skogan, Wesley G. (1990) *Disorder and Decline: Crime and the Spiral of Decay in American Neighbourhoods.* New York: The Free Press.

Smith, A.T.H. (1987) "The Public Order Act 1986 (1) Part 1: The New Offence", *Criminal Law Review,* March, 156–67.

Smith, D.J. (1997) "Ethnic Origins, Crime, and Criminal Justice in England and Wales", in M. Tonry, (ed.), *Ethnicity, Crime and Immigration. Comparative and Cross-National Perspectives.* Chicago, London: University of Chicago Press, 101–82, 174.

Sobremonte Martínez, José Enrique (1980) *Indultos y Amnistía.* Valencia: Universidad de Valencia.

Sola Dueñas, Ángel de (1983) "Política Social y Política Criminal", in R. Bergalli and J. Bustos. (eds), *El PensamientoCcriminológico II. Estado y Control.* Barcelona: Península.

Sopel, Jon (1995) *Tony Blair, The Moderniser.* London: Bantam Books.

Sørbye, Espen (1998) "Jødeforfølgelsene under den Annen Verdenskrig: Et Mørkt Kapittel I Statistikkens Historie?" (The Persecution of Jews During World War II: A Dark Chapter in the History of Statistics), *Samfunnsspeilet,* 12:4, 2–17.

Soros, George (1998) "The Economy: Toward a Global Open Society", *The Atlantic Monthly,* January, 20–32.

Stangeland, Per (1997) "La Delincuencia en España", in Per Stangeland, (ed.), *La Criminología Aplicada.* Madrid: Consejo General del Poder Judicial (CGPJ).

—— (1998) "La Criminología Europea: Entre la Utopía y la Burocracia. Esbozo para una Criminología Realista en España", *Revista de Derecho Penal y Criminología,* 1, 207–19.

Starr, J. (1992) *Law as Metaphor: From Islamic Courts to the Palace of Justice.* New York: SUNY Press.

Statewatch European Monitor, (1998) 1:1.

Statewatch. Published by Statewatch, London. A series of issues.

Steffen, W. (1996) "Ausländer als Kriminalitätsopfer", in Bundeskriminalamt, *Das Opfer und die Kriminalitätsbekämpfung. Vorträge und Diskussionen der Arbeitsagung des Bundeskriminalamtes vom 14–17 November 1995*. Wiesbaden: Bundeskriminalamt, 247–82.

Steinert, Heinz and Cremer-Schäfer, Helga (1998) *Straflust und Repression. Zur Kritik der Populistischen Kriminologie*. Münster: Westfälisches Dampfboot.

Stewart Committee (1983) *Keeping Offenders Out of Court: Further Alternatives to Prosecution*. Cm. 8958. Edinburgh: HMSO.

Stinchcombe, Arthur T., Adams, Rebecca, Heimer, Carol A., Scheppele, Kim Lane, Smith, Tom W. and Taylor, D. Garth (1980) *Crime and Punishment in America: Changing Attitudes in America*. San Fransisco: Jossey-Bass Publishers.

Stojkovic, Stan and Klofas, John (1995) "Preparing for the Year 2010", in J. Klofas and S. Stojkovic, (eds), *Crime and Justice in the Year 2010*. Belmont: Wadsworth, 281–96.

Stonequist, E.V. (1937) *The Marginal Man*. New York: Russell and Russell.

Straw, Jack (1995) "Put the Heart back into Communities", *The Times*, 8 November.

—— (1998a) "New Approaches to Crime and Punishment". Speech at the launch of the International Study for Prison Studies, 7 October 1997. *Prison Service Journal*, March, 116.

—— (1998b) "Crime and Old Labour's Punishment", *The Times*, 8 April.

Sutherland, E. (1949) *White Collar Crime*. New York: Holt, Rinehart and Winston.

Sutherland, E.H. and Cressey, D.R. (1978) *Criminology* (10th edn). Philadelphia: Lippincott.

Swaaningen, René van (1995) "Sociale Controle met een Structureel Tekort; Pleidooi voor een Sociaal Rechtvaardig Veiligheidsbeleid", *Justitiële Verkenningen*, 21:3, 63–87.

—— (1996) "Justitie als Verzekeringsmaatschappij; 'Actuarial Justice' in Nederland", *Justitiële Verkenningen*, 22:5, 80–97.

—— (1997a) *Critical Criminology; Visions from Europe*. London: Sage.

—— (1997b) "De Reclassering als Flexibel en Marktgericht Productiebedrijf", *Proces*, 76:11/12, 193–8.

Swaaningen, René van, Blad, John and Loon, Reinier van (1992) *A Decade of Criminological Research and Penal Policy in the Netherlands*. Rotterdam: Erasmus University.

—— and Beijerse, Jolande uit (1993) "From Punishment to Diversion and Back Again; The Debate on Non-custodial Sanctions and Penal Reform in the Netherlands", *The Howard Journal of Criminal Justice*, 32:2, 136–56.

—— and de Jonge, Gerard (1995) "The Dutch Prison System and Penal Policy in the 1990s: From Humanitarian Paternalism to Penal Business Management", in V. Ruggiero, M. Ryan and J. Sim, (eds), *Western European Penal Systems: A Critical Anatomy*. London: Sage.

Sykes, Gresham (1980) *The Future of Crime*. National Institute of Mental Health. Washington, DC: Government Printing Office.

Tarrius, A. (1997) *Fin de Siècle Incertaine à Perpignan. Drogues, Pauvreté, Communautés d'Etrangers, Jeunes Sans Emplois, et Renouveau des Civilités dans une Ville Moyenne Française*. Perpinyà: (ed.) Trabucaire.

Tejerina, Benjamin (1997) "Civil Society, Political Violence and Social Movements: The Case of the Basque Country", in Fernando Reinares, (ed.), *State and Societal Reactions to Terrorism*. Oñati: IISJ.

Telepolis, www.telepolis.de/tp/deutsch/special/enfo629/1.html.

Ter Wal, J. (1991) "Il Linguaggio del Pregiudizio Etnico", *Politica ed Economia*, 4.

Tham, Henrik, (1995) "From Treatment to Just Deserts in a Changing Welfare State" in Annika Snare (ed.), *beware of Punishment on the Utility and Futility of Criminal Law*. Oslo: Pax Furlag, 89–122.

Thaman, Stephen C. (1998) "Spain Returns to Trial by Jury", *Hastings International and Comparative Law Review*, 21, 2.

Thome, Herbert (1998) "Hilft uns die Kriminalgeschichte, Kriminalität in Gegenwartsgesellschaften zu Verstehen?". Paper presented at 6th Bielefelder Konferenz, *Gewaltkriminalität zwischen Mythos und Realität*. Zentrum für interdisziplinäre Forschung der Universität Bielefeld, Bielefeld, 7–9 October.

Tonry, Michael (1995) *Malign Neglect: Race, Crime and Punishment in America*. New York: Oxford University Press.

—— ed. (1997) *Ethnicity, Crime, and Immigration. Comparative and Cross-National Perspectives*. Vol. 21, Crime and Justice. Chicago: University of Chicago Press.

—— (1998) "A Comparative Perspective on Minority Groups, Crime, and Criminal Justice", *European Journal of Crime, Criminal Law and Criminal Justice*, 6, 60–73.

Tonry, Michael and Farrington, David P. (1995) *Building a Safer Society; Strategic Approaches to Crime Prevention*. Chicago: University of Chicago Press.

Tournier, P. (1997) "Nationality, Crime and Criminal Justice in France", in M. Tonry, (ed.), *Ethnicity, Crime, and Immigration. Comparative and Cross-National Perspectives*. Vol. 21, Crime and Justice. Chicago: University of Chicago Press, 523–51.

Trenz, H.J. (1997) "Governing Beyond Public Legitimation? Some Reflections on the Role of the Public Sphere in the Intergovernmental Framework of European Immigration and Asylum Policies". Paper presented at the International Conference on *Migrations, Interactions and Conflicts in the Making of a European Democracy*. Bologna and Reggio Emilia, 16–19 December.

Triffterer, Otto (1998) "Gewalt und Völkerstrafrecht. Ein neues Gewaltmonopol zur Bekämpfung von Gewalt?", in Klaus Lüderssen, (ed.), *Aufgeklärte Kriminalpolitik oder Kampf gegen das Böse? Vol. III: Makrodelinquenz*. Baden-Baden: Nomos, 272–376.

Tromp, Ruud (1998) "The Inner Workings of SIRENE". Paper delivered at the *Sixth Schengen Colloquium: Schengen's Final Days?* European Institute of Public Administration, Maastricht.

Tyler, Tom R. and Boeckmann, Robert J. (1997) "Three Strikes and You're Out, but Why? The Psychology of Public Support for Punishing Rule Breakers", *Law and Society Review*, 31:2, 237–66.

Ulfkotte, Ulrich (1998) "Im Visier der Datenjäger. Das Amerikanisch-britische Echelon-System überwacht die Weltweite Kommunikation", *Frankfurter Allgemeine Zeitung*, 2 June, 2.

Unzueta, Patxo (1997) *Qué era? Qué es? El terrorismo*. Barcelona: Destino.

Urbano, Pilar (1997) *Yo Entré en el Cesid*. Barcelona: Plaza y Janés.

Varona Martínez, Gema (1994) *Inmigración Irregular. Derechos y Deberes Humanos*. Vitoria: Ararteko.

Verhoef, N.J. (1994) "De Reclassering in Breder Perspectief", *Justitiële Verkenningen*, 20:4, 28–35.

Villagómez, Alfonso (1997) *Las Luerzas y Cuerpos de Seguridad: Del Orden Publico a la Seguridad Ciudadna*. Oleiros: Xunta de Galrai.

Vogel, Jos G. (1994) "Reclassering en Vrijwilliger 'Nieuwe Stijl' ", *Sancties*, 6, 343–50.

Vogler, Richard (1989) *Spain. A Guide to the Spanish Criminal Justice System*. Rochdale: Prisoners Abroad.

Wacquant, Loic (1996) "The Rise of Advanced Marginality: Notes on Its Nature and Implications", *Acta Sociologica*, 39, 121–39.

—— (forthcoming) "Blairism: Trojan Horse of Americanism?", in Keijo Rahkonen and Tapani Lausti, (eds), *Blairism: A Beacon for Europe?*. London: Institute for Public Policy Research.

Walgrave, Lode (1998/99) "Criminology, Criminal Policy and Democracy", *Criminal Justice Matters*, Winter, 23–4.

Walker, Nigel (1991) *Why Punish?* Oxford: Oxford University Press.

Waller, Irvin, Welsh, Brandon C. and Sansfacon, Daniel (1997) *Crime Prevention Digest 1997*. Montréal: International Centre for the Prevention of Crime.

Webber, Frances (1995) "Crimes of Arrival: Immigrants and Asylum-Seekers in the New Europe". Paper presented at the *23rd Conference of the European Group for the Study of Deviance and Social Control*. Crossmaglen, Northern Ireland. 1–4 September. Published by Statewatch.

Weber, Max (1930) *The Theory of Social and Economic Organisation*. (Trans. T. Parsons). London: Macmillan.

Weigend, Thomas (1983) "Prosecution: Comparative Aspects", in S.H. Kadish, (ed.), *Encyclopedia of Crime and Justice*. New York: The Free Press.

Wells, Celia (1997) "Stalking: The Criminal Law Reponse", *Criminal Law Review*, 463–70.

Werbner, P. (1996) "Essentialising Essentialism, Essentialising Silence. Debates on Ethnicity and Racism in Britain", in H.R. Wicker et al., (eds), *Das Fremde in der Gesellschaft*. Zurich: Seismos, 309–32.

Western, Bruce and Beckett, Katherine (1999) "How Unregulated is the US Labor Market? The Penal System as Labor Market Institution", *American Journal of Sociology*, 104:4, 1030–60.

White House (1984) *National Strategy for Prevention of Drug Abuse and Drug Trafficking*. Washington DC: US Government Printing Office.

—— (1989) National Drugs Control Strategy. Washington DC: US Government Printing Office.

Wilkins, Leslie T. (1973) "Crime and Criminal Justice at the Turn of the Century", *Annals*, 208, 13–20.

Wilson, James Q. (1974) "Crime and Criminologists", *Commentary*, July, 47–53.

—— (1975) *Thinking About Crime*. New York: Basic Books.

—— (1977) "The Political Feasibility of Punishment" in J. Cederblum and William Blizek, (eds), *Justice and Punishment*. Cambridge, Mass.: Ballinger, 107–23.

—— ed. (1983) *Crime and Social Policy*. San Fransisco: Institute for Contemporary Studies.

—— (1996) "Foreword" to George L. Kelling and Catherine M. Coles, *Fixing Broken Windows Restoring Order and Reducing Crime in our Communities*. New York: The Free Press.

—— and Kelling, George L. (1982) "Broken Windows: The Police and Neighbourhood Safety", *The Atlantic Monthly*, 249, 29–38.

Wilson, W.J. (1997) *When Work Disappears*. New York: Knopf .

Wimmer, A. (1997) "Explaining Xenophobia and Racism: A Critical Review of Current Research", *Ethnic and Racial Studies*, 20, 17–41.

Windlesham, Lord (1993) *Responses to Crime, Volume 2: Penal Policy in the Making*. Oxford: Clarendon Press.

—— (1997) *Responses to Crime, Volume 3: Legislating with the Tide*. Oxford: Clarendon Press.

Wittkämper, G., Krevert, P. and Kohl, A. (1996) *Europa und die innere Sicherheit: Auswirkungen des EG-Binnenmarktes auf die Kriminalitätsentwicklung und Sclußfolgerungen für die polizeiliche Kriminalitätsbekämpfung*. Wiesbaden: Bundeskriminalamt.

Woolf, Lord (1996) *Access to Justice*. London: HMSO.

Working Group to Examine the Issue of Telephone Control in Relation to Modern Telecommunication Systems (1996) *Report on Telephone Control and Modern Telecommunications Systems (The Aukrust Report)*. Norwegian Ministry of Justice. (Norwegian).

Wright, Steve (1997–98) *An Appraisal of Technologies of Political Control. Final Report*. European Parliament, Scientific and Technological Options Assessment, April 1997; revised report September 1998.

Yeager, M.G. (1997) "Immigrants and Criminality: A Cross-National Review", *Criminal Justice Abstract*, 145–71.

Young, H. (1982) "The Department of Civil Liberties in The Home Office: Perspectives on Policy and Administration". *A Collection of Essays to Mark the Bicentenary of the Department*. London: Royal Institute of Public Administration.

Young, Jock (1988) "Radical criminology in Britain: The Emergence of a Competing Paradigm". British Journal of Criminology, 28, 2, 159–83.

—— (1997a) "Left Realist Criminology: Radical in its Analysis, Realist in its Policy", in Mike Maguire, Rod Morgan and Robert Reiner, (eds), *The Oxford Handbook of Criminology*. Oxford: Clarendon Press, 473–98.

—— (1997b) "Foreword", in R. van Swaaningen, *Critical Criminology. Visions from Europe*. London: Sage.

—— (forthcoming) "Cannibalism and Bulimia", Ch. 13.

Zimring, Franklin E. and Hawkins, Gordon (1991) *The Scale of Imprisonment*. Chicago: University of Chicago Press.

—— (1997) *Crime is Not the Problem: Lethal Violence in America*. New York: Oxford University Press.

Zwaan, Jaap de (1998) "Schengen and Its Incorporation into the new Treaty: The Negotiating Process". Paper delivered at the *Sixth Schengen Colloquium: Schengen's Final Days?* European Institute of Public Administration, Maastricht.

Index